Limiting Bias in the Assessment of Bilingual Students

Limiting Bias in the Assessment of Bilingual Students

Edited by

Else V. Hamayan, Ph.D.
Coordinator of Training and Services
Illinois Resource Center
Des Plaines, Illinois

Jack S. Damico, Ph.D.
Associate Professor of Communication Disorders and Linguistics
Louisiana State University
Baton Rouge, Louisiana

pro·ed

8700 Shoal Creek Boulevard
Austin, Texas 78758

Printed in the United States of America

Library of Congress Cataloging-in-Publication Data

Hamayan, Else V.
 Limiting bias in the assessment of LEP students / Else V. Hamayan and Jack S. Damico.
  p.   cm.
 Includes bibliographical references.
 ISBN 0-89079-411-1
 1. Special education. 2. Handicapped—Education. 3. English language—Study and teaching—Foreign speakers. 4. English language—Remedial teaching. 5. Education, Bilingual. I. Damico, Jack Samual. II. Title.
 LC3965.H256   1990
 371.9—dc20   89-28783
                                                                            CIP

pro·ed

8700 Shoal Creek Boulevard
Austin, Texas 78758

1 2 3 4 5 6 7 8 9 10   95 94 93 92 91

Contents

Preface

Over the last several decades, there has been increased awareness of the problems faced by students entering the schools from culturally and linguistically diverse backgrounds. Depending on their histories and experiences, these students are identified under various labels: limited English proficient (LEP), non-English proficient (NEP), culturally and linguistically diverse (C/LD), and bilingual. In this volume, issues pertinent to these students—and students with dialectical differences—will be addressed. (For ease of reference, these students will be referred to as bilingual or LEP).

One problem in this area involves the placement of bilingual students in special education or remedial programs. Although some of these students are valid candidates for special education placement, many are inappropriately identified as exceptional students. A survey of the literature suggests a number of potential reasons for this inappropriate placement. First, there is a lack of knowledge among the professionals assessing bilingual students. They are frequently unaware of the special characteristics minority students bring to the testing situation; they are unaware of the normal process of second language development and of the limitations of many test instruments when assessing bilingual students. Second, there are difficulties with the referral process when dealing with bilingual students. Teachers may refer students without consideration of linguistic or cultural differences; they may have negative attitudes toward bilingual students, and they may ask naive or nonfeasible questions when doing the referral. In general, bilingual students are more quickly referred for academic and behavioral problems than are monolingual students. Third, the interpretation of test results is a problem when dealing with bilingual students. Unlike that of monolingual speakers, the interpretation of bilingual students' test results—both in traditional and nontraditional testing—must take into consideration a number of additional factors that are often not considered, such as language dominance, language transfer, rule fossilization, and cultural and interactional differences. Finally, difficulties arise when professionals from diverse fields work together to assess the bilingual student.

Too often, the special education assessor and the bilingual specialist do not interact in the best interests of the students. Recent calls for accountability, the increase in federal guidelines, and the legal remedies applied to instances of inappropriate special education placement have suggested the need for a book that would review and discuss the major concerns in the field of bilingual special education assessment. As teachers, psychologists, support personnel, and administrators continue to scrutinize current practices in bilingual special education testing, the following questions emerge:

1. How can we distinguish between temporary difficulties that students face in learning to function in a nonproficient language and more permanent perceptual and cognitive deficiencies that interfere with learning?
2. How can we assess bilingual students' abilities, and possibly disabilities, when the students are not proficient in the language of testing?
3. How can we accurately assess culturally different students' abilities, and possibly disabilities, when the students are unfamiliar with the social norms underlying tests?
4. What types of assessment not only satisfy the requirements of the law but also give service providers clear guidelines as to the components of instruction that a student needs?

The above questions directly concern only one aspect of bilingual special education—that of assessment. Numerous other questions that go beyond assessment and address instructional issues continue to plague educators and policy makers. The focus of this book, however, is primarily on assessment, the first step in providing quality education to all bilingual students.

These questions impinge on the daily working lives of a variety of professionals: school psychologists; speech and language clinicians; bilingual, English as a second language, and special education teachers; counselors; and nurses. The diversity of backgrounds and areas of specialization represented by these professionals reflect the multidisciplinary nature of the field of bilingual special education assessment, and consequently, the cross-disciplinary nature of this volume.

In the first chapter, Kretschmer, whose training is in special education but who is also interested in bilingual issues, provides a general context for nonbiased assessment by covering the history of bilingual special education and the legislative actions taken to guard against inappropriate bilingual testing and placement. This chapter also deals with issues of special education in general, the types of exceptionalities, and concerns specific to special education populations, with a focus on those characteristics unique to bilingual special education students. Kretschmer provides a sufficient knowledge base for professionals who are not familiar with the field of bilingual special education, emphasizes the seriousness of the problems of bilingual students, and sets a challenge for readers and authors of subsequent chapters for potential solutions.

Hamayan, a psycholinguist with interests in special education, explores the issue of second language acquisition in Chapter 2. She discusses the processes of second language acquisition and learning and the difference between first- and second-language acquisition. The variables affecting second-language acquisition and the various types of bilingualism are discussed in the context of their impact on nonbiased assessment. This chapter provides essential background information to enable the reader to progress through the remainder of the book.

Oller and Damico, both trained as linguists with a specific interest in theoretical aspects of language proficiency and language assessment, focus on the theoretical construct of language proficiency and its implications for nonbiased language assessment. They discuss the necessity for a valid theoretical construct and provide requirements that such a construct must meet. The construct of language proficiency they offer is logical, defensible, and practical for use within the school environment, allowing for a systematic transcription to actual testing procedures in later chapters.

These first three chapters provide sufficient background information so that any reader—whether a special educator, a bilingual specialist, a psychologist, or a speech-language pathologist—can acquire a working knowledge of the historical and legal context of the field of special education as it applies to bilingual students, second-language processes, and the concept of language proficiency. Having set the theoretical context for the assessment of bilingual students with special education needs, the remaining chapters deal with practical applications of the issues discussed in the first chapters.

In Chapter 4, Chamberlain and Landurand, who both have experience in bilingual education and an interest in students with special needs, continue the theme of "considerations for the assessment of bilingual students." Rather than deal with theoretical issues, however, they focus on practical considerations for this population, such as cultural differences and the importance of second-language proficiency in testing. Additionally, they emphasize the importance of using appropriate models of assessment and argue for the value of prereferral, the use of team evaluations, cooperative assessment, and interdisciplinary support.

Chapters 5 through 7 offer actual frameworks and practical procedures for nonbiased assessment. These three chapters provide the objectives and guidelines for assessment, based on the previous theoretical chapters. Specific assessment tools and techniques are described and demonstrated in an attempt to offer actual, useful tools for nonbiased assessment. These chapters cover three related but independent aspects: assessment of communicative abilities, assessment of cognitive ability, and educational assessment.

In Chapter 5, Damico incorporates his background in communication disorders and linguistics to focus on both language proficiency and communicative skills. He develops a general framework for conceptualizing language proficiency in test-oriented tasks, which is essential because language proficiency serves as a foundation for assessment and has an impact on other cognitive abilities. Specific assessment approaches and techniques utilizing discrete point, integrative, and pragmatic orientations are described in this chapter as well as the strengths of each approach and its role in the global evaluation of proficiency. Damico places the need for descriptive assessment of communication and the constraints required to assess communication in a consistent and defensible framework. He describes and demonstrates procedures and tests for a multipurpose and multiskill assessment, with an emphasis on psychometrically strong and pragmatically useful tools.

In Chapter 6, Cloud, a bilingual educator with special education expertise, discusses educational assessment. She focuses on the assessment of students with an interrupted or atypical school history, which could include students undergoing migration and reverse migration and refugees. This chapter also addresses the relationship between language proficiency and academic achievement and the importance of bilingual students' school background in interpreting academic performance. The use of criterion- and norm-referenced tests to measure academic performance is discussed, and selected tests in English as well as other languages are described.

Holtzman and Wilkinson, both with research and applied expertise in bilingual special education and psychology, discuss the assessment of cognitive ability by presenting traditional methods and tools of assessment as well as less traditional ones that may be more appropriate for bilingual populations. As with the chapters on assessment of communicative abilities, the assessment of cognitive ability is presented from a multipurpose and multiskill perspective. This chapter also addresses the basic issue of distinguishing between temporary problems due to normal second language development and more lasting cognitive deficiencies by reconfirming the value of a comprehensive assessment system that includes a prereferral phase and by demonstrating this with case studies.

Willig and Ortiz, who also have research and applied expertise in bilingual special education, deal with the overall interpretation of test data obtained from bilingual exceptional students. This chapter focuses on collection and analysis of data from various sources and on determining the source of any difficulties that a student may be encountering. The authors discuss the implications of the interpretation and the use of assessment profiles to create individualized education plans, and they suggest general instructional approaches that befit bilingual students with special education needs.

Finally, in the last chapter, Damico and Hamayan incorporate the information from the preceding chapters and discuss the methods for actually adopting the suggestions previously discussed for limiting bias in assessment. They suggest methods of integration and give examples of successful adaptations throughout North America. Additionally, they stress the importance of assessment in the educational process and the role of the assessor as advocate for the bilingual child.

While the assessment process is an extremely complicated one, it takes on greater complexity when assessment personnel must take cultural and linguistic diversity into account. Because of the biases of many formal testing procedures against students with diversity, the assessment process with the bilingual population requires a mixture of knowledge, skill, and creativity. It is felt that this book can help assessment personnel acquire and develop these traits and thereby assist in limiting bias in the assessment process.

E.V.H.
J.S.D.

Contributing Authors

Pat Chamberlain
Consultant, Illinois Resource Center, Des Plaines, IL

Nancy Cloud, Ed.D.
Special Assistant Professor, Department of Curriculum and Teaching, Hofstra University, Hempstead, NY

Jack S. Damico, Ph.D.
Associate Professor of Communication Disorders and Linguistics, Louisiana State University, Baton Rouge, LA

Else V. Hamayan, Ph.D.
Coordinator of Training and Services, Illinois Resource Center, Des Plaines, IL

Wayne H. Holtzman, Jr., Ph.D.
Adjunct Professor, Arizona State University

Robert E. Kretschmer, Ph.D.
Associate Professor of Education and Psychology, Teachers College, Columbia University, New York

Patricia Medeiros-Landurand, Ph.D.
Adjunct Associate Professor, Leslie College, Cambridge, Massachusetts

John W. Oller, Jr., Ph.D.
Professor of Linguistics, University of New Mexico, Albuquerque

Alba A. Ortiz, Ph.D.
Professor of Special Education, University of Texas, Austin

Cheryl Yelich Wilkinson, Ph.D.
Research Associate, Department of Special Education, University of Texas, Austin

Ann C. Willig, Ph.D.
Director,
MRC, Atlantic University, Boca Roca, FL

CHAPTER 1

Exceptionality and the Limited English Proficient Student: Historical and Practical Contexts

ROBERT E. KRETSCHMER

Although the direct connection between special education and bilingual education has come to the fore only recently, there has been an indirect relationship for at least a century. The early work of Binet, Montessori, and Sequin, for example, addressed issues concerning the welfare of people who were not, or could not, "compete" with the "norm" of the culture and of the times. These individuals came largely from the ranks of the poor and disadvantaged, which undoubtedly included individuals who were culturally and linguistically different from the prevailing culture and who were handicapped.

This long-standing (albeit indirect) relationship between special education and bilingual education recently has received direct recognition primarily because of certain legislation, litigation, sociopolitical trends, and advocacy actions intended to overcome problems arising from the lack of emphasis on bilingual special education. It has been well documented, for example, that certain categories of special education are overrepresented (as much as 60 to 80%) with individuals who are of lower social economic status (SES) (Dunn, 1968) and who are from minority and linguistically different populations (Mercer, 1973; Ortiz & Maldonado-Colon, 1986). Simultaneously, it has been shown that certain minority and linguistically different students are underrepresented in other categories and generally misdiagnosed throughout (Laosa, 1977; Plata & Santos, 1981).

Irrespective of whether the youngsters in question are legitimately placed within special education situations, they do suffer from a triple threat: They are treated as handicapped; they are often among the poor and disadvantaged; and they are of culturally, ethnically or linguistically diverse backgrounds. This last characteristic subjects them to various forms of biases. In recent years, possibly as an overreaction to the identified problems of misdiagnosis, a different problem has surfaced. Limited English proficient youngsters who typically (and, presumably, legitimately) would have been identified as needing special education services have not been receiving those services (Bergin, 1980). Even direct attention to this relationship apparently is not sufficient.

The solution to the identified problems in bilingual special education is direct attention focusing on specific issues within the appropriate sociopolitical context, including the analysis and discussion of evaluation strategies. This text explores these notions and provides the reader with some sense of what appropriate assessment of limited English proficient students might be. This chapter gives the reader background on bilingual special education and the sociopolitical, legal, behavioral, and pedagogical context in which to interpret the rest of this volume. The following topics will be discussed in this chapter: definitions of the various exceptionalities; definitions of bilingualism and limited English proficiency; the sociopolitical milieu surrounding bilingual special education; a historical legal perspective of bilingual special education; the notable behavioral characteristics in exceptional and bilingual students; and general pedagogical implications for special education and bilingualism.

DEFINITIONS AND DEMOGRAPHIC CONTEXT

DEFINITIONS

Categories and Definitions of Exceptionality

There are eight traditionally recognized categories of exceptionality: mental retardation; visual impairments; hearing impairments; communication disorders; learning disabilities; behavioral problems; physical handicaps; and giftedness. Each of these is purported to have its own set of unique characteristics and is treated as distinct from all of the other areas of exceptionality; however, this is oversimplified. Actually, many of these categories overlap greatly; there is considerable heterogeneity within each of these areas due to differences in the degree of impairment, the nature of the impairment, the age of onset, the etiology, and nature of the home environment.

Mental retardation refers to "significantly subaverage general intellectual functioning existing concurrently with deficits in adaptive behavior and manifested during the developmental period" (Grossman, 1983, p. 1). A mentally retarded individual, then, would score distinctly below average (i.e., in the bottom 2 to 3%) on an intelligence test; would have problems learning basic academic skills; would have difficulty participating in appropriate group activities; and would demonstrate difficulties in meeting standards of independence and social responsibility expected of the individual's age and cultural group.

Visual impairment refers to a handicap wherein visual acuity or visual field is sufficiently reduced so as to "interfere with optimal learning and achievement, unless adaptations are made in the methods of presenting learning experiences, the nature of the materials used, and/or in the learning environment" (Barraga, 1983, p. 25). This term subsumes two subgroups of individuals: students with low vision and those who are considered blind. Blind students have light perception but are unable to "project" or identify the source of the light whereas low vision students, while severely visually impaired even with glasses, can identify light sources and this enables them to use print.

The term *hearing impairment*, like visual impairment, refers to all degrees of hearing loss. Traditionally, this population comprises two groups: those who are deaf and those who are hard of hearing. "A deaf person is one whose hearing is disabled to an extent (usually 70 dB ISO or greater) that precludes the understanding of speech through ear alone, with or without the use of a hearing aid. A hard of hearing person is one whose hearing is disabled to an extent (usually 35 to 69 dB ISO) that makes difficult, but does not preclude, the understanding of speech through the ear alone, without or with a hearing aid" (Frisina, 1974, p. 3).

The term *communication disorder* refers to a group of "impairments in articulation, language, voice, or fluency. Hearing impairment may be classified as a communication disorder when it impedes the development, performance or maintenance of articulation, language, voice, or fluency" (Comprehensive Assessment and Service (CASE) Information System, 1976, p. 26). The term *learning disability* is a generic, exclusionary term that refers to a disorder in one or more of the basic psychological processes involved in understanding or using language (spoken or written), which may manifest itself in the imperfect ability to listen, think, speak, read, write, spell, or do mathematical calculations. It includes such conditions as perceptual handicap, brain injury, minimal brain dysfunction, dyslexia, and developmental aphasia. It does not include learning problems that are due primarily to visual, hearing, or motor handicaps; mental retardation; emotional disturbances; or environmental, cultural, or economic conditions.

Students with *behavior disorders* "are those who chronically and markedly respond to their environment in socially unacceptable and/or personally unsatisfying ways but also can be taught more socially acceptable and personally gratifying behavior" (Kauffman, 1977, p. 23). A person is considered *physically handicapped* "when he or she possesses a physical or health condition of such a severe nature that it substantially limits participation in one or more life activities" (United States Congress, 1977).

Gifted and talented students constitute a unique category of exceptionality in that they are identified not as a result of any "disability" but rather the antithesis, their outstanding ability. Traditionally, giftedness is defined by superior intellectual abilities, though giftedness also manifests itself in terms of highly creative or productive thinking, leadership ability, and talent and achievement in the visual and performing arts.

Bilingualism, Biculturalism, Ethnicity, and Limited English Proficiency

Bilingualism refers to proficiency in at least some aspects of two languages, and *biculturalism* is the participation in two cultures. *Ethnicity*, on the other hand, refers to the sharing of a unique social and cultural heritage passed on from one generation to the next, frequently identified by distinctive patterns of family life, language, recreation, religion, and other customs that cause certain individuals to be differentiated from others (Banks, 1987). Finally, *limited English proficiency* (LEP) refers to the lack of facility, fluency, or linguistic competence in English as a second language relative to a normal native speaker-listener of the language.

These seemingly straightforward definitions are simplistic. They also encourage inappropriate stereotyping or attribution. With reference to bilingualism and biculturalism, for example, one popular belief is that bilingual individuals have nativelike fluency and proficiency in both languages and that a bicultural individual is fully familiar with and can operate with equal efficiency within two distinct cultures. In fact, bilingualism and biculturalism may be viewed from different perspectives ranging from various descriptive continua based on the individual's degree of facility, knowledge, and acceptance within the linguistic and cultural context (Ortiz, 1984; Weinreich, 1953) to more complex stratification hierarchies of language ability and cultural knowledge (Paradis, 1978). These issues are developed more fully in Chapter Two.

DEMOGRAPHICS

Special Education in General

Reports by the Office of Special Education within the Federal Department of Education indicate that the prevalence of handicaps (i.e., excluding giftedness) to be approximately 10.6 to 15 percent of the total school population (see Table 1-1). According to the data, communication disorders rank as the most prevalent disorder, followed closely by learning disabilities, behavioral disorders, and mental retardation. The least prevalent area of exceptionality is visual impairment. By certain accounts, these are conservative estimates that may in part be due to the fact that these figures were based upon state compliance records and reports with regard to PL 94-142 (The Education for All Handicapped Children Act) and may reflect caps that have been imposed on certain categories, such as learning disabilities.

Bilingual Education in General

Although there are widely divergent estimates of the numbers of bilingual students in the United States school systems (Fradd, 1987), even moderate estimates reveal significant figures. For example, based on data from the National Summary of the 1980 Elementary and Secondary

Table 1-1. Prevalence figures by exceptionality for the general population

Area of exceptionality	Prevalence figures in percentage of population
Mental retardation	2.0–3.0
Visual impairment	0.1
Hearing impairment	0.5–0.7
Communication disorder	3.0–4.0
Learning disability	2.0–3.0
Behavioral disorder	2.0–3.0
Physical handicap and health impairment	0.5
Multiple handicap	0.5–0.7
Gifted and talented	4.0–6.0
Total	14.6–21.0

Adapted from U.S. Office of Education, Bureau of Education for the Handicapped, Washington, D.C. Based on 1982 population estimates.
Gifted figures source: Gallagher, J., Weiss, P., Oglesby, K., and Thomas, T. (1983). *The Status of Gifted & Talented Education: United States Survey Needs, Practices, and Policies.* Los Angeles: National Training Institute on the Gifted and Talented.

Schools Civil Rights Survey, Hispanics represent 8% of the total school age population; Asian or Pacific Islanders 1.9%; and American Indian/ Alaskan Native represent 0.8% (Office of Civil Rights, 1980). These groups comprise approximately 11% of the school age population; it is reasonable to assume that a large majority of the individuals in these groups are monolingual or bilingual speakers of a language other than English (Waggoner, 1988). When these numbers are linked with the other minority language speakers in the United States (e.g., French and German), there appears to be a significant bilingual population that must be educated in our schools. Further, this population is increasing. Walker (1985) has indicated that the Asian American population has grown 120% since 1972 and Oxford-Carpenter, Pol, Lopez, Stupp, Gendell and Peng (1984), using various sophisticated analytic and projection techniques, found that the overall number of Spanish speaking children in the schools will increase dramatically until the year 2000.

An analysis of the distributional patterns of language minority speakers based on the 1980 Census of Population indicate that potential bilingual students are present in large numbers throughout every state (Waggoner, 1988). The figures reveal that in 29 of the 50 states, at least 10% of the school-age population comes from a linguistically diverse family. The actual percentages of these students in each state range from a high of 56.4% in New Mexico to a low of 4.3% in Kentucky (see Table 1-2).

Even in the state with the lowest percentage, the actual numbers of school age children from minority speaking families is quite large (i.e.,

Table 1-2. Estimated distribution of school-age language minority students by state according to 1980 U.S. census (numbers in thousands)

State	Total school age	Language minority	Percentage of total
New Mexico	303	171	56.4
Hawaii	198	73	36.9
California	4,685	1,665	35.5
Arizona	579	202	34.9
Texas	3,143	1,062	33.8
New York	3,560	936	26.3
Rhode Island	187	43	23.0
New Jersey	1,531	339	22.1
Alaska	92	20	21.9
Connecticut	639	134	20.9
Colorado	594	122	20.5
Massachusetts	1,155	216	18.7
Louisiana	972	175	18.0
North Dakota	137	25	18.0
Florida	1,795	316	17.6
Maine	244	42	17.4
Nevada	160	28	17.3
New Hampshire	196	33	16.9
Illinois	2,407	395	16.4
Utah	350	50	14.4
South Dakota	148	20	13.4
Wyoming	101	13	12.6
Washington	834	105	12.5
Vermont	110	13	12.2
Idaho	214	23	11.0
Maryland	896	96	10.8
Pennsylvania	2,380	225	10.7
Oregon	526	53	10.1
Delaware	125	13	10.1
Michigan	2,068	205	9.9
Montana	167	16	9.8
Kansas	469	44	9.3
Wisconsin	1,013	90	8.9
Minnesota	867	77	8.9
Ohio	2,308	204	8.8
Virginia	1,114	96	8.6
Oklahoma	623	53	8.6
Nebraska	325	27	8.2
Indiana	1,201	96	8.0
Iowa	606	41	6.7
Missouri	1,011	64	6.4
South Carolina	706	43	6.0
Georgia	1,236	72	5.8
North Carolina	1,256	69	5.5
Tennessee	975	46	4.7
Mississippi	602	28	4.7

Table 1-2. *(continued)*

State	Total school age	Language minority	Percentage of total
Alabama	868	39	4.5
Arkansas	496	22	4.5
West Virginia	414	19	4.5
Kentucky	802	34	4.3
Total	47,385	8,022	16.9

Adapted from Waggoner, D. (1988). Language minorities in the United States in the 1980s: The evidence from the 1980 census. In S.L. McKay and S.C. Wong (Eds.), *Language diversity: Problem or resource?* (pp. 69–108). New York: Newbury House.

34,000 in Kentucky). Again, considering the fact that these estimates are somewhat outdated and probably conservative, it is clear that bilingualism must be stressed in every area of the United States.

Bilingual Special Education

McCormick (1980) suggested that there must be at least 250,000 bilingual students with learning disabilities in the country, given that there are approximately five million school age children whose parents' native tongue is not English (as reported by Reich, 1975) and using a conservative estimate of 5% for children with learning disabilities. Baca and Bransford (1981) estimated that 420,000 bilingual youngsters are mentally retarded, learning disabled, or hearing impaired. According to Fradd (1987), the numbers of handicapped limited English proficient students could be as high as 780,000. However, there appears to be little reliable demographic data on bilingual students with handicapping conditions, in part because there are still large numbers of LEP students whose impairments have been either misdiagnosed or undiagnosed (Laosa, 1977; Ortiz & Maldonado-Colon, 1986; Plata & Santos, 1981). Early reports showed an overrepresentation of black, bilingual, and multicultural students in special education, particularly in the category of educable mentally handicapped (Mercer, 1973). Horber (1976) reported on the overrepresentation of bilingual students in classes for the educable mentally handicapped but underrepresentation in classes for learning disabilities (see, e.g., Finn, 1982). Given the difficulties reported in the assessment and placement of LEP students in special education programs by local education authorities around the United States, these findings are not surprising (Dew, 1984; Nuttall, Landurand, & Goldman, 1983). Possibly as a backlash to overreferral and the placement of bilingual students in special education programs, there now seems to be an overrepresentation of handicapped students in bilingual programs who are not receiving special education services (Bergin, 1980).

Another potential difficulty in gathering accurate demographic data in bilingual special education is the disproportionate patterns of exceptionality that appear unique to certain minority groups. For example, a report submitted to the House Subcommittee on Select Education (1981) indicated that Hispanics and whites participated in classes for handicapped consistent with their numbers enrolled in school whereas Blacks were overrepresented in programs for the educable mentally handicapped, emotionally disturbed, and trainable mentally handicapped. However, Blacks had lower representation in the areas of learning disabilities and speech problems. American Indians were underrepresented in trainable mentally retarded classes (less than any other racial or ethnic group), although proportionately within their own ethnic group, they were reported to have more students identified as learning disabled. Asians have the highest proportion of special education participation in programs for speech impaired with the lowest participation in classes for the emotionally disturbed. Assuming that there is no reason for specific exceptionalities to be linked to ethnicity and given the overlap between classification of exceptionalities, such patterns are likely due to the inherent difficulties in the assessment and placement process (Reschly, 1988).

HISTORICAL CONTEXT

To appreciate the importance placed on limiting bias in language assessment and the role of such assessment in bilingual special education, it is necessary to understand the changes that have occurred in both special and bilingual education over the last several decades. In both of these areas, neglect and discrimination appear to have been the norm throughout American educational history until the 1970s (Levin, 1982–1983; Salomone, 1986). This pattern of neglect changed, however, due to the sociopolitical pressures placed on governmental officials and their reaction to this pressure in the form of judicial action and legislative initiative. The sociopolitical influence and the legislative and judicial reactions are discussed next.

SOCIOPOLITICAL MILIEU

As noted earlier in this chapter, legislative acts and litigative actions are reactive: They reflect reactions against current practice and attitudes. An understanding of the sociopolitical milieu, therefore, is needed to comprehend the motivations for the judicial and legislative responses to special and bilingual education concerns in the 1960s and 1970s.

While there has been a long-standing recognition of the problems faced by linguistically diverse groups (Grubb, 1974; Manuel, 1965) and handicapped students (Kirp, 1973; Martin, 1968) in the public schools, there was little done to aid these individuals until the 1960s. This was due partly to the then-held view in the United States (Salomone, 1986) and partly to the attitudes held regarding diversity in society in general (Walzer, 1983). With respect to speakers of a language other than English, there was a pervasive atmosphere of "American nativism" that arose as a reaction to the great wave of immigration to the United States between 1880 and 1920 (Molesky, 1988). This atmosphere, reflected in the rhetoric of presidents (e.g., T. Roosevelt), the rise of political organizations (e.g., Immigrants Resistence League), and passage of specific naturalization laws (e.g., petitioners for citizenship must be able to speak English), viewed non-English speakers with suspicion and saw the teaching of English in the schools as the most effective means of establishing American principles and values (Kloss, 1971). Education was viewed as the means of integrating the immigrants into the American mainstream and this integration required a focus on English, even to the exclusion of their first languages. "Teach them English and the natal cord which nourished their foreign ways in the U.S. would be severed" (Krickus, 1976 cited in Molesky, 1988). In this atmosphere, little concern was given to the instructional strategies used with non-English speakers in the schools. Typically, the instructional strategies embraced a "sink or swim" philosophy (Tawney, 1964).

The educational treatment of handicapped students during this time was no better. Since the educational system was structured to educate the mainstream of society, those who could not benefit from mainstream instruction were excluded from the process. For the handicapped, there were usually three alternatives: They were provided no educational services, were allowed to stay in the schools with little or no consideration of their handicapping conditions, or were placed in educational or residential settings outside of the regular school systems. Although these alternatives were discriminatory, they prevailed because the rights of the handicapped were not considered. As a result, it was estimated in 1975 that over 50% of the eight million handicapped students in the United States were receiving an inappropriate education or no education at all (Salomone, 1986).

The issue of rights for all citizens, however, received major attention during the late 1950s due to the Civil Rights Movement. Led by the National Association for the Advancement of Colored People (NAACP), the Southern Christian Leadership Conference (SCLC), and other organizations, the sociopolitical milieu of the late 1950s and 1960s in the United States was intent on ensuring the basic constitutional civil rights of American Blacks. Since the black minority was neglected and discriminated against in a manner similar to the linguistic minorities and the handicapped (particularly in educational matters), the movement and its resultant call to action benefitted each of these groups. The pressure exerted by the NAACP resulted in a number of lawsuits culminating in the appeal to the Supreme Court as *Brown v. Board of Education* (1954). In this landmark decision, the Court ruled that segregation by race in the public schools is a violation of the Fourteenth Amendment to the United States Constitution. Although the Brown decision and subsequent litigation did not result in immediate clarification of the rights of black citizens or end racial segregation in the schools (Salomone, 1986), it did galvanize the Civil Rights Movement and force legislative action (e.g., Civil Rights Act, 1957; 1964). Under the Johnson Administration, the War on Poverty legislation translated the post-Brown sociopolitical context into a movement for social reform. The Elementary and Secondary Education Act (1965) and the establishment of compensatory education programs such as Headstart and Title One provided federal funds for compensatory education for the disadvantaged. While this legislation had some unforeseen consequences (see Fradd & Vega, 1987), it did enable a greater focus on the problems faced by minorities and the disadvantaged in the school systems.

Another significant result of this sociopolitical context was modification of the concept of equal opportunity. During the social reform movement in early 1964, the U.S. Office of Education funded research to investigate the concept of equality of educational opportunity. In this research, Coleman redefined the concept: Rather than basing equality in education on the types of educational resources provided to students, he measured it according to the educational achievement of the students (Coleman, 1974). That is, the criterion of interest was not resource input but performance output. The implications of this "equality of results" rather than "equality of opportunity" was significant to all disadvantaged and minority students. The concept provided a rationale for providing the resources needed to overcome educational difficulties whether due to poverty, linguistic or cultural difference, or a handicapping condition. In effect, this new definition of equal opportunity in education set the stage for the significant entitlement programs of the next 15 years.

The success of the Civil Rights Movement for Blacks resulted in a greater awareness of all citizen rights, especially in education. Outside of the black community, these rights were advocated by political and professional organizations such as the National Association for Bilingual Education (NABE), the League of United Latin American Citizens (LULAC), the National Council of La Raza, the Center for Applied Linguistics (CAL), and the Mexican-American Legal Defense and Education Fund (MALDEF) for non-English speaking students in the promotion of bilingual education programs (Grubb, 1974) and by the National Association for Retarded Citizens (NARC), the Council for Exceptional Children (CEC), the American Speech-Language-Hearing Association (ASHA), the American Federation for the Blind and others who championed the rights of the handicapped (Kirp, 1973; Martin, 1968). The result of these advocacy efforts was that in the 1970s the concept of equality of educational opportunity and the resultant legislation was extended to education in general, including linguistically and culturally diverse students and handicapped individuals. Since the 1970s, the issue with special education has been one of normalization, whereas within bilingual education emphasis has been on establishing the notion of pluralism within the larger society.

LEGISLATIVE AND JUDICIAL MILIEU

In response to the sociopolitical context of the post-Brown era, there have been numerous legislative actions and lawsuits in both bilingual education and special education. Table 1-3 lists the most significant of these and earlier legislative acts that have occurred in the United States, along with their implications.

Once attention was focused on the plight of linguistically diverse and handicapped students, Congress developed a two-pronged attack in advancing equality in education for these populations (Salomone, 1986). One strategy involved the prohibition of discrimination in federally funded programs, while the other involved the enticement of federal funds for various programs to aid these populations (Wong, 1988).

STATUTORY PROHIBITION AGAINST DISCRIMINATION

In the area of bilingual education, there were two statutory acts that served to prohibit discrimination on the basis of race, color, sex, national origin, or language. The first, Title VI of the Civil Rights Act (1964), did not originally contain a prohibition against discrimination on the basis of language. However, this interpretation protecting linguistically diverse students from inappropriate program placement was added in an HEW policy guideline ("Identification of discrimination," 1970). The second statutory prohibition was attached to a controversial piece of legislation designed to achieve integration in education through busing (Equal Educational Opportunities Act of 1974). This inserted section, Section 1703(f), prohibits denial of equal educational opportunity due to the failure to overcome language barriers that impede instructional participation.

Table 1-3 Chronology and implications of legislation and litigation within special and bilingual education

Public law number	Year	Title	Implication
PL 19-8	1827	An act to provide for the location of the Deaf and Dumb Asylum of Kentucky	One of the early acts that reflected the federal government's involvement with handicapped individuals
PL 33-4	1855	An act to establish in the District of Columbia a government hospital for the insane	Governmental commitment to providing services to a nonsensory-impaired population
PL 38-52	1864	An act authorizing Columbia Institute for the Deaf and Dumb and Blind to confer degrees	Established the first and only liberal arts college (now university) for deaf individuals
PL 45-186	1879	An act to promote the education of the blind	Established the American Printing House for the Blind
PL 65-178	1918	Soldiers Rehabilitation Act	Offered vocational rehabilitation services
PL 66-236	1920	Citizens Vocational Rehabilitation Act	Expanded vocational rehabilitations services to physically handicapped nonmilitary personnel
PL 78-113	1943	Vocational Rehabilitation Act Amendments of 1943	Extended vocational rehabilitation services to mentally ill and mentally retarded persons
	1954	*Brown v. Board of Education*	Established that segregated education based on race was unequal and unconstitutional
PL 85-926	1958	An act to provide grants in aid to institutions of higher education to prepare personnel to prepare teachers of the mentally retarded	First financial commitment to leadership personnel preparation
PL 87-276	1961	An act to provide support for preparing teachers of the deaf	First financial commitment to recruiting teachers into the field of teaching handicapped youngsters
PL 88-164	1963	Mental Retardation Facilities and Community Mental Health Centers Construction Act	Amended PL 87-276 and extended this support to other disability areas
PL 89-10	1965	Elementary and Secondary Education Act	Funds provided to assist local education agencies to meet the needs of "educationally deprived children"

Table 1-3 (*continued*)

Public law number	Year	Title	Implication
PL 89-313	1965	Aid for Education of Handicapped Children in State Operated Institutions	Provided grants to state agencies responsible for free public education for handicapped children
PL 89-750	1966	Elementary and Secondary Education Act Amendments of 1966, Title VI	Expanded the ESEA to include handicapped children and established National Advisory Committee on Handicapped Children
PL 90-247	1967	Elementary and Secondary Education Act Amendments of 1967	Specifically earmarked funds from Title III and Title V to provide programs for handicapped students
PL 90-480	1968	Elimination of Architectural Barriers to Physically Handicapped	Mandates that architectural barriers in various federal buildings be eliminated
PL 90-538	1968	Handicapped Children's Early Education Assistance Act	Establishment of experimental preschool and early childhood programs for the handicapped
PL 90-247	1968	Elementary and Secondary Education Act Amendment of 1968, The Bilingual Education Act, Title VII	Provided funding to establish bilingual programs
	1968	*Arreola v. Board of Education Unified School District*	Established the due process rights of parents and children to have a hearing prior to placement
	1970	*Covarrubias v. San Diego*	Established the need to provide informed consent prior to placement
PL 91-230	1970	Elementary and Secondary Education Act Amendment of 1970	Extended previous aid programs and provided for research, training, and model centers for the education of learning disabled children
	1971	*Pennsylvania Association of Retarded Children v. Commonwealth of Pennsylvania*	Established the right of handicapped individuals to a public education commensurate with their ability to learn
	1972	*Mills v. The Board of Education of the District of Columbia 1972*	Established the right of handicapped children to a public education commensurate with their ability to learn

Table 1-3 (continued)

Public law number	Year	Title	Implication
	1973	*Diana v. State Board of Education*	Established that testing be done in the child's primary language, the use of "nonverbal" tests, and the requirement to obtain extensive supporting data to justify special education placement
	1974	*Lau v. Nichols*	Established that language programs were necessary to provide equal educational opportunities
	1974	*Wyatt v. Aderhlot*	Established right to adequate treatment, treatment/educational standards and the right to related services, all in the least restrictive environment
PL 93-112	1973	Rehabilitation Amendments of 1973 and Section 504 in particular	Provides for equal access to services provided by any federal or federally funded program or project
	1974	*Serna v. Portales Municipal Schools*	Mandated bilingual programs
	1974	*Aspira of New York, Inc. v. Board of Education of the City of New York*	Established the need to use proficiency tests to determine student eligibility for a bilingual program
PL 93-380	1974	Education Amendments of 1974	Forerunner of PL 94-142 providing for eligibility requirements in order to obtain federal funding, including full service goal, priority to unserved children, and evaluation-placement safeguards (nondiscriminatory testing). Also extended services to other bilingual groups
PL 94-142	1975	The Education of All Handicapped Children Act	Mandates that all children regardless of handicap are entitled to a free and appropriate education,

Table 1-3 (continued)

Public law number	Year	Title	Implication
	1976	*Keyes v. School District #1, Denver, Colorado*	along with appropriate monitoring and evaluative procedures. Established bilingual education as compatible with desegregation
	1978	*Rios v. Reed*	Established that bilingual programs must emphasize quality and must be effective in meeting students' needs
PL 95-561	1978	Elementary and Secondary Education Act Amendment of 1978	Reauthorized and reorganized programs funded under the ESEA. Also included Alaskan Natives as eligible for services
	1978	*Jose P v. Ambach*	Established the right to timely evaluations and placement procedures
	1979	*Dyrcia S, et al. v. Board of Education of the City of New York et al.*	Established the right to timely evaluations and placement procedures
	1981	*Castaneda v. Pickard*	Established court standards for reviewing remediation plans for programs
	1979	*Rowley v. Hendrick Hudson Central School District and the State of New York*	Addressed the issue of what constitutes a free and appropriate education
PL 98-511	1984	Elementary and Secondary Education Act Amendment of 1984, Amendments to the Bilingual Education Act, Title VII	Amended Title VII by expanding the programs to include special alternative instructional programs and to provide funds specifically for bilingual education for special populations (preschool, handicapped, and the gifted and talented)
PL 99-457	1986	The Education of All Handicapped Children's Act Amendments of 1986	Extended mandatory programming for handicapped children down to age 3 years and incentives for programming down to age 0 years.

These two acts were the basis of several lawsuits involving linguistically diverse students in the schools. The most famous of these suits was *Lau v. Nichols* (1974). In this class action suit, it was charged that LEP Chinese American students were being denied an education because they were not receiving special English classes with bilingual teachers. The Supreme Court ruled that the San Francisco school district had violated Title VI of the Civil Rights Act of 1964 and the HEW's 1970 regulating guideline addressing discrimination due to language. Stating that the system had failed to provide these students with a meaningful education because they did not take their LEP status into consideration, the Court stated that in this situation, ". . . students who do not understand English are effectively foreclosed from any meaningful education" (1974). In reaching this decision, the Court held that since English was the primary vehicle of instruction, it was not reasonable to require the students to learn English before they could effectively benefit from public education. It was a violation of their civil rights. The court further determined that there did not need to be proof of intentional discrimination but that the results of the educational practices used, no matter how well intentioned, were sufficient to find discrimination. That is, if the outcome of even well-intentioned instruction proved discriminatory, then there was a legal basis for discrimination. The Court ordered the development of district guidelines to meet the needs of LEP students; these guidelines were eventually developed as the Lau Remedies.

The Lau Remedies focused on the identification of linguistically diverse students, assessment of their language proficiency and academic performance, and their placement in appropriate educational programs, usually involving bilingual instructional strategies. This suit and subsequent ones (e.g., *Keyes v. Denver* in 1981 and *Rios v. Reed* in 1978) established bilingual education in the United States from the judicial perspective.

In the area of special education, the nondiscrimination strategy was preceded by two significant right-to-education lawsuits. The first of these suits was *Pennsylvania Association for Retarded Children (PARC) v. Pennsylvania* (1971). Here, the plaintiffs challenged a state law that excluded mentally retarded students from the public schools based on performance criteria. The plaintiffs argued that all mentally retarded individuals could benefit from education and training and that to deny them access to public education violated their constitutional rights. This suit was resolved by a consent decree whereby the state agreed to identify all school-age persons excluded from the public schools and give them access to a free public program of education and training appropriate to their learning capacities.

The second lawsuit, *Mills v. Board of Education* (1972), involved the District of Columbia school district's exclusion of a broad range of handicapped students from regular school assignment and the suspension and expulsion of handicapped students from the school system. The court judgment was against the school district and stated that these students could not be excluded from a regular school assignment unless provided with adequate alternative educational services, a prior hearing, and subsequent follow up of their status. This suit established the rights of all handicapped students, their parents, and the necessity of due process as a regular component of special education placement.

Perhaps as a reaction to these two judicial actions, Section 504 was added to the Rehabilitation Act (1973) the following year; it established statutory prohibition against discrimination on the basis of a handicapping condition. Before this section on non-discriminatory practice was added, the act was limited to employment situations. This section expanded the prohibition of discrimination on the basis of handicapped to any program or activity receiving federal financial assistance. The next year, the amendments to this act clarified the definition of handicapped to include handicapped children who may be denied admission to federally supported school systems. Although HEW failed to issue rules and regulations pursuant to this piece of legislation until 1977, it has had widespread influence on the federal civil rights policy for the handicapped (Salomone, 1986).

Appropriation of Federal Funds

The other prong of attack for support of both bilingual education and special education at the federal level involved appropriation of federal funds for services to the linguistically diverse and handicapped students. The initial federal resources for linguistically diverse populations were derived from the passage of Title VII of the Elementary and Secondary Education Act of 1968. This legislation, also known as the Bilingual Education Act of 1968, was written to provide discretionary funds on a competitive basis to school district projects targeting LEP students between the ages of 3 and 18 years whose socioeconomic level fell below the Title I poverty guidelines. This bill was amended in 1974 to clarify the focus on bilingual education; to remove the poverty factor; to include a bicultural component to the programs; and to provide monies for staff development, research, and greater technical assistance at the state level. The bill was amended again in 1978 to clarify which students were eligible for these services; to clarify and broaden the term *limited English proficiency* to include those who have difficulty reading, writing, or understanding English; and to correct some of the corruptions that had been reported at the local levels. Additionally, a ceiling was set at 40% for participation of native English-speaking students to avoid using these funds for foreign language instruction, and reevaluations were required for each LEP student in the program every 2 years. In 1984, the Bilingual Education Act was revised and enacted into law as Title II of the Educational Amendments of 1984 (PL 98-511). This act expands the programs to include Special Alternative Instructional Programs and to provide funds specifically for bilingual education for special populations (preschool, handicapped, and the gifted and talented).

The federal funding for handicapped students was initiated before the funding of bilingual education. Through the lobbying of advocacy groups, Title VI was added to the Elementary and Secondary Education Act of 1966 (PL 89-750). This act authorized monies to assist states in implementing and improving special education programs, and it established the Bureau of Education for the Handicapped (BEH). A majority of the monies authorized by Congress under Title VI of ESEA never materialized, however, and renewed pressure from advocacy groups and professional organizations resulted in new legislation in 1970. This legislation under ESEA was the Education of the Handicapped Act of 1970 (PL 91-230); it authorized the awarding of grants to institutions of higher education, state and local educational agencies, and other research- and training-oriented organizations for research and training in specific learning disabilities. Additionally, the funds allocated were significantly increased. Amendments were added to the Education of the Handicapped Act in 1974 (PL 93-380) requiring states to submit comprehensive plans for serving all handicapped students, implementation timetables, due process provisions, and instructional strategies for providing education in the least restrictive environments.

The year after the passage of PL 93-380, a much more comprehensive act was passed. This was the Education for All Handicapped Children Act (1975), also known as PL 94-142. A very detailed act, PL 94-142 increased funding for both states and local educational authorities but also required more documentation and monitoring. The act expanded the ages served to include students between 3 to 21 years of age; required placement in the least restrictive environment; and required an extensive identification, assessment, and placement process. Additionally, the law required an Individualized Education Program (IEP) for every identified student, approval of placement by the student's parent or legal guardian, and the right to due process and access to relevant records. Provisions were also made for the inclusion of supportive services such as speech-language pathology and physical therapy. This act has had a significant effect on the status of special education in the United States over the past fifteen years.

Clearly with respect to bilingual special education, the most significant legislative actions were PL 93-380 and PL 94-142. These acts and subsequent litigation addressed guidelines for appropriate assessment and placement in the least restrictive environment. In essence, they established that a student must be given a nonbiased multidimensional, multitask evaluation by qualified personnel and in the student's primary language; that the parents or guardians must give informed consent with regard to any action taken with respect to their child in their own native language; that the parents must be given due process; and that this process must be completed in a timely fashion. Additionally, with the passage of PL 98-511, there is the potential for even greater awareness of bilingual special education needs in the future.

GOALS OF BILINGUAL SPECIAL EDUCATION

As might be expected, the goals of bilingual special education are an amalgamation of the goals of special and bilingual education, which for the most part are similar. According to Baca and Cervantes (1984), the goals of bilingual education (and special education) are cognitive development, affective development, linguistic growth, and acculturation or culture maintenance. Although most experts emphasize the areas of cognitive and affective development as the primary goals of bilingual education (Blanco, 1977), it is clear that language instruction (more specifically, English as a second language), is a necessary part of bilingual education. The manner in which this instruction, acculturation, and culture maintenance are accomplished is reflected in the philosophy and pedagogical methods used.

The linguistic and cultural goals of bilingualism can be viewed from four different philosophical perspectives, according to Baca and Cervantes (1984): transition, maintenance, restoration, and enrichment. The transition approach uses the native language and culture only to the extent that it is necessary for the student to acquire English to function in the regular curriculum, whereas the maintenance approach encourages students to become literate in their native language and to develop bilingual skills throughout school and even into their adult lives. The cultural restoration approach attempts, as its name suggests, to restore the language and culture of the students' ancestors, which may have been lost through assimilation. Finally, the enrichment approach concerns itself with adding a new language and culture to a group of monolingual students.

In general, most experts tend to recommend or suggest a form of the maintenance approach for students who have some proficiency in the native language. Virtually all have accepted the approach described by Cummins (1984), which suggests that academic instruction should be conducted at least initially in the primary language, until sufficient English language facility is acquired to permit instruction in English as well. This approach assumes that information and skills learned in one language will eventually transfer to the other language. When applied to special education, at least in certain categories, this raises the question of whether complications can occur given that these students present certain difficulties either cognitively, linguistically, or affectively.

BEHAVIORAL CONTEXT

To understand more fully the problems involved in the assessment and placement of bilingual exceptional students, the behavioral context should be acknowledged. Students are referred by their teachers, evaluated, and placed in bilingual and special education programs on the basis of their behaviors in the school environment. That is, the behavioral characteristics exhibited by both special education students and bilingual students form a context for the expectations and evaluations, which are transformed into placement decisions and programmatic planning. Many of the problems faced in the assessment process result from superficial commonalities exhibited by exceptional students and by LEP students. Due to these apparent commonalities, students may be misdiagnosed as requiring special education when they are students with normal learning ability who are simply limited in English proficiency, or they may be inadvertently denied appropriate special education services because their behavioral characteristics are interpreted as being due solely to their limited English proficiency.

CHARACTERISTICS BY EXCEPTIONALITY

Given the high premium placed on conformity and achievement in our educational system (DeVos, 1980; Ogbu, 1982; Spindler, 1987), both exceptional students and LEP students are quickly set apart. This is due to their inability to meet the expectations established by the educational system. Regardless of whether the failure to meet expectations was due to an intrinsic impairment that we categorize as an exceptionality or whether the failure was due to linguistic or cultural differences, the outcome is the same: The student is treated as ineffective and may experience prejudice and bias in the form of lower expectations and placement in special programs. Further, some LEP students who are also exceptional experience the reverse bias of being denied special education services when they legitimately require such intervention.

While there are numerous behaviors that may be identified in students experiencing difficulty (for whatever reason) in the schools, seven categories of behavior may be effectively described: communicative functioning, sensory functioning, cognitive abilities, academic functioning, motoric functioning, social abilities, and affective factors. These categories will be helpful in understanding both the commonalities and the differences between the exceptional student, the LEP student, and the student who is both exceptional and LEP. To aid in this understanding, the behavioral context for each of the special education exceptionalities is provided and then contrasted with the behavioral context of the LEP student.

Students with Mental Retardation

Mental retardation exists on a continuum, ranging from mild to profound. It is not uncommon for mild retardation to go undetected until a child reaches school age, since our expectations and demands of a child during the preschool years often are not weighted intellectually. For the most part, mildly mentally retarded individuals (sometimes referred to as educable mentally handicapped individuals) are capable of academic achievement up to the primary and advanced elementary grade levels, of social independence, and of partial or total self-support as adults. There is a slightly higher incidence of vision, hearing, and neurological problems among mildly retarded individuals than among the nonretarded. Many mildly retarded individuals are found to be much more easily distracted, hyperactive, inattentive, and apt to engage in nonproductive activities, such as fighting and out-of-seat behavior, than nonretarded individuals (Bloom, 1974; Krupski, 1979). As the severity of the retardation increases, so does the apparent disability of staying on task. Mildly retarded individuals on the average perform motor tasks somewhat more poorly than "normal" individuals (Francis & Rarick, 1960; Rarick & Wilddop, 1970).

Moderately mentally retarded individuals typically are identified much earlier than mildly retarded ones and generally can learn academic skills for functional purposes, achieve some degree of social responsibility, and attain partial vocational self-support, though they often need assistance. While they typically acquire self-help and self-protective skills and strategies, they generally cannot be totally independent. The incidence of sensory impairments in moderately retarded individuals is much greater even than that in mildly retarded youngsters. Moderately retarded people often demonstrate problems involving coordination, gait, and fine motor skills as a result of some form of central nervous system disorder or damage (Rie & Rie, 1980). These students often have personal and social problems that arise as either a function of the retardation itself or the reaction of others to the retardation.

Most, if not all, severely and profoundly retarded children are identified during early infancy. Many have multiple handicapping involvements (including various sensory, neurologic, and motoric disabilities) of a sufficiently severe nature as to make establishing some level of social adaptation and appropriate personal control over their own person and the environment the primary goal of habilitation.

Regardless of the level of severity, mentally retarded individuals have difficulties in encoding, organizing, and retrieving information, though they do not seem to have difficulty with storage once they have the information. One major problem mentally retarded students seem to have concerns executive functioning (i.e., the ability to engage in meta-cognitive reflectivity or "on-line" monitoring of performance). While they can be taught to employ various learning and problem solving strategies, they often do not seem to pay attention to relevant aspects of a problem nor do they always chose the correct responses or strategies to use (Baumeister & Brooks, 1981). Their vocabularies reflect more concrete word usage than those of normally developing individuals (Shiefelbush, 1972), and they are apt to define words in more concrete, perceptual, or functional rather than categorical terms (Papania, 1954). They also experience difficulty with the morphological aspects of language, though the order of acquisition is similar to that of normal individuals (Newfield & Schlanger, 1968). With regard to syntax development, there is evidence that a strong relationship exists between mental age and syntactical skills and that the retarded follow a normal but delayed pattern of syntax acquisition. Many retarded individuals have difficulties in using language pragmatically for social functions. While they can be taught interactional skills, they tend to maintain passive communication roles (Calculator & Dollagahan, 1982).

Students with Visual Impairments

Given the nature of the etiologies that cause visual impairments, the incidence of multiple handicaps, including deafness, mental retardation, and neurological deficits is relatively high in this population. Intellectually, there is a differentiation of abilities. In the verbal portion of the Wechsler Intelligence Scale for Children (WISC), intact blind students perform within the expected range for nonhandicapped students, though a somewhat distinctive pattern of subscale scores has been noted: comparable performance on Arithmetic, Information, Vocabulary and Digit Span but poor performance on Comprehension and Similarities (Tillman, 1967; Tillman & Osborne, 1969). Behaviorally, there can be a tendency toward a lower self-esteem, passivity, and learned helplessness, as a consequence of restricted mobility and the attitudes of sighted people toward blind individuals. Other areas of difficulty are: motoric posturing, early parental bonding, object knowledge, spatial orientation, and the acquisition of self-help skills. Another problem blind individuals encounter is access to print, which is one of the main avenues of conveying information in our society. (This problem, incidentally, has spawned a whole industry of technologically inspired adaptive equipment.) Academically, if blind youngsters have adequate access to information, they generally succeed, and they are more than capable of social and occupational independence and success.

Because of their disability, visually impaired students rely more heavily on their remaining senses. (This does not imply, however, that by relying on these remaining senses they are "strengthened" in any way.) As a result of this "sensory organismic shift," blind and visually limited individuals process information somewhat differently than normally sighted individuals; they are far more reliant upon their auditory, tactic, and haptic senses. One might expect, then, that these individuals' episodic memories would be organized with respect to images obtained from their remaining intact senses and their long-term semantic memory might be organized slightly differently, reflecting the absence of visual connotations for lexical items.

In a series of case studies, Landau and Gleitman (1985) provided evidence that blind children exhibit an initial delay in language production, though they very quickly catch up and by age 3 they are similar to normally sighted children in syntactic organization, the use of case–grammar relations, and vocabulary. They also demonstrated that blind children are capable of defining and appropriately using various visual terms and suggested that this was possible through the language system itself. They noted, however, that when one takes into account the entire context of the child's utterances, including the youngster's nonverbal accompanying actions and reactions, it must be concluded that blind and sighted children must have partly different lexical entries for these visual terms, but that sufficient overlap exists to permit effective communication. Landau and Gleitman noted that young blind children often have difficulties in handling the patterns of everyday conversation for they often cannot figure out what is occurring in the ongoing social event. One common problem is a delay in appropriate use of the personal pronouns. The present author has also noted a general reluctance to participate in discussions and difficulties in knowing when and how to interrupt.

Students with Hearing Impairments

Although the primary sensory difficulty that hearing impaired youngsters have is reduced auditory capabilities, a great many of them also possess visual difficulties (but generally not to the extent that they might be classified as visually impaired). Intellectually, the hearing impaired youngsters' performance on various tasks is virtually the opposite of that of visually impaired youngsters, in that they do relatively better on performance tasks than on verbal tasks. Deaf students also demonstrate a characteristic profile on the WISC-R, which is as follows: average ability on Picture Completion; high average to above average ability on Object Assembly and Block Designs; but low average ability in Picture Arrangement and Coding (see Kretschmer & Quigley, 1988 for a complete review). Academically, deaf students typically do not succeed well, reaching a third- to fourth-grade reading level upon graduation from secondary school. For the most part, deaf students do not demonstrate gross motor difficulties, though it has been noted that certain students (e.g., those who lose their hearing due to meningitis), have balance problems. Generally speaking, deaf and hard of hearing children develop to be independent self-supporting adults, though as with many other areas of exceptionality they are underemployed (Quigley & Kretschmer, 1982). With regard to social maturity, they typically demonstrate low average performance. Behaviorally, they often demonstrate a pattern of impulsivity, rigidity, egocentricity, absence of inner controls, suggestibility (Meadow, 1980), and learned helplessness (McCrone, 1979). Given the nature of the typical caretaker-child interaction of hearing adults and deaf children, such personality development should not be surprising (Quigley & Kretschmer, 1982).

With regard to information processing, there seems to be a difference between deaf and hard of hearing students. The former, by definition, process information visually whereas the latter tend to do so auditorially. This is not to suggest that deaf students do not mediate verbally, since there is evidence that they do. No single communication or encoding system, however, predominates. Some individuals mediate through signs; others by fingerspelling; and still others, phonetically. One of the primary problems that deaf individuals have is learning auditory-oral language. To date, research in the area of language acquisition within the United States has been limited to either English or American Sign Language. In the acquisition of English, great difficulties have been noted in all areas, including delays in vocabulary, syntax, and virtually all areas of pragmatics (Kretschmer & Kretschmer, 1978). Syntactically, deaf children tend to produce simple sentences with functors and morphological markers omitted. With regard to English semantic memory, hearing impaired children seem to have fewer and less-well-defined concepts. Also, they seem to have difficulty in discriminating between synonymous relationships from other associative relationships (Kretschmer, 1982). As for metacognitive and metalinguistic skills, hearing impaired individuals often demonstrate a delayed ability to make judgments of grammaticality (Kretschmer, 1976; Quigley, Wilbur, Power, Montanelli & Steinkamp, 1976) and in summarizing and paraphrasing ideas and statements (Kretschmer & Kretschmer, 1978).

Students with Communication Disorders

Communicatively disordered students represent a number of impairments due to a wide range of etiologies. In general, however, these impairments can be divided into either speech disorders or language disorders. The speech disorders are traditionally divided into voice problems, stuttering, and articulation difficulties. Voice disorders are generally identified by deviations sufficient to interfere in communication in one or more of the following vocal parameters: pitch, resonance, intensity, and quality. Stuttering is a disturbance in the normal fluency and timing of speech and it usually is characterized by one or more of the following: sound prolongations, sound repetitions, silent or audible blocking, and difficulties secondary to the dysfluency such as visible tension, interactional avoidance, and circumlocution. Articulation disorders are speech deviations that involve substitutions, omissions, distortions and additions of speech sounds or phonemes, due possibly to inappropriate phonological development, poor auditory discrimination ability, oral sensation difficulties, and poor oral motor control. It is not uncommon for children with articulation disorders to also have other language problems.

In general, speech impaired individuals grow to be fully participating members of society. They typically exhibit no greater incidence of academic, cognitive, or information processing problems than the nonexceptional population. The only potential exceptions are when the speech impairments are due to some degree of neurological difficulty or manifest one of a number of genetic syndromes. While there may be social or affective problems linked to some speech impairments (e.g., severe stuttering), these difficulties are typically in response to pressure in the communicative situation rather than due to intrinsic emotional factors.

Students with language disorders may have difficulties in one or more of the following areas: phonology, morphology, syntax, semantics, and pragmatics (Fey & Leonard, 1983; Prutting, 1979). These difficulties may be manifested in their conversational interactions (Damico, 1985), narrative abilities (Westby, 1983), and academic performance (Ripich & Spinelli, 1985; Simon, 1985). Traditionally, there has been an overlap between the classification of language-learning disabled students as language disordered or learning disabled. When the focus is on conversational interaction and oral communication, these students are typically labelled "language disordered." When the focus involves academics, "learning disabled" is the classification employed. This overlap and the fact that there is conflict regarding classification and service delivery to these students further support a noncategorical approach to classification. Since this cross-classification does occur, a more elaborated discussion of students exhibiting these difficulties is presented in the subcategory of learning disabilities.

Students with Learning Disabilities and Language Disorders

The basic problem manifested by students with learning disabilities or a language disorder is the processing of information and the acquisition and use of language. Four broad types of learning disabilities have been identified (Mattis, French, & Rapin, 1975; Wiig & Semel, 1984): language deficits, articulatory and graphomotor coordination deficits, visuospatial perceptual deficits, and difficulties in mathematics. These students by definition do not have (peripheral) sensory deficits or generalized intellectual problems. Although these learning difficulties are purportedly not the result of behavioral problems, it is often the case that students with learning disabilities exhibit behavioral problems, presumably secondary to the frustrations associated with their learning problem. They may also have an external locus of control, attentional deficits, and learned helplessness. It has been shown that most learning disabled adolescents demonstrate social skill deficiencies (Deshler & Schumaker, 1983; Schumaker, Hazel, Sherman & Sheldon, 1982).

Unfortunately, often it is virtually impossible to distinguish behaviorally disordered students from learning disordered children, since both exhibit academic problems as well as behavioral problems. Presumably, the difference lies in which causes what: Did the learning problems cause the behavioral problem, or did the behavioral problem cause the learning problems? Although the data are equivocal, there is the suggestion that a relationship between learning disabilities and delinquency exists in some students (Kirk & Chalfant, 1984).

With respect to information processing, these students may manifest problems in stimulus discrimination and selectivity and in encoding, organizing, storing, or retrieving information. Language-learning disabled students often have difficulties in comprehending and using words, in noting and producing homophones and synonyms, and they tend to be limited to narrow and concrete word meanings. They also have difficulty with deictic spatial terms, and syntax. Seriously disordered students may have even more basic problems, including the development of semantic relationships and the generation of simple sentences. Less seriously disordered students manifest more "subtle" problems such as difficulties with linguistic refinements and modulations and with more complex sentence forms. Finally, these individuals have serious to mild problems with all aspects of pragmatics including maintaining and repairing conversations, inferencing, adjusting to the needs of the listeners, discourse/text organization, cohesion, and understanding body language.

Students with Behavioral Problems

Behavioral disorders subsume a number of distinct subcategories among which are conduct disorders, anxiety-withdrawal, immaturity, and socialized aggression. Conduct disorders manifest themselves in terms of hostility toward authority figures, cruelty, maliciousness, assaultive behavior, hyperactivity, restlessness and hyperkinesis, impulsivity, attentional deficits, and the inability to delay gratification (Wicks-Nelson & Israel, 1984; Gersten, Langner, Eisenberg, Simcha-Fagan & McCarthy, 1976). Students who suffer from anxiety-withdrawal and immaturity often demonstrate problems in self-esteem, resiliency, and learned helplessness, which eventually can result in depression and feelings of self-destruction. Such students are often unhappy, and they demonstrate reduced social skills. The extreme dependency, according to Maccoby and Masters (1970), is associated not with warmth and overprotection but its opposite; rejection or hostility on the parts of significant caregivers.

Socialized-aggressive students have some of the same characteristics as conduct disorders but are socialized within their peer group or gang. These behaviors may not be considered maladaptive within the specific environment in which these students exist. Bronfenbrenner (1979) maintains that the alienation of students reflects a breakdown in the familial and social system, with tension resulting from the conflict of values of the mainstream society and those of the subculture from which many of these youngsters come. A number of factors have been posited as being related to behavioral disorders, among which are certain biophysical factors, including temperamental styles; various environmental factors, including child-rearing practices (or lack thereof); and social environments, including modeling (Bandura, 1977) and social learning.

Students with behavioral disorders typically do not demonstrate any additional sensory or motor difficulties (or at least not any more than the population at large), nor do they demonstrate any particular cognitive limitations, though learning problems and reduced academic achievement are to be expected. It is not uncommon for these students to have concomitant difficulties in academic achievement, language learning, and processing information, so that much of the information provided in the other sections is relevant here as well. In addition, however, it appears that these youngsters may have reduced vocabularies and automatic associations between concepts and notions that are not the same as nondisturbed youngsters and that may lead to nonproductive thought patterns, which therapy and counseling are meant to address. They may also have pragmatic problems; there are those who suggest that therapy should be regarded as communication/discourse and a linguistic event to be used, understood, and possibly shaped (Bandler & Grinder, 1975; Burns, 1980; Labov & Fanshel, 1977).

Students with Physical Handicaps

This category, like the categories of learning disabilities and communication disorders, is an umbrella that subsumes a number of disparate conditions. Essentially, the category of physically handicapped students comprises four subgroups: those with cardiopulmonary conditions, musculoskeletal conditions, neurological conditions, and chronic or terminal illnesses. Students with cardiopulmonary problems have difficulty in breathing or pumping blood properly. As a result, physical activities (even sitting in class all day) are too difficult. This, in association with frequent illness and absences from school, often results in poor academic performance despite normal intelligence and otherwise-normal functioning.

Students with musculoskeletal conditions due to such conditions as muscular dystrophy, arthritis, amputation, severe burns, and scoliosis have limited motor skills. These youngsters do not necessarily encounter academic problems as a direct result of their disability or any intellectual difficulties, though they may manifest social and emotional difficulties that indirectly contribute to educational problems.

Neurological disabilities, including cerebral palsy, traumatic brain injury and spinal cord injury, and spina bifida, often result in a variety of motor skill deficits, ranging from mild incoordination to total paralysis. Epilepsy, often categorized as a neurological disability, typically does not result in any neuromuscular incoordination and does not result in any intellectual or academic problems other than that which occurs as a reaction to social stereotyping. Such is not the case with individuals who sustain head injuries or possess cerebral palsy, particularly if the condition is severe.

For the most part, those individuals with chronic illness do not demonstrate significant intellectual or academic problems as a direct result of the illness, although academic problems can ensue as a result of social and personal reasons and frequent absences from school.

New entries into this category of disabilities are students with AIDS and autistic students. Like other students in the area of chronic illness, those with AIDS are at risk primarily because of possible social or emotional difficulties (as a result of public and familial reactions to the condition and the possible realization of their impending death), fatigue, and frequent absences. A common problem shared by virtually all physically handicapped students is a sense of powerlessness and lack of control over their own personal well-being, which could result in social adjustment problems and learned helplessness.

Although the exact etiology of autism is yet unknown, it has been removed from the category of behaviorally disordered since there is growing sentiment that it is not due to any psychogenic factors. Autism is characterized by: (1) onset before 30 months of age; (2) pervasive lack of responsiveness to other people; (3) gross deficits in language development; (4) bizarre responses to various aspects of environment; and (5) the absence of delusions, hallucinations, and loosening of associations and incoherence as in schizophrenia (American Psychiatric Association, 1980).

The information-processing capabilities and the language abilities of those with cardiopulmonary conditions, musculoskeletal conditions, and who are chronically ill, should be no different than "normal" individuals, whereas those with neurological problems might well have difficulties similar to youngsters with language learning difficulties. In addition to general language problems, these students may also have difficulties with speech apraxia (the inability to intentionally or volitionally produce speech), dysarthria (difficulties in manipulating the speech musculature), respiration, phonation, articulation, and speech resonance.

Students Who Are Gifted and Talented

Gifted and talented students constitute a unique category in that they are identified not as a result of any "disability" but rather the antithesis, their outstanding ability. While they typically manifest high general intellectual capacity, this giftedness also manifests itself in terms of highly creative or productive thinking, leadership ability, and talent and achievements in the visual and performing arts. As opposed to the stereotype of gifted students as being puny, socially immature, or unstable, Terman (1954) established through a longitudinal study that as a group gifted individuals were healthy, above average in physique, well adjusted, and emotionally stable.

As might be expected, gifted and talented students typically do not have difficulties in processing information and are superior in aspects language and communication, unless they also possess a secondary disability.

CONTRASTING THE LEP AND THE EXCEPTIONAL CHILD BEHAVIORALLY

When comparing the LEP student and the exceptional student, it is essential to realize that the behavioral similarities are not usually due to the same underlying factors. Whereas many of the behaviors manifested by exceptional students are due to intrinsic impairments which, by definition, are not seen in the nonexceptional population, LEP students are usually normal in their cognitive, sensory, motoric, and affective abilities and their academic and social potential. The behaviors manifested by the LEP population are usually normal responses that occur when the English-dominant environment in which they are located is different from their own cultural or linguistic environments or experiences. In this sense, the behaviors that set LEP students apart and link them to the exceptional population are typically due to extrinsic rather than intrinsic factors. Still, the behavioral similarities should be recognized and documented as a portion of any assessment process. The ability to differentiate between the underlying causes of these behavioral manifestations is the essential factor in successfully limiting bias during assessment.

When considering the seven behavioral categories, the category that most frequently differentiates the LEP student from the mainstream is the area of communication. By definition, the communicative use of English typically is reduced in this population; it is easily noted by native English speakers, both within and outside of the school environment. If viewed from a monolingual English perspective, these students may be misidentified as exhibiting both speech and language disorders. With regard to speech characteristics, normal first language phonological interference or interlanguage phenomenon (Tarone, 1979) can be misdiagnosed as a voice problem (e.g., nasalization interference in Navajo LEP students) or an articulation disorder (Metcalf, 1979). Stuttering problems are typically not misdiagnosed in LEP populations.

Due to their reduced English proficiency, LEP students may also be misdiagnosed as language disordered when interacting in English. This difficulty may also be due to normal processes of second language acquisition (e.g., rule fossilization, first language interference, cultural interactional differences) but may result in misidentification because of the superficial similarities to language disordered populations. Despite these similarities, however, LEP students typically have normal language learning potential and can acquire the communicative proficiency necessary to function effectively in society. This is not always the case with exceptional students, and it is a major difference between the LEP student and language disordered student.

With regard to the other behavioral areas, the LEP youngster does not possess any special motor or sensory difficulties. Although it has been reported that bilingual children and adults have difficulties producing and discriminating some English speech sounds, this is likely explained by normal second language acquisition phenomena and predicable difficulties with cross-linguistic perception (Buckingham & Yule, 1987; Trubetzkoy, 1939).

When noting the LEP student's performance academically, cognitively, socially, or affectively, there may be apparent problems. Difficulties may arise in one or more of these behavioral areas if the LEP student's culturally determined learning styles, mediational coding, or perceptual strategies diverge from the mainstream English characteristics and if the schools are not responsive to these differences (Philips, 1983; Trueba, 1987). When this lack of educational responsiveness occurs, the burden and responsibility for apparent academic, social, and affective difficulties is placed on the LEP student rather than the educational process. This frequently results in misidentification of these students as disordered or as poor learners and this misclassification affects the overall expectations and educational opportunities provided to these individuals. The end result of such a process is that the LEP students are made to feel marginal in their ability to succeed, and they begin to act according (Sinclair & Ghory, 1987). This process can result in reduced academic performance, social difficulties, and affective problems. The student does become disabled, but the etiology is extrinsic to the student rather than due to some intrinsic exceptionality (Cummins, 1986; McDermott, 1974). In such situations, even LEP students with strong learning potential may begin exhibiting problems similar to the exceptional individual due to the pressures and barriers set before them. Finally, LEP students, particularly those new to the English-speaking environment, may exhibit academic difficulties as a result of the lack of previous formal education, the pedagogical orientation of the student's bilingual education program, or the extent and nature of the family support, involvement, and valuation of education.

CONCLUSIONS

This chapter has provided an overview on limiting bias in the assessment of the LEP student. General definitions and descriptions have been supplied to allow for a cross-disciplinary utilization, and the general issues to be addressed have been placed in the necessary demographic, historical, and behavioral contexts. While there are superficial behavioral similarities between exceptional students and LEP students, these are generally due to different underlying factors. It is the objective of fair and appropriate assessment to document any potential difficulties and then to differentiate between those due to intrinsic disorders and those due to cultural and linguistic differences and other extrinsic factors. Only through this process can the appropriate assessment, identification, and programming for exceptional LEP students versus nonexceptional LEP students be accomplished.

REFERENCES

American Psychiatric Association. (1980). *Diagnostic and statistical manual of mental disorder. 3rd ed.* Washington, DC: American Psychiatric Association.

Baca, L. M., & Brandsford, J. (1981). Meeting the needs of the bilingual handicapped child. *Momentum, 12*(2), 26–51.

Baca, L. M., & Cervantes, H. T. (1984). *The bilingual special education interface.* St. Louis: Times Mirror/Mosby.

Bandler, R., & Grinder, J. (1975). *The Structure of magic I.* Palo Alto, CA: Science and Behavior Books.

Bandura, A. (1977). *Characteristics of children's behavior disorders.* Columbus, OH: Charles E. Merrill.

Banks, J. (1987). *Teaching strategies for ethnic students.* Newton, MA: Allyn and Bacon.

Barraga, N. (1983). *Visual handicaps and learning.* Austin, TX: Exceptional Resources.

Baumeister, A., & Brooks, P. (1981). Cognitive deficits in mental retardation. In J. Kauffman & D. Hallahan (Eds.), *Handbook of Special Education.* Engelwood Cliffs, NJ: Prentice-Hall.

Bergin, V. (1980). *Special education needs in bilingual programs.* Arlington, VA: National Clearinghouse for Bilingual Education.

Bilingual Education Act of 1968. 20 U.S.C. Section 3221 *et seq.* (Supp. 1984).

Blanco, G. (1977). *Bilingual education: Current perspectives.* Arlington, VA: Center for Applied Linguistics.

Bloom, B. (1974). Time and learning. *American Psychologist, 29,* 682–683.

Bronfenbrenner, U. (1979). Content of child reading: Problems and prospects. *American Psychologist, 34,* 844–850.

Brown v. Board of Education, 347 U.S. 484 (1954).

Buckingham, H. W., & Yule, G. (1987). Phonemic false evaluation: Theoretical and clinical aspects. *Clinical Linguistics and Phonetics, 1,* 113–126.

Burns, D. (1980). *Feeling good: A new mood therapy.* New York: New American Library.

Calculator, S., & Dollaghan, C. (1982). The use of communication boards in a residential setting: An evaluation. *Journal of Speech and Hearing Disorders, 47,* 281–287.

Civil Rights Act of 1957, 42 U.S.C. Section 1975 *et seq.* (Supp. 1984).

Civil Rights Act of 1964, 42 U.S.C. Section 2000d *et seq.* (Supp. 1984).

Coleman, J. S. (1974). Inequality, sociology, and moral philosophy. *American Journal of Sociology, 80,* 739–764.

Comprehensive Assessment Service (CASE) Information System. (1976). Washington, DC: American Speech-Language-Hearing Association.

Cummins, J. (1984). *Bilingualism and special education: Issues in assessment and pedagogy.* Austin, TX: PRO-ED.

Cummins, J. (1986). Empowering minority students: A framework for intervention. *Harvard Eductional Review, 56,* 18–36.

Damico, J. S. (1985). Clinical Discourse Analysis: A functional language assessment technique. In C. S. Simon (Ed.), *Communication skills and classroom success: Assessment of language-learning disabled students* (pp. 165–206). Austin, TX: PRO-ED.

Deshler, D., & Schumaker, J. (1983). Social skills of learning disabled adolescents: A review of characteristics and intervention. *Topics in Learning and Learning Disabilities, 3,* 15–32.

DeVos, G. A. (1980). Ethnic adaptation and minority status. *Journal of Cross-cultural Psychology, 11,* 101–124.

Dew, N. (1984). The exceptional bilingual child: Demography. In P. C. Chinn (Ed.), *Education of culturally and linguistically different exceptional children* (pp. 1–42). Restin, VA: Eric Clearinghouse on Handicapped and Gifted Children.

Dunn, L. M. (1968). Special education for the mentally retarded: Is much of it justified? *Exceptional Children, 34,* 5–21.

Educational Amendments of 1984. PL No. 98-511.

Education for All Handicapped Children Act of 1975. PL No. 94-142, 20 U.S.C. Section 1401 *et seq.* (Supp. 1984).

Education of the Handicapped Act of 1974. PL No. 93-380, Section 611, 20 U.S.C. Section 1401 (Supp. 1984).

Elementary and Secondary Education Act of 1965. 20 U.S.C. Section 241 (1978).

Elementary and Secondary Education Act of 1966. PL No. 89-750, 80 Stat. 1204-08 (1966).

Elementary and Secondary Education Act of 1970. PL No. 91-230, 84 Stat. Section 241 (1970).

Equal Educational Opportunities Act of 1974. 20 U.S.C. Section 1703(f) (Supp. 1984).

Fey, M. E., & Leonard, L. B. (1983). Pragmatic skills of children with specific language impairment. In T.M. Gallagher & C. A. Prutting (Eds.), *Pragmatic assessment and intervention issues in language* (pp. 65–82). Austin, TX: PRO-ED.

Finn, J. D. (1982). Patterns in special education placement as revealed by OCR surveys. In K. Heller, W. Holtzman, & S. Messick (Eds.), *Placing children in special education: A strategy for equality* (pp. 322–381). Washington, DC: National Academy Press.

Fradd, S. H. (1987). The changing focus of bilingual education. In S. H. Fradd & W. J. Tikunoff (Eds.), *Bilingual education and bilingual special education: A guide for administrators* (pp. 1–44). Austin, TX: PRO-ED.

Fradd, S. H., & J. E. Vega. (1987). Legal considerations. In S. H. Fradd & W. J. Tikunoff (Eds.), *Bilingual education and bilingual special education: A guide for administrators* (pp. 45–74). Austin, TX: PRO-ED.

Francis, R., & Rarick, L. (1960). *Motor characteristics of the mentally retarded (Cooperative Research Monograph No. 1).* Washington, DC: Department of Health, Education, and Welfare, U.S. Office of Education.

Frisina, R. (1974). *Report of the Committee to Redefine Deaf and Hard of Hearing for Educational Purposes* (mimeo).

Gersten, J., Langner, T., Eisenberg, J., Simcha-Fagan, O., & McCarthy, E. (1976). Stability and change in types of behavioral disturbances of children and adolescents. *Journal of Abnormal Child Psychology, 4,* 111–127.

Grossman, H. (Ed.). (1983). *Manual on terminology and classification in mental retardation*. Washington, DC: American Association on Mental Deficiency.

Grubb, E. B. (1974). Breaking the language barrier: The right to bilingual education. *Harvard Civil Rights–Civil Liberties Law Review, 9,* 52–94.

Horber, J. (1976). *The bilingual child with learning disabilities*. Arlington, VA: ERIC Documents.

House Subcommittee on Select Education. (1981). *Disparities still exist on who gets special education, final report*. Washington, DC: United States Government Printing House.

Identification of discrimination and denial of services on the basis of national origin. (1970) *Federal Register, 35,* 11, 595.

Kauffman, J. (1977). *Characteristics of children's behavior disorders*. Columbus, OH: Charles E. Merrill.

Keyes v. Denver, 576 F. Supp. 405 (1981).

Kirk, S., & Chalfant, J. (1984). *Academic and developmental learning disabilities*. Denver: Love.

Kirp, D. L. (1973). Schools as sorters: The constitutional and policy implications of student classification. *University of Pennsylvania Law Review, 121,* 705–797.

Kloss, H. (1971). The language rights of immigrant groups. *International Migration Review, 5,* 250–268.

Kretschmer, R. E. (1976). *Judgements of grammaticality by 11-, 14-, and 17-year old hearing and hearing impaired youngsters*. Unpublished doctoral dissertation, University of Kansas.

Kretschmer, R. E. (1982). Reading and the hearing-impaired individual: summation and application. In R. E. Kretschmer (Ed.), *Reading and the hearing impaired individual* (pp. 107–122). Washington, DC: Alexander Graham Bell Association.

Kretschmer, R. E., & Quigley, S. P. (1988). Psychoeducational assessment of hearing impaired children. In R. J. Roeser & M. P. Downs (Eds.), *Auditory disorders in school children*. New York: Theime-Stratton, Inc.

Kretschmer, R., & Kretschmer L. (1978). *Language development and intervention with the hearing impaired*. Baltimore, MD: University Park Press.

Krupski, A. (1979). Are retarded children more distractible? Observational analysis of retarded and nonretarded children's classroom behavior. *American Journal of Mental Deficiency, 84,* 1–10.

Labov, W., & Fanshel, D. (1977). *Therapeutic discourse*. New York: Academic Press.

Landau, B., & Gleitman, L. (1985). *Language and experience: Evidence from the blind child*. Cambridge, MA: Harvard University Press.

Laosa, L. M. (1977). Nonbiased assessment of children's abilities: Historical antecedents of current issues. In T. Oakland (Ed.), *Psychological and educational assessment of minority children* (pp. 1–20). New York: Brummer/Mazel.

Lau v. Nichols, 414 U.S. 563 (1974).

Levin, B. (1982–1983). Equal educational opportunity for special pupil populations and the Federal role. *West Virginia Law Review, 85,* 159–185.

Maccoby, E., & Masters, J. (1970). Attachment and dependency. In P. Mussen (Ed.), *Carmichael manual of child psychology,* (Vol. 2). New York: Wiley.

Manuel, H. T. (1965). *Spanish-speaking children of the Southwest*. Austin, TX: University of Texas Press.

Martin, E. W. (1968). Breakthrough for the handicapped: Legislative history. *Exceptional Children, 33,* 493–503.

Mattis, S., French, J., & Rapin, I. (1975). Dyslexia in children and young adults: Three independent neuropsychological syndromes. *Developmental Medicine and Child Neurology, 17,* 150–163.

McCormick, D. (1980). "Occult" bilingualism in children with school problems. *The Journal of School Health, 50,* 2, 84–87.

McCrone, W. (1979). Learned helplessness and level of underachievement among deaf adolescents. *Psychology in the Schools, 16,* 430–434.

McDermott, R. (1974). Achieving school failure: An anthropological approach to illiteracy and social stratification. In G. Spindler (Ed.), *Education and cultural process* (pp. 82–117). New York: Holt, Rinehart and Winston.

Meadow, K. (1980). *Deafness and child development.* Berkeley: University of California Press.

Mercer, J. R. (1973). *Labeling the mentally retarded.* Berkeley: University of California Press.

Metcalf, A. A. (1979). Chicano English. *Language in Education: Theory and Practice, 21.*

Mills v. Board of Education, 348 F. Supp. 866 (D.D.C. 1972).

Molesky, J. (1988). Understanding the American linguistic mosaic: A historical overview of language maintenance and language shift. In S. L. McKay & S. C. Wong (Eds.), *Language diversity: Problem or resource?* (pp. 29–68). New York: Newbury House.

Newfield, M., & Schlanger, B. (1968). The acquisition of English morphology by normal and educable mentally retarded children. *Journal of Speech and Hearing Research, 11,* 82–95.

Nuttall, E. V., Landurand, P. M., & Goldman, P. (1983). *A study of mainstreamed limited English proficient handicapped students in bilingual education.* Newton, MA: Vazques Nuttall Associates. (ERIC Document Reproduction Service No. ED 246 583.)

Office of Civil Rights. (1980). *Elementary and secondary school civil rights surveys.* Arlington, VA: ERIC Document.

Ogbu, J. (1982). Cultural discontinuities and schooling *Anthropology and Educationa Quarterly, 13,* 290–307.

Ortiz, A. A. (1984). Choosing the language of instruction for exceptional bilingual children. *Teaching Exceptional Children. 16,* 208–212.

Ortiz, A. A., & Maldonado-Colon, E. (1986). Reducing inappropriate referrals of language minority students to special education. In A. C. Willig & H.F. Greenberg (Eds.), *Bilingualism and learning disabilities* (pp. 37–52). New York: American Library Publishing Co.

Oxford-Carpenter, R., Pol, L., Lopez, D., Stupp, P., Gendell, M., & Peng, S. (1984). *Demographic projections of non-English-language-background and limited-English-proficient persons in the United States to the year 2000 by state, age, and language group.* Rosslyn, VA: National Clearinghouse for Bilingual Education.

Papania, N. (1954). A qualitative analysis of the vocabulary responses of institutionalized, mentally retarded children. *Journal of Speech and Hearing Research, 25,* 171–177.

Paradis, M. (1978). The stratification of bilingualism. In M. Paradis (Ed.), *Aspects of bilingualism* (pp. 165–177). Columbia, SC: Hornbeam Press.

Pennsylvania Association for Retarded Children (PARC) v. Pennsylvania. 343 F. Supp. 279 (E.D. Pa. 1972) (consent decree).

Philips, S. (1983). *The invisible culture.* New York: Longman.

Plata, M, & Santos, G. (1981). Bilingual special education: A challenge for the future. *The Council for Exceptional Children,* 97–99.

Prutting, C. A. (1979). Process /pras/ses/n: the action of moving forward from one point to another on the way to completion. *Journal of Speech and Hearing Disorders, 44,* 3–30.

Quigley, S. P., & Kretschmer, R. E. (1982). *The education of deaf children: Issues, theory, and practice.* Baltimore, MD: University Park Press.

Quigley, S. P., Wilbur, R. B., Power, D. J., Montanelli, D. S., & Steinkamp, M. (1976). *Syntactic structures in the language of deaf children.* Urbana, ILL: Institute for Child Behavior and Development.

Rarick, L., & Wilddop, J. (1970). The physical fitness and motor performance of educable mentally retarded children. *Exceptional Children, 36,* 509–520.

Rehabilitation Act of 1973. 29 U.S.C. Section 701 *et seq.* (Supp. 1984).

Reich, M. (1975). *A comparison of scholastic achievement of Mexican-American pupils in regular and bilingual groups in Chicago public elementary school (1974–1975 School year).* Arlington, VA: ERIC Document.

Reschly, D. J. (1988). Minority MMR overrepresentation and special education reform. *Exceptional Children, 54,* 316–323.

Rie, H., & Rie, E. (Eds.). (1980). *Handbook of minimal brain dysfunctions: A critical view.* New York: Wiley.

Rios v. Reed, 480 F. Supp. 14 (E.D.N.Y. 1978).

Ripich, D. N., & Spinelli, F. M. (Eds.). (1985). *School discourse problems.* Austin, TX: PRO-ED.

Salomone, R. C. (1986). *Equal education under law: Legal rights and federal policy in the Post-Brown era.* New York: St. Martin's Press.

Schumaker, J., Hazel, J., Sherman, J., & Sheldon, J. (1982). Social skill performance of learning disabled, non-learning disabled and delinquent adolescents. *Learning Disabilities Quarterly, 5,* 388–397.

Shiefelbush, R. (1972). Language disabilities of cognitively involved children. In J. Irwin & M. Marge (Eds.), *Principles of childhood language disabilities.* Englewood Cliffs, NJ: Prentice-Hall.

Simon, C. S. (Ed.). (1985) *Communication skills and classroom success: Assessment of language-learning disabled students.* Austin, TX: PRO-ED.

Sinclair, R. L., & Ghory, W. J. (1987). Becoming marginal. In H. T. Trueba, (Ed.), *Success or failure? Learning and the language minority student* (pp. 169–184). New York: Newbury House.

Spindler, G. (1987). Why have minority groups in North America been disadvantages by their schools? In G. Spindler (Ed.), *Education and cultural process: Anthropological approaches. (2nd ed.)* (pp. 160–172). Prospect Heights, IL: Waveland Press.

Tarone, E. (1979). Interlanguage as chameleon. *Language Learning, 29,* 181–191.

Tawney, R. H. (1964). *Equality* (4th ed.). London: Allen and Unwin.

Terman, L. M. (1954). The discovery and encouragement of exceptional talent. *American Psychologist, 9,* 221–230.

Tillman, M. (1967). The performance of blind and sighted children on the Wechsler Intelligence Scale for Children. *International Journal for the Education of the Blind, 16,* 65–74, 106–172.

Tillman, M., & Osborne, R. (1969). The performance of blind and sighted children on the Wechsler Intelligence Scale for Children: Interaction effects. *Education of the Visually Handicapped, 1,* 1–4.

Trubetzkoy, N. S. (1939 1969). *Principles of phonology* (Translated by C.A.M. Baltaxe). Berkeley: University of California Press.

Trueba, H. T. (Ed.). (1987). *Success or failure? Learning and the language minority student.* New York: Newbury House.

United States Congress. PL 93-112, Section 504, 290 O.S.C. (698). Federal Register 42:86, May 1977.

Waggoner, D. (1988). Language minorities in the United States in the 1980s: The evidence from the 1980 census. In S. L. McKay & S. C. Wong (Eds.), *Language diversity: Problem or resource?* (pp. 69–108). New York: Newbury House.

Walker, C. L. (1985). Learning English: The Southeast Asian refugee experience. *Topics in Language Disorders, 5*(4), 53–65.

Walzer, M. (1983). *Spheres of justice.* New York: Basic Books.

Weinreich, U. (1953). *Languages in contact.* New York: Linguistic Circle of New York.

Westby, C. E. (1983). Development of narrative abilities. In G. P. Wallach & K. G. Butler (Eds.), *Language-learning disabilities in school-age children* (pp. 103–127). Baltimore: Williams & Wilkins.

Wicks-Nelson, R., & Israel, A. (1984). *Behavior disorders of children.* Englewood Cliffs, NJ: Prentice-Hall.

Wiig, E., & Semel, E. (1984). *Language disabilities in children and adolescents.* Columbus, OH: Charles E. Merrill.

Wong, S. C. (1988). Educational rights of language minorities. In S. L. McKay and S. C. Wong (Eds.), *Language diversity: Problem or resource?* (pp. 367–386). New York: Newbury House.

CHAPTER 2

Developing and Using a Second Language

ELSE V. HAMAYAN
AND JACK S. DAMICO

Unlike first-language acquisition, learning a second language is often difficult. Not everyone who attempts to learn a second language can become proficient. In fact, it is the exception rather than the rule that learners attain nativelike proficiency in the second language, even after years of study. The road to second-language proficiency is arduous and long; beginning learners constantly make errors in both the production and comprehension of the second language and invariably have difficulty processing information presented in that language. Even in the best of circumstances, this state of apparent "incompetence" may last as long as 6 years (Cummins, 1980). When the learner is a youngster in a school where that second language is used as the medium of instruction, a lack of proficiency in the second language is bound to lead to academic difficulties which can resemble difficulties encountered by special education students.

Consequently, one of the most difficult tasks facing educators of limited English proficient (PEP) students is to distinguish between difficulties due to operating in the second language and those due to intrinsic learning impairments that would necessitate legitimate special education intervention. Obviously, this ability to distinguish between these causal factors has considerable implications for assessment of PEP students who experience difficulty in school. To determine whether the sources of problems are normally occurring second-language learning difficulties or cognitive or perceptual disabilities, the educators responsible for assessment must be familiar with the factors and patterns inherent in the process of second-language acquisition. This chapter addresses the types of bilingualism, the factors affecting second-language proficiency, the process of second-language proficiency development, the patterns of second-language use, and some ways that this process of second-language acquisition can complicate the assessment process.

TYPES OF BILINGUALISM

When addressing types of bilingualism, it is necessary to clarify the term *language proficiency*. This term has a theoretical and a practical usage. The theoretical usage refers to one's underlying capacity to handle language ability in general, regardless of the actual language spoken. That is, theoretical language proficiency focuses on the underlying psychologi-

---

The term "potentially English proficient" (PEP) is used in lieu of the more traditional term "limited English proficient" (LEP) in order to emphasize the positive aspects of adding English to another language rather than to stress any perceived limitations of students with a primary language other than English. However, "limited English proficient" remains the legal descriptor for those students in the federal guidelines as well as in most states.

cal construct of language as an explanatory device for what is observed; it forms the general basis for our behavior when attempting to assess and teach language. This theoretical perspective of language proficiency is the primary focus of the next chapter and will not be discussed here (see Chapter Three).

The practical usage of the term *language proficiency* refers to the degree of control one has over the language in question. It typically focuses on the four major manifestations, or skills, of language ability: listening, speaking, reading, and writing. These skills are interrelated in that the ability to comprehend oral language is related to the ability to speak that language; similarly, how well one writes a language varies as a function of how proficient one is in reading it. This interrelatedness is likely due to the way language proficiency is organized as a psychological construct (see Chapter Three). Still, these four skills have some independence from one another in that one skill may develop separately from the others. For example, a learner may develop oral proficiency in the second language without having literacy skills in that language.

Aspects of the four skills can be broken down further into other components that typically involve syntax, phonology, and other traditional aspects of language. Paradis (1978), for example, discusses the stratification of language into different levels of organization involving the encoding and decoding of conceptual, sememic, lexemic, morphemic, phonemic, and phonetic elements. These levels interact to form one's actual language proficiency and, as noted by Macnamara (1967), the ability to speak a language proficiently comes with mastery of these elements (e.g., the sounds, the grammar rules, and the vocabulary of the language). Additionally, proficient use of a language involves mastery of the discourse rules that govern acceptable communication among members of the society where that language is commonly used. These traits of language proficiency also include what Canale and Swain (1980) call sociolinguistic skills, such as the ability to make requests, suggestions, and complaints. These particular traits appear independent of one another, especially in second-language learning. Thus, it is not uncommon for a learner to have little mastery of the sounds of the second language but to be proficient in the grammar and vocabulary as well as the social rules of communication in that language. In fact, pronunciation of sounds seems rather independent of the other traits of language proficiency, especially in older learners (Hammerly, 1982). Although children seem to retain the ability to acquire second-language pronunciation perfectly (an ability that begins to deteriorate at puberty [Krashen, 1973]), quality of pronunciation in English by linguistically diverse students also varies as a function of the time of their arrival in the United States (Asher & Garcia, 1969). That is, the younger the arriving students, the closer to nativelike their pronunciation proves to be.

Language proficiency, then, is a complex, multifaceted, multileveled, and variable phenomenon, making discussions of bilingualism equally complex since the measure of a speaker's language proficiency in each language is the defining factor in describing that individual's bilingualism. Because of this complexity and because only some people who attempt to learn a second language become highly proficient, the term *bilingualism* typically refers in this chapter to different levels of proficiency in the two languages involved. The two major types of bilingualism (balanced versus nonbalanced, and additive versus subtractive) are discussed in the following sections.

BALANCED VERSUS NONBALANCED BILINGUALISM

One type of bilingualism is exemplified by the learner who has attained an equal level of proficiency in more than one language, referred to as "balanced bilingualism." An important aspect of balanced bilingualism is the learner's feeling of comfort in the two languages; that is, feeling at home with both of them. A second feature concerns actual language skills. Truly balanced bilinguals have an equal proficiency in both languages in all aspects of language use; that is, their receptive skills and expressive skills as well as their oral and written skills are equal in both languages, and they are equally able to function in a variety of settings (both formal and informal). Given the complexity of language proficiency, it is not surprising that so few people attain balanced bilingualism.

It is more likely for bilinguals to have one dominant language, that is, to have a higher level of proficiency in one language. This is referred to as "nonbalanced bilingualism." An PEP student who is clearly dominant in the primary language has higher levels of proficiency in that language than in English in all four skills (listening, speaking, reading, and writing) and functions better in the primary language in all settings. However, it is possible for a bilingual person to have a mixed dominance in the two languages: that is, to be dominant in one particular skill or in one specific language setting. For example, a bilingual student might be dominant in one language in speaking skills yet have equal proficiency in listening skills in both languages. In fact, this type of dominance is not atypical for some bilingual students in the United States who have been exposed to English at school and to the native language (such as Spanish) at home. The parent addresses the child in Spanish, and the child responds in English. Consequently, the child's speaking ability in Spanish is at a lower level than in English, while listening ability may be equal in both languages.

The dominant language in linguistically diverse students is not always the non-English language. In recent years, many ethnic communities have suffered loss of the ethnic language, and rapid shifts toward English have been reported (Lieberson, Dalto, & Johnston, 1975; Veltman, 1979). Hakuta (1986) describes this instability of bilingualism in the United States as a transitional stage toward monolingualism in English. Thus, many students who come from a language background other than English may actually be dominant in English rather than the "primary or native" language, which may or may not have been the language that was acquired first or the language that is most commonly used at home.

That this proficiency imbalance is so typical in bilinguals, and that the dominant language is not always easily identifiable, has significant implications for assessment. First, due to the multifaceted nature of language proficiency, careful analysis of an individual's specific skills in particular settings should be accomplished. Second, since the individual's first language may not be the dominant language, both languages should be analyzed when determining dominance.

Context Specific Analysis

Because language proficiency consists of many skills and traits, the particular combination of skills or traits that are necessary for success in a given setting must be clearly delineated. The underlying assumption here is that it is not necessary to attain maximum proficiency in all aspects of language. Rather, it may be sufficient to specialize in those that are crucial to a particular setting. For example, the linguistic performance demands placed on a student in a school are different from those placed on a mechanic. Thus, we need a clear model of language proficiency (such as the one presented in Chapter Three) for a specific population of second-language learners in order to guide the assessment process and to delineate the optimum levels of proficiency expected of those learners.

For PEP students in a school setting where English is the medium of instruction, expectancies for proficiency include the use of formal language in an academic context: for example, the ability to comprehend content area information both orally and in written form. Since school is also a social setting, another set of expectations includes the use of vernacular language, which is more appropriate when communicating with peers (Milroy, 1987). For a group of adults in a vocational program, the expectations would be different. Here, we would expect oral proficiency of a more informal nature, and literacy ability would center on the needs of the particular vocation for which the students are being trained.

Based on this awareness, the implication for assessment resulting from the multifaceted nature of bilingual proficiency is that we must assess all those aspects of language proficiency a student should have attained in the context of interest. We cannot reliably predict proficiency in one aspect of language on the basis of proficiency in another (Oller, 1979). Assessment procedures for PEP students must yield information on their oral proficiency as well as on literacy skills in both formal and informal contexts. Further, these procedures must include the measurement of language proficiency in specific content areas such as math and science.

Analysis in Both Languages

While there has been a tendency in the United States for assessment personnel to assume that a PEP student's dominant language is the non-English language (Shore, 1974; Valdez, 1969), this is not always the case. Since language dominance actually refers to a comparison of the language proficiencies in the two or more languages in question (Burt, Dulay, & McKeon, 1980), actual analysis must occur in each of these languages. Neither language dominance nor, more importantly, language proficiency can be automatically assumed. The need arises, therefore, for a comprehensive assessment of both the student's ethnic language and English.

ADDITIVE VERSUS SUBTRACTIVE BILINGUALISM

The attainment of bilingualism manifests itself in different ways. When a second language is learned after acquiring the first, two types of bilinguism may occur: "additive" or "subtractive" (Lambert, 1977). In additive bilingualism, learners who have attained the expected level of proficiency in their first language simply add on a second language to their existing repertoire in the first language. For example, a child who begins to learn the second language upon entering school at age 6 would, in an additive environment, continue developing in the first language while building proficiency in the new one. Similarly, an adult whose first language development is largely complete, would, in an additive environment, develop proficiency in the second language without significantly affecting his or her proficiency in the first language.

In contrast to additive bilingualism, subtractive bilingualism is a process wherein the development of proficiency in the second language has inhibiting and sometimes detrimental effects on the first language (Lambert, 1977). Thus, when a child begins to learn a second language, the development of the first language may slow down and perhaps, at some point, even cease. Some learners' proficiency level in their first language may even decrease as proficiency in the second language increases. Subtractive bilingualism may even result in skills that are below expected levels of proficiency in both languages: a state that Skutnabb-Kangas and Toukomaa (1976) called "semilingualism." That is, a low level of competence is achieved in two languages when early exposure to both has occurred but when no adequate training has been given in either language. Skutnabb-Kangas and Toukomaa documented the performance of Finnish migrant workers in Sweden, many of whom showed evidence of semilingualism. They found that the extent to which the native language had been developed prior to formal exposure to the second language was strongly related to how well the second language was learned. That is, a threshold level of linguistic competence may have to be attained by bilingual children in order for them to benefit maximally from both languages (Cummins, 1978, 1979; Jacobson, 1985; Swain & Cummins, 1986).

Semilingualism has detrimental effects on a child's emotional, cognitive, linguistic, and academic development (Paulston, 1975). To counter this, schools must promote additive forms of bilingualism. The educational strategy that best overcomes semilingualism is that of valuing and developing the child's first language (Alvarez, 1984; Cummins, 1986). By enhancing or solidifying children's native language, children become cognitively capable of developing competence in both languages. This is especially germane to PEP students who come from a linguistic minority and who may not have adequately developed their native language to that threshold level. Unless these individuals attain a threshold level of competence in the native language, they may not have the cognitive ability to fully develop the second language (in this case, English). This holds true even if only relatively low levels of proficiency in English are attained (Diaz, in press).

The fact that many language learners attain additive bilingualism shows that it is psychologically and cognitively possible. Human cognitive capacity does not limit a person's ability to become proficient in two languages. In many societies, fluency in two languages (and sometimes even three or four languages) is expected (Hakuta, 1986). Unfortunately, however, a sizable body of research prior to the 1950s drew largely false conclusions regarding the detrimental effects of bilingualism on cognition. Much of this research appears to show that bilingualism had a detrimental effect on intelligence, as assessed by IQ tests (for a review of the issue, see Cummins & Swain, 1986; Hakuta, 1986; for a review of the studies, see Peal & Lambert, 1962). Although most studies confounded bilingualism with the effects of age, sex, degree of bilingual proficiency, and socioeconomic class, research that has controlled these variables has strongly refuted these early conclusions (Hakuta, 1986; Peal & Lambert, 1962). However, the myth that bilingualism may be harmful still persists in some quarters.

Current research indicates not only that there is no cognitive price to pay for bilingualism but that there may be positive consequences of additive bilingualism. Under many circumstances, bilingual abilities accelerate the development of verbal and nonverbal abilities (Bain, 1975; Peal & Lambert, 1962) and increase cognitive flexibility (Ben-Zeev, 1977, Ianco-Worrall, 1972). Peal & Lambert (1962) suggested that bilinguals have more cognitive flexibility than those who are monolingual because bilinguals are forced to conceptualize objects and events in terms of general properties rather than on the basis of specific linguistic symbols. Further evidence for the acceleration of abstract thought in a bilingual environment was reported in studies conducted by Liedke and Nelson (1968) and by Bain (1975). Children who had become bilingual before entering school showed higher levels of concept formation than did their monolingual counterparts. Additive bilingualism, which occurs in many bilingual speakers, may thus confer important cognitive advantages (McLaughlin, 1984).

The fact that only some learners experience the subtractive type of bilingualism raises the question of the conditions under which subtractive versus additive bilingualism occur. The answers lie in the social, affective, and political milieu in which language learning takes place.

The Subtractive Milieu

Children who undergo subtractive bilingualism generally come from lower socioeconomic status homes where they do not have the opportunity for extensive one-on-one language use with an adult in either language. It is also the case that in these settings, objects are not labeled for children consistently or adequately in either language. As a consequence, such children may not develop a full conceptual system in either language (Nelson, 1985). Children who experience subtractive bilingualism are also likely to come from homes in which literacy itself plays a minimal role; the parents may not read much and may not be able to share with their children valuable story-reading time. Subtractive bilingualism is also more likely to occur in societies where members of the minority or majority community have negative attitudes toward a minority language (Skutnabb-Kangas & Toukomaa, 1976). Children in that kind of environment receive the message that their native language (their parents' language) is to be shunned and, as a result, develop negative attitudes and lowered self-esteem (Trueba, 1987). This environment may, in turn, prohibit the smooth development of proficiency in the two languages to which the child is exposed.

In addition to these societal factors that make it likely for some children to show lack of growth, or even loss of proficiency in the native language, characteristics of individual learners also affect the language learning process. Research on learner characteristics associated with native language loss, or subtractive bilingualism, is scant (but see Haugen, 1953, for a sociological perspective). Yet findings from a related body of research that addresses another important issue may shed some light on this question. This body of research, dealing with predictors of success in second language acquisition, will be discussed in the following section.

FACTORS AFFECTING SECOND-LANGUAGE PROFICIENCY

Because the vast majority of monolingual children become at least adequately proficient in their native language, it is interesting to find that many who attempt to learn a second language are unable to do so. This may be a source of frustration for teachers of students who encounter difficulties in learning a second language, since this inability leads many to wonder whether such difficulties are due to "normal" second-language proficiency problems or due to more permanent perceptual or cognitive deficits. Since students differ considerably regarding the ease with which they are able to attain proficiency in a second language, the question of which learner characteristics underlie success in learning a second language has very important educational implications. Learner characteristics that contribute to the rate of second-language proficiency attainment will be discussed in two categories: the individual learner and the learner's home and community. The characteristics within each category and between the two categories are interrelated, but they will be discussed separately for the sake of clarity.

INDIVIDUAL CHARACTERISTICS

Cognitive Factors

The first set of individual characteristics affecting second-language learning involve cognitive skills. As an overall measure of cognitive skill, intelligence was long thought to play an important role in second-language proficiency. This assumption was not surprising given the fact that intelligence has traditionally been measured by IQ tests, and these tools may primarily be tests of language proficiency. There has been substantial research indicating that language proficiency accounts for a large portion of the test variability in IQ tests (Oller & Perkins, 1978; 1980). However, intelligence as measured by IQ tests appears to account for a relatively small percent of success in second-language learning (Pimsleur, 1980). Further, intelligence (as defined by IQ tests) contributes significantly to only specific academic second language skills, such as grammar analysis (Genesee, 1976). It is possible that the impact of intelligence as measured by IQ tests only has a significant and negative impact on second-language acquisition when the individual learner has a real and significant intellectual impairment (e.g., genetically based mental retardation). In such cases, all aspects of acquisition and learning are impaired (see Chapter One). However, when dealing with the normal and above-normal range of variation, it is not always the "intelligent" students who master the second language easily. The students who may be identified as having "low intelligence" are not necessarily the ones who will have more than the usual difficulties with the second language. Factors other than intelligence seem to play a larger role in these cases.

A cognitive characteristic that has a stronger effect than intelligence is learning style: that is, the manner in which a student processes information from the surrounding environment. Individual differences in learning style affect second-language learning to the extent that there is a match (or mismatch) between the student's learning style and the style in which the second language is being taught. For example, students who are field independent (who can extract relevant details from a complex configuration) have success in learning a second language largely within an academic setting where the focus is on rule analysis (Naiman, Frohlich & Stern, 1975).

Another learning style that has been suggested as an influence in second-language learning success involves reflectivity versus impulsivity. Some students tend to approach the second language analytically, to reflect on whatever task they happen to be engaged in, and to monitor their language use extensively (Krashen, 1981). This type of student would likely thrive in an academically oriented second-language classroom where the focus is on the form of language. More impulsive students, on the other hand—who tend to approach the second language more intuitively—would gain proficiency more efficiently in settings that impelled students into natural use of the second language in a communicative context.

Another learning style that has been addressed in the literature (although research on it is scarce) involves the preference for processing information through one modality over another (e.g., through oral as opposed to visual modes). Students who can process information more effectively through visual means would be more likely to succeed in a second-language classroom where new material is presented visually or pictorially.

Affective and Personality Factors

A second major set of learner characteristics concerns affective or emotional states, particularly relating to students' attitudes. Extensive studies with English-Canadian students learning French (Gardner & Lambert, 1972), as well as with linguistically diverse students in the United States learning English as a second language (Oller, Baca, & Vigil, 1978), have led to the conclusion that positive attitudes toward self, one's own native language group, and the target language group significantly enhance the attainment of proficiency in the second language.

Attitudes toward the target language and its speakers are likely to have their effect through different levels of motivation. Negative attitudes may lead to decreased motivation to learn the language and, consequently, to unsuccessful attainment of proficiency. On the other hand, positive attitudes are likely to lead to increased motivation, resulting in a high likelihood of second-language proficiency. Affective or attitudinal factors are also mediated by the perceived social distance (Schumann, 1976) that exists between members of two linguistic communities. If second-language learners are part of a cohesive community, if they perceive themselves as subordinate to the native speakers of the target language, and if they have negative attitudes toward the target language community, the resulting perceived social distance is great and would likely hamper the attainment of proficiency either through negative attitudes or decreased motivation. This difficulty is less likely to occur when the attitudes held by different group members are at least neutral toward the student's group and when the student's group identity is not paramount.

Personality traits may also affect second-language learning. In particular, the traits of extroversion and the need for control are related to the attainment of second-language proficiency. Students who are outgoing and adventurous seem to learn the second language faster than those who are shy and introverted (Tucker, Hamayan, & Genesee, 1976). However, there is also evidence (Naiman, Frohlich, & Stern, 1975) that extroversion does not always characterize the "good language learner." These conflicting findings may be explained by the notion that extroversion may facilitate expressive ability, such as speaking and writing, but not listening and reading comprehension. Similarly, students who feel that they are adequately in control of their environment are better second-language learners than those who feel the need for control (Genesee & Hamayan, 1980). These traits may simply be secondary predictors of success in second-language learning, in that they are likely to lead the learner toward more exposure to the target language and consequently to create more opportunities for practice. Students who are outgoing as well as those who feel in control are likely to seek out speakers of the target language or at least not to escape situations in which they are exposed to them.

Anxiety is a related trait. Just as high levels of anxiety interfere with learning in general, being too anxious while learning the second language may interfere with attainment of proficiency in that language. Students who feel a high level of anxiety in a second-language environment (particularly in the second-language classroom) are not as likely as less anxious students to become highly proficient in that language (Stevick, 1976). This is probably because anxious students are less likely to take risks and are more likely to feel threatened in a situation in which they are bound to make mistakes.

Thus, there are a number of related attitudes or traits that affect second-language learning. Just as it is important that students have basic proficiency in their native language, it is necessary for them to have basic positive attitudes toward their own language group. Similarly, attitudes that encourage students to approach language learning situations or the new language group can facilitate second-language learning.

First-Language Proficiency

A final and crucial individual characteristic is proficiency in the first language. The level of proficiency that students have attained in their native language at the time they begin to learn the second language directly affects how easily and efficiently they will attain proficiency in the second language. In general, students who come to school with a shaky foundation in their native language may encounter more than the average number of problems when they begin to tackle a second language. One of the major premises for bilingual education in the United States has been that linguistically diverse students are given instruction in their native language before they receive formal instruction in English as a second language. In particular, students who have developed only the social interpersonal skills in their native language (which Cummins [1980] has called "basic interpersonal communication skills") rather than conceptually higher-order or cognitively demanding skills (which Cummins has called "cognitive academic language proficiency") are likely to have difficulty in learning the second language. These students are similar to those described earlier in terms of subtractive bilingualism. Students who have a low literacy level or those who are nonliterate in their native language are likely to find it difficult to learn a second language, especially in a formal classroom setting.

HOME AND COMMUNITY CHARACTERISTICS

Parental and Community Attitudes

The attitudes that an individual's parents have toward the English language or toward English speakers in general are likely to affect that individual's own attitudes, and hence will influence the ability to learn English. Parental attitudes themselves are likely to reflect the attitudes held by their own community and may depend on the perceived social distance between members of the linguistically diverse community and members of the mainstream population. Community attitudes toward English also vary as a function of the role that the ethnic language plays in the larger community and the needs that it serves in both the linguistically diverse and in the mainstream communities. The more vital and viable the ethnic language, the more important it might be for the children to learn and maintain it, sometimes at the expense of the second language (Taylor, 1980).

Literacy in the Home

The level of literacy maintained in the home may influence the student's achievement in school generally. Literacy level strongly affects second-language learning facility, such that students who come from a literate home have a significant advantage over those who do not (Weinstein, 1984). Students who are surrounded by literacy, regardless of whether it is in the native language or English, develop the necessary prereading skills and literacy orientation that produce successful readers. For example, by having an adult read to them out of attractive storybooks, children learn that written language is a representation of meaningful speech and that certain configurations correspond to meaningful words or sounds. These skills, and a general orientation toward literacy, do not simply constitute a set of mechanical coding and decoding skills; rather, they represent a way of processing information. The skills emerge as a result of specific socialization patterns acquired in the home, which prepare students for the cognitive and social demands made on them in a classsroom setting (see Weinstein, [1984] for a review of the research).

In addition to the acquisition of the prereading skills and an orientation to literacy, exposure to reading and writing in the home results in students' attitudinal changes. By seeing people important to them (such as siblings and parents) engrossed in a book or a magazine, students learn to value reading. They learn that reading can be fun and that it is a privilege to enjoy rather than a chore to be completed.

These types of influences are important because prereading skills (such as the orientation to and attitudes toward literacy) are transferable from one language to another (Cummins, 1979). Hence, students who are exposed to literacy in their native language are much better off than those who do not have that exposure. However, many students may lack exposure to literacy in the native language either because the parents themselves are not literate or because they are intent on "teaching the children English." Being limited in English proficiency, parents can only offer their children limited exposure to English. Such parents need to be assured that using the native language and reading books to their children in their native language will not harm their children's English language development. In fact, it is much more preferable for them to give their children extensive exposure to the native language than to expose them to inadequate or inappropriate English.

IMPLICATIONS OF FACTORS AFFECTING SECOND LANGUAGE PROFICIENCY

The research summarized in this section makes it clear that many of the difficulties encountered by second-language learners are due to far more than simple cognitive or academic factors. Such difficulties may result from curricular factors (e.g., a mismatch between students' learning styles and the teaching style utilized) or from personal factors like negative attitudes or low motivation. Further, the personality of a student may not be the most conducive for second-language learning, the student may be experiencing much anxiety in the second-language learning environment or the student's proficiency in the native language may not be adequate to support the processing of information through a second language. Finally, home variables may affect second-language learning: For example, the social atmosphere in the student's home may contribute to lower proficiency due to the parental and community attitudes or practices; the home environment, if it is not linguistically stimulating, may also contribute to inadequate second-language learning opportunities.

This research has a critically important implication for assessment. Educators who are faced with the difficult task of determining whether a problem is due to commonplace second-language difficulties or to more permanent perceptual or cognitive deficits need to consider each of these characteristics of the student. These characteristics must be assessed, even if only informally, and they must be included systematically in any prereferral procedures that a school district or school may have established. The checklist in Table 2-1 may be helpful as a first step in ruling out a second-language difficulty as the source of problems that

Table 2-1. Factors affecting second-language proficiency: A checklist

Individual characteristics

1. Cognitive factors. Does the student's learning/cognitive style match the teaching style? Consider:
   a. Field dependence/independence
   b. Impulsive/reflective styles
   c. Visual/aural preference
2. Attitudinal factors. Does the student have positive attitudes toward:
   a. learning English?
   b. English-speaking peers?
3. Motivational factors. Is the student motivated to:
   a. become a proficient speaker of English?
   b. become a proficient reader and writer of English?
4. Personality factors. Does the student have characteristics that are conducive to attaining proficiency in a second language?
   a. Is the student outgoing?
   b. Does the student feel comfortable in the classroom?
   c. Does the student make friends easily with English-speaking peers?
5. Native-language proficiency. Does the student have the level of native-language proficiency expected of his or her age in:
   a. informal oral communicative settings?
   b. reading and writing?

Home and community characteristics

1. Attitudinal factors. Do the student's parents have positive attitudes toward:
   a. their child's learning of English?
   b. English-speaking persons?
2. Home literacy. Do the parents:
   a. read on a regular basis (daily or at least weekly)?
   b. read to their child (for younger students), or encourage their child to read (for older students)?

This checklist is meant to be an informal guide and an initial step in discovering the reasons for difficulty in developing English proficiency.

a PEP student might be having in school. The three chapters detailing communicative assessment (Chapter Five), educational assessment (Chapter Six), and cognitive assessment (Chapter Seven) have incorporated much of these data into the assessment process.

THE SECOND-LANGUAGE LEARNING PROCESS

Although there are obvious individual differences in students' rate of second-language learning, the basic process through which second-language proficiency is attained is similar for all learners. Many issues have been addressed in the research completed in the last two decades on the process of second-language acquisition. The following questions have the most significant implications for limiting bias in the assessment of PEP students who may be in need of special education services:

1. What role does age play in second-language acquisition?
2. Is second-language acquisition qualitatively different from first-language acquisition?
3. What role does the first language play in second-language acquisition?
4. What are the processes used in second-language learning?

These questions will be answered in the following sections.

THE ROLE OF AGE IN SECOND-LANGUAGE LEARNING

The predominant view among educators is that the general process of learning is qualitatively different for children than it is for adults. Unfortunately, the research evidence on this question specifically regarding second-language learning is complex and demonstrates that some aspects of this type of learning are qualitatively different for children vis-a-vis adults whereas other aspects do not appear to differ. The differences in second-language learning between children and adults can be summarized as follows (Ervin-Tripp, 1974):

1. Children show a greater readiness to learn the language of their peers in a new linguistic environment. Children may be less threatened by a situation in which they are likely to make mistakes than are adults.
2. Children are more perceptive to the sounds of a new language. Various studies of immigrants to the United States have consistently found that younger learners acquire better pronunciation in English than those for whom second-language learning is delayed (Krashen, Long, & Scarcella, 1979).
3. Children usually learn new words through sensory activity and in a tangible immediate context, while adults tend to learn in a purely verbal and abstract context. That is, children learn a new language by "doing it," whereas adults learn a new language by learning about it. To some extent, this may be an artifact of the way English as a second language is usually taught; children are usually taught through hands-on activities and adults through paper and pencil tasks.
4. Children can make linguistic abstractions and learn about struc-

tures never directly presented to them, while adults have a greater capacity to remember explicitly stated grammatical rules.
5. Children seem less subject to interference from their native language than are adults.

Research findings in general indicate that people who begin learning English as a second language during early childhood reach a higher level of proficiency than do adults (Krashen, Long, & Scarcella, 1979). However, recent research also indicates that two assumptions about age differences in second-language learning that have long been held are not true. First, it has been assumed that a young child acquires a language more quickly and easily than an adult because the child is biologically programmed to acquire languages whereas the adult is not. Second, it has been further assumed that even among children, those who are very young have an easier time acquiring the second language than do older children. Research shows both of these beliefs to be unsubstantiated (Genesee, 1987).

While child–adult differences in second-language acquisition exist, evidence for a specifically biological advantage for children in second-language acquisition is lacking, and the current views and conclusions among neurolinguists remain unsettled (Krashen, 1981). The basic premise for the biological advantage hypothesis is that the development of cerebral dominance (specialization of the left and right hemispheres of the brain) regarding language functions is not complete until around puberty. It has been suggested that while this cerebral specialization is taking place, a child's brain has a plasticity and a flexibility that gives a facility to acquire a second language. However, it is unclear just how long the period of plasticity lasts. The evidence from recent neurolinguistic research implies that much of the development of cerebral dominance may be complete much earlier than puberty, and perhaps soon after birth (Genesee, 1982). Thus, whatever age differences there are in second-language acquisition, they are probably unrelated to basic biological factors.

Not only has the hypothesis of a biological advantage for children over adults regarding second-language learning not been supported, some data refute this hypothesis outright. Many researchers, perhaps now a majority, conclude that older learners can, in fact, acquire a second language faster than can younger ones. It usually takes children about 6 months to a year to catch up to those who acquire a second language when older (Snow & Hoefnagel-Hohe, 1978). Older learners are also able to use "the rules" better to consciously learn the language, and they are faster learners because they can use production strategies younger learners do not have (Krashen, Long & Scarcella, 1979). Perhaps more importantly, older learners have a greater knowledge of the real world; this extralinguistic information gives them a better chance to understand what they hear, both in and out of school.

Children typically receive simple linguistic input that is already comprehensible. We tend to use concrete language with children, where the meaning of the utterances is made obvious by the context in which language occurs. In contrast, older learners tend to be exposed to more complex and abstract linguistic input but are able to make that input more comprehensible. This is because older learners can use their native language structure and apply second-language vocabulary to that structure quickly; they are also able to manipulate their linguistic environment by asking questions, slowing down conversation, or keeping the conversation going. By doing so, they make their linguistic input more pedagogically effective. (For an extensive collection of papers on input, see Gass & Madden, 1985.)

Nevertheless, the evidence remains strong that children learning a second language eventually outperform adults in the long run; that is, children attain higher levels of proficiency in the second language than do adults (Krashen, Long, & Scarcella, 1979). Still, the superior performance of children is not a function of biological differences but stems from the affective domain. Children's affective state while approaching the second-language setting is more conducive to learning than is the affective state of the typical adult. Younger learners are less likely than older learners to experience anxiety in using language that they are not proficient in (Stevick, 1976). As a result, younger learners may have strong motivation to learn the second language and high self-confidence to use it—both important conditions for attaining proficiency (Hamayan, Genesee, & Tucker, 1977). Older learners are more likely to be anxious, defensive, or unmotivated; as a consequence, second-language acquisition is impaired. Finally, older learners' attitudes are more likely than younger ones to be firmly set; if those attitudes happen to be negative toward the second language or speakers of that language, learning will be impeded.

DIFFERENCES AND SIMILARITIES BETWEEN FIRST- AND SECOND-LANGUAGE LEARNING

The belief that second-language acquisition is a qualitatively different process from first-language acquisition is not substantiated by research and has probably been generated by comparing the native-language acquisition of *children* to the second-language acquisition of *adults* (Garcia, 1983). Similarities between first- and second-language learning are especially evident when the two languages are learned simultaneously. Studies of childhood bilingualism suggest that the simultaneous acquisition of two languages does not differ significantly from the acquisition of a single language (Swain, 1972): That is, young children being raised bilingually follow the same paths in developing proficiency in the two languages as do children acquiring a single language. Following an initial period of code mixing, the rules of each code begin to be differentiated by the learner. Swain suggests that bilingual language development is 4 to 5 months behind monolingual-language development because the bilingual child has more to acquire and differentiate than does the monolingual child. This disparity is bound to affect young students' performances in the classroom but should not be a source of alarm for teachers of PEP students.

Despite basic similarities between first- and second-language learning (especially when the two languages are being learned simultaneously) there are important differences between the two processes that emerge when the second language is learned after the first. Differences appear in the order of acquisition of certain aspects of language, as well as the extent to which the grammar, the sounds, and the vocabulary of the student's first language interfere in the learning and the use of the grammar, the sounds, and the vocabulary of the second language.

THE ROLE OF THE FIRST LANGUAGE IN SECOND-LANGUAGE LEARNING

The student's first language plays an important role in learning English as a second language. If the first language is adequately developed, it provides the necessary foundation on which to build the second language. In addition, much of what is already mastered in a student's first language (grammatical structures, vocabulary, and phonological rules) can be transferred to the second language, especially if the second language is related to the first.

The need for the student's first language to serve as a foundation for developing the second can best be summarized through the threshold hypothesis, discussed earlier in this chapter in terms of additive and subtractive bilingualism. Briefly, a PEP student's native language must be developed to a level proficient enough to support the addition of another language; below this threshold level, the student is likely to suffer negative consequences both cognitively and academically (Cummins, 1979).

The second way in which the first language contributes to the learning of the second is in the transfer that occurs between languages. We know little about the transfer of skills from one language to another, but there is some evidence for its occurrence at different levels, and especially between languages that are similar. The more similar the two languages are, the more transfer is possible. For example, children speaking Indo-European languages are more accurate in their production of English morphology and their use of English syntax than are speakers of non-IndoEuropean languages (Saville-Troike, 1984). Transfer also occurs in reading so that among PEP students who are learning English as a second language, reading achievement in English is more dependent on students' native language reading ability than on their oral proficiency in English (Saville-Troike, 1984). The underlying principle that allows for transfer between languages is that certain processes are basic to reading and speaking; once these are mastered in one language, they can be applied to another language (Genesee, 1987; Oller, 1979). Also, it has been suggested that cognitive academic language proficiency (CALPS), which includes literacy-related aspects of language, is common or "interdependent" across languages (Cummins & Swain, 1986). This interdependence principle implies that experience with either language can promote the development of proficiency basic to both languages (referred to as common underlying proficiency [CUP] by Cummins).

Transfer between two languages can be both a help and a hindrance. When a structure, word, or sound is common to a student's two languages, the transfer is positive and is advantageous to the learner. For example, a Spanish-speaking student can produce the sound /p/ in English without too much trouble because that same sound (or an allophone) exists in Spanish. However, wherever differences exist between the two languages, and transfer occurs, interference may result.

This form of language transfer, known as linguistic interference, may result in difficulty for the second-language learner acquiring the phonological patterns (Mulford & Hecht, 1980; Wolfram, 1985), grammatical rules (Cancino, Rosansky, & Schumann, 1978; Madrid & Garcia, 1985), or discourse patterns (Young, 1982) of English. In this process, the more dominant native language form interferes with the mastery of the correct form in the second language. The student may have to overcome the linguistic patterns of the first language while learning the second. For example, a Spanish-speaking student is likely to use the wrong word order in English (such as "the house big") as a result of word order in Spanish, where the adjective typically follows the noun. Another form of interference is the case of a sound not existing in the student's native language. For example, an Arabic-speaking student might have difficulty pronouncing the sound /p/ because it does not exist in Arabic, and might say "bill" for "pill."

Even though interference does occur—and there is little doubt that language transfer plays a role in the creation of some of the errors exhibited in second-language learners—the actual impact of interference in second-language error production is controversial (Chun, 1980; Richards, 1971; Tarone, 1976). A prevailing myth suggests that it is an inevitable and universal part of second-language acquisition (McLaughlin, 1984). Research has not always supported this belief; fewer than 5% of all errors in English as a second language are directly traceable to "interferences" from the first language (Dulay & Burt, 1974). Observed errors in second-language learning are more likely related to confusion arising from the target language rather than confusion arising from the structural differences between the two languages. Second-language errors reflect the way in which English as a second language is learned. Consequently, this process should be discussed.

SECOND-LANGUAGE LEARNING PROCESS

Three types of processes underlie the attainments of proficiency in the second language: automatic habit formation, conscious rule learning, and natural acquisition of meaningful language. Evidence for these processes comes from research on the learning strategies used by PEP students and other second-language learners. Although there is no clear definition of learning strategies, they generally refer to activities or plans used by second-language learners to improve their competence in that language (O'Malley, Chamot, Stewner-Manzana-Res, Kupper, & Russo, 1985).

Through habit formation, learners pick up "chunks" of language (usually phrases that are frequently used in everyday conversation) or, in the case of students in a classroom setting, passages that are the focus of an English as a second language lesson. These are then made part of students' automatic verbal repertoire. For example, students often chant "Hello, how are you, fine, thank you" in response to a simple "Hi!", clearly an example of determined memorization of a lesson. Initially, students may not understand the exact meaning of the chunk of language and may use it inappropriately. Automatic language habits, which are based on repeated exposure to a word, phrase, or sentence, give the learner access to automatized responses in specific situations, and are particularly useful to (and typical of) beginning level PEP students.

The second process reflects a more conscious knowledge of the rules of a language (in Krashen's 1981 terms, the product of *learning*). Through this process, the learner develops explicit knowledge *about* the second language and is able to reflect on the rules of grammar, phonology, and semantics. Older students, especially those with a strong native language basis and a solid educational background, are more likely to develop this abstract awareness of language, although children as young as 9 years of age have been known to talk about language rules (Hamayan, 1978). This type of linguistic awareness may well underlie the type of language proficiency that Cummins (1980) refers to as cognitive academic language proficiency. Knowledge of the rules of a language develop primarily through formal instruction where the focus of the lessons is on language per se.

The third process is similar to first-language development in young children and reflects an implicit knowledge of a language or, rather, the ability to use it (in Krashen's terms, the product of *acquisition*). Through this process, language is picked up naturally and emerges through natural stages of development. Thus, students begin with a silent stage that precedes production. When production finally occurs, it emerges in stages. In the earlier stages students might produce no more than single-word utterances, which eventually turn into longer phrases and sentences. When a second language emerges naturally, errors are likely to occur and are a necessary part of the process. Thus, the expectation that many teachers have for PEP students to produce near-perfect sentences in English as a second-language is far from realistic.

Rather than try to stop PEP students from making errors in English, teachers can actually make use of valuable information that second-language errors represent. Two types of errors are notable. The first type of error is due to the interference of verbal habits, well established in students' native language, into their second language. This type of error results when a sound, structure, or word in English is somewhat different from the corresponding sound, structure, or word in the student's native language. Thus, similar interference errors occur among learners with the same native language background.

The second type of error is developmental, in that the errors made by second-language learners are the same as those made by native speakers while acquiring their first language. These errors arise from difficulties within the language itself. For example, both English-speaking children and learners of English as a second language produce sentences such as, "Where she is going?" It has been suggested that such errors reflect general characteristics of learning the particular language regardless of whether it is being acquired as a mother tongue or as a second language. Developmental errors, then, are common to all persons learning English.

IMPLICATIONS OF THE SECOND-LANGUAGE LEARNING PROCESS

Three conclusions from the review of the literature on the second language learning process have implications for educators of PEP students who may have special education needs. First, because of the important role that a student's native language plays in learning English, difficulties exhibited by a PEP student in an English-speaking environment may be due to a lack of a solid foundation in the student's native language. This is distinct from perceptual or cognitive deficits that may lead to learning disabilities. Second, the evidence that second-language learning is similar to first-language acquisition implies that second-language learning is a time consuming process which needs to emerge naturally through a series of developmental stages. Finally, as in first-language acquisition, errors are an inevitable part of the second-language learning process. Rather than attempting to avoid them, teachers of PEP students should be attuned to the specific nature of errors. Such errors are clues to the language-learning and language-use strategies applied by the student and can be used to provide the student with a better linguistic environment.

PATTERNS OF SECOND-LANGUAGE USE

Use of English by nonproficient PEP students often leads educators to wonder whether a student's language difficulties are inordinate or not. Two features of PEP students' language use have particular relevance in distinguishing normal from exceptional second-language use: interlanguage and code switching.

INTERLANGUAGE

As PEP students attempt to communicate in English, their language production reflects an internal language system that consists of combinations of English rules, the students' native language rules, and ad hoc rules adapted from either or both languages (Selinker, 1972; Selinker, Swain, & Dumes, 1975; McLaughlin, 1977). This hybrid language system results in the production of English as a second language that is not like the English of native speakers but only approximates it. The development of this interlanguage, however, is a normal and systematic state of acquisition and not a case of poor or impaired English language learning. Further, this interlanguage production may vary in a speaker due to a number of factors such as the linguistic context, psychological factors, social factors, and the differing functions that some linguistic forms perform in discourse (Tarone, 1988). Consequently, what may seem to be random and incorrect performance (if the PEP student's performance is compared with the target second language [English]) may actually be evidence of a normal language-learning process (Huebner, 1985; Larsen-Freeman, 1975).

Additionally, the resulting interlanguage is a transitional system that constantly changes. It changes within a limited period of time as a function of the context in which language is used (Tarone, 1985). It also changes over time: PEP students in a classroom setting add new words and master new structures and ways of saying things on a daily basis. If a student's English proficiency increases, the interlanguage approximates more closely the language used by a native speaker of the same age. Similarly, the interlanguage of a student who is removed from the second language environment may suffer some backsliding, as aspects of the language that were previously mastered are forgotten.

Some interlanguage forms may reach stability and permanence even though they only approximate the nativelike proficiency level that a learner is aiming for. In this case, errors may seem impossible to correct and may persist regardless of practice and instruction given to the student. This tendency to maintain a less than perfect interlanguage form, also known as fossilization or stabilization (Selinker, 1972), is to be expected. Fossilization is due more to the experiences and motivations of the learner than to some intrinsic language-learning capacity (Schumann, 1978; Vigil & Oller, 1976). Although both backsliding and fossilization are part of the normal second language learning process, fossilization of interlanguage forms and the forgetting of correct language forms have not been studied extensively. It is not clear, for example, whether there are some aspects of language generally, or English specifically, that are particularly prone to fossilization and forgetting. A particularly interesting question for educators of PEP students who may be in need of special education services is whether an inordinate amount of fossilization indicates a long-term perceptual or cognitive deficit in a given student or is simply the way in which that student's particular interlanguage is developing.

That interlanguages are systematic may help to resolve this often-troubling issue. Due to this systematicity, interlanguages follow a predictable pattern, which helps identify the source of difficulty that students may be encountering. Changes in the interlanguage are due to a complex interaction of five central processes: language transfer, transfer of training, strategies of second-language learning, strategies of second-language communication, and generalization of target-language material (for a discussion of these processes, see Selinker, 1972). Teachers of PEP students would do well to observe a student's interlanguage and the changes that occur in that interlanguage when they need to determine the source of difficulty that a student might be having.

CODE SWITCHING

Code switching, another feature of the speech of bilingual students, is a commonly observed type of verbal interaction in bilinguals that involves shifting from one grammatical system to another (Sanchez, 1983). For example, a Spanish-English bilingual might begin an utterance in English and end in Spanish, "I put the forks en las mesas" (Lipski, 1985:18). This behavior may occur within one utterance, as is the case with the previous example (referred to as *intrasentential code switching*), or it may occur across several utterances. That is, the individual might begin an utterance in one language, complete a sentence or two in that language, and then shift to the other language at a true sentence boundary, "I have much to be grateful for. He was responsible for my knowledge of music. Carlitos da para la musica." (Lipski, 1985:26). This is termed *intersentential code switching*.

A common misconception, especially among teachers, is to take code switching as an automatic indicator of inadequate language development or a weak language system that reveals poor bilingual ability. Extensive research on code switching, however (particularly among Spanish-speaking persons in the United States), shows the contrary (Penalosa, 1981). Numerous studies have demonstrated that code switching is a complex, rule-governed phenomenon that carries significant social and psychological implications (Auer, 1984; Genesee, 1984; McClure, 1981; Poplack, 1982). It is also systematically influenced by various contextual and situational factors (Jacobson, 1977; Sanchez, 1983; Sprott & Kemper, 1987). According to the research, the main reason for switching is not inability to come up with the right word or phrase in one language; rather, code switching is a skill that evolves through high levels of proficiency in both languages. Switching takes place so that the speaker may be better able to convey meaning to the listener or to emphasize change of topic. Subtle social messages are also sent by means of code switching, to convey humor, ethnic solidarity, or attitudes toward the listener. Thus, code switching is a complex ability that involves the application of sociolinguistic norms operating within the speaker's speech community (Ramirez, 1985). Because of the important social role that code switching plays, the social situation in which it happens must be taken into account when analyzing bilingual student's language behavior.

The fact that code switching does not necessarily indicate inadequate language development does not mean that students who have lower than optimal proficiency in both languages do not code switch out of necessity. In addition to skilled code switching, there is evidence of forced code switching among young children and learners who are weak in at least one of the languages being used. Educators who are concerned about their PEP students' code switching may want to observe students' use of each language separately in a setting where the use of the other language would be socially inappropriate.

COMPLICATING VARIABLES DURING PEP ASSESSMENT

Due to the nature of second-language acquisition and the phenomena unique to this process, there are a number of behavioral and learning variables that complicate the assessment of limited English proficient students. These variables and how they affect assessment in general must be addressed. The most noteworthy, superficial similarities between PEP versus learning-impaired communication, the transitional and unique behaviors noted in the second language, the need to assess in both the first and the second language, the effects of cultural differences, and listener attitudes toward second language performance, will be discussed in the following sections.

SIMILARITIES IN PROBLEMATIC BEHAVIORS

The first variable of concern involves the way in which a communicative difficulty is exhibited in English. It is well documented that a PEP student learning English will exhibit difficulties in the language (see Chapter One). These difficulties may range from a limited English repertoire that affects grammatical form, lexical selection, fluency, and comprehension on a basic level (Omark & Watson, 1985; Paradis, 1978) to more subtle problems involving conversational and academic discourse (Cheng, 1987; Damico, Oller, & Storey, 1983; Iglesias, 1985; Larsen-Freeman, 1980). Given the nature of the language-learning process, these difficulties are not unexpected.

The problem, however, is that regardless of the underlying cause (normal second language acquisition or a language-learning impairment), communicative difficulties in English have a limited range of observable manifestations and these "problematic behaviors" are exhibited whenever there are communicative problems. Typically, the PEP population exhibits the same superficial manifestations of communicative and academic difficulty in English (e.g., phonological miscues, reduced verbal output, grammatical errors, comprehension difficulties, interactional problems) that are observed in language-learning disordered monolingual English speakers. As a result, observation of these superficial manifestations of communicative difficulty (behaviors which are routinely used as indices of language-learning impairment in monolingual English populations) cannot be utilized in the same way with the PEP population. When these problematic behaviors are observed in PEP students, they only indicate difficulty in English and not necessarily an intrinsic language-learning impairment. Consequently, they cannot be used to effectively differentiate between normal and impaired PEP communicators. This is an important point. If these problematic communicative behaviors are utilized as indices of intrinsic language impairment in the PEP population, many students exhibiting apparent language or communicative difficulties as a normal aspect of the process of second language acquisition may be misdiagnosed as having a speech, language, or learning disorder and may be inappropriately placed into special education programs (Cummins, 1984; Kayser, 1987).

Due to the similarities in superficial manifestations of difficulty, therefore, assessment in the PEP population must employ a different set of evaluative criteria than those used for monolingual English speakers. As noted by Westby (1985) and Seymour (1985), traditional indices of language impairment are not sufficient when assessing culturally and linguistically diverse (C/LD) students. The evaluator must also take into account apparent difficulties due to cultural and interactive differences that may make the normal C/LD student appear impaired.

THE COMPLEXITY OF SECOND-LANGUAGE ACQUISITION

A second complicating variable involves the complexity of second-language acquisition as a process. As previously discussed, this complexity reveals itself in the transitional nature of second language acquisition and in the numerous behaviors and phenomena that are not evident in first-language acquisition but that may occur as a normal aspect of second language acquisition.

Unlike monolingual English-speaking students who bring a relatively stable English language system to the schools, PEP students acquiring English as a second language are typically in a more dynamic stage of language acquisition. Consequently, the English performances of these students may vary greatly between individuals, across settings, and over time (Dulay, Burt, & Krashen, 1982; Hyltenstam, 1985; Wong-Fillmore, 1979). This degree of variation is dependent on many factors. In addition to a student's intrinsic language-learning potential, for example, the individual's motivation (Schumann, 1978; Wald, 1985), exposure to English (Goldstein, 1987; Krashen, 1982), the feedback received from others (Beebe and Zuengler, 1983; Schumann, 1978; Vigil & Oller, 1976), the opportunity to use the language (McLaughlin, 1977; Swain &

Wesche, 1975), and the behavioral context (Bell, 1984; Tarone, 1988) all help structure the normal process of acquisition. Due to this complex transitional aspect of second language acquisition, the assessment process must be designed to individually describe each PEP student's current level of English proficiency and to determine which variables have affected the student's acquisition. Careful description of the PEP student's attitudes and experiences (data that cannot be obtained by a test) must be conducted to determine which variables have influenced the individual's second language acquisition. As suggested by Mattes and Omark (1984), a PEP student's language performance should be compared with the performances of students that share common cultural and linguistic experiences if valid assessment is to occur. This guideline, however, does not go far enough. The evaluator must also attempt to determine the individual student's reaction to these experiences (Kayser, 1987; Omark, 1981).

In addition to the dynamic and transitional nature of second language acquisition, the evaluator must also be aware of the several second language phenomena discussed previously. These phenomena—linguistic interference, interlanguage development, rule fossilization or stabilization, and code switching—are all normal factors in acquiring a second language. The primary concern with each, of course, is that these normal phenomena may lead the uninformed evaluator or teacher to form the mistaken impression that the student is a poor language learner when this is not necessarily the case. For example, due to language transfer or interference, the normal learner may undergo "U-shaped development" in English acquisition whereby early accuracy is followed by significantly poorer performance before further improvement is noted (Kellerman, 1985; Yule, Damico, & Hoffman, 1988). Such "backsliding" should not be interpreted as evidence of poor language-learning ability but, rather, as a normal process of overcoming various types of interference (Selinker, 1972).

KNOWLEDGE AND PROFICIENCY IN THE FIRST LANGUAGE

Given the previous discussion on the complexity of second language acquisition and the ways in which the first language might affect the acquisition of English, the importance of a working knowledge of the PEP student's first language should be clear. Assessment of PEP students must include analysis of the ways in which the first language has potentially affected the student's English performance. Typically, this will require enough knowledge of the first language to conduct an error analysis to differentiate between expected problems due to interference or transfer and problems of a more general type, which might suggest true learning deficits (Eblen, 1982; Wolfram, 1985). Additionally, it is essential that the communicative evaluation occur in the PEP student's first language as well as in English (Juarez, 1983). In order to identify a true language-learning impairment in the PEP population, indices of communicative difficulty must be present in both the first language and in English. This is a logical implication of the construct of language proficiency (see Chapter Three). As noted by Oller (1979), Cummins (1984), Shuy (1981) and others, there is a common language proficiency underlying the surface-level aspects of both the first and the second language. This underlying proficiency is affected by an intrinsic language-learning impairment, which will be manifested in both languages. Consequently, it is necessary to conduct an evaluation in both languages to identify a true language-learning impairment.

This requirement is problematic given that most special educators and evaluators in the United States, Canada, Great Britain, and Australia are monolingual English speakers. For example, in the United States, speech-language pathologists conduct most communicative assessments in the schools; members of this profession typically are not bilingual (Cole, 1985). It is possible, however, to use the services of the monolingual speech-language pathologist trained in assessment and linguistic analysis techniques and the services of another professional or paraprofessional proficient in the PEP student's first language (see Chapter Four).

EFFECTS OF CULTURAL DIVERSITY

Individuals learn language and communication at their local levels; this learning is embedded in the cultural contexts that surround the individuals when the first language is acquired (Heath, 1983; Nelson, 1985; Vygotsky, 1962). A learner's context structures the interactions, assumptions, and expectations used in the development of language and forms that person's knowledge of the world and the skills needed to achieve comprehensibility (Oller, 1989; Smith, 1982). It is not surprising, therefore, that changes in the cultural context experienced by PEP students when entering the schools will significantly affect these students. As discussed by Chamberlain and Landurand (see Chapter Four), the mismatch between a student's native culture and that of the schools may have a profound impact on these students' communication, motivation, and performances.

These cultural differences between the PEP student's native context and that of the mainstream schools complicate the assessment process (but not in the manner expected). Instead of complicating test selection or administration, cultural diversity issues complicate test interpretation.

It should be expected that PEP students from diverse cultural backgrounds typically will perform more poorly on formal English tests and will experience difficulty in English interactions (Oller, 1979). By design, tests are biased against those who do not speak the language or do not come from the same cultural context. That is the purpose of testing: to discriminate between various levels of skill regardless of the causal factors. When interpreting the results of testing and drawing implications from these results, however, the evaluator must account for cultural diversity as an explanatory mechanism (Adler, 1981; Carpenter, 1986; Troike, 1984; Wolfram, 1983). This requires a strong knowledge of the cultural variables that might contribute to the PEP student's poor performance. The evaluator, therefore, must have knowledge of any cultural differences and must understand how these cultural mismatches might be expressed.

EFFECTS OF LISTENER ATTITUDES

The last major complicating variable involves the well-documented effects of listener attitudes toward nonnative English speakers. As demonstrated in the work of Williams (1973), Taylor (1973), and others (see Eisenstein, 1983), negative attitudes held by school personnel toward the speech of nonnative (and nonmainstream) speakers present major pedagogical barriers to both PEP and C/LD students. Whether consciously or unconsciously applied, these attitudes can result in the lowering of expectations (Brophy, 1983; Cummins, 1986) and inappropriate referrals (Rodriguez, Prieto, & Rueda, 1984).

Once a student is referred, negative attitudes can further affect the PEP students due to evaluators' language attitudes. Test selection and all aspects of test adminstration, scoring, and interpretation may be affected. Gerken and Deichmann (1979), for example, found that the ability to accurately record and score something as concrete as responses on a vocabulary test was affected by dialectal and attitudinal factors. Figueroa (1983) has expressed similar concerns about the effects of attitudinal bias when assessing Hispanic children. Unless evaluators are aware of the potential biasing effects of language attitudes, PEP students may be misidentified and placed into special education inappropriately.

CONCLUSIONS

Educators of PEP students who are attempting to determine whether a student is having problems due to normal and temporary second-language learning difficulties or to more permanent deficits must be aware of features and types of bilingualism and the process of second-language learning. This information is also crucial for those who are faced with the task of assessing PEP students' abilities and skills. The following implications for limiting bias in assessment of PEP students emerge from the issues discussed in this chapter.

First, the complexity of language proficiency and the various types of bilingualism that exist indicate the need for a comprehensive assessment of both English and the student's other language(s). Both oral and literacy skills must be assessed in a variety of formal and informal settings.

Second, the findings that second-language proficiency is affected by a variety of affective and social factors imply that problems encountered by PEP students in the second language may be due to a large number of individual characteristics of the learner and the home environment, many of which are not concerned with cognitive ability.

Third, because of the complexity of the second-language learning process, errors and difficulties in English encountered by PEP students are to be expected.

Fourth, an analysis of the patterns of second-language use indicates that it is not only natural but expected for PEP students to switch from one language to another within a conversation.

Considerable controversy surrounds bilingualism. Many opponents of bilingualism propose that students would progress in English more rapidly if they were to let go of their first language. However, the research literature clearly demonstrates that this is false. Instead, the development of basic skills in the native language as well as the development of positive attitudes toward the native language itself and the native ethnolinguistic group are important prerequisites for the full development of English language skills. Thus, while many of the factors that impede the learning of English as a second language are outside the control of the teacher or even the parents or the school system as a whole, it is nonetheless clear that an atmosphere wherein the students themselves and their native language are fully valued and developed facilitates achievement by PEP students. Attention to specific deficits, learning style, and the creation of a nonanxiety provoking and non-threatening language-learning setting can be extremely helpful in the development of English language skills. Only when these factors have been fully attended to can one consider the presence of more fundamental cognitive or perceptual deficits as the cause of PEP students' underachievement.

REFERENCES

Adler, S. (1981). Testing: Considerations in cultural differences. *Seminars in Speech, Language, and Hearing, 2,* 77–90.

Alvarez, M.D. (1984). Puerto Ricans and academic achievement: An exploratory study of person, home and school variables among high-risk bilingual first graders. (Doctoral dissertation, New York University, 1983). *Dissertation Abstracts International*, DA 8325197.

Asher, J., & Garcia, R. (1969). The optimal age to learn a foreign language. *Modern Language Journal*, 53, 334–341.

Auer, J. C. P. (1984). *Bilingual Conversation*. Amsterdam: John Benjamins Publishing Company.

Bain, B. (1975). Toward an integration of Piaget and Vygotsky: Bilingual considerations. *Linguistics*, 160, 5–20.

Beebe, L., & Zuengler, J. (1983). Accommodation theory: An explanation for style shifting in second language dialects. In N. Wolfson and E. Judd (Eds.), *Sociolinguistics and language acquisition* (pp. 195–213). Rowley, MA: Newbury House.

Bell, A. (1984). Language style as audience design. *Language in Society*, 13, 145–204.

Ben-Zeev, S. (1977). The effects of Spanish–English bilingualism in children from less privileged neighborhoods on cognitive development and cognitive flexibility. *Working Papers on Bilingualism*, 14, 83–122.

Brophy, J.E. (1983). Research on the self-fulfilling prophecy and teacher expectations. *Journal of Educational Psychology* 75, 631–661.

Burt, M., Dulay, H., & McKeon, D. (1980). *Testing and teaching communicatively handicapped Hispanic children: The state of the art.* Sacramento, CA: California Department of Education.

Canale, M., & Swain, M. (1980). Theoretical bases of communicative approaches to second language teaching and testing. *Applied Linguistics*, 1, 1–47.

Cancino, H., Rosansky, E. J., & Schumann, J. H. (1978). The acquisition of English negatives and interrogatives by native Spanish speakers. In E. M. Hatch (Ed.) *Second Language Acquisition* (pp. 207–230). Rowley, MA: Newbury House.

Carpenter, L. (1986). Influence of examiner knowledge on decision making with language minorities. A miniseminar presented at the American Speech-Language-Hearing Association Convention. Detroit, MI, November.

Cheng, L. L. (1987). *Assessing Asian language performance*. Rockville, MD: Aspen.

Chun, J. (1980). A survey of research in second language acquisition. In K. Croft (Ed.), *Readings on English as a second language* (pp. 181–198). Cambridge, MA: Winthrop Publishers.

Cole, L. (1985). Minority concerns: Progress and challenge. A miniseminar presented at the American Speech-Language-Hearing Association Convention. Washington, DC, November.

Cummins, J. (1978). Educational implicaitons of mother tongue maintenance in minority-language groups. *The Canadian Modern Language Review*, 34, 395–416.

Cummins, J. (1979). Linguistic interdependence and the educational development of bilingual children. *Review of Educational Research*, 49, 222–251.

Cummins, J. (1980). The entry and exit fallacy in bilingual education. *NABE Journal*, 4, 25–59.

Cummins, J. (1984). *Bilingualism and special education: Issues in assessment and pedagogy*. Austin, TX: PRO-ED.

Cummins, J. (1986). Empowering minority students: A framework for intervention. *Harvard Educational Review*, 56, 18–35.

Cummins, J., & Swain, M. (1986). *Bilingualism in education*. New York: Longman.

Damico, J. S., Oller, J. W., Jr., & Storey, M. E. (1983). The diagnosis of language disorders in bilingual children: Pragmatic and Surface-oriented criteria. *Journal of Speech and Hearing Disorders, 48,* 385–394.

Diaz, R. (in press). Bilingual cognitive development: Assessing three gaps in current research, *Child Development.*

Dulay, H. C., & Burt, M. K. (1974). Errors and strategies in child second language acquisition. *TESOL Quarterly, 8,* 129–136.

Dulay, H., Burt, M., & Krashen, S. (1982). *Language Two.* New York: Oxford University Press.

Eblen, R. E. (1982). Some observations on the phonological assessment of Hispanic-American children. *Journal of the National Student Speech Language Hearing Association, 10,* 44–54.

Eisenstein, M. (1983). Native reactions to nonnative speech: A review of empirical research. *Studies in Second Language Acquisition, 5,* 160–176.

Ervin-Tripp, S. (1974). Is second language learning like the first? *TESOL Quarterly, 8,* 111–127.

Figueroa, R. (1983). Test bias and Hispanic children. *Journal of Special Education, 17,* 431–440.

Garcia, E. (1983). *Early childhood bilingualism.* Albuquerque, NM: University of New Mexico Press.

Gardner, R. C., & Lambert, W. E. (1972). *Attitudes and motivation in second language learning.* Rowley, MA: Newbury House.

Gass, S., & Madden, C. (Eds.) (1985). *Input in second language acquisition.* Rowley, MA: Newbury House.

Genesee, F. (1976). The role of intelligence in second language learning. *Language Learning, 26,* 267–280.

Genesee, F. (1982). Experimental neuropsychological research on second language processing. *TESOL Quarterly, 16,* 315–322.

Genesee, F. (1984). The social-psychological significance of bilingual code switching for children. *Applied Psycholinguistics, 5,* 3–20.

Genesee, F. (1987). *Learning through two languages: studies of immersion and bilingual education.* Cambridge, MA: Newbury House.

Genesee, F., & Hamayan, E. (1980). Individual differences in second language learning. *Applied Psycholinguistics, 1,* 95–110.

Gerken, K. C. & Deichmann, J. W. (1979). The ability of listeners to report oral responses of Black and White children. *Language, Speech, and Hearing Services in Schools, 10,* 35–46.

Goldstein, L. M. (1987). Standard English: The only target for nonnative speakers of English? *TESOL Quarterly, 21,* 417–436.

Hakuta, K. (1986). *Mirror of language.* New York: Basic Books.

Hamayan, E. (1978). *Acquisition of French syntactic structures: production strategies and awareness of errors by young native and nonnative speakers.* Ph.D. Dissertation, McGill University, Montreal.

Hamayan, E., Genesee, F., & Tucker, G. R. (1977). Affective factors and language exposure in second language learning. *Language Learning, 27,* 225–241.

Hammerly, H. (1982). *Synthesis in second language teaching: an introduction to Linguistics.* Blaine, WA: Second Language Publications.

Haugen, E. (1953). *The Norwegian language in America: A study in bilingual behavior.* Philadelphia: University of Pennsylvania Press.

Heath, S. B. (1983). *Ways with words.* Cambridge, MA: Cambridge University Press.

Huebner, T. (1985). System and variability in interlanguage syntax. *Language Learning, 35,* 141–163.

Hyltenstam, K. (1985). Second language variable output and language teaching. In K. Hyltenstam and M. Pienemann (Eds.), *Modelling and assessing second language acquisition* (pp. 113–136). Clevedon, Avon: Multilingual Matters Ltd.

Ianco-Worrall, A. (1972). Bilingualism and cognitive development. *Child Development, 43,* 1390–1400.

Iglesias, A. (1985). Cultural conflict in the classroom: The communicatively different child. In D. N. Ripich and F. M. Spinelli (Eds.), *School discourse problems* (pp. 79–96). Austin, TX: PRO-ED.

Jacobson, R. (1977). The social implication of intra-sentential code-switching. *The New Scholar, 6,* 227–256.

Jacobson, R. (1985). Uncovering the covert bilingual: How to retrieve the hidden home language. In E. E. Garcia and R. V. Padilla (Eds.), *Advances in bilingual education research* (pp. 150–180). Tucson: The University of Arizona Press.

Juarez, M. (1983). Assessment and treatment of minority-language children: The role of monolingual speech–language pathologist. *Topics in Language Disorders, 3,* 57–66.

Kayser, H. G. (1987). A study of three Mexcian American children labeled language disordered. *NABE Journal, 12,* 1–22.

Kellerman, E. (1985). If at first you do succeed . . . In S. Gass and C. Madden (Eds.), *Input in second language acquisition* (pp. 345–353). Rowley, MA: Newbury House.

Krashen, S. D. (1973). Lateralization, language learning, and the critical period: Some new evidence. *Language Learning, 23,* 63–74.

Krashen, S. D. (1981). *Second language acquisition and second language learning.* Oxford: Pergamon Press.

Krashen, S. D. (1982). *Principles and practice in second language acquisition.* Oxford: Pergamon.

Krashen, S. D., Long, M., & Scarcella, R. (1979). Age, rate and eventual attainment in second language acquisition. *TESOL Quarterly, 13,* 573–582.

Lambert, W. E. (1977). The effects of bilingualism on the individual: Cognitive and sociocultural consequences. In P. A. Hornby (Ed.), *Bilingualism: psychological, social and educational implications* (pp. 15–27). New York: Academic Press.

Larsen-Freeman, D. (1975). The acquisition of grammatical morphemes by adult ESL students. *TESOL Quarterly, 9,* 409–419.

Larsen-Freeman, D. (1980). *Discourse analysis in second language research.* Rowley, MA: Newbury House.

Lieberson, S., Dalto, G., & Johnston, M. E. (1975). The course of mother-tongue diversity in nations. *American Journal of Sociology, 81,* 34–61.

Liedke, W. W. & Nelson, L. D. (1968). Concept formation and bilingualism. *Alberta Journal of Educational Research, 14,* 225–232.

Lipski, J. M. (1985). *Linguistic aspects of Spanish-English language switching.* Tempe, AZ: Center for Latin American Studies.

Macnamara, J. (1967). The bilingual's linguistic performance—a psychological overview. *Journal of Social Issues, 23,* 58–77.

Madrid, D. L., & Garcia, E. E. (1985). The effect of language transfer on bilingual proficiency. In E. E. Garcia and R. V. Padilla (Eds.), *Advances in bilingual education research* (pp. 53–70). Tuscon, AZ: University of Arizona Press.

Mattes, L. J., & Omark, D. R. (1984). *Speech and language assessment for the bilingual handicapped.* Austin, TX: PRO-ED.

McClure, E. (1981). Formal and functional aspects of the code-switched discourse of bilingual children. In R. Duran (Ed.), *Latino language and communicative behavior* (pp. 69–94). Norwood, NJ: ABLEX.

McKirnan, D. J., & Hamayan, E. V. (1984). Speech norms and attitudes toward outgroup members: A test of a model in a bicultural context. *Language and Social Psychology, 3,* 31–38.

McLaughlin, B. (1977). Second language learning in children. *Psychological Bulletin, 84,* 438–459.

McLaughlin, B. (1984). *Second-language acquisition in childhood. Vol. I, Preschool children.* Hillsdale, NJ: Lawrence Erlbaum Associates.

Milroy, L. (1987). *Language and social networks* (2nd ed.). Oxford: Basil Blackwell.

Mulford, R., & Hecht, B. F. (1980). Learning to speak without an accent: Acquisition of a second language phonology. *Papers Representing Child Language Development, 18,* 16–74.

Naiman, N., Frohlich, M., & Stern, H. H. (1975). *The good language learner.* Toronto: Ontario Institute for Studies in Education.

Nelson, K. (1985). *Making sense: The acquisition of shared meaning.* New York: Academic Press.

Oller, J. W., Jr. (1979). *Language tests at school.* London: Longman.

Oller, J. W., Jr. (1989). *Language and Experience.* Lanham, MD: University Press of America.

Oller, J. W., Jr., Baca, L., & Vigil, A. (1978). Attitudes and attained proficiency in ESL: A sociolinguistic study of Mexican Americans in the Southwest. *TESOL Quarterly, 11,* 173–183.

Oller, J. W., Jr., & Perkins, K. (Eds.), (1978). *Language tests at School: Testing the tests.* Rowley, MA: Newbury House.

Oller, J. W., Jr., & Perkins, K. (Eds.), (1980). *Research in language testing.* Rowley, MA: Newbury House.

O'Malley, J. M., Chamot, A. U., Stewner-Manzana-Res, G., Kupper, L., & Russo, R. P. (1985). Learning strategies used by beginning and intermediate ESL students. *Language Learning, 35,* 21–46.

Omark, D. R. (1981). Pragmatics and ethnological techniques for the observational assessment of children's communicative abilities. In J. G. Erickson and D. R. Omark (Eds.), *Communicative assessment of the bilingual bicultural child* (pp. 249–284). Baltimore: University Park Press.

Omark, D. R., & Watson, D. L. (1985). *Assessing bilingual exceptional children: In-service manual.* San Diego: Los Amigos Research Associates.

Paradis, M. (1978). The stratification of bilingualism. In M. Paradis (Ed.), *Aspects of bilingualism* (pp. 165–175). Columbia, SC: Hornbeam Press.

Paulston, C. B. (1975). Ethnic relations and bilingual education: Accounting for contradictory data. *Working Papers on Bilingualism, 6,* 1–44.

Peal, E., & Lambert, W. E. (1962). The relations of bilingualism to intelligence. *Psychological Monographs, 76,* 1–23.

Penalosa, F. (1981). *Introduction to the sociology of language.* Rowley, MA: Newbury House.

Pinsleur, P. (1980). *How to learn a foreign language.* Boston: Heinle and Heinle.

Poplack, S. (1982). Sometimes I'll start a sentence in Spanish y termino en español: Toward a typology of code-switching. In J. Amastae and L. Elias-Olivares (Eds.), *Spanish in the United States: Sociolinguistic Aspects* (pp. 230–263). Cambridge University Press.

Ramirez, A. (1985). *Bilingualism through schooling: Cross-cultural education for minority and majority students.* Albany, NY: State University of New York Press.

Richards, J. C. (1971). Error analysis and second language strategies. *Language Sciences, 17,* 12–22.

Rodriguez, R., Prieto, A., & Rueda, R. (1984). Issues in bilingual multicultural special education. *NABE Journal, 8,* 55–66.

Sanchez, R.(1983). *Chicano Discourse.* Rowley, MA: Newbury House.

Saville-Troike, M. (1984). What really matters in second language learning for academic achievement? *TESOL Quarterly, 18,* 199–219.

Schumann, J. (1976). Social distance as a factor in second language acquisition. *Language Learning, 26,* 135–143.

Schumann, J. H. (1978). *Second language acquisition: The Pidginization hypothesis.* Rowley, MA: Newbury House.

Seligman, C. F., Tucker, G. R., & Lambert, W. E. (1972). The effects of speech style and other attributes on teachers' attitudes towards pupils. *Language and Society, 1,* 131–132.

Selinker, L. (1972). Interlanguage. *International Review of Applied Linguistics, 10,* 209–231.

Selinker, L., Swain, M., & Dumas, G. (1975). The interlanguage hypothesis extended to children. *Language Learning, 25,* 139–152.

Seymour, H. N. (1985). Pragmatics and inter-dialectal dissonance: Clinical implications. A miniseminar presented at the American Speech-Language-Hearing Association convention, Washington, DC, November.

Shore, M.S. (1974). *The content analysis of 125 Title VII Bilingual Programs funded in 1969 and 1970.* Bilingual Education Research Unit, Project BEST. New York City Bilingual Consortium, Hunter College Division.

Shuy, R. (1981). A holistic view of language. *Research in the teaching of English, 15,* 101–111.

Skutnabb-Kangas, T., & Toukomaa, T. (1976). *Teaching migrant children's mother tongue and learning the language of the host country in the context of the sociocultural situation of the migrant family.* Helsinki: The Finnish National Commission for UNESCO.

Smith, F. (1982). How children learn? *Interdisciplinary Voice, 1.* Austin, TX: Society for Learning Disabilities and Remedial Education.

Snow, C., & Hoefnagel-Hohe, M. (1978). The critical period for language acquisition: evidence from second language meaning. *Child Development, 49,* 1114–1128.

Sprott, R. A., & Kemper, S. (1987). The development on children's code-switching: A study of six bilingual children across two situations. In E. F. Pemberton, M. A. Sell, and G. B. Simpson (Eds.), *Working Papers in Language Development: 1987, 2,* 116–134.

Stevick, E. (1976). *Memory, meaning and method.* Rowley, MA: Newbury House.

Swain, M. (1972). *Bilingualism as a first language.* Ph.D. Dissertation, University of California, Irvine.

Swain, M., & Cummins, J. (1986). Bilingualism, cognitive functioning and education. In J. Cummins and M. Swain (Eds.), *Bilingualism in education.* New York: Longman.

Swain, M., & Wesche, M. (1975) Linguistic interaction: A case study. *Language Sciences, 37,* 17–22.

Tarone, E. (1976). Some influences on interlanguage phonology. *Working Papers in Bilingualism, 8,* 87–111.

Tarone, E. (1985). Variability in interlanguage use: a study of style-shifting in morphology and syntax. *Language Learning, 35,* 373–403.

Tarone, E. (1988). *Variation in interlanguage.* London: Edward Arnold.

Taylor, D. (1980). Ethnicity and language: A social psychological perspective. In H. Gles, W. P. Robinson, and P. Smith (Eds.), *Language: Social psychological perspective.* Oxford: Pergamon Press.

Taylor, O. (1973). Attitudes toward Black and nonstandard English as measured by the language attitude scale. In R. Shuy and R. Fasold (Eds.), *Language attitudes: Current trends and prospects* (pp. 174–201). Washington, DC: Georgetown University Press.

Troike, R. C. (1984). SCALP: Social and cultural aspects of language proficiency. In C. Rivera (Ed.), *Language proficiency and academic achievement* (pp. 44–54). Avon, England: Multilingual Matters.

Trueba, H. (Ed.) (1987). *Success or failure? Learning and the language minority student.* Cambridge, MA: Newbury House.

Tucker, G. R., Hamayan, E. & Genesee, F. (1976). Affective, cognitive and social factors in second language acquisition. *Canadian Modern Language Review, 23,* 214–226.

Valdez, R. (1969). The fallacy of the Spanish surname survey. *CTA Journal, 65,* 29–30.

Veltman, C. (1979). *The assimilation of American language minorities: Structure, pace and extent.* Washington, DC: National Center for Education Statistics.

Vigil, N. A., & Oller, J. W., Jr. (1976). Rule fossilization: A tentative model. *Language Learning, 26,* 281–295.

Vygotsky, L. S. (1962). *Thought and language.* Cambridge, MA: MIT Press.

Wald, B. (1985). Motivation for language choice behavior of elementary Mexican American children. In E. E. Garcia and R. V. Padilla (Eds.), *Advances in bilingual education research* (pp. 71–95). Tucson: University of Arizona Press.

Weinstein, G. (1984). Literacy and second language acquisition: Issues and perspectives. *TESOL Quarterly, 18,* 471–484.

Westby, C. E. (1985). Cultural differences in adult-child interaction: Assessment and intervention implications. A miniseminar presented at the American Speech-Language-Hearing Association convention. Washington, DC, November.

Williams, F. (1973). Dialect attitudes and stereotyping. In R. W. Shuy & R. W. Fasold (Eds.), *Language Attitudes: Current trends and prospects* (pp. 113–128). Washington, DC: Georgetown University Press.

Wolfram, W. (1983). Test interpretation and sociolinguistic differences. *Topics in Language Disorders, 3,* 8–20.

Wolfram, W. (1985). The phonologic system: Problems of second language acquisition. In J. M. Costello (Ed.), *Speech disorders in adults* (pp. 59–76). Austin, TX: PRO-ED.

Wong-Fillmore, L. (1979). Individual differences in second language acquisition. In C. J. Fillmore, D. Kempler, & W. S. Y. Wang (Eds.), *Individual differences in language ability and language behavior* (pp. 203–228). New York: Academic Press.

Young, L. W. L. (1982). Inscrutability revisited. In J. J. Gumperz (Ed.), *Language and social identity* (pp. 72–84). Cambridge: Cambridge University Press.

Yule, G., Damico, J., & Hoffman, P. (1987). Learners in transition: Evidence from the interaction of accuracy and self-monitoring. *Language Learning, 37,* 511–521.

CHAPTER 3

Theoretical Considerations in the Assessment of LEP Students

JOHN W. OLLER, JR. AND
JACK S. DAMICO

When preparing to evaluate LEP students, teachers need a theoretical foundation. Every assessment procedure, every test developed, every attempt to interpret test scores, even the belief in assessment itself, is based (either explicitly or implicitly) on a theory of the ability or behavior to be evaluated. If language assessment is involved, a theory of language is necessary. That theory will determine to a large extent what type of test to use (e.g., discrete point or pragmatic), how and where to do the testing or observation (e.g., in a contrived situation or in a natural environment), and how to interpret the results (e.g., as an academic problem or a language impairment).

Such decisions hinge on a theory of what language is and how it relates to other mental abilities or behaviors. The determining factor is a conception, a theory, of what language proficiency is. This chapter addresses the question of language theory and its practical bearing on the assessment of LEP students. First, Cronbach's idea of the need for theoretical constructs and their interaction with experimental or observational evidence is presented. The point is to give an idea of how an accountable theory can be developed and how it should guide and, at the same time, be shaped by practice. Next appears a review of empirical research with language assessment procedures and tests leading into an overview of three theoretical paradigms of language testing: (1) discrete point theory based on the hypothesis that language proficiency (and mental abilities in general) can be divided into distinct bits and pieces; (2) integrative theory based on the idea that language proficiency may be holistic and unified in important respects; and (3) pragmatic theory, which aims to absorb the best of both worlds (i.e., discrete point and integrative ideas).

After reviewing three decades of research and practice and overhauling several competing theoretical positions, a hierarchical model of representational (semiotic) capacities following C. S. Peirce (1839–1914) and, more recently, Noam Chomsky is presented. John B. Carrol (1983a) and Vollmer and Sang (1983) have expressed hope for a hierarchical model along with acknowledging that no one of the currently popular theories of language is adequate to meet educators' everyday requirements (Bachman, 1989; Crystal, 1987; Cummins, 1981). This chapter, therefore, is a step toward filling the need for a more adequate theory.

After presenting a hierarchical model, various sorts of empirical and theoretical evidence in its favor are offered. These include the theory's straightforward explanation of human ability to translate representations from one modality (e.g., visual) into another (e.g., linguistic) and to distinguish different kinds of representations such as immediate experience from memory, or memory from imagination. The theory is also shown to suggest heuristically appealing explanations of the interrelatedness of different sorts of cognitive capacities (such as consciousness and short-term and long-term memory) and diverse representational systems (e.g., sensory-motor, gestural or kinesic, and linguistic ones). It explains well-known facts about the interrelationship of primary and nonprimary language acquisition and hypotheses about the role of primary language development in intellectual growth. Transfer and interference, Krashen's input hypothesis (Krashen, 1982; 1985), Cummins' threshold hypothesis, his CALP/BICS distinction (Cummins, 1976; 1984), and a potentially inexhaustible plethora of componential models of language proficiency are explained. The ultimate end in view is a theory that will reduce bias and enhance assessment procedures employed with LEP students.

CONSTRUCT VALIDITY

It is axiomatic that human behavior is guided by internal states that to some extent conform to or help determine external conditions. For rational individuals, actions are influenced by beliefs, expectancies, cognitive structures, attitudes, and mental abilities (Dewey, 1938; Piaget, 1970; Oller, 1989b). Depending in large measure on such internal factors, human beings make decisions, react to their environments, and expect certain outcomes (Cummins, 1985; Savage, 1978).

According to Cronbach (1970), it is necessary to develop theoretical notions, which he called "constructs": theoretical factors posited as organizers or controllers of some aspect of behavior. The "construct(s)" posited must with some determinable reliability be seen in real life performances. It (or they) must allow measurement or testing that will enable an educator, clinician, or other interpreter to predict or explain certain aspects of human performance.

For instance, a person who possesses a certain ability (defined by the theoretical construct) can be expected to perform, at a given level, a range of tasks with a certain probability (Cronbach & Meehl, 1955). As far as a postulated construct enables accurate predictions, it is judged to be valid: It has construct validity (Cronbach & Meehl, 1955). Wherever a construct fails to predict accurately, it will be modified. Each construct, then, acts as part of a theory of cognition and behavior. It must be sustained by experience or revised (Cronbach, 1971). In this way, measurement theory guides assessment procedures and yet is also subject to improvement as the constructs of the theory and their interrelationships are shaped by observed results (Piaget, 1970).

In the assessment of LEP students, the impact of beliefs about human abilities (the theoretical constructs posited) will have the same sort of effects as beliefs in general have. They will affect what educators do. If language ability is the focus, then a theory of language proficiency is required. To the extent that the theory is on the right track and the assessment procedure is a valid implementation of the theory, results obtained will enable consistent (reliable) and accurate (valid) predictions about actual capabilities and performances of students. This is the same as saying that the "test" (or assessment procedure) will be a valid measure of its construct(s) and that it will enable accurate prediction beyond the testing situation. The acid test of any theory, of any construct that is part of a theory, or of any test or measurement procedure based on the theory is its behavioral relevance (Cronbach, 1970).

In the assessment of LEP students, it would be impossible to deny a central role to the construct of language proficiency. It will be at the heart of any valid assessment procedure or test. Because of its importance to language acquisition and language use in general, language proficiency has been the focus for the last 30 years of an increasing quantity of published research (Bachman & Palmer, 1983; Canale & Swain, 1980; Carroll, 1961; Oller, 1979; Spolsky, 1968a) and a growing number of national and international conferences and symposia (Alderson & Hughes, 1982; Oller, 1983b; Palmer, Groot & Trosper, 1981; Rivera, 1984). Whether the theoretical issue is explicitly addressed as construct validity (Cronbach, 1970; Hanley, 1981; Messick, 1975; 1980; Muma, 1984) or is approached less directly (Crystal, 1987; Cummins, 1984; Damico, 1988; Kirchner & Skarakis-Doyle, 1983), there is a serious need for a defensible theory that will also define and determine an appropriate approach to assessment (Bachman, 1989; Cummins, 1981; 1983a; 1983b; 1983c; Cummins & Swain, 1986; Krashen, 1982; Oller, 1983b).

The need for a theory with construct validity is particularly acute when it comes to assessing LEP students. Unfortunately, policies have often been made on an ad hoc basis. In some cases, no theory has ever been articulated; more often than not, where an explicit theory has been proposed, it is either too cumbersome, too simplistic, or based on some well-intentioned guess rather than reasoning from evidence. Although it is widely agreed that language proficiency is a crucial factor in school assessment across the broad spectrum, it remains to be determined just what language proficiency is and how it relates to other abilities (e.g., memory, intelligence, knowledge, consciousness; Cummins, 1983c) as well as to disabilities or exceptionalities (Cummins, 1984). More particularly, how does a theory of language proficiency relate to the LEP student vis-à-vis special education?

These questions are addressed here and elsewhere (Oller, 1986; 1989a; 1989b) in a theory of language proficiency along the lines of classic pragmatism. As such, language proficiency is seen in dynamic relation to other representational (semiotic) capacities. Before evaluating the theory to be proposed, in terms of (a) its capacity to embrace and unify disparate ideas and research evidences and (b) the extent to which it suggests appealing and empirically testable hypotheses about human capacities in general, it will be useful to have a brief look at the three decades or so of prior research that have led up to it.

EMPIRICAL BACKGROUND

As surprising as it may seem, there is no clearly defined literature on the measurement of "language proficiency" per se: that is, native-, primary-, or first-language proficiency. Although verbal intelligence measurement and verbal achievement testing (see Gould, 1981; Oller & Perkins, 1978) deal more or less directly with the measurement of primary language proficiency, they do not purport to address the theoretical construct of language proficiency. Other areas of study where primary-language ability is likely to be the principal construct measured but where ostensibly the focus is on something else would include many investigations of exceptionalities, especially those that focus on "language disorders" and "learning disabilities."

The explicit empirical study of language proficiency, as a construct of interest in its own right, remained undeveloped until the 1960s, when foreign-, or second-language testing forced the issue (Carroll, 1961; Lado, 1961; Valette, 1964; 1967). At that time, applied linguists and evaluators were generally operating within a taxonomical framework regarding language. Nevertheless, during the 1960s language proficiency came to be regarded as a construct in its own right and the need for a better-grounded theory began to come into focus.

It was almost a decade later, however, that language testing research began to flourish (Anderson, 1969; Oller, 1970; Oller & Conrad, 1971; Savignon, 1971; Spolsky, 1968a; 1968b; Upshur, 1967; Upshur & Fata, 1968). With the studies conducted, new testing techniques were explored, old ones were tested experimentally for the first time, and new theoretical issues were raised. Various theories of language proficiency were proposed. All aimed to describe the organization of language abilities and their manifestations in language use (Spolsky, 1968b; Carroll, 1961; 1983b).

The various theories that emerged over three decades of study (roughly from 1960 until the present) can be classed according to three ways of viewing language proficiency: discrete point, integrative, and pragmatic approaches. These are also roughly coincident in historical development with the three decades in question, the 1960s, 1970s, and 1980s.

DISCRETE POINT ALTERNATIVE: ANALYSIS INTO BITS AND PIECES

In the 1960s, the extreme possibility of dividing language proficiency into ever smaller domains, components of domains, and elements of components dominated the scene. Language proficiency was seen as an inexhaustible taxonomy of taxonomies, a profusion of distinct bits and pieces of knowledge and/or specific abilities. This perspective was appropriately dubbed the *discrete point approach* by John B. Carroll (1961) and was best exemplified in the book by Lado (1961). The result in theory and practice was one of mind-stretching complexity that made test construction and interpretation about as difficult as could be.

Based on the taxonomic perspective of the American structuralists (roughly from 1933 through 1955 [Newmeyer, 1980]), language and other human abilities had been viewed as conglomerations of many distinguishable elements, each pertaining to some distinct domain or component of language ability. Language proficiency, according to such a perspective, consisted of separable components of phonology, morphology, lexicon, syntax, and so on, each of which could be further divided into distinct inventories of elements (e.g., sounds, classes of sounds or phonemes, syllables, morphemes, words, idioms, phrase structures, etc.).

The most enthusiastic proponents of this view argued that each test item should focus on only one element of one domain and skill at a time (e.g., Lado, 1961). It was urged that items testing phonemic contrasts should not be mixed with those aimed at testing vocabulary knowledge, which should in turn be distinguished from items aimed at syntactic patterns and so forth. Besides distinguishing domains of structure (such as phonology, lexicon, and syntax), discrete point testers also distinguished skills (listening, speaking, reading, and writing).

Following the discrete point model, a test could not be valid if it mixed several skills or domains of structure (Lado, 1961). By this model, presumably the ideal assessment would involve the evaluation of each of the domains of structure and each of the skills of interest. Then, all the results could be combined to form a total picture of language proficiency. It may be useful to note that the whole scope of educational and mental measurement was dominated by the same sort of thinking.

Discrete point theory, however, in the final analysis was more of an ideological perspective than a practical one. Had it been influenced much by empirical evidence, it would have had to be adjusted. In practice, it was always difficult (and sometimes impossible) to restrict performance to a single skill (listening, speaking, reading, or writing) without implicitly involving another. Writing, for instance, almost inevitably involves reading, just as speaking involves listening. Things were even more difficult when it came to distinguishing domains of grammar as perfectly as the theory required. Who ever heard of a word not defined in terms of its sounds and its potential of entering into semantic and syntactic relations with other words? Or what would a test item aimed at a single sound be like?

Nevertheless, tests purporting to meet the demands of discrete point thinking were produced in abundance, and the field of speech-language pathology was not exempt. For example, tests aimed at receptive syntax and expressive morphology were clearly derived from taxonomic, discrete point thinking. Upon closer scrutiny, however, it became obvious that discrete elements of language, in the absence of the rich and dynamic tensional context of discourse, are like the dimensionless points of a line. Without the line, the points become mere fictions.

In context, discrete elements of distinct domains of language structure, or distinct skills, are valuable as objects for analysis. Without context, the elements themselves become undefinable fictions. Besides its appeal to such fictions (i.e., useful in context but undefinable without it), discrete point theory made no reference to semantic and pragmatic aspects of language. This was because meaning is not a discrete point affair. Meaning spills over into the whole continuum of experience: a continuum that the very existence of meaning both presupposes and implies.

AN INTEGRATIVE OR HOLISTIC APPROACH

It was Carroll (1961) who introduced the term "discrete point"; and also it was he who commented on the artificial character of that approach. It is impossible in principle, to devise fully discrete items in real testing situations. There is no way to guarantee that the test taker will not appeal to some bit of knowledge or skill or to some other element of language structure besides the one the item is supposed to focus on. Compensating for this weakness, Carroll referred to another kind of test, one aimed at more global properties of language ability: what he called the *integrative approach*.

The integrative approach, which viewed language proficiency as a composite construct with holistic qualities, became increasingly prominent throughout the 1970s. According to this view, language proficiency cannot be assessed adequately except in a fairly rich context of discourse. Pushing this idea to its extreme limit led to the unitary factor hypothesis: the view that language proficiency might not be decomposable at all and that it could be assessed with nearly equal validity in a great variety of ways.

In contrast with the complexity of discrete point theory, this extreme view of integrative theory was the simplest conceivable possibility. Just as any extreme version of discrete point theory proved unworkable in principle and in practice, the unitary factor hypothesis was also wrong. Research soon established that language proficiency involves a variety of components that may be viewed in many different ways (Bachman, 1989; Bachman & Palmer, 1983; Carroll, 1983a; Upshur & Homburg, 1983).

Less extreme versions of integrative theory, however, had some validity. While the items of discrete point tests aimed at a single element of one component of grammar and just one skill, integrative tests required the use of many elements and more than one component and skill simultaneously. This approach was more consistent with the way language is actually used and seemed to yield more valid measurements of language proficiency (Oller, 1973; Sommers, Erdige, & Peterson, 1978; Spolsky, 1986a; Upshur, 1967; Valette, 1964).

As empirical research accumulated in the 1970s, it became apparent that integrative tests were measuring some traits and abilities of language users unreached by tests based on discrete point thinking. When the empirical evidence was examined, greater reliability and validity was found in more integrative tests. For instance, tests of particular phonemic contrasts, or inflectional morphemes, or syntactic rules, might generate reliabilities in the range of 0.6 to 0.7 (e.g., Evola, Mamer, & Lentz, 1980), but more integrative tests yielded reliabilities in the 0.8 to 0.9 range (e.g., Oller, 1972).

Another argument against any extreme form of discrete point thinking was that there are no completely focused discrete point items. Carroll (1961), Rand (1976), and Farhady (1983a) suggested that the dichotomy—discrete point versus integrative—formed a continuum whose end-points were fully distinct only in theory. In practice, there are no completely discrete point tests or even items. All real test items are more or less integrative in character. This theoretical discovery led inevitably to a search for a different kind of distinction, based not so much on the surface appearance of tests or items, but on the deeper character of language processing itself.

PRAGMATIC LANGUAGE TESTING

Between the theoretical extremes of demanding ever-more-finely tuned discrete items and the holism of integrative testing, a variety of alternatives were perceived. One that gained ground in the 1980s was called a *pragmatic approach*. It incorporated ideas from both integrative and discrete point approaches and at the same time defined a much clearer line between them. The hierarchical theory proposed in this chapter derives from this third approach. Before introducing the model, however, it will be useful to consider what motivated pragmatic theory in the first place.

For one thing, it was noted that normal language use always involves meaning beyond the theoretically discrete elements of surface forms. There is a linking with persons, places, things, events, and relations that invariably implicate the whole continuum of experience. If meaning beyond surface form is admitted, no test item can meet the demands of discrete point theory. Another insurmountable difficulty for discrete point theory was that language use occurs in real time and is always constrained, in one fashion or another, by temporal factors.

Time and meaning, respectively, constitute the pragmatic naturalness constraints that led to the identification of an indefinitely large subclass of integrative tests. This subclass, which is entirely distinct from discrete point tests, may be properly called *pragmatic* (Cohen, 1980; Oller, 1973; 1979; Savignon, 1983). In fact, the pragmatic naturalness criteria would eliminate any strictly discrete point item (or test) as unnatural. Such items do not involve normal language use any more than reciting numbers is mathematical reasoning.

What was more important about pragmatic tests, and what is yet to be appreciated fully by theoreticians and practitioners (e.g., Spolsky, 1983), is that all of the goals of discrete point items (e.g., diagnosis, focus, isolation) are better achieved in the full rich context of one or more pragmatic tests. As a result, it was argued that the valid objectives of discrete point theory could be completely incorporated within a pragmatic framework. This would necessitate, however, abandonment of the goal of separating every element of structure or skill from the fabric of experience. As a method of linguistic analysis, the discrete point approach had some validity, but as a practical method for assessing language abilities, it was misguided, counterproductive, and logically impossible. Furthermore, neither discrete point thinking nor mere integrative theory could explain the strong correlations among language tests aimed at widely different skills and/or domains of structure commonly observed throughout the 1970s (Cummins, 1976; Oller, 1970; 1972; 1976; 1979; Savignon, 1971; Stump, 1978).

The development of pragmatic theory was reminiscent in some respects to the early work of Charles Spearman (1927) on intelligence. By inventing the statistical technique of factor analysis, Spearman showed that it was possible to identify a general factor underlying most intelligence tests and accounting for a huge chunk of variance in nearly all of them. This controversial general factor became known as "g" or "the g-factor." In 1976, following Nunnally (1967), Oller revived the question of the g-factor and extended it to the case of language tests. One of the most obvious and compelling facts apparent from the examination of correlation matrices involving three or more language tests was the consistent positive strength of the interrelationships (Jones & Spolsky, 1975; Oller, 1983b; Oller & Perkins, 1978; 1980; Palmer, Groot, & Trosper, 1981; Palmer & Spolsky, 1975). In almost all cases, diverse language tests were observed to be positively and substantially correlated. This was especially obvious in the case of the pragmatic tests and this work provided initial, though false, hope for the unitary hypothesis.

In some studies, a single g-factor did seem to account for the bulk of the reliable variance in a diversity of language measures. Oller (1976; 1979) read this as evidence against additional factors. This was due in part to certain weaknesses in Nunnally's interpretation of Spearman's statistical methods and in part to the difference between classical factor analysis and principal components analysis. Almost immediately, it was shown (Bachman & Palmer, 1983; Farhady, 1983b; Upshur & Homburg, 1983; Vollmer & Sang, 1983) by a variety of methods that almost any language measure contains some reliable variance beyond what it shares with other measures. The unitary hypothesis of language proficiency, therefore, was rejected (Alderson, 1983; Davies, 1984; Oller, 1983; Spolsky, 1983).

Still, there remained an undeniably powerful general factor associated with a considerable diversity of language tests (Carroll, 1983a; Bachman, 1989). This fact was sustained in studies with more powerful confirmatory factoring techniques (Bachman & Palmer, 1983; Purcell, 1983) and led to a discussion of a variety of ways of dividing language proficiency into interrelated components. It became apparent, especially as urged by Upshur and Homburg (1983) and by Carroll (1983a) that the existence of a general factor does not preclude its decomposition in a great variety of ways (as Oller, 1976; 1979; Oller & Hinofotis, 1976, had incorrectly supposed).

On the contrary, the componential resolution of a general factor into a plurality of contributing components is not incompatible with the notion that language proficiency may be a coherent and integrated totality (Carroll, 1983a; 1983b; Oller, 1983a). Otherwise, the meaning of total scores on tests with diverse subtests, would evaporate. No one denies that communicative abilities interact in complex ways to produce composite results. Therefore, it is clear that both general and specific factors are required in an adequate theory of language proficiency. This sort of thinking led to the development of the hierarchical theory that will be examined next.

A HIERARCHICAL MODEL OF LANGUAGE PROFICIENCY

A new theoretical perspective is required (Bachman, 1989). It must account for the powerful general factor underlying a great diversity of language tests and the substantial relationship that appears to be evident between a factor of language proficiency and presumed measures of intelligence (Gunnarsson, 1978; Oller, 1981; Stump, 1978; Vygotsky, 1987). As already shown, the taxonomic models underlying discrete point theory were incompatible both with sound reasoning and empirical evidence. Moreover, they cannot compete in scope or power with generative theories along the lines of Noam Chomsky's thinking. They are logically too impoverished to even begin to account for the facts of human language ability or other semiotic capacities (Chomsky, 1956, 1980a, 1980b, 1988).

The possibility of such a hierarchical approach was proposed independently by Carroll (1983a) and by Vollmer and Sang (1983); it is not a new idea. Theories of intellect from Aristotle onward have attempted to come to grips with the human capacity for language and with closely allied representational and interpretive abilities. The hierarchy to be considered here (Oller, 1983a, 1986, 1989b) has its roots in the philosophy and logic of C. S. Peirce, the scholar with whom Chomsky also identifies most. See Oller (1989b:224, f.n. 1) where Chomsky says, "The scholar to whom I feel closest . . . is Charles Sanders Peirce."

The germ of the proposed model and its relation between language and intellect is suggested by Albert Einstein in the following remarks about language and thinking:

. . . Everything depends on the degree to which words and word-combinations correspond to the world of impression.

What is it that brings about such an intimate connection between language and thinking? Is there no thinking without the use of language, namely in concepts and concept-combinations for which words need not necessarily come to mind? Has not everyone of us struggled for words although the connection between "things" was already clear?

We might be inclined to attribute to the act of thinking complete independence from language if the individual formed or were able to form his concepts without the verbal guidance of his environment. Yet most likely the mental shape of an individual growing up under such conditions would be very poor. Thus we may conclude that the mental development of the individual and his way of forming concepts depend to a high degree upon language. (1941, in Oller 1989b: 62)

Peirce, Saussure, and Vygotsky (presumably for similar reasons) agreed in this assessment. Each contended that language is the canonical semiotic medium and that by the systematic study of it we should be able to optimize our understanding of representational processes in general.

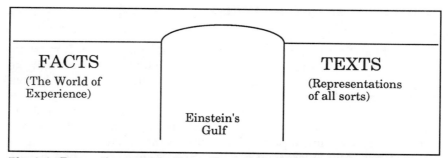

Fig. 3-1. Pragmatic mapping. From "Language and Experience: Classic Pragmatism" by J. W. Oller, Jr., 1989. Reprinted with permission of University Press of America.

PRAGMATIC MAPPING

This central theme can best be elaborated through the concept of Pragmatic Mapping. Figure 3-1 pictures the primary representational problem, as outlined in the above remarks by Einstein, and more fully by Peirce in the nineteenth century. On the left-hand side of the diagram, the raw uninterpreted facts of experience are pictured; on the right-hand side, representations of them. The question for a theory of intellect is how the connection between the two realms is accomplished. How does an individual take raw sensory data (uninterpreted facts) and convert it into experience (interpreted facts), and eventually, into comprehensible text(s) in a natural language? This is the pragmatic mapping problem: the primary problem of intelligence.

THE GULF

Einstein described this problem and defined a certain "gulf" between the physical world and representations of it:

. . . the concepts which arise in our thought and in our linguistic expressions are all—when viewed logically—the free creations of thought which cannot inductively be gained from sense experiences. This is not so easily noticed only because we have the habit of combining certain concepts and conceptual relations (propositions) so definitely with certain sense experiences that we do not become conscious of the gulf—logically unbridgeable—which separates the world of sensory experiences from the world of concepts and propositions. (1944, in Oller 1989b:22)

The question is how human beings are able to bridge the gulf and to communicate with others who may not share the same sensory experiences or even interpretations of them. What enables the linking of facts to internalized and externalized texts? Or, how is pragmatic mapping achieved?

Pragmatic mapping is accomplished, the gulf is bridged, through the powerful (and to some extent, innate and species-specific) semiotic capacity that mediates between sensory-motor images and their interpretations. There must be a deep and general representational capacity that unites the various surface forms of sensation, imagery, gesture, and ultimately, language.

THREE KINDS OF REPRESENTATIONAL CAPACITIES

Figure 3-2 elaborates on the process of pragmatic mapping by proposing a hierarchy of three distinct kinds of representational capacities: sensory-motor, kinesic, and linguistic. Sensory-motor representations are more or less directly, and iconically, related to the facts of experience. Someone skiing down a mountain not only represents the terrain ahead in a continuous flow of images but must also represent at some level bodily postures and internal commands for motor adjustments. Without

Fig. 3-2. Different kinds of semiotic capacities from "Language and Experience: Classic Pragmatism" by J. W. Oller, Jr., 1989. Reprinted with permission of University Press of America.

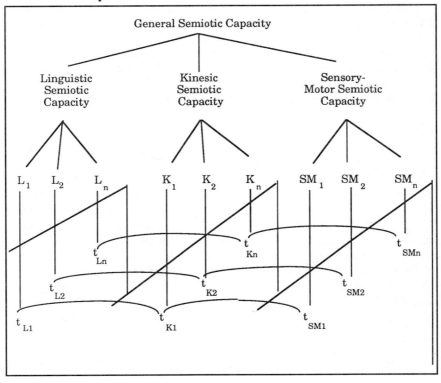

such representations, it would be impossible to explain the volitional control of the body to accommodate the changing terrain. The skier feels (i.e., represents in sensory-motor fashion) the skis, movements, the slope, the texture of the snow, and more.

As Peirce showed, sensory-motor representations are analogues, copies, or icons of the facts they represent; as such, they are degenerate. If a person looks away from an object, its image quickly fades. Details are lost or may be wrongly reconstructed in the mental picture.

Kinesic, or gestural representations differ in several ways from sensory-motor ones. Kinesic representations, such as pointing with the index finger, or brandishing a fist, are conventional and arbitrary to some extent but involve iconic (analogical) elements. For instance, a brandished fist suggests more or less iconically the act of punching someone. Unlike an icon, it is usually addressed to a certain audience and may acquire a meaning different from the one iconically suggested (e.g., the fist may be a sign of solidarity). Peirce contended that gestural representations are "reactionally degenerate"; that is, it may be difficult to tell what is pointed at, or whether the brandished fist means a threat or brotherhood, or whether a smile is genuine or feigned.

The third kind of representations pictured in Figure 3-2 are linguistic. By contrast with the other types, these achieve a higher level of abstraction and greater potential validity. While sensory-motor representations are iconic (analogues of what they mean) and kinesic representations are often ambiguous and require leaps of inference, linguistic representations are typically more abstract and potentially more determinate. For example, there is far less doubt about the meaning of the proposition that "humans are mortal" than about whether a certain act of pointing is aimed at this object or that.

Because of their abstractness and virtual independence of contextual determination, unlike sensory-motor icons (visual, auditory, or other images), linguistic representations are not qualitatively degenerate. That "humans are mortal" is a representation as good today, tomorrow, or next year, as it was yesterday, or seven centuries ago whereas a person's recollection of a reflection in a mirror fades quickly. Nor is a linguistic representation reactionally degenerate in the same way that a kinesic gesture is apt to be. While it may be difficult to say just who is pointed out when someone points at someone else in a crowd, the proposition that "humans are mortal" or that "cars are used for transportation" or any number of similar linguistic representations have a more determinate meaning.

Further, language may be used to represent any imaginable, or even unimaginable, idea. Linguistic forms that depend on sensory-motor representations of nonlinguistic states of affairs (e.g., factual or fictional contexts), or that appeal to indexical or deictic relations (e.g., pointing or naming or referring) involve the same kinds of degeneracy associated with icons and indexes respectively. Still, there is a potential for an indefinite and unlimited increase in determinacy (a nondegenerative sort) with linguistic representations that is missing in sensory-motor and kinesic representations. For this reason, Peirce called the abstract propositional forms (or texts) of language, "the relatively genuine genus." For these, he reserved the term *symbol* as contrasted with *icon* (a copy or image) or *index* (a sign that represents something by pointing it out).

SUBORDINATE TERMS: PARTICULAR SYSTEMS AND THEIR TEXTS

Having defined the three kinds of semiotic capacity (linguistic, kinesic, and sensory-motor) that are subordinate to general semiotic capacity in Figure 3-2, we must explain the terms subordinate to them. Under Linguistic Semiotic Capacity, an ability that Chomsky claims is innate and species specific to human beings, come terms that correspond to the grammars of particular language systems, L_1, L_2, through L_n. These systems, to the extent they are not already specified by innate knowledge of universal grammar, must be acquired if they are to be known at all.

Each specific language system in its turn corresponds to a class of textual representations in experience: t_{L1}, t_{L2}, through t_{Ln}. These latter terms stand for the texts of the primary language, or second language, and nth language. For monolinguals, there will be no L_2. The same sort of hierarchical arrangement is hypothesized under kinesic semiotic capacity. Although it is not entirely species-specific to human beings, again, the innate and universal kinesic capacity dominates or branches into a plurality (or at least a potential plurality) of subordinate acquired systems. Each of these subordinate systems dominates a class of texts, (or sequences of forms), in experience; these tend to be loosely tied to linguistic texts.

For example, English speakers are apt to accompany the statement that a certain person is about "so tall" with a corresponding gesture, palm down, hand extended. A Latin American Spanish-speaker by contrast is apt to use a very different gesture for the same meaning. The Latin, for instance, may hold the elbow of the right arm with the upturned fingers of the left hand. The position of the right elbow, hand extended in a vertical orientation, thumb up, corresponds to the height of the person spoken of.

More important, research shows that the sequence of gestures is delicately coordinated with the sequence of linguistic forms and meanings. Condon and Ogston (1971) showed that this is true not only of the speaker but also of the audience. Their body movements appear to be under the control of one and the same puppeteer.

The case for Sensory-Motor Capacity, if anything, is more dramatic. There is no question that much of our ability to perceive the world and our body as part of it, must be innate (Bower, 1971; 1974; Piatelli-Palmarini, 1980). However, every normal person operates in ordinary experience by so many routines and patterns that it would be impossible to estimate how many distinct sensory-motor systems an ordinary individual possesses. There are sensory-motor programs for almost every imaginable aspect of routine experience (e.g., chewing gum, brushing your teeth, grooming in general, dressing, driving a car, riding a bicycle, playing basketball, going to class, giving a talk, writing a letter, typing). Each of these routines is divisible into subroutines.

To the extent that such programs can be made explicit as rule-governed systems, they are like grammars of natural languages. They also have their own sensory-motor texts, t_{sm1}, t_{sm2}, and so forth. For instance, our ability to recognize a game of basketball and to distinguish it from a tennis match, or to distinguish either of these from a boxing match, depends in part on our knowledge of the corresponding sensory-motor systems. But none of these knowledge systems is the same as an actual game of basketball, or tennis, or a particular boxing match. Yet the general rule-systems underlying the particular manifest forms (t_{sm}'s in Figure 3-2) are at least as different from one another as are their diverse "textual" manifestations. Sensory-motor texts, in their turn, are also coordinated in ordinary experience in delicately articulate ways with kinesic and linguistic texts.

PRAGMATIC MAPPING AS INFORMATION PROCESSING

Another way of viewing the same pragmatic process of linking representations or texts of various sorts with the facts of experience is given in Figure 3-3. The focal element in this diagram is consciousness or immediate awareness. The question addressed is how information from the senses is processed through the kinds of grammatical structure that are supplied by the various semiotic systems: linguistic, kinesic, and sensory-motor. The idea is that the determination of the meaning of texts is chiefly a matter of relating them through representational capacity with the facts of experience and vice versa. As new texts or representations are processed, they are fed into short-term memory, and possibly from there into a longer-term memory. Consciousness and memory, together, then, may interact with particular semiotic systems to produce modifications of them. Presumably, this is the primary basis for the acquisition of the conventional aspects of semiotic systems.

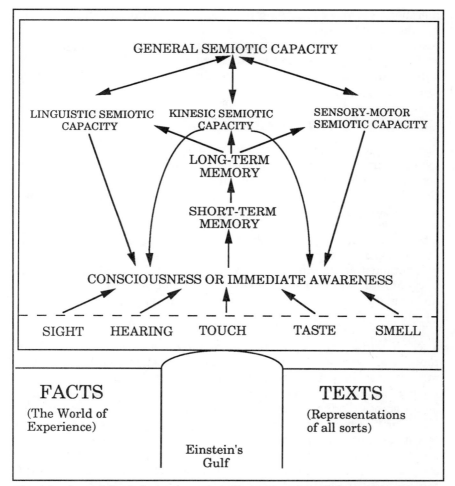

Fig. 3-3. A modular information processing expansion of the pragmatic mapping process from "Language and Experience: Classic Pragmatism" by J. W. Oller, Jr., 1989. Reprinted with permission of University Press of America.

EVIDENCE SUPPORTING THE THEORY

Empirical evidence in favor of the theory sketched out is abundant. First, the theory gives a plausible explanation of the ability to translate information from one semiotic system into another. Second, it provides a heuristically appealing basis for the common distinctions made between such cognitive processes as experiencing something versus remembering it versus recalling the memory, and so on. Third, systems are shown to be related in ways that correspond to what is known from research. Fourth, the special case of the interaction between primary and nonprimary languages is explained in a straightforward way. Finally, a number of intuitively appealing hypotheses can be incorporated.

GENERAL SEMIOTIC CAPACITY

A major question handled immediately is how the model explains the general semiotic capacity that enables the intertranslatability of representations across the various semiotic systems. The chief evidence for this aspect of the model is that individuals can usually work up in their imaginations appropriate sensory-motor representations in response to a narrative, for instance, told by someone else. Similarly, an observer of a boxing match may dodge punches: or, more commonly still, someone may grimace in response to someone else's discomfort. Such phenomena demonstrate the undeniable intertranslatability of at least some aspects of representations across diverse semiotic systems. There must be an intimate connection between the several representational systems hypothesized.

It is also possible to paraphrase meanings that have been expressed in a certain surface form by putting them into other surface forms that give more or less the same result. For instance, the statement that "Men are mortal" may be paraphrased by saying that "All humanity must ultimately face death" or that "Mortality is a trait of human beings." Translation across distinct language systems (e.g., "Los hombres son mortales" or "La mortalidad es una de las calidades de los hombres"), or translation into any language or other form that can be imagined, is ample evidence for a general factor of semiotic capacity. Apart from such a capacity, all translations (even quite imperfect ones) would be inexplicable.

DESIRABLE THEORETICAL DISTINCTIONS SUSTAINED

The model under consideration also allows certain distinctions that are important to any theory of intellect that aims for explanatory adequacy (Chomsky, 1956). For instance, it allows for a differentiation between innate and acquired knowledge. Innate knowledge is that which is present before any experience occurs, or which is triggered by experience and matures more or less automatically and somewhat independently of experience (Piatelli-Palmarini, 1980).

The difference between innate and acquired knowledge can be seen in all three of the semiotic systems proposed to underlie the general semiotic capacity. For instance, universal aspects of linguistic capacity that could not be acquired from experience but are in fact prerequisite to it would have to include such things as the subject-predicate relation, as well as the capacity for negation, conjunction, and disjunction of propositional meanings.

Universal aspects of kinesic systems would include such things as smiles, laughter, tears, and cries of joy or pain. Universal aspects of sensory-motor capacity would include the intimate association of the senses as demonstrated in the work of Bower (1971, 1974). It would extend to the physiological character of the senses and their tuning to facts external to the organism. All of these, it would seem, are prerequisite to any explanation of the common experiences shared by human beings across a vast range of cultures and backgrounds.

RELATIONSHIP BETWEEN SYSTEMS EXPLAINED

Each of the universal systems of knowledge—and no claim is made as to the completeness of the ones postulated, only their necessity—though distinct, is related to the others through the domination of the general capacity. Each also subordinates one or more particular systems that are acquired and are to some extent conventional in character. For example, the acquisition of the primary language at once fleshes out the universal aspects of language that are realized in that system and at the same time results in the addition of conventional features that are unique to the primary language. Much the same will be true in the acquisition of the kinesic system that accompanies the first language.

Even sensory-motor systems have noteworthy conventional aspects. For instance, in one culture it is customary for automobiles to drive on the right-hand side of a roadway while in another motorists stay to the left. If it is hypothesized that conventional aspects of the various semiotic systems in question must be acquired, this sort of acquired knowledge will be distinguished from innate knowledge to the extent that the former is a product of experience involving the senses. It is suggested that information from the sensory-motor system passes to consciousness where the sensory-motor texts (i.e., sequences of sensory-motor images) are interpreted. As they are understood, they are passed through various stages of memory.

The depth of the comprehension in question determines the degree of impact on semiotic systems. The acquisition of grammar is thought to be a process of comprehending a particular kind of texts so as to develop the sort of intuitive feel that constitutes knowledge of a language. By this reckoning, the acquisition of a particular grammar is a process of comprehending texts in that language at a sufficient depth so as to acquire the conventional aspects of the grammatical system.

PRIMARY- AND NONPRIMARY-LANGUAGE ACQUISITION RELATED

The theory under consideration hypothesizes that nonprimary-language acquisition will proceed in a manner much like primary-language acquisition except that acquisition of a second language will benefit greatly (and suffer minor interferences) from the prior acquisition of the first language (Asher & Price, 1967; Asher & Garcia, 1969). Similarly, the acquisition of a third language will benefit mainly, and suffer a little, from the first and second, and so on.

The fact that nonprimary-language acquisition usually falls short of the mark achieved in primary-language acquisition (Gregg, 1988) should be explained not by positing a radical difference in the physiology or even the internal strategies of the person involved in one or the other task (Selinker, 1972), but by noting the radical differences across the two cases in access to target language texts and the relative motivations to comprehend and produce them (see Chapter Two, also Schumann, 1975, 1978). A child acquiring a primary language experiences pressures and rewards based on the need to achieve comprehensibility through the primary language (Brown, 1973; Nelson, 1985; Vygotsky, 1987) that may not be present to the same degree or at all in the second-language case (Schumann, 1975; Vigil & Oller, 1976).

Exceptional cases, where nonprimary-language acquisition succeeds dramatically are those where access to target language texts and susceptibility to pressures and rewards, are both provided for. For instance, the person who marries across language boundaries and then moves to the country where the nonprimary language predominates is far more apt to achieve nativelike ability in the non-primary language than someone whose sole experience is a college course. In fact, continuing progress toward native competence in any language is more a function of internally defined motives and sensitivities than of methods of teaching or modes of exposure (Schumann, 1978; Vigil & Oller, 1976). Access to pragmatically rich and meaningful texts in the target language is requisite, but insufficient by itself. Motivation to conform to the communal conventions of the target language system is also required.

CONSENSUAL HYPOTHESES INCORPORATED

The hierarchical model under consideration not only supports the kinds of theoretical distinctions that are required in practice (e.g., the distinction between innate and acquired knowledge, memory and grammatical knowledge, grammar and text, comprehension and production, and so forth). It also suggests some explicit hypotheses about relationships within the proposed hierarchy that are susceptible to testing.

Role of the Primary Language in Intelligence

Since linguistic representations are the most abstract and general ones considered in the model, it follows that the primary language is the most likely basis for the development of general semiotic capacity. Observers have noted that mathematics as a kind of reasoning is parasitic and derivative inasmuch as it is dependent upon language (Peirce, in Hartshorne & Weiss, 1931–1935; Lotz, 1951; Church, 1951; Russell, 1919). As noted earlier, Einstein stressed the closeness of language development and cognitive growth in general (1941). This point was also developed by Vygotsky (1978; 1987), Piaget (1947), Luria and Yudovich (1959) and Luria (1961).

Empirical evidence may be seen in the remarkable accomplishments of deaf children with hearing parents. In cases where the children, for whatever reasons, are deprived of access to visual sign language they face a language acquisition problem far more difficult than that of the hearing child. Such children face special sensory difficulties. Typically, they acquire a natural visual-manual sign system (Lane, 1984; Wilcox, 1988) such as American Sign Language (ASL).

Deaf children deprived of this opportunity and forced to acquire speech directly are placed at a serious disadvantage (Lane, 1988). The difficulties they face, as well as the innate propensities they possess to help them in overcoming those difficulties (Bickerton, 1981), are predicted by the model under consideration. If children are deprived of a full and rich primary-language system, they will suffer consequences throughout the cognitive hierarchy, especially in areas that depend on communication such as social development.

Transfer and Interference Predicted

Another hypothesis suggested by the theory under consideration is that neighboring elements of the hierarchy are more apt to influence each other than distant ones. For example, the primary language is expected to have greater impact on a second language than on a third. The second, similarly, would influence the third, and so on. Again, experience of polyglots bears out these predictions. Typically, "padding" (Newmark, 1983), the use of known language forms in place of target language forms, is more often from the most recently acquired language rather than from any other.

Similarly, transfer in general would be expected to occur from more developed systems to less developed ones. For example, the primary language would be expected to influence a nonprimary language rather than the reverse. The situation would be altered in favor of the nonprimary language just when greater proficiency was achieved in the non-primary system. However, then the nonprimary system would be promoted to the status of the primary system, and the former primary system would presumably be demoted to a secondary status.

Input Hypothesis Vindicated

Another consequence of the postulated hierarchy is that distinct representational systems provide the means in some cases for comprehending what would otherwise be incomprehensible. For instance, a discourse in a target language that might be entirely incomprehensible if one had to rely on knowledge of that particular language alone can be made comprehensible if one has access to a translation provided in some other semiotic system.

In normal language acquisition, by the same token, meanings of new surface forms are often made obvious by context (Bruner, 1983; Krashen, 1985). The child first understands the context, perhaps by representing it in a comprehensible sensory-motor form, and subsequently understands the utterances associated with the context. This use of other semiotic systems to acquire the primary language is well documented. From the early 1930s, Vygotsky described this process as the primary mechanism for the development of thought and language (Vygotsky, 1987). His concept of "the zone of proximal development" is dependent on this intertranslatability. More recently, Nelson's focus on contextual scaffolding (1985), Bruner's insistence on the need for a language acquisition support system (1983), and Feuerstein's emphasis on mediation (1980) are further indications that acquisition is dependent on interaction between semiotic systems.

In successful nonprimary-language acquisition, a similar scaffolding is always supplied, whether by the environment or the learner/acquirer. In a classroom, scaffolding may be through dramatization, film, or translation into a language that the subject already knows. In more natural settings, physical, social and other contextual factors supply the scaffolding.

By this line of reasoning, Krashen's input hypothesis (Krashen, 1985) is vindicated (Oller, 1988). The input hypothesis in its most basic form says simply that language acquisition progresses as the acquirer comprehends texts that are slightly beyond his or her current level of development in the target language (precisely Vygotsky's notion of the "zone of proximal development"). Spolsky (1985) and Gregg (1988) have contended that the input hypothesis is either false or trivially true. If it means we must understand what is beyond our understanding, it is false; if it means merely that we must comprehend in order to learn, it is trivially true. However, the theory advocated here disposes of both of these interpretations.

New representations such as target language texts, which are out of reach in one system (namely, the target language) are understood by appealing to representations in another semiotic system. The one provides an interpretation of the other. Therefore, because of the intertranslatability of semiotic representations, and the potential interaction between primary and non-primary languages, the input hypothesis remains viable.

Threshold Hypothesis Incorporated

Cummins (1976) proposed the threshold hypothesis, an idea that relates to the impact of bilingualism on cognitive development. Subsequently, this hypothesis was modified and extended (Cummins, 1984:107). The threshold hypothesis suggests that the student's starting level of proficiency in one or both languages may be an important mediating variable in avoiding a burden in becoming bilingual or in benefitting from bilingualism once achieved. There are actually two hypotheses.

At the low end, it is claimed that a student may have to achieve a certain minimal level of proficiency in one or both languages in order to avoid deficits. In other words, if the student falls below threshold in both languages, presumably it will be difficult or even impossible for that child to benefit from instruction in either language. Further, it follows that a student who has not acquired threshold level in the primary language will only receive an unnecessary additional burden by being instructed in a second language. Therefore, the lower threshold is presumably important in the determination of when instruction might be beneficially introduced in a nonprimary language.

At the other end of the scale, a high threshold is also posited. In order for a bilingual student to experience the expected benefits of bilingualism (e.g., greater ability to appreciate and use symbols and greater "metalinguistic awareness"), the student must have surpassed the high threshold in one or both languages.

Admittedly, the idea of one or more thresholds is loosely stated, but the research seems to support it (Cummins & Mulcahy, 1978; Duncan & DeAvila, 1979; Kessler & Quinn, 1980). In fact, as Hakuta (1986; also see Lambert, 1975) has shown, there is a long history of debate concerning the deleterious versus beneficial effects of bilingualism (see Chapter Two). The weight of evidence properly interpreted sustains the view that bilingualism is advantageous to cognitive development on the whole, just at the hierarchical theory predicts.

The model explains the available evidence concerning the threshold hypothesis and provides a convenient framework within which to understand the interrelationships of semiotic systems in general. Within a hierarchical model, the threshold hypothesis can be incorporated and elaborated in terms of transfer and interference (see above), and in terms of a more explicit theory of the role of language proficiency in relation to cognition in general. Bilingualism, indeed multilingualism, deserves special consideration since it is bound to play a role in the education of culturally and linguistically diverse LEP populations.

CALP and BICS Distinction Accommodated

In response to consideration of the possibility of a general language proficiency factor, Cummins hypothesized a distinction between what he called *cognitive academic language proficiency* (CALP) and *basic interpersonal communicative skills* (BICS). This idea was appealing to educators in bilingual or multilingual contexts who often observed evidence in its favor. A student that gets along satisfactorily on the playground, where cognitive demands are presumably lessened by the immediacy of physical and social context, may encounter difficulty in the classroom when it comes to reading, writing, solving word and math problems, and generally acting on a more abstract level. The student may have adequate BICS without sufficient CALP.

Cummins (1983c) clarified that he did not intend to argue that the two kinds of ability were unrelated, but rather that they were apt to appear as such at the surface. To illustrate, he adapted an "iceberg" model (from Shuy, 1978; 1981) where the two visible points, CALP and BICS, were clearly distinct, but were joined below the surface in what he called "common underlying proficiency" (Cummins, 1984:143).

There was a further implication that the two kinds of ability might be developed in different contexts and by using distinct strategies. Cummins (1983c) quoted David Olson (1977) who said:

. . . language development is not simply a matter of progressively elaborating the oral mother tongue as a means of sharing intentions. The developmental hypothesis offered here is that the ability to assign meaning to the sentence per se [as in a written text], independent of its nonlinguistic context, is achieved only well into the school years (p. 275, Cummins 1983c:116, our interpolation).

What Cummins and Olson apparently intended to emphasize was the greater degree of inference required to link up a written text with its author's intended meanings than is required in the case of an interactive discourse in the here and now. The latter, presumably the typical context for the exercise of BICS, is less cognitively demanding than the former, a typical context for the use of CALP.

Within the more elaborate Peircean perspective proposed here, Olson's phrase "independent of its nonlinguistic context" might be reformulated to "without firsthand access to its nonlinguistic context." This does no violence to Olson's argument nor to Cummins application of the idea in reference to CALP. However, it is a necessary modification if Peirce's view of interpretation as translation from one form of semiotic representation to another is accepted. The translation is not viciously circular only because sensory-motor representations enable the investment of all other sorts of representation with material content. Otherwise they would be devoid of any practical meaning at all.

Strictly speaking, there is no such thing as a meaningful "sentence" without a "nonlinguistic" context. With that in mind, we assume that Olson and Cummins might accept the interpretation that CALP (or in Olson's argument, literacy) requires a larger inferential leap from the perceptible form of a written text in the case under consideration (representation) and an appropriate interpretation that associates it with experiential context. A representation that has no inferential relation to any experiential context is necessarily meaningless and would be entirely uninterpretable (Einstein, 1944 & Peirce, in Oller, 1989b).

In the Peircean perspective advocated here, the CALP/BICS dichotomy can be understood as follows. The overlapping part of the iceberg beneath the surface is similar to the general factor of language proficiency that incorporates whatever aspects of intelligence are necessary to that proficiency. For BICS, also, it is clear that the use of both sensory-motor information and linguistically coded representations simultaneously would require a pragmatic linking that could only be accomplished by access to general semiotic ability. However, with BICS, sensory-motor information is immediately accessible to aid the pragmatic linkage.

In the exercise of CALP, on the other hand, say in reading an unillustrated text (e.g., the one on this page), any necessary sensory-motor representations would have to be supplied by the reader. This is a more difficult semiotic task. It requires a higher degree of inference based on a more abstract semiotic system (namely, a linguistic one) from which the sensory-motor type images must be inferred where they are needed. The move from graphological representations to a more abstract linguistic form is already a difficult inferential process (reading), and the absence of sensory-motor images that might give some clue concerning reference, deixis, and the whole pragmatic mapping process demands a complex of inferences.

Thus, CALP, with its special emphasis on literacy and abstract reasoning would presumably require the development of reading and writing skills in the primary or some nonprimary language. Whereas BICS might benefit indirectly from such a development, literacy and specialized abstract reasoning skills (e.g., ability to do arithmetic leading on to higher mathematical skills) would not be necessary to BICS. To this extent, BICS and CALP are usefully distinguishable, which suggests an important amplification of Cummins's threshold hypothesis—one that he has commented on (Cummins, 1984:117).

Cummins attributes the initial distinction between "surface fluency" and "conceptual-linguistic knowledge" to Skutnabb-Kangas and Toukomaa (1976). They, no doubt, were influenced by the distinction between "surface" structure and "deep" structure from Chomskyan linguistics. A student might develop routing facility with greetings, leave-takings, playground games, and the like, and still fall short of the level of language proficiency and concept development necessary to read, write, and do arithmetic. Therefore, some students might do well in conversation but fail as readers (Olson, 1977).

The low threshold for language skill, then, might be construed as a completely general requirement applying as much to monolinguals as to multilinguals. Presumably, this was what another generation of specialists in another paradigm meant by "reading readiness" and what the field of speech-language pathology means by an intrinsic "language-learning impairment." The higher threshold, too, would have a more general interpretation in this context. Presumably, "metalinguistic awareness" is another way of referring to what psychologists and educators called "learning to learn" or "talking about talk" and so on.

Componential Models Required

One of the most difficult things to see about language proficiency is that it may be conceptualized in a considerable variety of different but mutually compatible ways. For instance, evaluators may think of language proficiency in terms of the various components of grammar that constitute it in theory, or they may think of language proficiency in terms of the traditional skills. What is difficult to see is that these are not incompatible ways of viewing the phenomena of interest. They are and there are many others.

If evaluators focus on primary language ability as represented in Figure 3-2 above, that portion of the diagram might be amplified as shown in Figures 3-4 or 3-5. In Figure 3-4, language proficiency is seen as divisible, more or less, into domains of grammar. Pragmatics may be defined as pertaining to those aspects of meaning that concern actual, particular, concrete contexts of experience. Semantics embraces those aspects of meaning that are virtual, universal, or abstract. Syntax is concerned with the sequential or simultaneous arrangement of categories of grammar

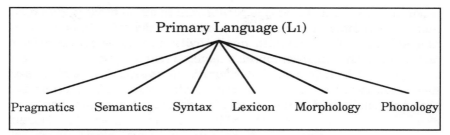

Fig. 3-4. Language proficiency in terms of domains of grammar.

into texts. Lexicon comprises those inventories of elements that are acquired as whole units (e.g., words, idioms, pat phrases, verbal routines). Morphology in English is a question of inflections, (e.g., pluralization, tense and number marking on verbs) and derivations (e.g., adding a morpheme to make a verb of an adjective such as "real" plus "-ize" to get "realize"). Phonology is a matter of determining the surface forms of phonemes, syllables, lexical items, and larger structures.

Figure 3-5 shows a similar breakdown with reference to skills such as listening, speaking, reading, writing, and verbal thinking. It may be argued without risk of contradiction that such hypothetical domains of structure, or distinct skills, are as valid as the theories upon which they are based. However, such divisions can never be finally determined anymore than Immanuel Kant could determine once for all the ultimate categories of reason. As Peirce, Einstein, and others have shown, such categories are intrinsically arbitrary and cannot be finally fixed or completely determined by any amount of empirical research (see especially Einstein, 1941, 1944, and the papers by Peirce in Oller, 1989b). While it may be possible to fix upper and lower limits within which the simplicity and complexity of the model must fall, its specifics will always retain a substantial arbitrariness nonetheless.

Fig. 3-5. Language proficiency in terms of modalities of processing.

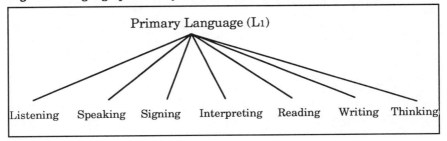

For instance, there is no conceivable argument that would prove either of the componential breakdowns of Figure 3-4 or 3-5 to be intrinsically superior to the other. For one purpose, one model might be preferred, for some other purpose, another. What is more, many other componential models may be conceived. For example, modes of processing (productive versus receptive) may be distinguished, modalities of processing (articulatory-auditory versus visual-manual), stages of processing (consciousness, short-term, long-term memory), and so forth. In principle, there is an infinite variety of possible componential models. Within the proposed hierarchy, this fact can be construed as a natural outcome of different ways of combining and parsing up various of the proposed elements.

Relation of Bilingualism to Intelligence

While it was long maintained that cognitive development might be hindered by becoming bilingual, the evidence clearly points in the other direction (Cummins, 1984; 1986; Hakuta, 1986). Dabbling in nonprimary-language acquisition may have little or no impact on intellect, but the acquisition of a second or third or fourth language to a substantial degree of proficiency is apt to result in significant, though modest, cognitive gains. In particular, evidence suggests that bilinguals achieve some kinds of flexibility in reasoning and a capacity to appreciate certain kinds of abstract relations that might remain outside the reach of some monolinguals. This result (see the research cited above with reference to the "threshold" hypothesis) is predicted on the basis of the hierarchy under consideration.

Moreover, as in the case of the threshold hypothesis, a more general hypothesis is suggested. If bilingualism contributes to mental growth only after some threshold is passed, it follows that simply attaining proficiency in one's primary or native language must be important to normal mental maturation. Further, if language is a window through which researchers may get a clear look at the mind, it follows that the development of language proficiency must be linked to normal cognitive development. Putting this hypothesis in its most general form (Oller, 1986) following Peirce, Einstein, Dewey, Piaget, Vygotsky, and others as noted above, we predict that normal development of deep semiotic abilities may depend in subtle ways on the development of the primary language.

While it may be possible for deep semiotic abilities to be developed to a high degree with reference to some other mainfest form (e.g., sensory-motor representations), since linguistic representations achieve a more complete level of logical abstractness and conventional arbitrariness, it seems likely that in normal human beings language development in all of its diversity is the fulcrum on which intellect attains its greatest leverage. It also follows that language abilities will be central to any definition of human exceptionalities ranging from giftedness in all its varieties to disabilities of all types.

CONCLUSIONS

This chapter has proposed a theory of language proficiency and representational abilities based on the work of C. S. Peirce. The theory is consistent with empirical research on language testing and hypotheses about multilingualism. It follows from such a theory that tests, or observational assessment procedures, should always involve performances in rich and engaging contexts. It will usually be necessary to examine a variety of sources of evidence (e.g., multiple languages, dialects, kinesic representations, and sensory-motor performances). The objective should always be to look for the student's optimal capabilities rather than to try to define a permanent set of disabilities. Judgments should always be subject to updating, revision, and rechecking. Any single test should form the basis only for a small part of a complete assessment. In the final analysis, the goal is to set the student up for success, not failure. Educators should find paths and build bridges rather than merely define impossibilities.

REFERENCES

Alderson, J. C. (1983). The cloze procedure and proficiency in English as a second language. In J. W. Oller, Jr., (Ed.), *Issues in language testing research* (pp. 205–217). Rowley, MA: Newbury House.

Alderson, J. C., & Hughes, A. (Eds.). (1982). *Issues in language testing.* ELT Documents No. 111. London: British Council.

Anderson, J. (1969). *Application of cloze procedure to English learned as a foreign language.* Doctoral dissertation, University of New England, Australia.

Asher, J. J., & Garcia, R. (1969). The optimal age to learn a foreign language. *Modern Language Journal 53,* 334–341.

Asher, J. J., & Price, B. S. (1967). The learning strategy of the total physical response: Some age differences. *Child Development, 38,* 1219–1227.

Bachman, L. (1989). *Fundamental considerations in language testing.* Reading, MA: Oxford University.

Bachman, L., & Palmer, A. S. (1983). The construct validity of the FSI Oral Interview. In J. W. Oller, Jr. (Ed.), *Issues in language testing research* (pp. 154–169). Rowley, MA: Newbury House.

Bickerton, D. (1981). *Roots of language.* Ann Arbor, MI: Karoma.

Bower, T. G. R. (1971). The object in the world of the infant. *Scientific American, 225,* 30–38.

Bower, T. G. R. (1974). *Development in infancy.* San Francisco: Freeman.
Brown, H. D. (1973). Affective variables in second language acquisition. *Language Learning, 23,* 231–244.
Bruner, J. S. (1983). *Child's Talk.* New York: W. W. Norton.
Canale, M., & Swain, M. (1980). Theoretical bases of communicative approaches to second language teaching and testing. *Applied Linguistics, 1,* 1–47.
Carroll, J. B. (1961). Fundamental considerations in testing for English proficiency of foreign students. In *Testing the English proficiency of foreign students* (pp. 31–40). Washington, D.C.: Center for Applied Linguistics.
Carroll, J. B. (1983a). Psychometric theory and language testing. In J. W. Oller, Jr. (Ed.), *Issues in language testing research* (pp. 80–107). Rowley, MA: Newbury House.
Carroll, J. B. (1983b). Studying individual differences in cognitive abilities: Through and beyond factor analysis. In R. Dillon and R. Schneck (Eds.), *Individual differences in cognition* (pp. 1–28). New York: Academic Press.
Chomsky, N. (1956). Three models for the description of language. In *I.R.E. Transactions on Information Theory,* Vol. IT-2 (pp. 113–124).
Chomsky, N. (1980a). On cognitive structures and their development. In M. Piatelli-Palmarini (Ed.), *Language and learning: The debate between Jean Piaget and Noam Chomsky* (pp. 35–54). Cambridge, MA: Harvard.
Chomsky, N. (1980b). *Rules and representations.* New York: Columbia University.
Chomsky, N. (1988). *Language and problems of knowledge.* Cambridge, MA: MIT Press.
Church, A. (1951). The need for abstract entities in a semantic analysis. *Daedalus, 80,* 100–112.
Cohen, A. (1980). *Testing language ability in the classroom.* Rowley, MA: Newbury House.
Condon, W. S., & Ogston, W. D. (1971). Speech and body-motion synchrony of the speaker-hearer. In D. L. Horton and J. J. Jenkins (Eds.), *The perception of language* (pp. 150–173). Columbus, OH: Merrill.
Cronbach, L. J. (1971). Test Validation. In R. Thorndike (Ed.), *Educational Measurement* (pp. 443–507). Washington D.C.: American Council on Education.
Cronbach, L. J., & Meehl, P. (1955). Construct validity in psychological tests. *Psychological Bulletin, 52,* 281–302.
Crystal, D. (1987). Towards a "bucket" theory of language disability: Taking account of interaction between linguistic levels. *Clinical Linguistics and Phonetics, 1,* 7–22.
Cummins, J. (1976). The influence of bilingualism on cognitive growth: A synthesis of the research findings and explanatory hypotheses. *Working Papers on Bilingualism, 9,* 1–43.
Cummins, J. (1984). Wanted: A theoretical framework for relating language proficiency to academic achievement among bilingual students. In C. Rivera (Ed.), *Language Proficiency and Academic Achievement* (pp. 2–19). Clevedon, England: Multilingual Matters.
Cummins, J. (1983a). Functional language proficiency in context: Classroom participation as an interactive process. In W. J. Tikunoff (Ed.), *Compatibility of the SBIS features with other research on instruction for LEP students* (pp. 109–131). San Francisco: Far West Laboratory.
Cummins, J. (1983b). *Heritage language education: A literature review.* Toronto, Canada: Ministry of Education.
Cummins, J. (1983c). Language proficiency and academic achievement. In J. W.

Oller, Jr. (Ed.), *Issues in language testing research* (pp. 108–130). Rowley, MA: Newbury House.

Cummins, J. (1984). *Bilingualism and special education: Issues in assessment and pedagogy*. Austin, TX: PRO-ED.

Cummins, J. (1986). Empowering minority students: A framework for intervention. *Harvard Educational Review 56*, 18–35.

Cummins, J., & Mulcahy, R. (1978). Orientation to language in Ukrainian-English bilingual children. *Child Development, 49*, 1239–1242.

Cummins, J., & Swain, M. (1986). *Bilingualism in education: Aspects of theory, research, and practice*. London: Longman.

Cummins, R. (1985). *The nature of psychological explanation*. Cambridge, MA: MIT Press.

Damico, J. S. (1988). The lack of efficacy in language therapy: A case study. *Language, Speech, and Hearing Services in Schools, 19*, 51–66.

Davies, A. (1984). Review of J. W. Oller, Jr. (Ed.), *Issues in language testing research* (Newbury House, 1983). *Language Testing, 1*, 111–114.

Dewey, J. (1938). Judgment as spatial-temporal determination: Narration-description. In *Logic: The theory of Inquiry* (pp. 220–244). New York: Holt, Rinehart and Winston.

Duncan, S. E., & DeAvila, E. A. (1979). Bilingualism and cognition: Some recent findings. *NABE Journal, 4*, 15–50.

Einstein, A. (1941). The common language of science. In *Out of my later years* (pp. 111–113). Secaucus, NJ: Citadel.

Einstein, A. (1944). Remarks on Bertrand Russell's theory of knowledge. In J. W. Oller, Jr. (Ed.), *Language and experience: Classic pragmatism* (pp. 21–29). Lanham, MD: University Press of America.

Evola, J., Mamer, E., & Lentz, B. (1980). Discrete point versus global scoring for cohesive devices. In J. W. Oller, Jr. and K. Perkins (Eds.), *Research in language testing* (pp. 177–181). Rowley, MA: Newbury House.

Farhady, H. (1983a). The disjunctive fallacy between discrete-point tests and integrative tests. In J. W. Oller, Jr. (Ed.), *Issues in language testing research* (pp. 311–322). Rowley, MA: Newbury House.

Farhady, H. (1983b). On the plausibility of the unitary language proficiency factor. In J. W. Oller, Jr. (Ed.), *Issues in language testing research* (pp. 11–28). Rowley, MA: Newbury House.

Feuerstein. R. (1980). *Instrumental enrichment: An intervention program for cognitive modifiability*. Baltimore: University Park Press.

Gunnarsson, B. (1978). A look at the content similarities of between intelligence, achievement, personality and language tests. In J. W. Oller, Jr. and K. Perkins (Eds.), *Language in education: Testing the tests* (pp. 17–35). Rowley, MA: Newbury House.

Gould, S. J. (1981). *The mismeasure of man*. New York: W. W. Norton.

Gregg, K. (1988). Epistemology without knowledge: Schwartz on Chomsky, Fodor, and Krashen. *Second Language Research, 4*, 66–76.

Hakuta, K. (1986). *Mirror of language: The debate on bilingualism*. New York: Basic Books.

Hanley, W. (1981). Validity, vaudeville, and values. *American Psychologist, 36*, 1021–1034.

Hartshorne, C., & Weiss, P. (Eds.), (1931–1935). *Collected writings of C. S. Peirce*, Volumes I and VI. Cambridge, MA: Harvard University.

Jones, R. L., & Spolsky, B. (Eds.) (1975). *Testing language proficiency*. Arlington, VA: Center for Applied Linguistics.

Kessler, C., & Quinn, M. E. (1980). Positive effects of bilingualism on science problem-solving abilities. In J. E. Alatis (Ed.), *Georgetown University roundtable on languages and linguistics*. Washington, D.C.: Georgetown University.

Kirchner, D., & Skarakis-Doyle, E. (1983). Developmental language disorders: A theoretical perspective. In T. Gallagher and C. Prutting (Eds.), *Pragmatic assessment and intervention issues in language*. (pp. 43–74) Austin, TX: PRO-ED.

Krashen, S. D. (1982). *Principles and practice in second language acquisition*. Oxford: Pergamon.

Krashen S. D. (1985). *The input hypothesis: Issues and implications*. London: Longman.

Lado, R. (1961). *Language testing*. New York: McGraw Hill.

Lambert, W. E. (1975). Culture and language as factors in learning and education. In A. Wolfgang (Ed.), *Education of immigrant students* (pp. 43–74). Toronto: OISE.

Lane, H. (1984). *When the mind hears*. New York: Random House.

Lane, H. (1988). Educating the American Sign Language Minority of the United States: A paper prepared for the Commission on the Education of the Deaf. In S. Wilcox (Ed.), *Academic acceptance of American sign language: Sign language studies, Special Issue, 59* (pp. 221–230). Silver Spring, MD: Linstok.

Lotz, J. (1951). Natural and scientific languages. *Daedalus, 80,* 87–88.

Luria, A. R. (1961). *The role of speech in the regulation of normal and abnormal behavior*. New York: Irvington.

Luria, A. R., & Yudovich, F. A. (1959). *Speech development and the mental processes of the child*. London: Staples.

Messick, S. (1975). The standard problem: Meaning and values in measurement and evaluation. *American Psychologist, 30,* 533–546.

Messick, S. (1980). Test validity and the ethics of assessment. *American Psychologist, 35,* 1012–1027.

Muma, J. R. (1984). Semel and Wiig's CELF: Construct validity? A letter to the editor. *Journal of Speech and Hearing Disorders, 49,* 101–104.

Nelson, K. (1985). *Making Sense*. New York: Academic Press.

Newmark, L. (1983). How not to interfere with language learning. In J. W. Oller, Jr. and P. Richard-Amato (Eds.), *Methods that work: A smorgasbord of ideas for language teachers* (pp. 49–58). Rowley, MA: Newbury House.

Newmeyer, F. (1980). *Linguistic theory in America*. New York: Academic Press.

Nunnally, J. (1967). *Psychometric theory*. New York: McGraw-Hill.

Oller, J. W., Jr. (1970). Dictation as a device for testing foreign language proficiency. *Workpapers in TESL: UCLA, 4,* 37–42.

Oller, J. W., Jr. (1972). Scoring methods and difficulty levels for cloze tests of proficiency in English as a second language. *Modern Language Journal, 56,* 151–158.

Oller, J. W., Jr. (1973). Cloze tests of second language proficiency and what they measure. *Language Learning, 23,* 105–118.

Oller, J. W., Jr. (1976). Evidence for a general language proficiency factor: An expectancy grammar. *Die Neuren Sprachen, 76,* 165–174.

Oller, J. W., Jr. (1979). *Language tests at school*. London: Longman.

Oller, J. W., Jr. (1981). Language as intelligence? *Language Learning, 31,* 465–492.

Oller, J. W., Jr. (1983a). A consensus for the 80's? In J. W. Oller, Jr. (Ed.), *Issues in language testing research* (pp. 351–356). Rowley, MA: Newbury House.

Oller, J. W., Jr. (Ed.). (1983b). *Issues in language testing research*. Rowley, MA: Newbury House.

Oller, J. W., Jr. (1986). Communication theory and testing: What and how? In C. Stansfield (Ed.), *Proceedings of the second international invitational Conference on the Test of English as a Foreign Language* (pp. 99–179). Princeton, NJ: ETS.

Oller, J. W., Jr. (1988). *The input hypothesis: Issues and implications by S. D. Krashen (1985) London and New York: Longman. Language*, 64, 171–173.

Oller, J. W., Jr. (1989a). Conclusions toward a rational pragmatism. In J. W. Oller, Jr. (Ed.), *Language and experience: Classic pragmatism* (pp. 223–250). Lanham, MD: University Press of America.

Oller, J. W., Jr. (Ed.). (1989b). *Language and experience: Classic pragmatism*. Lanham, MD: University Press of America.

Oller, J. W., Jr., & Conrad, C. (1971). The cloze procedure and ESL proficiency. *Language Learning*, 21, 183–196.

Oller, J. W., Jr., & Hinofotis, F. B. (1976). Paper presented at the Annual Meeting of the Linguistic Society of America, Philadelphia. Reprinted with some changes in J. W. Oller, Jr. and K. Perkins (Eds.), *Research in language testing* (pp. 13–23). Rowley, MA: Newbury House.

Oller, J. W., Jr., & Perkins, K. (Eds.). (1978). *Language in education: Testing the tests*. Rowley, MA: Newbury House.

Oller, J. W., Jr., & Perkins, K. (Eds.). (1980). *Research in language testing*. Rowley, MA: Newbury House.

Olson, D. (1977). From utterance to text: The bias of language in speech and writing. *Harvard Educational Review*, 47, 257–281.

Palmer, L., & Spolsky, B. (Eds.). (1975). *Papers on language testing: 1967–1974*. Washington, D.C.: TESL.

Palmer, A. S., Groot, P. J. M., & Trosper, G. A. (Eds.). (1981). *The validation of oral proficiency tests: Selected papers from The Colloquium on the Validation of Oral Proficiency Tests*. Washington, D.C.: TESOL.

Piaget, J. (1947). *The psychology of intelligence*. Totowa, NJ: Littlefield Adams.

Piaget, J. (1970). *Genetic Epistemology*. New York: W. W. Norton.

Piatelli-Palmarini, M. (1980). *Language and learning: The debate between Jean Piaget and Noam Chomsky*. Cambridge, MA: Harvard.

Purcell, E. T. (1983). Models of pronunciation accuracy. In J. W. Oller, Jr. (Ed.), *Issues in language testing research* (pp. 133–153). Rowley, MA: Newbury House.

Rand, E. (1976). A factored homogeneous items approach to the UCLA ESL Placement Examination. Paper presented at the Tenth Annual TESOL Convention, New York City.

Rivera, C. (Ed.). (1984). *Language proficiency and academic achievement*. Avon, England: Multilingual Matters.

Russell, B. (1919). *Introduction to mathematical logic*. New York: George Allen and Unwin.

Savage, (1978). *Perception and cognition: Issues in the foundation of psychology*. Minnesota Studies in the Philosophy of Science, 9. Minneapolis: University of Minnesota Press.

Savignon, S. (1971). *A study of the effect of training in communicative skills as part of a beginning college French course on student attitude and achievement in linguistic and communicative competence*. Doctoral dissertation, University of Illinois, Champaign-Urbana.

Savignon, S. (1983). *Communicative competence: Theory and classroom practice (Texts and contexts in second language teaching)*. Reading, MA: Addison-Wesley.

Schumann, J. (1975). Affective factors and the problem of age in second language acquisition. *Language Learning*, 26, 135–143.

Schumann, J. (1978). *Second language acquisition: The pidginization hypothesis.* Rowley, MA: Newbury House.

Selinker, L. (1972). Interlanguage. *International Review of Applied Linguistics, 10,* 209–231.

Shuy, R. W. (1978). Problems in assessing language ability in bilingual education. In H. Lafontaine, H. Persky, and L. Golubchick (Eds.), *Bilingual education.* Wayne, NJ: Avery.

Shuy, R. W. (1981). Conditions affecting language learning and maintenance among Hispanics in the United States. *NABE Journal, 6,* 1–18.

Skutnabb-Kangas, T., & Toukomaa, T. (1976). *Teaching migrant children's mother tongue and learning the language of the host country in the context of the socio-cultural situation of the migrant family.* Helsinki: The Finnish National Commission for UNESCO.

Sommers, R. K., Erdige, S., & Peterson, M. K. (1978). How valid are children's language tests? *The Journal of Special Education, 12,* 393–407.

Spearman, C. (1927). *The abilities of man.* New York: Macmillan.

Spolsky, B. (1968a). Language tests: The problem of validation. *TESOL Quarterly, 2,* 88–94.

Spolsky, B. (1968b). What does it mean to know a language? Or how do you get someone to perform his competence? Paper read at the Second Conference on Problems of Foreign Language Competence, University of Southern California, Los Angeles. Also in J. W. Oller, Jr. and J. C. Richards (Eds.), (1973), *Focus on the learner* (pp. 164–176). Rowley, MA: Newbury House.

Spolsky, B. (1983). Comments on a general factor. In A. Hughes and D. Porter (Eds.), *Current developments in language testing* (pp. 63–74). London: Academic Press.

Spolsky, B. (1985). A critical review of Krashen. Lecture presented at the Universtiy of New Mexico.

Stump, T. A. (1978). Cloze and dictation tasks as predictors of intelligence and achievement. In J. W. Oller, Jr. and K. Perkins (Eds.), *Language in education: testing the tests* (pp. 36–64). Rowley, MA: Newbury House.

Upshur, J. A. (1967). English language tests and the prediction of academic success. In *National Association of Foreign Student Affairs, Selected conference papers of the Association of Teachers of English as a Second Language.*

Upshur, J. A., & Fata, J. (1968). *Problems in foreign language testing. Language Learning,* Special Issue Number 3. Ann Arbor: University of Michigan.

Upshur, J. A., & Homburg, T. J. (1983). Some relations among language tests at successive ability levels. In J. W. Oller, Jr. (Ed.), *Issues in language testing research* (pp. 188–202). Rowley, MA: Newbury House.

Valette, R. (1964). The use of dictee in the French language classroom. *Modern Language Journal, 39,* 431–434.

Valette, R. (1967). *Modern Language Testing.* New York: Harcourt, Brace, Jovanovich.

Vigil, N., & Oller, J. W., Jr. (1976). Rule fossilization: A tentative model. *Language Learning, 26,* 281–295.

Vollmer, H. J., & Sang, F. (1983). Competing hypotheses about second language ability: a plea for caution. In J. W. Oller, Jr. (Ed.), *Issues in language testing research* (pp. 29–79) Rowley, MA: Newbury House.

Vygotsky, L. S. (1978). *Mind in society: The development of higher psychological processes.* Edited by M. Cole, V. John-Steiner, S. Scribner, and E. Souberman. Cambridge, MA: Harvard.

Vygotsky, L. S. (1987). *The collected works of L. S. Vygotsky, Vol. I.*

Wilcox, S. (Ed.). (1988). *Academic acceptance of American Sign Language: Sign Language Studies,* Special Issue. 59. Silver Spring, MD: Linstok.

CHAPTER 4

Practical Considerations for the Assessment of LEP Students with Special Needs

PAT CHAMBERLAIN
AND
PATRICIA MEDINOS-LANDURAND

Assessment is a subjective process that is highly influenced by the socio-political, cultural, and linguistic context. Apart from any theoretical considerations (see Chapter Three), these contextual variables result in practical concerns that subvert the common (and erroneous) notion of assessment as being an objective enterprise. As any experienced evaluator of culturally and linguistically diverse students can attest, there are a host of confounding variables and problematic factors that must be identified and resolved when assessing this population. Failure to do so may result in an invalid and potentially harmful set of evaluative conclusions and recommendations.

For example, a rural Portuguese 7-year-old boy, considered intelligent and well-adjusted by Portuguese educators, may not be similarly viewed by American educators assessing him in a suburban, upper socioeconomic status (SES) educational context. Based on expectations of how mainstream upper SES students should perform and on presuppositions of how Portuguese immigrants will perform, the evaluators may not adjust their assessment approach to potential experiential and linguistic differences between the two cultures. Due to testers' expectations, test interpretation may result in an inappropriate placement of this student into a special education program. In this case, the lack of awareness regarding the actual implications of cultural and linguistic diversity results in a devaluation of both the student's cultural/linguistic background and his intrinsic learning potential. Unfortunately, there are numerous examples of such incidences in the literature (e.g., Cummins, 1984; Miller, 1984; Trueba, 1987).

Due to the significant impact of cultural and linguistic variables on the assessment process, it is crucial that all educators invnolved in the assessment of culturally and linguistically diverse students recognize the extent to which these variables operate to affect test results and the interpretation of those results. This chapter addresses those cultural and linguistic factors from a practical viewpoint, discusses how they affect the assessment process, and includes strategies for controlling these variables during evaluation.

CONTEXTUAL FACTORS INFLUENCING ASSESSMENT

Although the pragmatic influences on the assessment process are numerous, contextual variables can be separated into two general categories for ease of discussion: cultural factors and linguistic factors. Within these two categories, sociopolitical agendas, experiential factors, communicative patterns, societal expectations, and parental hopes can be subsumed. While division into these two categories may seem arbitrary given various definitions of culture (Geertz, 1973; Hall, 1978; Hymes, 1967), such division allows a focus on these two most relevant aspects of the assessment process.

CULTURAL INFLUENCES ON ASSESSMENT

Culture can be defined as the values, norms, and traditions that affect how individuals perceive, think, interact, behave, and make judgments about their world. More simply, culture may be described as whatever an individual must know to function in a particular society. Due to the pervasiveness of this definition, a discussion of cultural influences may seem difficult. All aspects of human behavior (including the assessment process) must be included in this definition. We can, however, discuss cultural influences in a more explicit manner.

From a methodological perspective, culture may be divided into three general categories: cultural behavior, cultural artifacts, and cultural knowledge (Spradley, 1980). Cultural behavior may be considered the observable patterns of behavior within some social group or displayed by a specific individual from that group. The types of religious practices, the ways that an individual dresses, how that individual eats, how someone celebrates, and how an individual interacts with others are examples of cultural behavior. More specific to assessment concerns, the learning strategies that a student employs, the student's adaptive strategies when faced with failure, the student's reactions to teachers and testing situations, and even the overt acceptance of testing are further examples of cultural behavior patterns. Cultural artifacts are the actual products created by a culture. For example, the food that an individual eats or the music that an individual sings as well as books, newspapers, ditto sheets, report cards, artwork, homework, and buildings are all artifacts. They can reveal much about the culture which produced these forms. Together, these two categories make up the overt characteristics of a culture.

Cultural knowledge is more implicit and can only be inferred from the overt behaviors and artifacts. It is the tacit information, beliefs, and ideas that structure an individual's actions, reactions, and products. From an assessment perspective, cultural knowledge is critical. Correct inferences regarding the underlying reasons for a student's performance in school and during assessment reflects on that individual's knowledge base. That knowledge, in turn, is acquired by experience in a culturally specific environment that may differ from the evaluator's or the school system's. Since cultural knowledge is tacit, however, it is generally revealed through cultural behavior and artifacts. The evaluator, therefore, must look beyond the overt external behaviors and artifacts and explore the internal knowledge that strongly influences how individuals behave, how they learn, and how they use what they have learned. For example, when observing for behavioral disorders, whether a student who has been pushed by another student decides to tell the teacher, push the other child back, walk away and/or try to act on his or her own behalf will be determined, in part, by the student's cultural knowledge. Failure to consider such knowledge may result in inappropriate diagnosis.

All three of these cultural categories are important in the consideration of how cultural factors may affect the assessment process. Based upon one's experience and cultural knowledge, certain behaviors may occur or particular artifacts might be produced during the assessment process. Whether or not students can identify a light filament, an elevator, or a skyscraper on an intelligence test depends upon their culturally based experiences and knowledge. Such considerations make it imperative for judgments about intelligence or other cognitive characteristics to be interpreted through a cultural filter. Failure to do so will typically result in problems.

Problems Due to Cultural Insensitivity

If teachers and evaluators are insensitive to cultural diversity, several problems may occur. First, there may be *misperceptions* between the culturally diverse student and the teacher or evaluator. This may result in the two parties having different understandings regarding their roles and expectations in a specific situation. This, in turn, may lead to actual poorer performance or the perception of poorer performance in the testing situation or classroom. Deyhle (1987), for example, reported that Navajo second-graders had a different perception of what a test was than did Anglo second-graders. While the Anglo students recognized testing as an activity linked to demonstrating learning for promotion and evaluation, the Navajo students perceived tests as distinct events only due to their unique procedural rules. Not one of the Navajo second-graders linked testing to the learning process. Consequently, while the Anglo second-graders attempted to do their best in the testing situation, the Navajos were less motivated by performance criteria. In another setting, Philips (1983) reported on teacher misperceptions that resulted in a negative evaluation of Native American students on the Warm Springs Indian reservation. The non-Indian teachers perceived and defined the students as relatively inattentive in the classroom since Indian students convey attention in different ways than do Anglo students. Such misperceptions resulted in the belief that the Indian students were poorer students with more comprehension problems than their Anglo peers. Such misperceptions could result in inappropriate referrals, test interpretations, and placements into special education programs.

The second problem that may occur due to cultural insensitivity is the creation of *cross-cultural stereotyping* (Tannen, 1984). Due to a lack of awareness of cultural differences, certain groups may be stereotyped as possessing particular intrinsic traits when they merely exhibit behavioral differences. Scollon (as reported by Tannen, 1984) provides an example of such stereotyping: Athabaskan Indians consider it inappropriate to talk to strangers. Consequently, when they meet non-Athabaskans who do not understand this cultural difference, this Native American group is considered to be sullen, uncooperative, or even stupid. Interestingly, Basso (1979) points out that this negative stereotyping works both ways. Western Apache (another Athabaskan group), noting the willingness of Anglos to talk when meeting strangers, stereotype these Anglos as ridiculously garrulous and hypocritical.

A third problem that may arise from cultural insensitivity is *miscommunication*. Lacking shared background and an understanding of the interactional patterns exhibited in the other culture, a student or parent from one culture and a teacher or evaluator from another culture may misinterpret attempts at communication. This may result in confusion and misinformation, particularly if the miscommunications are not recognized, that affect the educational or the assessment process. For example, a student from a different culture may not share similar background knowledge with the teacher and/or the other students. Lessons and examples couched within this background may be confusing to the culturally different student and serve as a barrier to learning rather than an aid. In another case, the teacher reporting to the parent that there is a potential learning disability that may necessitate special education may be totally misinterpreted. Since the parent's culture has different conceptions of disabled, the parent may interpret the conversation as a suggestion that their child is severely retarded or insane. Varonis and Gass (1985) discuss this problem between native and nonnative conversational partners at length and suggest that such problems are surprisingly frequent.

Finally, another effect of cultural insensitivity is *assessment bias*. This problem results when the educational personnel involved in the assessment process do not take the potential cultural differences into account when assessing culturally diverse students. In an excellent account of this potential problem, Miller (1984) suggests biasing factors that are extrinsic to the tests themselves and factors that are intrinsic to the tests. Some of the extrinsic factors that should be considered are child-rearing and schooling differences, the sociocultural position and role of the test population within society as a whole, attitudes in test-taking and response styles, the value of competition in the student's culture, and adjustment to the artificiality of the testing situation. Intrinsic biasing factors include the use of culture-bound stimuli, background knowledge not accessible to the student, language and conceptual differences, and selection practices for determining normative samples. Although this issue of assessment bias is handled in the chapters of this volume specific to communicative assessment (Chapter Five), educational assessment (Chapter Six), and cognitive assessment (Chapter Seven), a more general discussion based on cultural implications is warranted.

Tests used in American schools are generally written by middle class individuals and reflect on Anglo middle-class experiences (Mercer, 1979). A student from a rural Portuguese village will most likely not be able to identify an elevator, a tennis racket, or a snowman. Students who do not have Euro-American middle class values and who have not experienced that culture are at a serious disadvantage in taking standardized tests. Furthermore, when asked a value-based question such as, "What would you do if you found a lost wallet?" the response will depend on the student's culturally learned values. For example, in one school district, a Portuguese student answered the above question by saying, "Give the wallet to the priest." The assessor did not give the student full credit for this response because he was unaware of the fact that in a small, rural, Portuguese village, the priest would be the best authority figure. A second child responded to the same question by saying, "Keep the wallet." This response was obviously given no credit by the assessor, who was following the scoring guidelines in the test administration manual. The assumption is that the student lacked the knowledge to answer this question correctly, yet the concern that the student was taught a different value was never considered. The appropriate interpretation of test performance is critical for the culturally or linguistically different student: The assessor must probe the possible reasons for the student's low score to determine whether the student was unfamiliar with the testing context, lacked the skills needed to take the test, or had values that clashed with those implied in the test items.

In addition to item bias, most tests used in the United States are normed on the mainstream population. Even when tests claim to have included culturally diverse populations in their standardization procedures, those populations are included in such small ratios that the results are insignificant. Assessors need to be aware of this problem when interpreting a culturally diverse student's performance in the context of norms.

Given the potential occurrence of these types of problems, assessors need to learn about a student's culture in order to interpret responses appropriately within the student's cultural framework. Without this cultural understanding, assessors will not be able to make appropriate interpretations of a student's performance and suggest recommendations that will encourage students to perform more successfully in a typical public school setting.

Because of the multifaceted nature of culture and because many facets of culture influence how a student behaves and performs in a school setting, it is necessary to detail several other variables that may affect the assessment process.

Influence of Specific Cultural Variables

Although there are numerous variables that may be detailed when discussing cultural diversity, the following appear to have sufficient impact to warrant discussion. Before this is done, however, two points must be made. First, although these variables typically play an important role in the assessment process, they are by no means the only cultural variables with potential impact. This discussion merely serves to highlight several variables and to draw attention to the impact of these and other variables. Second, although these variables may be discussed in terms of differences between cultures, there are differences within cultures as well. It can be argued that there are no actual universals in any culture. Because culture is learned at a local level, there are always exceptions due to individual differences in experience and motivation. The variables are detailed in the following sections.

Cooperation Versus Competition

Cultures vary as to the value placed on competition, as opposed to cooperation, among individuals. American mainstream classrooms generally encourage competition; doing better than others is often proof of mastery (Goldman & McDermott, 1987). Most games played in the United States have a winner and a loser and students learn early in life to compete in order to win. This attitude pervades all areas of society, including the classroom. In contrast, for students raised in cooperative societies, competition is generally not understood or valued; for these students, working together is a mutual goal. For example, students from particular cultures have been taught to wait until all their classmates have finished an assigned task before raising their hands. In this way, no student is placed in the embarrassing situation of being last. Similarly, other students are often taught by their parents that individual competition can often hurt significant others such as peers or family members.

In American society, students who do not value or are not skilled in competition are at a serious disadvantage in the testing process (Seymour, 1981). These students do not understand or accept the concept of doing their "best" and working to do better than others during a test. "Timed" tests, the roles of the examiner and the examinee, and the rule of silence and the privacy of answers are all learned concepts and behaviors that may be alien to students from cooperative societies. For example, students from cooperative societies may be accused of cheating in a group testing situation because they are seen helping a friend with a test item. The extent to which competition is valued in a culture, therefore, may have an impact on the student's performance.

Time

Time is viewed differently in various cultures. While in most North American societies, time "runs," it "walks" in many Latin American cultures. Generally, North Americans place great emphasis and importance on being on time and using time efficiently. In contrast, time is more expendable in other cultures; there, quality of interpersonal relationships may take priority over punctuality.

Since assessment is based on a degree of respect for and adherence to the constraints of time, most standardized tests are "speed" tests; and students are judged by how many correct responses they have made in a given amount of time. The assumption that all students value time in a similar fashion and have learned to move as quickly as possible in answering questions on timed tests does not hold true for all students. Students who have been taught that it is appropriate to take as much time as they need to respond to a question or that it is proper to refrain from giving an immediate response may be judged to be slower thinkers. Students who complete the test and thus have the most correct answers are perceived as more competent than students who, although they answered many questions correctly, did not finish the test (Kurt, 1976). Simply put, the concept of time varies across cultures and different culture groups hold different rules regarding the use of time. These rules strongly affect a student's test performance and may result in the inaccurate conclusions that particular students are limited in intelligence because they have answered fewer questions correctly on a timed test.

Polychronic Versus Monochronic Orientation

Another cultural variable tangentially related to the concept of time involves the preference toward a polychronic versus a monochronic orientation. Some cultures are polychronic, meaning that people are generally used to handling several interactions and activities at the same time. Other cultures are monochronic in that they encourage people to deal with one activity at a time. The maxim "business before pleasure" reflects a monochronic orientation, whereas in many polychronic cultures, business and pleasurable activities are seen as a whole (Kurt, 1976).

North American students are generally taught to be monochronic and are encouraged to focus on interactions and activities one at a time. For example, teachers with monochronic styles will insist on starting and completing an activity before beginning another one. A student who is tapping a pencil, listening to the radio, and studying at the same time may be accused of not paying attention to work.

The assessment process often operates on a monochronic basis. Students must operate methodically one step at a time within specified time frames. Students with a polychronic orientation will have difficulty adhering to monochronic operating procedures inherent in a test. This difficulty and lack of experience in monochronic functioning often adversely affects a student's testing performance.

Bodily Movements

Bodily movements vary across cultures both in their types and their range. The way that people move their arms, the extent to which they move them, their walking pace, and the restrictiveness or expansiveness of their motions are all examples of what Almanza and Mosley (1980) refer to as a person's movement repertoire. Movement repertoires vary from person to person, but some are more typical in one culture than another.

In many North American schools, a passive style is rewarded (Almanza & Mosley, 1980), and students whose style is more active may be referred for behavior problems. Similarly, students are expected to talk or move about only when directed to do so by the teacher. Those students who adopt a passive style in a testing situation and who respond according to the teacher's or assessor's directions meet normative standards and expectations in the assessment process. On the other hand, those students whose style is much more active and who talk and move about without adult directions may be labeled as having a behavior problem. Furthermore, when required to sit for long periods and quietly perform tasks, certain students may perform poorly because they have difficulty functioning in a traditional testing situation that restricts their active style.

Proximity

Individuals from different cultures use, value, and share space differently (Condon, Peters, & Carmen, 1979). In some cultures, it is considered appropriate for people to stand close to each other while talking. In other cultures, such proximity is considered a violation of one's personal space. Differences in the norms regarding space may give rise to misperceptions. For example, Latin Americans often view North Americans as distant because they prefer more space between speakers. On the other hand, North Americans often view persons who come "too close" as pushy because they are invading private space.

In the educational environment, students and teachers of some cultures prefer a small, close working space while those of other cultures prefer wide-open, spacious working areas. In the assessment process, the formal relationship between the assessor and the student dictates that a certain distance be kept between the assessor and the student(s) during both individual and group testing. For students who value proximity, the physical distance makes the testing situation stressful and consequently, test performance may suffer.

Touching

Rules regarding touching vary from culture to culture. For example, in the Portuguese and Italian cultures, it is acceptable for men to embrace upon greeting each other. In other cultures, people exhibit more physically restrained greetings. Students in certain cultures are used to having frequent physical contact with adults and other students. In other cultures, students are less demonstrative and prefer to have a more formal relationship with adults as well as with other students.

In the testing situation, problems can arise when cultural norms of the assessor and the student do not match for touching. Restrictions are typically placed on physical contact in formal testing situations. These restrictions can affect students who have been culturally conditioned to be in frequent physical contact with others. This lack of contact may result in misperceptions regarding the examiner's attitudes about the student and his ability and may result in an uncomfortable testing condition that can hamper a student's performance.

Eye Contact

Students in many Latin American and Asian cultures show respect by not looking persons of authority in the eye. North American teachers who have different expectations regarding eye contact may perceive this as disrespect. In such cases, students may be erroneously labeled as having behavioral problems. These same students, when placed in a testing situation, may miss directions requiring them to look directly at the teacher and, subsequently, make unnecessary errors while being tested. These errors may lead assessors to misinterpret responses as indicative of the student's poor comprehension. The student may also be perceived as being inattentive or displaying a "bad" or resistant attitude in a testing situation.

Gender

Expectations about how boys and girls should behave differ among cultures. Most cultures exhibit gender stereotypes. For example, in many traditional Columbian and Asian families, young boys are fed, dressed, and pampered; yet they may be allowed more independence than girls outside the home at an earlier age. Girls, on the other hand, care for younger siblings, clean, cook, and are given a great deal of responsibility within the home; however, they are often restricted in their independence outside the home.

In the assessment process, such gender differences can significantly affect a student's performance. If the eldest Chinese son is evaluated for adaptive behavior, he may be judged incapable of performing common tasks such as tying his own shoes rather than acting as a pampered eldest son. Often, behaviors that are not condoned within a student's culture generally will not be performed successfully by the student. Not only will the student lack experience in performing the task, but the emotional barrier to performing a task that the student views as inappropriate for his or her gender or culture will hamper performance.

A further example of how difference in sex roles may affect assessment is that a male student may perform better for a male assessor than for a female assessor because of his higher regard for the male adult model (Gollnick & Chinn, 1988). Although sex role expectations differ across cultures and can influence the assessment process, traditional values concerning gender-determined roles are in flux in many areas of the world. Consequently, two students from the same culture group may hold different views about gender-determined roles.

Individual Versus Family Orientation

Individual achievement in the assessment process does not motivate all students. An underlying assumption in the assessment process is the belief that students value their roles as individuals and can be motivated by the assessment process (Deyhle, 1987; Philips, 1983). Many students will perform poorly if they are not given a motivational rationale acceptable to their value system that goes beyond the individual. For example, students whose roles as family members are viewed more importantly than their roles as individuals may be better motivated to perform on a test by encouraging them to do their best so that their family will be proud of them (Gallimore, 1981). Others will be sufficiently motivated to perform as best as they can simply as individuals.

Verbal and Nonverbal Communication Norms

Underlying the assessment process is an assumption that the student both understands the common meanings in nonverbal communication and knows and respects the verbal rules considered acceptable in the classroom. Both these assumptions may be erroneous. The importance of nonverbal communication is often overlooked during assessment (Mehrabian, 1972). A common nonverbal gesture such as a smile or nod may be interpreted by the assessor as indicative of a student's agreement or understanding when in fact neither has occurred. The student may be nodding in agreement or smiling in order to show respect for the assessor or because the assessor is an adult. For example, a teacher once reported her frustration when testing a Greek kindergarten child who burst into tears halfway through the testing and refused to continue with the testing. Later, she discovered that the child became upset because her nod of approval was interpreted by him as disapproval.

In the verbal domain, discourse rules vary from culture to culture. Some cultural groups may regard verbosity as rude whereas other groups interpret it as an indicator of high verbal ability and/or friendliness. Some students are taught to remain quiet in front of adults (Birdwhistell, 1970). Talking is discouraged between children and adults, and children learn at an early age to talk to other children and not adults (Crago, 1988). Other students, reared in a different culture, may hesitate to speak in an elaborate language to adults. These students may have been conditioned to speak to adults in a limited fashion and only in response to specific questions. Students who have been taught not to talk to adults, or to respond in a limited fashion to adult questions are at a disadvantage in individual testing situations where they are being judged by the verbal responses they give to an adult. Some students, on the other hand, are encouraged to talk as an interactive responsibility even if they have not had time to reflect on the task at hand (Heath, 1983). Consequently, they may arrive at many incorrect answers in a formal testing situation and are often penalized and judged as less capable because they have not been culturally conditioned to reflect before they respond. Socially learned language behavior such as the quickness or slowness of verbal responses varies across cultures, which may affect an accurate interpretation of a student's performance.

Fate Versus Individual Responsibility

Most North American societies place a great emphasis on individual rights and responsibilities. The general belief in this society is that individuals have some control over both the environment and what may happen to them. In contrast, other cultures believe that control lies outside of the individual and that outside factors are largely responsible for what happens to people. For students who come from such cultures, fate, religion or some outside source greater than them will control their life. For example, Spanish or Portuguese students, explaining in their own language that they were late for the bus would say, "the bus left," not, "we missed the bus." In both languages, there is not a direct translation for "I missed the bus." The language reflects the outside focus of control.

The strong contrast of belief systems between fate (or greater force) versus individual responsibility creates serious problems for students and educators in North American mainstream classrooms. Students who do not see themselves as having control cannot be easily motivated to do their best because they do not believe they can control and influence their own performance through their own efforts. They believe the outcome of the testing will be predetermined by a force outside of them and nothing they can do will change the outcome. The amount of responsibility students are willing to assume in a test-taking situation and the degree of persistence they will show may be a direct reflection of their view regarding locus of control.

Perceptual Style

Students' cultural background influences what and how they perceive their environment (Luria, 1976). Even a student's recognition of basic shapes is influenced by the environment. While an urban student may more readily identify squares and rectangles as representations of buildings, another student will recognize a triangle as analogous to a tepee and still another will recognize and associate a half circle with an igloo.

Furthermore, all three students, if presented with a picture of a horse, would perceive the horse differently. A student reared in a culture where horses are used for work and transportation may focus on the horse's teeth or feet. A second student whose only familiarity with a horse is a memory of a carousel ride may focus on the horse's tail and thus have little recollection of the horse's teeth. Simply put, a student's environment and cultural knowledge affect that student's familiarity with what they are seeing. The greater the familiarity with the object perceived, the more apt the student is to give the correct response.

Witkin, Moore, Goodenough, and Cox (1977) suggested that perceptual styles varied along the dimension of field independence/dependence. The term *field independence* refers to the ability of an individual to perceive specific details within a complex pattern as discrete entities. A person with a field-independent perceptual style is able to see details apart from the whole. In contrast, a person with a field-dependent perceptual style is able to see details only in relation to the whole. This individual has difficulty making critical discriminations among competing perceptual stimuli. Certain cultures cultivate field-independent learners who are able to selectively discriminate details from the perceptual whole. In contrast, other cultures tend to cultivate global perceptions and tend to see details in relation to the whole (Leftcourt & Telegdi, 1971). For students from these cultures, identifying individual items in isolation from the total context is difficult. In general, the formal testing process favors students with a field-independent perceptual style. Students who are able to perceive details, for the most part, perform better on standardized objective tests than students who have difficulty discriminating the parts from the whole context.

Cognitive Style

Cognitive style refers to the way in which an individual processes information in particular tasks. Processing information involves taking what is perceived and abstracting, categorizing and forming concepts about it. Childrearing practices within different cultural groups greatly influence cognitive styles. Some students can be characterized as global, relational, and intuitive learners. In contrast, there are students who can separate elements of a situation from the context and can methodically process information (Kagan; 1965, Ramirez & Castenada, 1974). Their cognitive style can be characterized as reflective, methodical, and analytical.

Although there are many classifications used to describe differences in cognitive styles, discussion of such classifications is outside the scope of this chapter. It is important to note, however, that any classification must be viewed on a continuum. Although most students have a predominant cognitive style, they may respond with a variety of styles according to the demands of the situation. Although no one always behaves one way or another, there are tendencies for students of a particular culture to display behavior that is predominantly one style (Almanza & Mosley, 1980). Academically successful students in the United States typically display an analytical, reflective, cognitive style (Kagan, 1965). These students are able to critically and methodically analyze information using a rational, step-by-step approach.

In the testing situation, students with global/relational and more impulsive cognitive styles are at a disadvantage. These students are more apt to guess at answers and may display poor problem solving skills. Although these students may be as competent as those with a reflective, analytical cognitive style, their spontaneous, more intuitive style may cause them to be perceived in a different light.

Overall Effects of Cultural Diversity on Assessment

Variations in students' values, experiences, and perceptual and cognitive styles greatly affect learning and performance in formal assessment. The monocultural process of assessment requires: (1) a formal relationship between the tester and the student(s); (2) analytical, reflective thinking skills; (3) experience in and acceptance of the value of competition; (4) a detailed perceptual style; (5) knowledge and skill in taking standardized, timed tests; (6) familiarity and experience with the culturally influenced content; (7) a high degree of acculturation to mainstream culture; and (8) shared verbal and nonverbal meanings within the assessment context. Unfortunately, as demonstrated by this discussion, many students from different cultural backgrounds do not fit these assessment requirements. Within the mainstream educational context, therefore, these students are seen as different, or even disabled (see Chapter One), and are referred for further assessment. During assessment, their performance may be inappropriately evaluated.

LINGUISTIC INFLUENCES ON ASSESSMENT

Just as the cultural context of assessment, the linguistic context of the interactions that comprise assessment must not be overlooked. In order to assess students accurately, both cultural and linguistic information about the students, the task at hand, and the testing situation must be analyzed. One of the most serious problems with the assessment of culturally and linguistically different students who are referred for special education testing is that they frequently are not identified as limited

English proficient (LEP) prior to the assessment (Cummins, 1986). As a result, the apparent problems these students may exhibit as a manifestation of their limited English proficiency may be misinterpreted as an indication of an intrinsic learning problem (see Chapters One and Two). Linguistic variables are important in defining a specific student's capabilities. The way in which subsequent phases of the assessment process are structured and the ways that the student will respond to this structure are dependent on these variables and the linguistic profile they create for each student. Although discussed in general terms elsewhere in this volume (see Chapters Two and Five), the direct impact of the linguistic variables of language use patterns, language loss, use of code switching, and dialectal variation on the assessment process warrants further discussion.

Language Use Patterns

The two major reasons for referral of culturally and linguistically diverse students are poor academic performance and language impairment (Rueda, Mercer, & Cardoza, 1987). Both of these performance variables are related to language use patterns. The term *language use patterns* refers to the manner in which a person uses a language, with whom it is used, and the conditions in which it is used. As demonstrated by Fishman (1968), numerous factors (e.g., setting, purpose, audience, political views, emotional state) interact to determine the actual language or register that a speaker selects when interacting with others. Often, the intentions and perspectives of the teacher in the classroom or the evaluator during testing differ from the student's. Consequently, the professional may require a particular language or register and the student may use a different one. For example, students may prefer to use English to initiate play with classmates in school. If observational data were collected only within that context, we can assume that the students were incapable of using their other language for that purpose. However, when the same students interact with their siblings at home, they may use the first language exclusively to initiate play. The topic, the setting, and the interactors influence which language is used for what purposes (Genesee, 1987; Hakuta, 1986).

Language use patterns vary from community to community as well. For example, a mother in one linguistic community may ask her children to repeat an example, asking the child to tell the father, the grandmother, and the aunt individually about a doctor's visit. The mother may mediate, prompt, rephrase, and model appropriate language on each of those occasions. Children who have participated frequently in these "event casts" may seem to have better language proficiency if it is measured by the ability to retell a story than children whose language use patterns do not include event casts regularly (Heath, 1983). Thus, performance on one type of linguistic task such as story retelling, even used across languages, may not lead to generalizable conclusions regarding the relative strength of a particular language. Consequently, it is not sufficient to draw conclusions about students' language proficiency based on one test or task. This could lead to inappropriate judgments of the student's proficiency since language use patterns are not taken into consideration.

Language use patterns are also used in the interpretation of assessment results to help identify the student's particular stage in the second-language acquisition process. However, caution is necessary in interpreting those patterns, especially when language use patterns of second-language learners are compared with those of monolingual English speakers. Such comparisons are likely to result in misinterpretation of levels of cognitive functioning. For example, if a student's ability in English as a second language is described as being similar to that of an English-speaking 3-year-old child, erroneous implications may be drawn with respect to that student's cognitive abilities that may be detrimental to school success (Diaz, 1986). The more appropriate comparison group for second-language learners ought to be other second-language learners.

Language Loss

Another linguistic consideration relates to the dynamic nature of languages interacting with one another. The language proficiency of school-age students changes over time; some proficiency is gained, and some may be lost. Loss of proficiency in a first language while still learning a second language may affect a person's general ability to learn (Ovando & Collier, 1985). The following (example) demonstrates the variability of results that can be obtained when children are assessed over time.

Irma came to school at age 5 with very limited English language skills and age-appropriate Spanish language skills; however, by age 8, she had partial control of the two languages. She had gained in her English skills but lost some of her Spanish skills. Her reading achievement showed a pattern of decline as her second language grew. Many factors may influence the decline: she has had no first-language instruction in school, she speaks Spanish only to her mother who works nights and is cared for by an English speaking sister, and she is encouraged to speak only English in school. Her teacher feels that a referral should be made before it is too late. Irma is in a language-loss situation: She is losing her first language. Irma's language learning situation should be seen from an historical perspective. If the influence of language loss due to bilingual environmental factors is not noted, Irma's profile may resemble that of a monolingual learning-disabled student. The remediation plan for a student experiencing language loss due to bilingualism should be drastically different from that of a learning-disabled student. Irma needs an enriched language environment full of literacy experiences in school. An analytic approach such as the one used to teach phonics may only exacerbate the situation. In Irma's case, an inappropriate remediation approach may lead to the creation of still another problem to be resolved.

Code Switching

As discussed in Chapter Two, code switching was once viewed as a disability resulting from inappropriate development of two languages and the subsequent lack of appropriate words in one language, which are substituted with a known word in the other language. As linguists have studied code switching from a sociolinguistic perspective, however, they have found that the way in which bilinguals code switch is predictable and regular. The rules of both languages are maintained throughout code switching. Since traditional assessment of bilingual students typically occurs in one language or the other, there is no provision for students who regularly, predictably, and appropriately code switch. If a question is asked in one language and answered correctly by the student using code switching, evaluators may mark the response as incorrect because of the use of more than one language or mark the response as correct regardless of the language used. The first choice clearly penalizes the student because of language. The second may lead to an overestimation of a student's ability in situations (e.g., monolingual classrooms) where only English can be used. Due to the overwhelming reliance on standardized tests and the concomitant utilization of prescriptionism in the scoring of responses (see Chapter Five), normal code switching behavior becomes a barrier to the student's effectiveness in test-taking.

Dialectal Variance

Another linguistic consideration relates to dialectal variation. *Dialect* refers to the variations within a language that can occur at the phonemic level, the lexical level, or the syntactic level (Sapir, 1921). For example, in Spanish, a banana may be referred to as banana, guineo, or platano, depending on the country or region of origin. Dialects vary in the way they are used as a function of numerous factors such as geographical location, social status, learning experience, and the contexts in which the language is used. If the student is from a linguistic situation different from the evaluator's or if the test was designed and normed on a population speaking a different dialect than the student being tested, the student may be wrongly judged. This may occur because the use of certain words or grammatical constructions is viewed as incorrect by an examiner whose standards reflect only educated middle class usage rather than the standards of the student's linguistic community. Additionally, students' performance on a test will be hampered if the dialect that they feel most comfortable using differs from the one being used in the assessment setting. This is particularly crucial for languages such as Arabic, where dialects can be mutually incomprehensible. An overreliance on certain variables such as phonemes, which are particularly subject to dialectical variations, may skew assessment results. In cases where the student's language use varies strongly from the assessor's expectations, a close look at the family and community language is needed (Wolck, 1978).

SUMMARIZING CULTURAL AND LINGUISTIC INFLUENCES

As demonstrated by this discussion, cultural and linguistic influences can have a practical impact on the assessment process in many ways. These effects range from the reasons for a teacher referral, through the actual evaluation process, until the interpretation of the test results, and the placement of the student into a program. For this reason, even the most well-intentioned (but uninformed) evaluators may engage in assessment practices that result in inappropriate placement of culturally and linguistically diverse students. To limit the potential for bias during assessment, evaluators must be aware of the roles played by these cultural and linguistic variables. With that knowledge, the evaluators must seek to overcome the adverse effects of these variables. The next section of this chapter provides some practical ideas for achieving this objective.

ADDRESSING CULTURAL AND LINGUISTIC INFLUENCES DURING ASSESSMENT

Numerous strategies may be used to limit assessment bias due to cultural and linguistic variables. Linked with background knowledge of the process of second-language acquisition (see Chapter Two) and specific direction regarding communicative assessment (Chapter Five), educational assessment (Chapter Six), and cognitive assessment (Chapter Seven), these strategies may be used effectively in all evaluative settings. Five general strategies will be discussed; this information will then be integrated into a stage model of assessment.

GENERAL STRATEGIES FOR OVERCOMING BIAS IN ASSESSMENT

Increasing Knowledge and Awareness

The first strategy involves learning about the student's cultural and linguistic background and then focusing on how this background potentially influences assessment. It is axiomatic that the evaluator must possess some knowledge of the student's cultural and linguistic features if potential biases are to be reduced.

After information is gathered along the cultural and linguistic dimensions outlined earlier in this chapter, it is useful for evaluators to apply this knowledge to the broader assessment context. In Figure 4-1, cultural and linguistic factors that should be examined prior to formal assessment of potentially handicapped LEP students are listed. Beside each factor is a continuum with descriptors that represent opposing views. To determine the suitability of an assessment approach for any particular student, add the scores for each characteristic. The higher the score, the closer the match between the student and a traditional psychometric approach. The lower the score, the greater the need for nonstandard assessment approaches. These guidelines will help individual evaluators and assessment teams gauge the level of appropriateness of assessment methods to the characteristic of individual students.

Determining the Student's Level of Acculturation

The second strategy fits with the first. After the variables in Figure 4-1 are examined, the evaluator should apply this information and information from other sources to determine the student's level of acculturation. Acculturation results "when groups of individuals having different cultures come into continuous, first-hand contact with subsequent changes in the original pattern of either or both groups" (Redfield, Linton, & Heskovits, 1936, p. 149). Individuals in the process of acculturation differ not only in the degree to which they acculturate, but also in the level of stress that they experience in making the required behavioral adjustments. Level of acculturation has become an important characteristic to study in evaluating mental health status, cognitive and personality development, and psychological and educational functioning of acculturating individuals.

Fig. 4-1. A continuum of cultural and linguistic dimensions

1. |————————————— Movement —————————————|
   Active   Passive

2. |————————————————— Space ——————————————|
   Close   Distant

3. |————————————————— Time ————————————————|
   Adherence   No strict time
   To strict time   Schedules
   Schedules

4. |——————————————— Interactions ———————————|
   Polychronic   Monochronic

5. |——————————————— Goal/Structures ————————|
   Cooperative   Competitive

6. |——————————————— Gender/Role ——————————|
   Inequality   Equality

7. |————————————————— Role —————————————|
   Group   Individual

8. |——————————————— Locus of Control ————————|
   External   Internal

9. |——————————————— Perceptual Style ————————|
   Field-Development   Field-Independent

10. |——————————————— Cognitive Style ————————|
    Intuitive   Reflective

11. |——————————————— Language Patterns ————————|
    Mismatch   Match

12. |———————————————— Language Loss —————————|
    Extensive   Minimal

13. |——————————————— Code Switching ————————|
    Frequent   Infrequent

14. |——————————————— Language Variance ———————|
    Nonstandard   Standard

Every culturally and linguistically diverse student will exhibit certain behaviors and preferences in different circumstances and at different times. However, specific beliefs, styles, and behaviors may predominate at a particular stage in the acculturation process. Figure 4-1 can be used as a guide in determining where on the continuum a student fits within a particular cultural or linguistic dimension. This information is very important in establishing procedures for assessing culturally and linguistically diverse students and in interpreting results.

Acculturation, both as a group and an individual process, is composed of three phases: contact, conflict, and adaptation. Individual acculturation may be viewed as a linear function of the amount of time, extent to which, and purposes for which a person has been exposed to the host culture (Berry, 1980). The rate of which the process takes place is seen to be a function of variables such as educational level, income level, age, and sex. This process is affected as well by ethnic density of the neighborhood in which the acculturating individual resides (Milroy, 1987). Evaluators need to consider these variables in order to predict the level of acculturation of the student being tested. A student who is totally unacculturated to the mainstream culture is clearly at a disadvantage in the assessment process. Evaluators should interpret poor performance cautiously and retest students as they become more acculturated. Evaluators who are able to determine which acculturation phase students are experiencing can better interpret their test performances (Olmedo, 1980; Padilla, 1980). For example, a student who is in the conflict stage in the acculturation process may exhibit many performance inconsistencies that might be misinterpreted as manifestations of intrinsic learning problems.

Controlling for Cultural Variables

Once a student's level of acculturation is clear, the evaluator must manage the factors in the testing environment that can hamper student performance. This is the third general strategy. The first step in managing the factors is to recognize and identify the specific cultural variables that may affect the assessment results (see Figure 4-1). Second, evaluators must analyze formal tests for the specific cultural content and style(s) they require of students.

In the third step, cultural variables that work against students performing to the best of their ability need to be taken into account, and testing procedures should be changed so as not to interfere with the testing outcomes. For example, when addressing the cultural variable of competition versus cooperation, the examiner must explore students' attitudes toward competition and their experience with competition. If students do not value or understand competition, a formal assessment approach will yield inaccurate interpretations about their ability to perform. The decision may be to teach the students how to compete before expecting them to use this skill in a testing situation or to establish a noncompetitive situation in order to accurately determine what knowledge and skills they have or do not have. In another instance, the evaluator may be aware of differences in students' movement repertoires and adapt the testing environment to allow students who need more movement this freedom so as not to have this variable interfere with a student's performance. A fourth step in managing cultural factors would be to teach students test-taking strategies to enhance their performance during traditional assessment.

Determining the Languages Used in Testing

The next strategy is determining which languages to use during the evaluation. Whether or not two languages are to be used in the formal assessment of LEP students will depend on various factors: the purposes of testing, the skills of the evaluator, the availability of tests, and the skills of the students. For example, if the purpose of testing is to diagnose a learning disability, both languages must be used. The exclusive use of a weak second language will not yield an accurate diagnosis (see Chapter Three). Ideally, the selection of which language(s) to use in testing should reflect the nature of the questions to be answered rather than constraints such as availability of personnel, tests, and cost. Informal assessment using the student's first language prior to referral may eliminate the need for highly specialized bilingual evaluators such as speech-language pathologists or psychologists. However, when a complete evaluation is needed, the manner in which the student's two languages are used must be consistent with the purpose of testing and the skills of the student.

Determining the student's skills necessitates collecting data that define the specific characteristics of each student's bilingualism. To accomplish this, data must minimally be collected: (1) in several settings at home and at school; (2) with several different types of interactors, both adults and peers; and (3) on a variety of different topics ranging from simple to complex, which reflect the students' linguistic experience (see Chapter Two).

This is important because assessing students in only one language when they are limited in one or both of the languages compromises the intent of PL 94-142 and is not defensible from the student's perspective. When students are referred and a problem has been identified, the assessment that follows ought to sample behavior which will yield information regarding the problem. If LEP students suspected of having disabilities are assessed in English only, the result will be an incomplete profile no matter how excellent the assessment. When assessing in only one language, a disability cannot be accurately distinguished from limited English proficiency. The law states that testing must be multifacted and that it must be conducted by a multidisciplinary team of qualified personnel using tests that are valid for their intended purpose (Ambert & Dew, 1982).

Matching the languages used for assessment with the student's skills and purposes becomes more problematic as English proficiency improves. Some LEP students have good control of English for social purposes and can use English for academic purposes to a limited extent as well. When there is no opportunity or reinforcement of the use of the first language in school, these student's language-minority background may be overlooked or dismissed as not relevant to their poor academic performance. The risk of misdiagnosing these students is great from both a cultural and linguistic perspective. These students are typically good candidates for complete bilingual assessments. Another common scenario for LEP students is this: The student receives specialized ESL or bilingual services and then is exited into mainstream educational program. Over time, many of the "early exit" students fall farther and farther behind their classmates and cannot be accommodated within regular education. When a referral is made on this type of student, the issue of limited English proficiency may not be discussed because they are program graduates. However, evaluators must be cognizant of the parameters of the program in which the student participated. For example, many bilingual programs do very little direct instruction in first language but use it rather to mediate English learning. Some ESL programs are designed to teach social skills in English and not deal with the academic needs of the students. Assumptions with respect to the goals of any particular program must be clarified before assessment proceeds. Both languages may be needed to accurately diagnose learning difficulties.

Another decision that has to be made when assessing LEP students is the manner in which the languages will be used during testing. Each language may be used separately, one at a time, or both languages may be used simultaneously. If a single language is used, a decision has to be made as to which language is used first. Pollack (1980), found that young bilingual children who were tested in Spanish and then in English performed higher on the English tests than those tested first in English and then Spanish. Her findings suggest that in using each language separately, the stronger of the two languages should be the first language of administration to obtain optimum scores. Using each language separately in assessment is most effective for students who are young and come from primarily monolingual homes, have been enrolled in a quality bilingual program where academic instruction has been consistently delivered in the first language (Krashen, 1988) and who are recent arrivals to the United States.

Comparing performance on tasks in both the first and the second language may well provide important clinical insights into a student's problem. Students who have developed some cognitive/academic language proficiency (Cummins, 1984) in English are most accurately assessed by a bilingual/bicultural evaluator who has access to both languages and cultural knowledge that reflects the student's efficiencies.

Evaluators may use two languages simultaneously in assessment. In testing students whose relative language proficiency is low in both languages, evaluators have found that when the use of the two languages was allowed, the overall performance of these students improved over single-language administration (Commins, 1986). Using both languages during assessment is most effective for students who have limited control of both languages, who have a native language that combines two languages, who have lived in New York City for their entire lives, and who are young and have difficulty separating one language from the other.

Items may be administered in one language; if the test fails, the items are then translated into the other language. However, students may notice that only items that are incorrect are changed or translated, which may increase anxiety or reduce motivation. This, in turn, may depress performance over time. There are a variety of ways to use two languages during testing. Items and directions may be translated before assessment begins, and both languages used one after the other before the student responds. In this situation, however, some students, who have difficulty switching from one language to another, may be confused.

Another method is to administer all items according to standard procedures until the student begins to fail. Then, the assessment proceeds in the other language to determine if the student could pass the failed items. Students who have relatively low proficiency in the initial language of administration may benefit from this method.

The variability in the bilingual administration of tests is evident from the previous examples. Consequently, the administration of assessment instruments following standard procedures is likely to result in overidentification of LEP students as handicapped. If an LEP student is handicapped, evaluators should use means other than the standard administration of test batteries to confirm the diagnosis. When this occurs, it is imperative that each bilingual assessment be accompanied by a detailed description of the procedure used. When tests are administered in nonstandard ways, such as allowing for code switching, scores should not be reported in standard ways. Procedures for nonstandard administration should be written in the report and performance described rather than scores being reported. This may be problematic in many school districts where eligibility criteria include a score, but it is a more valid and appropriate strategy given the need to diverge from standard procedures.

Unfortunately, there are very few assessment instruments designed to be administered bilingually. This is primarily due to the fact that language tests are typically unique to a single culture (see Chapter Five). When a nonstandard approach such as bilingual administration is used, the psychometric properties of the tests are violated. Thus, scores should not be reported as if the test administration was not conducted in the standard manner. A detailed description of a student's performance rather than a score will yield more valid data. Additionally, evaluators should include their interpretation of the performance with respect to language and/or culture.

Use of Interpreters

The fifth general strategy to limit bias involves the use of interpreters. The paucity of trained bilingual evaluators in languages other than English has led to a widespread use of interpreters during the evaluation process (Wiener, 1986). As discussed by Perlman (1984), interpreters can greatly improve the diagnosis and assessment of exceptional LEP students. Due to the potential ethnolinguistic bonds that the interpreter shares with the students being assessed, the interpreter can be effective in many ways. The interpreter may gather entry-level data on academic performance, sociocultural background, emotional adjustment, cognitive development, and data from other important areas. Additionally, the interpreter may serve as a cultural informant for the monolingual/monocultural evaluator. Several studies have reported positive results when using interpreters in very different cultural and linguistic situations (Crago & Annahatak, 1985; Godwin, 1977; Marr, Natter, & Wilcox, 1980).

If interpreters are used in the evaluation of potentially handicapped students, however, great care must be taken to involve them early in the process and to train them adequately. When poorly trained interpreters are used, they may err in their translations, in their role definition, in analysis and interpretation activities, and in building rapport and transmitting information to a student's parents (Juarez, 1983; Langdon, 1988; Marcos, 1979). Toliver-Weddington and Meyerson (1983) suggest that if less than adequate training is provided an interpreter, the results may be worse than if no interpreter is used. The selection and training of interpreters, therefore, is an important issue.

Selection of Interpreters. In an excellent discussion of selection procedures, Langdon (1988) suggested a number of competencies that are preferred when selecting interpreters. Although these competencies need not be present when the individual is selected, they are essential once the individual functions as an interpreter in the assessment process. These competencies may be organized into three general categories.

Linguistic Competencies. First (and most importantly), there are required *linguistic competencies.* The interpreter must possess a high degree of language proficiency in all relevant areas of language use in both first language and second language. This means that the individual should be able to comprehend and converse effectively and be proficient in both reading and writing in the two languages. Additionally, since interpreting requires specific abilities and skills, this individual must also be able to paraphrase effectively, adjust to different levels of language usage, and have a working knowledge of technical educational terminology. Since, by definition, an interpreter is used to overcome language barriers, this individual must have the proficiency to accomplish this task.

Ethical/Professional Competencies. The second set of competencies may be considered *ethical/professional competencies.* Interpreters must function as members of a professional team if they are to be successful. This means that they must conduct themselves as cooperative professionals by maintaining confidentiality, respecting the feelings and beliefs of the students and their parents, respecting the roles of the other professionals, and striving to maintain impartiality or neutrality. Additionally, they should be realistic and straightforward about their abilities and skills. Just as with other professionals, the interpreter should not accept an assignment beyond that individual's capabilities. When a problem of confusion arises, the interpreter must be willing to ask for help or seek clarification. Otherwise, the student being assessed or that student's parents are typically the ones who are negatively affected.

Other Competencies. The final set of competencies is a general category termed *other competencies.* These are cognitive, experiential, and personality variables that help individuals function effectively in the interpreter role. For example, interpreters should have some knowledge of child development, cross-cultural variables, and educational procedures. This knowledge will help the interpreter understand the requirements of the assessment professional and understand testing. Additionally, cognitive skills such as the ability to memorize and retain information, and personality traits such as flexibility, trust, and patience are considered under this general category.

Some of these competencies are clearly dependent on the cognitive and personality traits of the interpreter. Other competencies, however, may be learned through a carefully organized training program.

Training of Interpreters. There are a number of suggestions regarding the training of interpreters (Hoppe & Villarreal, 1987; Langdon, 1988; Mattes & Omark, 1984; Toliver-Weddington & Meyerson, 1983). Figueroa, Sandoval, and Merino (1984) detail a model for training interpreters that consists of three parts: pre-assessment, assessment, and placement. Prior to the testing session, interpreters must be trained in the rules that govern assessment in general and with the specific test procedures. They also need to be introduced to technical language and shown how to simplify it for communication with parents. The interpreter must get to know the students and to meet with the parents prior to any testing. This pre-assessment is essential for setting up the context of assessment.

The evaluator and interpreter review the potential linguistic and cultural variables and how these variables should be handled. In this discussion, the evaluator typically draws upon professional expertise while the interpreter draws upon experiential knowledge. Once these variables are discussed, appropriate rapport-building strategies are reviewed. For example, decisions on how to pronounce the student's name, how introductions are accomplished, what language is to be used, what topics to discuss, and whether touching or eye contact is appropriate all contribute to the building of rapport. Additionally, the actual assessment procedures are reviewed so that the interpreter can anticipate potential difficulties and appropriate clarification strategies are determined.

During the actual testing that may occur with different professionals, the primary interaction is between the student and the interpreter, while the evaluator records the proceedings and observes, so that scoring and analysis can be completed immediately after the testing. The same interpreter ought to communicate the assessment results to the parents during the parent conference. In this way, the interpreter participates throughout the entire process and conflicts are less likely to occur.

Evaluator's Responsibilities. The success or failure of the interpretive strategy does not depend on the interpreter alone. The evaluator has a number of responsibilities that must be fulfilled for success to occur. First, the evaluator must recognize the limitations of translation in the assessment process. Regardless of the interpreter's ability, there are many problems with this strategy due to the nature and complexity of the linguistic, interactional, cultural, and psychometric variables (see Chapters Two, Three, and Five). Second, the evaluator must select individuals with potential to be effective interpreters and then carefully and completely train the individuals selected. Third, the evaluator must exhibit the same professional/ethical competencies required of the interpreter. Competencies such as cooperation, respect for another's perspective, and impartiality are even more important traits for the evaluator if assessment is to be effective. Fourth, it is the responsibility of the evaluator to prepare the interpreter before each assessment and to debrief the interpreter after each assessment. While training is a general activity that may occur infrequently, adequate preparation and review must occur for every evaluation. Finally, the evaluator should facilitate effective interpretation by keeping the interactional language as simple as possible, by avoiding extra words and professional jargon, and by monitoring the behaviors of the interpreter and student during the evaluation. By carefully observing for changes in body language, apparent mismatches between the length of the original stimulus and the interpretation, and excessive repetition, potential difficulty can be identified and the evaluator and the interpreter can work to clarify (Langdon, 1988).

As a general strategy, interpretation may be very effective if carefully implemented. It should be noted, however, that there is a great deal of controversy over the legitimacy and adequacy of the strategy. The controversy is partly political: Some bilingual evaluators feel that many school administrators opt for use of interpreters even when bilingual specialists are available because that is the easier and less costly option. This may be a real danger in urban areas where bilingual evaluators are more plentiful, especially in languages with high concentrations of speakers. However, in more rural areas with low-incidence languages, the use of interpreters is oftentimes the only solution available to a school district.

IMPLEMENTING A STAGE MODEL OF ASSESSMENT

According to PL 94-142, an assessment model that is most appropriate for culturally and linguistically diverse students must meet two conditions: First, it must be sufficiently comprehensive to diagnose and appraise suspected disabilities; second, it must employ a multidisciplinary approach. In the case of culturally and linguistically diverse students, several steps need to be accomplished prior to beginning the specialized formal assessment process. Based on the previous influences and the strategies to address them, a stage model may be discussed.

Identifying Linguistic Diversity

Identification of linguistically diverse students is the first stage of assessment; it involves screening all students in order to identify students who come from a language background other than English. These students need not speak a language other than English but must come from a home where a language other than English is spoken by someone. Frequently, the language use patterns of linguistically diverse students who speak English at home are very different from their mainstream peers. Many linguistically diverse students are addressed by their parents in a language other than English, and they respond in English. Teachers must be aware of the students' background if effective instruction is to occur.

A simple procedure for identifying language minority students is to send a home language survey to every parent in the school system. The form typically asks three or five questions regarding the language(s) used in the home by the parents, the family, and the student. It may be necessary to translate the forms or interview nonliterate parents to obtain reliable information.

Collection of Background Information

The second stage of assessment involves surveying parents, teachers, family members, and students in order to collect basic information regarding students' experiences. Age, grade, educational experience, report card grades, family configuration, family history, previous educational difficulty, level of literacy in the home, and literacy skills of the student are typically obtained. An interview with parents upon registration is the easiest way to collect background information; older students can also provide valuable information. If informations are not available at registration, the resources of the local community may be explored so that an interview in the home or over the phone an be conducted later. All background information collected should be recorded, shared with all appropriate personnel, and placed with the student's official school records. Information may need verification over time as rapport improves between school and home. To ensure that the appropriate background information is obtained, survey forms have been provided on language (Chapter Two), educational history (Chapter Six), and cognitive background (Chapter Seven).

Identification of Limited English Proficient Students

The third stage of assessment prior to special education assessment involves assessing students' language proficiency. Both social and academic language proficiency should be assessed across a wide variety of tasks and across languages to construct a valid picture of student's relative language proficiency. Based on the relative language proficiency profile, an instructional program can be designed to take into account strengths and weaknesses in both the first and second languages. The appropriateness of the instructional program often has a direct effect on whether a student encounters academic difficulties. When programs do not take into account the student's background and relative language proficiency, learning problems often surface in the regular education context.

Collection of Prereferral Information

Prereferral takes place when a student is experiencing difficulty in school. The purpose of the prereferral is to intervene early to identify possible reasons for the problem and to provide alternatives for alleviating the problem. According to Garcia and Ortiz (1988), this process is a powerful method for preventing inappropriate referrals to special education. During prereferral, more background data is usually collected and the instructional environment is examined to ascertain whether the problem may be explained by factors unrelated to a disability. Consultation seems to facilitate the prereferral process, since the distinction between temporary second-language learning difficulties and more permanent cognitive or perceptual deficiencies that interfere with learning is often unclear. Informal data that expand upon the background data previously collected need to be gathered before the student is referred for formal assessment. The caution at the prereferral stage is to collect just enough information so that decisions can be made but not so much information that the process becomes too cumbersome. When dealing with culturally and linguistically diverse students, the collection of background information continues at the prereferral stage. Several factors should be considered.

Student's age, according to the traditional definition used in schools in the United States, must be verified because the concept of age may vary from culture to culture. For example, in some cultures, children may be considered 1-year-old on the day they were born, or at the beginning of the new year. Miscalculations of a student's age may contribute to inappropriate placements or misperceptions of a student's developmental level or other abilities. Other relevant personal information may include the number of siblings in a family, the student's position within the family, other people living within the student's household, and length of time a student has been in the United States. Other information may be collected as well, as each case dictates.

The educational history of culturally and linguistically diverse students may have been less consistent than their mainstream peers. During prereferral, the number of schools a student has attended, the attendance pattern and the types of educational programs in which the students have participated are important data. Culturally and linguistically diverse students may not have been taught with the same curriculum as their English-speaking counterparts and thus would not be expected to be achieving at the same level and rate. Migrant students often change schools twice a year, and there may be little or no coordination between the curricula and materials from one school to the next. Low achievement may result, but it does not necessarily suggest a handicapping condition.

Family history also must be amplified. Some recent immigrants have lost family members in warlike conditions. The families may be suffering from a drastic change in status; for example, a former high government official might be working now as a custodian. Any of these conditions could adversely affect a student's school performance. The language use pattern of LEP students should also be studied at this stage. Observations of students' language with friends, family, teachers, and others in the classroom as well as on the playground and at home will provide a brief overview of the language use pattern.

The classroom situation should also be examined at prereferral. Both academic and behavioral difficulties exhibited in the learning environment should be described by the teacher and observed by other professionals. The tasks and subject areas in which difficulties are exhibited should be noted. The student's successful and unsuccessful problem-solving efforts should be recorded. Specific interventions and their results should be noted. Teacher assistance teams may provide support during this process; these teams may include teachers, principals, social workers, speech therapists, and psychologists who meet informally to suggest alternative intervention strategies, provide observational data, give feedback about the implementation of the interventions, and meet with parents.

Parents and school records should be consulted regarding general health information. Particularly important are the results of the vision and hearing screening; however, other health information such as a history of chronic ear infections or diseases such as diabetes or other relevant data such as being involved in a car accident may provide a unique perspective on a child's school performance. Parents may also provide normative data with respect to their child's intellectual functioning and behavior. Reports comparing their child's relative strengths and weaknesses in cognitive and social areas frequently may be obtained from an interview with the parents.

Additionally, it is important to compile the results from all testing that exists. Students who have been identified as LEP will have been tested in a bilingual and/or ESL program, as well as the nonbilingual classroom. Examining all the testing results may well provide useful insights.

Patterns of achievement may offer clues to student difficulties, especially when they are examined across language and academic settings. Many professionals may contribute to the collection of prereferral data. The more people that are involved, the broader the perspective at the prereferral stage. After data has been collected and interventions tried, assessment may be required.

Identification Of LEP Students with Special Needs

The comprehensive evaluation process for LEP students requires that a multidisciplinary staff (MDS) be involved formally and informally in assessing students in each of the following areas: language, psychoeducational performance, adaptive behavior, medical/developmental history, and intellectual functioning. An MDS includes a psychologists, a social worker, a speech-language pathologist, a nurse, a diagnostician, an administrator, and a teacher. A bilingual or ESL specialist must also be included if the team typically does not include such professionals when culturally and linguistically diverse cases are brought to the team.

Some suggest that all team members simultaneously begin their assessment. This approach is problematic for LEP students in that they may feel overwhelmed by the number of adults and the variety of tasks that they are required to perform. In addition, it is difficult to identify competent bilingual individuals who can conduct such a complete assessment simultaneously. A more realistic approach includes a systematic sequential assessment of each area in turn or no more than two at a time: language, psychoeducational performance, adaptive behavior, medical/developmental history, and intellectual functioning (Baca & Cervantes, 1984). Using this approach, the assessment results could be reviewed after each step is completed in order to decide whether continued assessment is warranted. Data are interpreted more frequently, and interventions can be made as assessment proceeds. Since formal approaches to assessing potentially handicapped LEP students are fraught with technical problems, a closer examination of interventions and their results in each area will produce more reliable results.

Frequently, assessments are not considered complete unless all of the professionals have administered their test battery even though the results may not be directly relevant to answering the questions posed for the assessment. For example, a full psychological assessment would not be indicated if the student is suspected of having a language disorder. If a sequential approach to assessment rather than a simultaneous approach were used, much unnecessary testing would be eliminated. Input from all MDS members would still be provided during team meetings. The cost in dollars and hours would be greatly reduced with minimal effect on the quality of the assessment.

The procedures that occur at each phase of the culturally and linguistically diverse students' assessment will greatly influence the results. The roles of key personnel during each phase of the assessment process are discussed in the following section.

Language Evaluation

The determination of relative language proficiency in a wide variety of social and academic tasks should be done prior to this stage of assessment. During the language evaluation phase of assessment, the speech-language pathologist collects language information from a variety of sources in the language or languages appropriate and across the dimensions that will answer the assessment questions. An analysis of vocabulary, pragmatic skills, grammatical structures, processing ability or articulation, may be indicated in any particular case (see Chapter Five for a discussion of communicative assessment).

Often, speech-language pathologists become the case managers for special education evaluations. As a result, a monolingual speech-language pathologist may need to organize the data collection effort for a bilingual language evaluation. The pieces of information that need to be collected should be outlined and the locally available resources identified.

Assessment personnel in other school districts may be available locally to work on a contractual basis. Local hospitals or social service agencies may have assessment personnel on staff, or they may be able to make referrals within the community. To use parents as resources, the speech-language pathologist may need to teach them how to listen, to observe language use, or may ask parents specific questions about linguistic interactions (Erickson & Omark, 1981).

As discussed in an earlier section of this chapter, areas of cultural conflict must be identified prior to assessment whenever possible. Also, an LEP specialist must ensure that the findings are interpreted within the appropriate cultural context.

Classroom data may confirm or conflict with the results of formal assessment. When formal results differ from teacher observations, particularly in first language or ESL settings, the LEP specialist must note such conflicts and suggest solutions for conflict resolution such as continued assessment focusing on interactions in a variety of settings. Students may be much more verbal and open in an informal environment, and richer data could be gathered. Other MDS members may also note signs of problems or areas of strength during the prereferral stage. Their observations related to a student's language performance should be included during this phase of the assessment process. For example, the psychologist may notice difficulties with problem-solving tasks that require language during a classroom observation. Then the psychologist may formulate additional questions if processing difficulties appear.

Data collected during the language assessment phase must be reviewed to comment on the pattern of strengths and weaknesses. Interventions typically include changes in materials, interaction patterns, teaching style, and language of instruction. After the instructional changes have been effectively implemented and monitored, their effects must be examined. If the interventions have not brought about anticipated changes in student performance, then psychoeducational assessment may be necessary.

Psychoeducational Assessment

An educational diagnostician typically assesses the current academic achievement of students who are having learning difficulties. In some settings, a psychologist fills this role. In others, a diagnostician who usually has a learning disabilities background, acts as the evaluator. The diagnostician assesses strengths and weaknesses in the areas of math and reading using a wide variety of tests and procedures. To a lesser extent, other content areas may be sampled such as science, vocational subjects, or social sciences. Additionally, psychoeducational diagnosticians examine strengths and weaknesses in the perceptual-motor, psycholinguistic, and learning styles areas. There are questions regarding the validity of some of the more common formal measures used in assessment because they were not developed or normed on culturally and linguistically diverse populations. However, a good evaluator can acquire valuable descriptive data based on test administration results. Caution must be exercised when LEP students' profiles show a discrepancy between achievement and potential especially in verbal areas, when tested only in English. Such a discrepancy should be viewed as an artifact of the testing situation unless data from testing in first language verify such findings. Results of psychoeducational assessment must be carefully interpreted to avoid misclassification of LEP students in mild/ moderate categories since these are very vaguely defined. Ysseldyke (in Reynolds, Wang, & Walberg, 1987) reports that more than 80% of normal English-speaking students could be classified as learning disabled by one or more definitions now in use in the United States.

Locally determined cut-off scores that define program eligibility are not generally adjusted to reflect the special circumstances of LEP students. Diagnosticians working with LEP populations should report their findings based on formal assessment, judiciously. An alternative clinical approach offers richer data than traditional approaches. When a test-teach-retest method is employed, a student's potential may be more accurately described because strategies used in learning are the focus rather than the areas of weakness. Additionally, actual academic performance in a classroom setting must be observed and documented in every case. When more than one classroom is involved, performance in each must be recorded. The results that different teaching methods and materials, use of culturally relevant content and language of instruction have on achievement should be documented. Cultural factors may also confound results in the area of academic achievement particularly if the LEP student has not had a lot of experience in U.S. schools. The match between background knowledge of the student and the background knowledge assumed by the content of the test has a great impact on performance.

When a bilingual diagnostician is unavailable, the LEP specialist may assist a diagnostician by highlighting linguistic and cultural factors that may affect test results. Under the direction of a diagnostician, a bilingual teacher or trained interpreter may administer certain formal tests that are available in the student's native language. (see Appendix B.) Monolingual diagnosticians may also play the role of consultant for the classroom teacher. In that role they may need to explain particular behavior patterns or characteristics that are common for a particular disability. They may also assist the teacher in searching for evidence of their existence in a variety of settings across languages within the student's normal learning tasks. Data regarding native language achievement may also be collected by a bilingual teacher using criterion-referenced tests, curriculum based assessment (see Chapter Six), anecdotal records and assignments. Instructional interventions are again formulated to modify a student's existing educational plan. The effectiveness of the interventions are evaluated over time. If the interventions that are designed based on a student's language assessment and diagnostic assessment do not produce sufficient growth, then further investigations would be warranted. The next level of assessment would include adaptive behavior.

Adaptive Behavior Assessment

The goal of adaptive behavior assessment is to ascertain the degree to which a student's behavior conforms to a set of standards that are acceptable within a specific community such as the home, school, church, or neighborhood. Certain student behaviors may appear aberrant when compared to a middle class, monolingual English-speaking majority student. However, they may be acceptable within another community context. Behavior patterns also change over time. Language minority students progress through phases of acculturation upon entering a new community. The predictable changes should not be confused with poor adaptive behavior.

The social worker's task in assessing adaptive behavior is to identify the person's ability to function in different settings appropriately. Individuals with certain handicapping conditions may find it more difficult to adapt to their bicultural world. Other students may have developed a pattern of learned helplessness, if they have been repeatedly told implicitly and explicitly, that they are not capable of certain things; they then believe that they are incapable and become increasingly restricted in the activities they attempt. Culture often plays an important role in the development of learned helplessness. An ecologically based assessment takes into account the types of behavior that have been expected and rewarded in all of the settings where the students function.

In conducting an adaptive behavior assessment, the social worker needs to become familiar with the student's environment. Social workers collecting behavioral information especially in a cultural setting with which they are less familiar, must be given the time necessary to visit homes if a valid assessment is to be obtained. Currently, parents are expected to come to school in order to be interviewed. Heavy caseloads are cited as the cause for this practice. This arrangement has not been very effective with minority parents for a variety of reasons: work schedules, transportation and language. An interview at school with a stranger frequently yields incomplete information and the results could lead to erroneous conclusions. Personal information of this kind should be obtained under the best of conditions.

Social workers who are not familiar with the norms, values, and mores of a particular community must rely on LEP specialists to provide a basic framework for understanding LEP students' behavior. For example, some teachers may consider a long silent period upon entering school a deviant behavior; however, within the LEP population, that behavior would be considered normal. LEP specialists can identify other informants that will provide a broader perspective on student behavior using the language of the family. When informants are used, they must understand the type of data that is being sought as well as acceptable methods of data collection; thus, some preparation and training are necessary before actual cases are begun. Informants must establish rapport with the parents or other knowledgeable people, learn how to ask questions without leading the answers and keep personal bias and prejudice from interfering with the collection of information. When social workers and informants work as a team the quality of data collection is high. When community members have been identified as reliable informants, their compensation should be commensurate with the tasks they are asked to perform.

By this stage of the assessment process, many professionals will have also become acquainted with the student. Their perspectives on the student's behavior add another dimension to the understanding of the individual. Interviews or discussions with each person regarding students' behavior should be included during this phase of assessment. Results are reviewed by the team to decide if further assessment is warranted. If further information is needed to design an appropriate educational plan, then a completed medical and developmental history will need to be collected. Some general information in these areas have already been gathered during the prereferral stage. During assessment, however, a very thorough and complete picture of the student's history must be obtained.

Medical/Developmental Assessment

The nurse typically conducts an interview with the student's mother or with both parents to collect medical and developmental histories. The social worker may also participate in the interview, particularly if the social worker is bilingual and the nurse is not. Medical records may also prove useful at this phase of assessment.

The collection of accurate medical/developmental information may include a history of childhood diseases, traumas, chronic health problems, the age of certain developmental milestones (first step, first word, family history, physical and mental problems), conditions during mother's pregnancy, birth and delivery, and types of medication or home remedies used regularly. A more in-depth assessment of vision and hearing may be indicated at this point. During the interview, it may also be beneficial to discuss general living conditions, medical facilities and health practices if the student was born or spent a large portion of his life in another country. This information must be collected in a culturally sensitive manner. For example, it may be difficult to ascertain developmental milestones because many other cultures do not keep track of time in as rigorous a manner as the school system prefers. Consequently, questions that ask parents to compare children's growth patterns may lead to more complete information.

Specialists in the education of LEP students, or informants who are identified by them, must understand the purpose of the assessment. The type of questions and answers that are useful, and general interviewing techniques, should be reviewed with an informant. The use of medical terminology may add confusion rather than clarify the information-gathering process. The level of rapport and the style of the interviewer may greatly influence the type of information that is obtained. Nurses should accompany the informant to the interviews until they feel comfortable with the informant's ability to collect complete and accurate information. Whenever possible, trained informants should be maintained over time because they will learn the values and customs of the community and conduct better assessments. They should, of course, be adequately compensated for their services.

After the histories have been compiled, the team reviews the findings. If it is felt that the cognitive abilities of the student should be assessed then the final phase of assessment commences.

Cognitive Assessment

During the final phase of assessment, the intellectual abilities of the student are examined. Some researchers suggest that the type of IQ that is measured by instruments such as the WISC-R is very narrow (Gardner, 1984). Many of the psychological instruments currently used in the public schools are based on Western thought and to a large degree reflect culture-specific knowledge and thought patterns. Performance may be related to success in the United States school system, but not necessarily to intellectual potential (Feuerstein, 1979). The challenge during the final assessment phase is to sample a wide range of abilities using a variety of methods in order to verify and clarify the previous findings. (See discussion in Chapters Six and Seven.)

The psychologist is charged with the task of assessing a student's cognitive abilities. Since this is a very powerful position within the MDS team, psychologists must be exceptionally careful in their choice of an approach and in selecting their test battery. Psychologists must not act merely as psychometricians, but must observe the student's responses and analyze them within a culturally and linguistically appropriate framework.

Optimally, all monolingual psychologists should attempt to become familiar with one of the languages spoken by the students they assess. Figueroa, Sandoval, and Merino (1984) suggest that this broadens the assessor's sensitivity and provides more avenues for obtaining information. When an LEP student's cognitive abilities are assessed, the native language of the student should be used whenever feasible. However, when monolingual English-speaking psychologists are responsible for an LEP's psychological assessment, then the LEP specialist plays an important role. The LEP specialist may act as an interpreter or assist in the identification of appropriate candidates. The LEP specialist may also be able to evaluate in cultural and linguistic terms the appropriateness of particular approaches, instruments, and linguistic items. They may also assist assessors in techniques for establishing rapport and maximizing a student's potential during test administration. If the LEP specialist or another person is used as an interpreter during a psychological assessment, caution must be exercised to ensure valid assessment. Interpreters must be trained in the roles that they will perform. This is a complex and time consuming process that cannot be undertaken without a strong commitment from the interpreter as well as the psychologist with whom he or she will work. Under optimum conditions, this procedure offers insights into the way students learn. Under less than optimum conditions, a misdiagnosis may occur under the guise of appropriate procedures.

In an ideal situation, well-trained psychologists who are knowledgeable in second language acquisition, bilingualism and the cultures of the students whom they assess, conduct assessments using a variety of approaches, ranging from psychometric to developmental to dynamic. After a psychological interpretation assessment has been completed, all the MDS members reconvene to evaluate the results and plan for the education of the LEP student.

Interpreting Assessment Data

The final stage in the evaluation process is the interpretation phase. During this phase, all of the professionals pool their knowledge and findings to understand a student's strengths and weaknesses in learning. Ideally, interpretations of assessment data are then synthesized and operationalized, and an Individualized Educational Plan (IEP) can be designed to provide for appropriate instruction. Specific programs can then be identified which would allow the implementation of the suggested interventions (see Chapter Eight).

The adequacy of the interpretation, and thus the placement decision as well, rests heavily upon the team's ability to function cohesively as a team. Rueda, Mercer, and Cardoza (1987) found that the services that were to be provided as a result of team meetings were frequently not delivered, partly because of the difficulty of getting a team to function as a team. When teams are cohesive, they will be able to monitor their recommendations and see that they are carried out. When teams are splintered, their ability to monitor their recommendations is reduced. When LEP students and specialists are involved, the possibilities for the dysfunction multiply because the dynamics of the team influence the types of programming and placements decisions that are made (Bailey, 1984). The following examples illustrate ways in which team dysfunction may affect decision-making. A team member other than the leader may emerge as a dominant force in team functioning. Frequently, a psychologist assumes the dominant position. In cases where the psychologist is the bilingual "expert," other team members may feel pressured to acquiesce during group discussions, and their expertise may be lost in the decision-making process. An English-speaking psychologist may make a diagnosis regarding an LEP student's capabilities based on results from an all-English test battery. When the psychologist dominates the group, there would likely be no dissent.

A team may also dysfunction if one team member is accorded inferior status. Certain individuals are more at risk than others: Teachers, paraprofessionals, and parents are frequently perceived as having inferior knowledge and understanding of special education problems and issues. Added to that, some of those associated with LEP students may be minority group members and LEP themselves. Those perceived as being inferior members may withdraw and become nonparticipatory; or it may be culturally appropriate to assume a passive role, which, in turn, reinforces the perception of inferiority. A valuable perspective may be lost to the team if this type of dysfunction persists.

Sometimes, two team members may disagree philosophically or may have personality conflicts that cause friction during team meetings. This may lead to disagreement simply for the sake of disagreement. In cases involving LEP students, one person may advocate more native language instruction, while the other person favors English-only instruction. Students' needs may not receive as much attention as the disagreement itself.

Occasionally, a single member is frozen out of a group. Groups that have been together for a long time may find it difficult to accept new members. For example, in districts with low numbers of language-minority students, bilingual/ESL programs may be moved from school to school. A teacher who becomes the language-minority specialist on a new team may find it difficult to break into a well-established group. This may make it difficult for the LEP specialists' perspective to be meaningful.

Another factor that may influence the quality of the interpretation of assessment results is related to the dynamics of the team. Teams grow in four stages. During the first stage, professionals deal with students in an autonomous way and they may not even meet as an entire team. If language-minority students are involved, professionals with expertise in issues related to bilingualism should be represented on the team (Ortiz, 1986). When they are not, the LEP student's needs may be ignored if each professional's perspective does not include a bilingual filter. LEP specialists must be empowered to assert their perspective to ensure that their concerns are voiced. During the second stage of team development, team members meet, but each discipline remains independent. When teams at this stage receive bilingual recommendations from out-of-district personnel who are hired to assess LEP students, they may be ignored because team members function independently and do not integrate all of the available data. They focus on their area of specialization. For example, a bilingual psychologist may recommend one hour of native language instruction, but when the team develops the IEP, no native language instruction is included because it does not represent any team member's area of expertise. During the third stage of team development, the input and collaboration of all the participants is required. A team cannot achieve this level unless all group members are perceived as having equal status.

Ogbu and Matute-Bianchi (1988) suggest that achieving equal status in the United States is difficult to do for certain Blacks, Hispanics, or Native Americans. Teams that have minority group members must actively encourage collaboration in order to realize their goals. During the fourth stage of team development, all services are coordinated. Group members actively teach each other about their discipline. A team that is functioning at this stage will consider all of the options and weigh their benefits in order to provide the best possible program. Team members are free to interchange their roles. In teams functioning at this stage, an observer would hear questions regarding the cultural appropriateness of a certain behavior being raised by someone other than the language-minority specialists. Interpretations would consistently be made that integrate all existing data and yet are flexible and creative in terms of service-delivery options. MDS teams ought to strive for the improvement of their group dynamics because higher-quality interpretations will result. These will translate into more appropriate services and better learning environments for all LEP students.

CONCLUSIONS

Evaluation procedures designed for monolingual, mainstream populations cannot continue to pervade school systems composed of growing numbers of minority students. The results of an unchanging system will be more and more language-minority students identified as handicapped. The delivery systems currently used for special education cannot accommodate such large numbers. Culturally and linguistically relevant approaches to evaluation must be explored if language-minority students who are handicapped are to be accurately identified and provided with appropriate services. Only through the flexible use of the best from both traditional and nontraditional approaches can meaningful linguistically and culturally sensitive assessment emerge. Designing the LEP students' optimum learning environment should be the ultimate goal of the evaluation process.

REFERENCES

Alamanza, H. P., & Mosley, W. J. (1980). Curriculum adaptations and modifications for culturally diverse handicapped children. *Exceptional Children, 48,* 808–814.

Ambert, A., & Dew, N. (1982). *Special education for exceptional bilingual students: A handbook for educators.* Dallas, TX: Evaluation, Dissemination and Assessment Center.

Baca, L., & Cervantes, H. (1984). *The bilingual special education interface.* St. Louis, MO: Times Mirror/Mosby.

Bailey, D. B. (1984). A triaxial model of the interdisciplinary team and group process. *Exceptional Children, 51,* 17–26.

Basso, K. (1979). *Portraits of the "The Whiteman."* Cambridge: Cambridge University Press.

Berry, J. W. (1980). Acculturation as varieties of adaptation. In A. M. Padilla (Ed.), *Acculturation: Theoretical models and some new findings* (pp. 9–26). Boulder, CO: Westview Press.

Birdwhistell, R. L. (1970). *Kinesics and context.* Philadelphia: University of Pennsylvania Press.

Brice-Heath, S. (1986). Sociocultural contexts of language development. In California Board of Education, *Beyond language: Social and cultural factors in schooling language minority students.* Los Angeles, CA: Evaluation, Dissemination and Assessment Center.

Commins, N. L. (1986). *A descriptive study of the linguistic abilities of four low achieving hispanic bilingual students.* Unpublished Dissertation Abstract, Boulder, CO: University of Colorado.

Condon, E., Peters, J. Y., & Carmen, S. (1979). *Special education in the Hispanic child: Cultural perspectives.* Philadelphia, PA: Temple University Teacher Corps Mid-Atlantic Network.

Crago, M. (1988). *Cultural context in communicative interaction of Inuit Children.* Unpublished Dissertation. Montreal: McGill University.

Crago, M., & Annahatak, B. (1985). Evaluation of minority-language children by native speakers. A paper presented at the American Speech-Language-Hearing Association Convention. Washington, DC, November.

Cummins, J. (1984). *Bilingualism and special education: Issues in assessment and pedagogy.* Clevedon, Avon, England: Multilingual Matters.

Cummins, J. (1986). Empowering minority students: A framework for intervention. *Harvard Educational Review, 58,* 18–36.

Deyhle, D. (1987). Learning failure: Tests as gatekeepers and the culturally different child. In H. E. Trueba (Ed.), *Success or failure?* (pp. 85–108). Rawley, MA: Newbury House.

Diaz, R. M. (1986). Bilingual cognitive development: Addressing three gaps in current research. *Child Development.*

DiPrieto, R. J. (1978). Code switching as a verbal strategy among bilinguals. In Michael Paradis (Ed.), *Aspects of bilingualism.* (pp. 101–110). Columbia, SC: Hornbeam Press.

Dunn, L. (1976). *Test de Vocabulario y Imagenes Peabody. Examiner's Manual.* Circle Plains, MN: American Guidance.

Erickson, J. G., & Omark, D. R. (Eds.). (1981). *Communication assessment of the bilingual bicultural child.* Baltimore, MD: University Park Press.

Feuerstein, R. (1979). *The dynamic assessment of retarded performers.* Baltimore, MD: University Park Press.

Figueroa, R. A., Sandoval, J., & Merino, B. (1984). School psychology and limited English-proficient children: New competencies. *Journal of School Psychology*, 22, 131–143.

Fishman, J. (1968). Sociolinguistic perspective on the study of bilingualism. *Linguistics*, 39, 21–49.

Gallimore, R. (1981). Affiliation, social contexts, industriousness and achievement. In R. Monroe, R. Monroe, and B. Whiting (Eds.), *Handbook of cross-cultural human development*. New York: Garland.

Garcia, S. B., & Ortiz, A. A. (1988). Preventing inappropriate referrals of language minority students to special education. *New Focus: Occasional Papers in Bilingual Education*, 5, 1–12. Wheaton, MD: The National Clearinghouse for Bilingual Education.

Gardner, H. G. (1984). The seven frames of mind. *Psychology Today*, 18, 28–33.

Geertz, C. (1973). *The interpretation of cultures*. New York: Basic Books.

Genesee, F. (1987). *Learning through two languages: Studies of immersion and bilingual education*. Cambridge, MA: Newbury House.

Godwin, D. C. (1977). The bilingual teacher aide: Classroom asset. *Elementary School Journal*, 77, 265–267.

Goldman, S., & McDermott, R. (1987). The culture of competition in American schools. In G. Spindler (Ed.), *Education and cultural process*, 2nd ed. (pp. 282–299). Prospect Heights, IL: Waveland Press.

Gollnick, M. & Chinn, P. (1983). *Multicultural education in a pluralistic society*. St. Louis: C. V. Mosby.

Hall, E. T. (1978). *The hidden dimension*. Garden City, NY: Anchor & Doubleday.

Hakuta, K. (1986). *The mirror of language: The debate on bilingualism*. New York: Basic Books.

Heath, S. B. (1983). *Ways with words*. Cambridge: Cambridge University Press.

Hoppe, M. R., & Villarreal, J. (1987). *Nonbiased assessment manual for limited English proficient speakers: Special projects for reaching the exceptional and disadvantaged*. New Orleans: Jefferson Parish Public School System Bilingual/ESL Program.

Hymes, D. (1967). Models of the interaction of language and social setting. *Journal of Social Issues*, 23, 8–28.

Juarez, M. (1983). Assessment and treatment of minority language handicapped children: The role of the monolingual speech-language pathologist. *Topics in Language Disorders*, 3, 57–66.

Kagan, J. (1965). Impulsive and reflective children: Significance of conceptual tempo. In J. D. Krumboltz (Ed.), *Learning and the education process* (pp. 133–160). Chicago, IL: Randy McNally.

Krashen, S., & Biber, D. (1988). *On course*. Sacramento: California Association for Bilingual Education.

Kurt, C. J. N. (1976). *Teacher training packet for a course on cultural awareness*. Cambridge, MA: National Dissemination and Assessment Center.

Langdon, H. W. (1988). Working with an interpreter/translator in the school and clinical setting. A presentation at the Council for Exceptional Children Symposia on ethnic and Multicultural Concerns, Denver, October.

Leftcour, H., & Telegdi, M. (1971). Perceived focus of control and field dependence as predictors or cognitive activity. *Journal of Consulting and Clinical Psychology*, 37, 53–56.

Leiter, R. G. (1979). *Leiter International Performance Scale: Instruction manual*. Chicago, IL: Stoelting Company.

Luria, A. R. (1976). *Cognitive Development: Its cultural and social foundations*. Cambridge, MA: Harvard University Press.

Marcos, L. (1979). Effects of interpreters on the evaluation of psychopathology in non-English speaking patients. *American Journal of Psychiatry, 136,* 171–174.

Marr, M. K., Natter, R., & Wilcox, C. B. (1980). Testing a child in a language you don't speak. A miniseminar presented at the American Speech-Language-Hearing Association convention. Detroit, November.

Mehrabian, A. (1972). *Nonverbal communication.* Chicago, IL: Aldine and Atherton.

Mercer, J. R. (1979) *SOMPA: System of Multicultural Pluralistic Assessment: Technical Manual.* New York: Psychological Corporation.

Miller, N. (1984). Some observations concerning formal tests in cross-cultural settings. In N. Miller (Ed.), *Bilingualism and language disability: Assessment and remediation* (pp. 107–114). Austin, TX: PRO-ED.

Milroy, L. (1987). *Language and social networks.* Oxford: Basil Blackwell.

Ogbu, U., & Matute-Bianchi, M. E. (1986). Understanding sociocultural factors: knowledge, identity, and school adjustment. In California Board of Education, *Beyond language: Social and cultural factors in schooling language minority students.* Los Angeles: Evaluation Dissemination and Assessment Center.

Olmedo, E. L. (1980). Quantitative models of acculturaton: An overview. In A. M. Padilla (Ed.), *Acculturation: Theory, models and some new findings* (pp. 27–45). Boulder, CO: Westview Press.

Ortiz, A. (1985, Spring). Characteristics of limited English proficient Hispanic students served in programs for the learning disabled: Implications for policy and practice (part II). *Bilingual Special Education Newsletter* (Available from University of Texas at Austin, Department of Special Education, Austin).

Ovando, C. J., & Collier, U. P. (1985). *Bilingual and ESL classrooms: Teaching in multicultural contexts.* New York: McGraw-Hill.

Padilla, A. M. (Ed.). (1980) *Acculturation: Theory, models and some new findings.* Boulder, CO: Westview Press.

Perlman, R. (1984). Bilingual teacher aids: Diagnosis and assessment. *IABBE Forum, 2.*

Philips, S. (1972). Participant structures and communicative competence: Warm Springs children in community and classroom. In C. B. Cazden, V. P. John, and D. Hymes (Eds.), *Functions of language in the classroom* (pp. 370–394). New York: Teachers College Press.

Philips, S. (1983). *The invisible culture.* New York: Longman.

Pollack, M. D. (1980). *The effects of testwiseness language of test administration, and language competence on readiness test performance of low socio-economic level, Spanish speaking children.* Ann Arbor: University of Michigan, University Microforms International Microfiche #80-16031.

Ramirez, M. & Castenada, A. (1974). *Cultural democracy, bicognitive development, and education.* New York: Academic Press.

Ravens, J. C. (1960). *Guide to using the standard progressive matrices.* London: Lewis.

Redfield, R., Linton, R., & Herskovits, M. T. (1936). Memorandum for the study of acculturation. *American Anthropologist, 38,* 149–152.

Reynolds, M. C., Wang, M. C., & Walberg, H. S. (1987). The necessary restructuring of special and regular education. *Exceptional Children, 53,* 391–398.

Rueda, R., Mercer, J. R., & Cardoza, D. (1987, May). Special education decision making with Hispanic students in large urban school districts. Paper presented at the Special Education for Changing Population Conference, Los Angeles.

Sapir, E. (1921). *Language: An introduction to the study of speech.* New York: Harcourt Brace.

Seymour, S. (1981). Cooperation and Competition: Some issues and problems in cross cultural analysis. In R. Monroe, and B. Whiting (Eds.), *Handbook of cross cultural human development.* New York: Garland.

Spradley, J. P. (1980). *Participant observation.* New York: Holt, Rinehart and Winston.

Tannen, D. (Ed.). (1981). *Analyzing discourse: Text and talk.* Washington, DC: Georgetown University Press.

Tannen, D. (1984). The pragmatics of cross-cultural communication. *Applied Linguistics, 5,* 189–195.

Toliver-Weddington, G., & Meyerson, M. D. (1983). Training paraprofessionals for identification and intervention with communicatively disordered bilinguals. In D. R. Omark and J. G. Erickson (Eds.), *The bilingual exceptional child* (pp. 379–395). Austin, TX: PRO-ED.

Trueba, H. E. (Ed.) (1987). *Success or Failure?* MA: Newbury House.

Varonis, E. M., & Gass, S. M. (1985). Miscommunication in native/nonnative conversation. *Language in Society, 14,* 327–343.

Wechsler, D. (1984). *Manual for the Wechsler Intelligence Scale for Children–Revised.* New York: The Psychological Corporation.

Wiener, F. D. (1986). The non-native speaker: Testing and therapy. In F. H. Bess, B. S. Clark, and H. R. Mitchell (Eds.), *Concerns for minority groups in communication disorders* (pp. 40–45). Rockville, MD: American Speech-Language-Hearing Association.

Witkin, H. A., Moore, C. A., Goodenough, D. R., & Cox, P. W. (1977). Field-independent cognitive styles and their educational implications. *Review of Educational Research, 47,* 1–64.

Wolck, W. (1978). Towards a classificatory matrix for linguistic varieties, or . . . the dialect/language problem revisited. In Michel Paradis (Ed.), *Aspects of bilingualism* (pp. 211–220). Columbia, SC: Hornbeam Press.

Young, L. W. L. (1982). Inscrutability revisited. In J. J. Gumperz (Ed.), *Language and social identity* (pp. 72–84). Cambridge: Cambridge University Press.

CHAPTER 5

Descriptive Assessment of Communicative Ability in Limited English Proficient Students

JACK S. DAMICO

A key aspect of the assessment process in the schools involves the determination of a student's language and communicative abilities. Since underlying language proficiency and its use for communication is so important to social interaction and academic success (Heath, 1983; Norris & Bruning, 1988, and see Chapter Three), evaluators must conduct communicative assessment cautiously. This is especially true when addressing the language and communicative abilities of limited English proficient (LEP) students. These students frequently are placed in situations where they cannot comprehend or use English effectively or where the cultural norms of communication vary from their own. While they may be proficient in their own cultures and languages, their communicative interactions in English are less effective. Therefore they may be perceived as different, or even disabled by monolingual English speakers (Miller, 1984a; Rueda, 1987; Padilla, 1979; Young, 1982). These perceptions are problematic in all environments but are especially significant in the academic setting. As documented by Ortiz and Wilkinson (1987), an observed lack of communicative proficiency in English is a primary reason for LEP student referral for possible special education placement.

When such referrals occur, the evaluator's objective is to determine the reasons for the student's lack of communicative effectiveness. The evaluation should differentiate between difficulties that result from normal second-language-learning processes or differences due to experiential and cultural factors versus those caused by intrinsic language-learning impairment. While this objective may appear simplistic and straightforward, this is rarely the case.

As discussed in Chapter Two, observation of LEP students acquiring English as a second language (L2) suggests a number of complicating variables. First, there are similiarities between the problematic communicative behaviors observed in LEP students and those in monolingual-language-learning impaired students. Care must be taken, therefore, in deciding how to identify true language-learning difficulties in this population. Second, the process of L2 acquisition is complex and different from first-language acquisition. Consequently, there must be a greater awareness of the linguistic, social, and psychological factors involved in L2 acquisition. Third, to adequately assess a LEP student's language-learning ability, the evaluator must be fluent in the student's first language. Fourth, when assessing LEP students, the evaluator must be aware of any cultural differences between the LEP student's primary cultural context and that of the mainstream schools. Cultural differences can affect communicative and academic performance. Finally, it is essential to recognize that listener attitudes regarding a LEP student's first language can significantly affect that student's communicative performance, motivation, and self-confidence.

This chapter suggests how effective communicative assessment of LEP students can be accomplished. By initiating a descriptive approach to communicative assessment that uses a number of recently developed techniques and procedures, the evaluator can differentiate between normal language learners in the process of learning English versus those with intrinsic language-learning impairments. In order to appreciate this descriptive approach to assessment, however, we must review the current assessment approach and its practices. This discussion clarifies that this assessment approach is not sufficient and that an alternative approach should be used.

CURRENT APPROACH TO COMMUNICATIVE ASSESSMENT

The most popular assessment approach in special education today is a discrete point approach (Acevedo, 1986; Day, McCollum, Cieslak, & Erickson, 1981; Mattes & Omark, 1984). In this approach, language is viewed as an autonomous cognitive ability that can be separated from other cognitive and environmental variables and that can be divided into numerous, easily discernible and measurable linguistic components. Since this assessment approach is used widely, it is helpful to review its underlying perspective, defining characteristics, and clinical applications.

MODULAR PERSPECTIVE

The discrete point approach is based on a detailed historical development that has occurred over the past 60 years. Throughout this development, the primary defining construct has been a modular perspective of language proficiency (see Chapter Three). This perspective gives rise to two specific implications. First, language is viewed as a separate and closed system that is only indirectly influenced by such cognitive skills as intelligence, memory, and motivation. Additionally, since this autonomy also implies that language is a closed system, extraneous variables such as fatigue, experience, anxiety, and learning are considered separate variables that do not affect language proficiency directly. Based on this autonomy of language, then, the perspective assumes that language can be analyzed and tested apart from the influence of intrinsic and extrinsic factors.

Second, the modular perspective conceptualizes the internal structure of language proficiency as consisting of numerous components, which are themselves separate and autonomous. Consequently, these components (e.g., syntax, phonology, semantics, pragmatics, reception, and expression) are felt to be observable and analyzable apart from one another. Although these components may interact to some extent, they are basically divisible and discrete in their functioning. This fragmentation of the observable components of language allows for the practice of isolating one component to better describe it without the complexity that would exist if several components were considered together.

This modular perspective has resulted in an assessment process and concomitant practices typified by six overlapping characteristics. These include a discrete point method of analysis, the focus on the structural aspects of language and communication to the exclusion of other language dimensions, a prescriptionistic view of language performance, an emphasis on quantification as the assessment objective, the use of norm referencing as an interpretation technique, and the strict standardization of language data obtained for analysis and assessment. Each of these will be described in the following sections.

CHARACTERISTICS OF THE CURRENT APPROACH

Discrete Point Methodology

In the modular perspective, the assessment of communication is based on the belief that the evaluator can fragment language into its components, analyze these components separately, and then bring the individual analyses together to comment on the student's communication skills. With this methodology, communicative assessment need not focus on actual communication but, rather, on the components believed to make up communicative effectiveness. For example, the LEP student's skill with expressive syntax and the ability to ask for clarification (both necessary for communication) will be assessed separately and the data from separate tests combined to comment on the student's communicative ability. Although evaluators do not analyze real communicative behavior through this approach, neither do they sufficiently analyze the discrete components necessary for communication. Rather than administer numerous tests or probes designed to exhaust the components important in communication, evaluators will administer only those tests with which they are familiar or they will administer commercially available tests. The result is a determination of communicative or language effectiveness that may be based on insufficient data. Regardless of how well the discrete point method is applied, however, its influence on the current assessment approach is pervasive.

Focus on Structural Aspects

The second characteristic of the discrete point approach is the focus on the structural aspects of communication to the virtual exclusion of other dimensions of language and communicative proficiency. Language is coded into observable units through its superficial structure and, consequently, these data are readily accessible for the development of discrete point tests and probe techniques. This focus on the structural aspects of communication has a practical implication. Since these tests are intended to indicate potential language or communicative difficulty and since they are designed to focus on these superficial structural characteristics, these behaviors become the indices for determining whether an individual exhibits a language or communicative disorder. In effect, through the reliance on structural units for discrete point analysis, the definition of a communicative disorder becomes a structural one.

Prescriptionism

The third characteristic is a prescriptionistic view of language and communicative behavior. Prescriptionism is based ". . . on an ideology (or set of beliefs) concerning language which requires that in language use, as in other matters, things shall be done in the 'right' way" (Milroy & Milroy, 1985:1). This characteristic is evident in many tests designed to elicit predictable, discrete responses and where responses are scored as "correct" or "incorrect." Due to the characteristic of standardization (see below), the responses accepted and the way that they are scored is restricted. That is, the tests are designed to elicit a limited range of responses. One response form is typically designated as the "correct" form, which is based either on the written language form or the structural norms of the mainstream population (Milroy & Milroy, 1985; Mims & Camden, 1986).

This prescriptionism is also evident in the interpretation of test results where the emphasis is on the test score. In turn, these tests are typically interpreted through a norm-referenced procedure (see below) based on the numbers of "correct" and "incorrect" responses. While these tests do not directly state that poor performance indicates a language or communicative disorder, this message is frequently implied.

Quantification

Since the current assessment approach views language proficiency as a series of discrete components that are observable through the correct use of structural forms, the absence of normal language proficiency or communicative effectiveness may be noted in the specific errors made during test performance. The evaluation of performance, therefore, may be based on a counting of the actual errors produced; this process of quantification becomes the objective of the testing process. Tests, therefore, are designed to provide numerical scores for interpretation rather than a detailed description of performance. This characteristic of the current approach, quantification, is believed to increase the objectivity of language and communicative assessment because the focus on actual numbers of incorrect responses reduces the need for subjective judgments and interpretations by the evaluator.

Norm-referencing

In order to interpret test scores, the current assessment approach stresses normative data as the best way to determine the student's performance level. That is, once the evaluator obtains the student's scores, they are compared to the performance expected of a particular chronological age level or peer group. The comparison data is obtained by administering the test to a large number of other individuals who are assumed to be similar to the student being assessed. If the student scores at the lower end of the distribution curve created from the norming population, then that student has performed poorly. Among other possibilities, this may indicate some type of intrinsic impairment.

Standardization

The use of norm-referencing gives rise to the last characteristic: the requirement of strict standardization of the test format. To compare an individual with peers over time, in various testing locations, and with different evaluators, it is necessary to collect the discrete point data through set tasks in controlled situations. Evaluators must take care in administering the test, in the possible responses that the student can give in reaction to a test stimulus, and in the way they score and interpret the responses. Each of these conditions are necessary to increase the replicability of results and to reduce error variance.

CLINICAL APPLICATION OF THE CURRENT APPROACH

The direct application of the current assessment approach and its modular perspective is evident in the actual assessment process and the testing procedures used in communicative assessment. The assessment process focuses attention on the discrete components of speech and language and orients the evaluator to a specific type of testing instrument.

Assessment Process

Based on the modular perspective, the process of assessment is directed toward the division of communicative behavior into its subcomponents. The evaluator's task is to collect objective and reliable data in as many of the components as is feasible (Carrow, 1974; Lado, 1961). Typically, this involves determining which specific subcomponents of speech and language to assess and then selecting discrete point tests that can evaluate these behaviors (see Figure 5-1). When assessing LEP students, the evaluator first selects a discrete point test to determine language dominance. Then, based on the results of this testing, the evaluator selects other tools to analyze various subcomponents of the speaker's dominant speech (articulation, voice, fluency) and language (receptive and expressive ability). Once these scores are obtained, the evaluator reviews all of the test scores and interprets them together. This gives a clear picture of the student's overall communicative ability in the dominant language. The evaluator may also decide to administer similar tests and procedures in the nondominant language as a basis for comparison between the two languages. The process, then, uses standardized and norm-referenced discrete point tests in the dominant language to break communication down and determines the proficiency of each subcomponent of interest based on the test results. These data are then combined to give an overall picture of communicative effectiveness.

At times, evaluators may not consider a LEP student's language dominance during assessment. The monolingual evaluators may only admin-

Fig. 5-1. Current Assessment Process

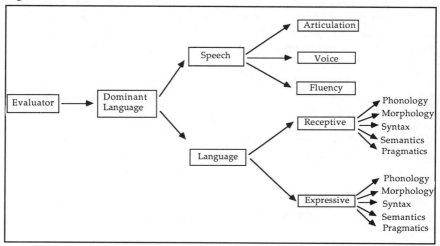

ister English tests and may ignore the bilingual considerations, an inappropriate practice that invariably leads to invalid conclusions and should not be condoned. It is also a violation of the federal mandates, which require testing in the appropriate language (e.g., P.L. 94-142). Even in these instances, however, the current process is used. Although the first step of determining language dominance is omitted, discrete point tests are selected in English and the process continues as previously described.

Language Tests

The second application of the current assessment approach involves the actual language testing instruments and procedures used during communicative assessment. Since the 1950s, language tests have been designed that adhere to the modular perspective of language proficiency and its six resulting characteristics. Among the most frequently used instruments designed to focus on receptive language abilities in English are: the *Peabody Picture Vocabulary Test* (Dunn & Dunn, 1982); the *Test for Auditory Comprehension of Language–Revised* (Carrow-Woolfolk, 1985); the *Assessment of Children's Language Comprehension* (Foster, Giddan, & Stark, 1969); the *Goldman-Fristoe-Woodcock Test of Auditory Discrimination* (Goldman, Fristoe, & Woodcock, 1970); and the *Boehm Test of Basic Concepts* (Boehm, 1971). To focus on expressive aspects of language structure or on both receptive and expressive abilities, the *Northwestern Syntax Screening Test* (Lee, 1970), the *Carrow Elicited Language Inventory* (Carrow, 1974), the *Oral Language Sentence Imitation Screening Test* (Zachman, Huisingh, Jorgensen, & Barrett, 1976), the *Grammatical Analysis of Elicited Language* (Moog & Geers, 1979), and the *Structured Photographic Language Test* (Werner & Kresheck, 1974) were developed. While these tools focus only on specific language structures, other tests were developed that focus on superficial aspects of language structure along with other related language skills. Instruments that are considered test batteries, such as the *Illinois Test of Psycholinguistic Abilities* (Kirk, McCarthy, & Kirk, 1971), the *Test of Language Development* (Newcomer & Hammill, 1977), the *Test of Adolescent Language* (Hammill, Brown, Larsen, & Wiederholt, 1980), and the *Clinical Evaluation of Language Function* (Semel-Mintz & Wiig, 1982) were also developed within the modular framework. Each of these tests is designed with a focus on discrete items of language structure, rigid standardization, and some attempt at norm-referencing. As a result, the data for analysis is obtained by using artificial tasks in contrived and structured situations.

Adaptations for LEP Students

As greater emphasis was placed on the evaluation of LEP students, a need developed to ensure that these formal tests could be used with the LEP population. Federal mandates required that assessment occur in the appropriate linguistic and cultural contexts (see Chapter One) and numerous researchers discussed the problem of using tests designed for the monolingual English population when assessing LEP children (Evard & Sabers, 1979; Grill & Bartel, 1977; Matluck & Mace, 1973; Mercer, 1981; Oakland, 1977; Samuda, 1975). Consequently, several types of adaptations were applied to the current testing instruments developed for the English population to make this approach more appropriate for LEP assessment. These adaptations consisted of the creation of language dominance tests; modification of the content, stimuli, and performance criteria used in English tests; scoring modifications in the English tests; modifications of English test norms; direct translations of the English tests or the use of interpreters during the actual test administration; and the development of formal and modular tests in other languages. Each of these will be discussed in the following sections.

Creation of Language Dominance Tests. One adaptation for LEP students was the construction of discrete point tests designed to determine a student's dominant language. Although the need to determine language dominance for instructional purposes was established several decades ago (Hoffman, 1934), the emphasis on discrete point testing measures is of more recent origin due in part to the litigation referred to as the "Lau Decision" (see Chapter One), which required a rating of bilingual proficiency on a five-point scale. Similar to the English discrete point language tests, some language dominance tests focus on specific components whereas some are designed as test batteries (Jakobovits, 1968; Zirkel, 1974). The *James Language Dominance Test* (James, 1975) and the *Dos Amigos Verbal Language Scales* (Critchlow, 1974), for example, are picture-elicitation instruments that assess receptive and expressive single word vocabulary in both English and Spanish to derive a dominance rating. The *Crane Oral Dominance Test* (Crane, 1976) uses word and sentence repetition in English and Spanish to determine language dominance where the *Bilingual Syntax Measure* (Burt, Dulay, & Hernandez-Chavez, 1976) is designed to assess syntactic ability.

There are several formal and modular language batteries that attempt to determine dominance based on several different tasks. The most widely used is the *Language Assessment Scales* (DeAvila & Duncan, 1977). This battery consists of subtests involving sound discrimination, phoneme production, vocabulary usage, sentence comprehension, and story telling. Two other dominance batteries are the *Spanish/English Language Performance Screening* (Evans, 1976) and the *Shutt Primary Language Indicator Test* (Shutt, 1974). Both of these tests use picture description and picture elicitation to evaluate receptive and expressive vocabulary and other structural language components (see Appendix A).

Once an evaluator makes a determination of a student's dominant language, assessment may proceed. If the tests indicate that the LEP student is English-dominant, for example, then assessment can be in English and the student's performance in this "stronger" language may be used as a basis for determining a potential language-learning impairment.

Content Modification of Existing English Tests. A second adaptation is to use the existing English tests with content, stimuli, and performance criteria modifications. These modifications are intended to make existing tools more appropriate for the LEP population (Cheng, 1987; Evard & Sabers, 1979; Vaughn-Cooke, 1986). The first type of modification involves the actual test content. In attempting to adapt the existing tests for LEP students, evaluators need to make the tool as culture-fair as possible (Miller, 1984b). This means that the content presented in the test must not be biased against LEP students because an item or set of items is culturally or linguistically inappropriate. In these instances, items in conflict with the student's normal cultural or linguistic background are omitted or changed (Rosenbluth, 1976).

A second modification of existing tests involves the modification of actual test stimuli. Even when test content is appropriate, the elicitation stimuli may represent barriers to the student's performance. The stimuli used to elicit responses should represent situations that are familiar to the LEP student rather than alien or in conflict with the student's experience. Test stimuli depicting only white characters performing middle class tasks, for example, may not be as appropriate to Black, Asian, or Native American students as stimuli derived from their own cultures (Cheng, 1987; Harris, 1985). Changes in actual stimuli (e.g., pictures and tasks) may result in a more culture-fair testing procedure.

The third modification is accomplished by changing the performance criteria. LEP students may be given more time before responding, may be allowed the opportunity to ask for more repeats, or may be able to code switch when responding. These modifications are generally intended to overcome the bias inherent in a student's need to translate from English to the first language during testing.

Scoring Modifications of Existing English Tests. Rather than changing the test content or performance criteria to create a more culture-fair test, the third type of adaptation involves using the existing English tests while changing the scoring criteria or procedures (Evard & Sabers, 1979; Matluck & Mace, 1973). Alternative scoring criteria are created that attempt to take linguistic and cultural differences into account. Advocated most often when dealing with dialectal differences, the scoring criteria are based on consistent language response patterns noted in the student's cultural or linguistic peer group. Arnold and Reed (1976), for example, suggested using a modified scoring system for Vernacular Black Engish (VBE) speakers when administering the Grammatic Closure subtest of the *Illinois Test of Psycholinguistic Abilities*. When this was done, many of the differences noted between white and black children on this subtest were eliminated. Similar findings regarding the *Test of Language Development* (Wiener, Lewnau, & Erway, 1983), the *Carrow Elicited Language Inventory* (Hemingway, Montague, & Bradley, 1981), the *Developmental Sentence Scoring* analysis procedure (Nelson, 1983), and even a speech discrimination task with Spanish bilinguals (Danhauer, Crawford, & Edgerton, 1984) have been reported in the literature.

Modifications of Existing English Test Norms. Due to the reliance on normative data for interpretative purposes, another frequently used adaptation involves a modification of the test norms (Brown & Bryant, 1984). Such modification is necessary because of the assumptions required when norm-referencing is used. Norm-referencing assumes that the student tested is similar in all significant aspects to the normative population with which that student is compared. This allows the basic premise that since all individuals being tested had similar experiences and opportunities to learn English, the differences in test performance must be due to actual language-learning potential (Omark, 1981a; b). Since this assumption of homogenity is obviously not correct when using mainstream norms to test LEP students with differing cultural and linguistic backgrounds, modifications are needed.

One type of modification is the use of stratified norms. That is, the normative data is collected from subjects selected on the basis of their group identity and according to their representative percentages in the total population. For example, if race is a variable of concern and the general population consists of 70% Anglo students, 18% Black students, 9% Hispanic, and 3% Native American, then the normative sample would consist of each of these groups in these percentages. The *Peabody Picture Vocabulary Test—Revised* uses stratified normative data.

A second type of modification is the development of local norms (An-astasi, 1976; Evard & Sabers, 1979). Examiners use the standardized pro-cedure but develop a new set of norms with their local students as the sample population (Mares, 1980; Nelson-Burgess & Meyerson, 1975; Norris & Juarez 1985). This allows the tester to compare a student's performance with the performances of individuals in the local area where the experiences and patterns of language use are presumably similar (Toronto, 1973; Toronto, Leverman, Hanna, Rosenzweig, & Mal-donado, 1975). There are a number of advocates for the development of local norms if the formal and modular language tests are used. Omark and Mattes (1984) and Toronto and Merrill (1983), for example, give excellent and detailed procedures for developing such norms.

The third modification involves the use of pluralistic norms that are more specific and focused than the stratified or local norms. This modifi-cation involves collecting all of the normative data from the actual socio-cultural group being targeted so that there is a real match between the LEP student and the normative sample. This allows an interpretation of performance in relation the individual's ethnic, linguistic, cultural, or socioeconomic group (Cummins, 1984). This approach has been widely encouraged by Jane Mercer (1979; 1984) with the development of the *System of Multicultural Pluralistic Assessment* (see Chapter Six). Mus-selwhite (1983) has demonstrated the need for pluralistic norms when administering the *Test for Auditory Comprehension of Language* to different socioeconomic groups. She advocates using dual sets of norms that would allow comparison of the targeted student with both the standard group and the student's peer group. This procedure enables the as-sumption of homogenity while also providing a measure against the mainstream standards of performance.

Direct Translations of Existing English Tests. The fifth adaptation of the English language tests to the LEP population involves the direct translation of the English tests into the other languages. This has been accomplished in two ways. First, a number of the existing English tests have been directly translated into another language by making a parallel translation of each stimulus item from one language to the other: For example, the Spanish version of the *Test for Auditory Comprehension of Language*, the Spanish version of the *Boehm Test of Basic Concepts*, the *Assessment of Children's Language Comprehension* (Foster, Giddan, & Stark, 1978; Maison, 1973), the *Receptive One-Word Picture Vocabulary Test-Span-ish* (Gardner, 1980), and several versions of the *Peabody Picture Vocabulary Test* (Ickes & Brown, 1976; Moreau, 1967, as reported by Evard and Sa-bers, 1979; Weiner, Simon, & Weiss, 1978). Although these early transla-tions involved receptive language components, direct translations of expressive language tests or tests combining both expressive and receptive abilities have also been completed. The best examples of these are the *Expressive One-Word Picture Vocabulary Test-Spanish* (Gardner, 1980), the *Preschool Language Scale-Spanish* (Zimmerman, Steiner, and Pond, 1976), and the *Los Ninos, A Screening Test of Communicative Disorders, English/Spanish* (Crosland-Real, 1978) in Spanish and the *Test of Oral Language Development–Primary* into Navajo (Nye, 1987).

The second modification of the language used in an existing English language test is to employ a proficient bilingual in the LEP student's first language as an interpreter during the test administration. This individual is trained in test administration and in scoring procedures unique to the targeted tests and may even be given time to prepare for the translation. The bilingual person then acts as a mediator between the examiner and the examinee during the actual assessment. Though not generally advocated in the literature, this modificational strategy is used a surprising amount of the time (see Chapter Four).

Development of New Modular Tests in the Other Languages. The last adaptation does not involve modification of the English tests but, rather, the development of a new set of discrete point tests in languages other than English. There are a number of formal tests that fit into this category. Although most are described in Appendix A, some warrant further attention.

To assess superficial aspects of expressive phonology (articulation) in Spanish, the *Southwestern Spanish Articulation Test* (Toronto, 1972), the *Austin Spanish Articulation Test* (Carrow, 1974), and the *Medida Espanola de Articulacion* (Mason, Smith, & Henshaw, 1976) are available. These tests resemble their counterparts in English in that they elicit single-word productions from picture-naming activities. To assess single-word receptive vocabulary, the *Mexican-American Inventory of Receptive Abilities* and the *Toronto Tests of Receptive Vocabulary* (Toronto, 1977) have been designed. These tools are also based on a picture-elicitation format requiring a pointing response.

Available tests designed specifically for morphological and syntactic assessment are: the *Screening Test for Spanish Grammar* (STSG) (Toronto, 1973); the *Developmental Assessment of Spanish Grammar* (DASG) (Toronto, 1976); and the *Oral Language Evaluation* (Silvaroli & Maynes, 1975). Though not parallel translations, the STSG and the DASG are closely patterned on two English language assessment procedures. The STSG is based on the elicitation and scoring format used in the *Northwestern Syntax Screening Test*. Consequently, it focuses on both receptive and expressive morphological elements and syntactic units. The DASG is patterned after the scoring procedures used with *Developmental Sentence Scoring*

(Lee & Canter, 1971) and is based on data from Spanish-speaking Mexican-American and Puerto Rican children. The *Oral Language Evaluation* assesses a LEP student's ability to use superficial aspects of language structure during a picture-elicitation task and some picture-description activities. The student's performance is compared to a list of five language development steps and a set of "typical" response patterns in both Spanish and English.

Similar to the trend in English language assessment, there are also a number of tests developed in languages other than English that are actually test batteries consisting of various discrete point subtests. One of the first test batteries developed along these lines in Spanish was the *Del Rio Language Screening Test* (Toronto, Leverman, Hanna, Rosenzweig, & Maldonado, 1975). This tool consists of five subtests (receptive vocabulary, sentence repetition for length, sentence repetition for complexity, memory, and story comprehension) administered in a structured testing environment with norm-referenced interpretative criteria. These norms, however, are local norms collected in Del Rio, Texas and are not necessarily appropriate to other situations. The *Short Tests of Linguistic Skills* (Fredrickson & Wick, 1976), constructed in the Chicago Public Schools, is a battery consisting of four sections (speaking, listening, reading, and writing) with further division into discrete point tasks. Although this tool has been designed for use in 11 different languages (English, Spanish, Arabic, Chinese, Greek, Italian, Japanese, Korean, Tagalog, Polish, & Vietnamese), there is little direction given for the interpretation of the scores obtained from these tools so caution is advised (Day, McCollum, Cieslak, & Erickson, 1981).

The *Pruebas de Expresion Oral y Percepcion de la Lengua Espanola* (PEOPLE) (Mares, 1980) is another test battery developed for local use but adopted throughout the country. This test, intended for Spanish-speaking students in Southern Calfornia, includes five discrete point subtests that enable the examiner to obtain scale scores of the LEP student's performance. This test is well designed and highly standardized and, consequently, has strong internal consistency and reliability indices.

Two other language assessment batteries constructed in Spanish closely parallel the test formats of well-known English language tests. The *Prueba del Desarrollo Inicial del Lenguaje* (Hresko, Reid, & Hammill, 1982) is similar in construction to the *Test of Early Language Development* (Hresko, Reid, & Hammill, 1981). This battery focuses on both receptive and expressive components of language structure and content. Test scores are reported in both percentiles and language quotients; there are limited norms for Mexican children, Puerto Rican children, and Spanish speaking children in the United States. The Spanish version of the *Compton Speech and Language Screening Evaluation* (Compton & Kline, 1983) parallels the English version by the same name. The data collection procedures are similar, and the same superficial aspects of language are analyzed.

A number of other modular tests have been constructed in languages other than Spanish. However, many of these tools are not yet widely available or are still being developed. In addition to the information available in this volume (see Appendix A), there are a number of excellent testing bibliographies. For example, an important resource for Asian language tests is Cheng's *Assessing Asian Language Performance* (1987) whereas the *Nondiscriminatory Assessment Test Matrix* (Watson, Grouell, Heller, & Omark, 1987) and the American Speech-Language-Hearing Association's *Resource Guide to Multicultural Tests and Materials in Communicative Disorders* (Deal & Rodriguez, 1987) provide brief listings and addresses. For actual test critiques, the work of Dulay, Burt, and McKeon (1980), Day, McCollum, Cieslak, and Erickson (1981), Juarez, Hendrickson, and Anderson (1983), and Acevedo (1986) includes reviews of a number of the commonly used modular language tests.

CONCERNS ABOUT THE CURRENT ASSESSMENT APPROACH

In recent years, many researchers have discussed the difficulties inherent in the current assessment approach when testing LEP students. Mercer (1983), for example, suggested that the current assessment approach does not assess enough dimensions of language proficiency, does not take into consideration important sociocultural and motivational factors, and exhibits little discriminant validity. The results of these problems are routinely described in the literature through the demonstration of inappropriate identification and placement of LEP students into special education (see Chapter One).

A review of the literature suggests four primary concerns with the current communicative assessment approach. Each of these may be traced to one or more of the six defining characteristics of the current approach and may be summarized as consequences of an even more basic difficulty with the construct validity of the modular perspective on language proficiency. Each of these issues will be discussed in the following sections.

LACK OF LINGUISTIC REALISM

The initial concern relates to the treatment of language and communication in the tests derived from the current assessment approach. These tests are based on a simplistic conception of language that violates the principle of linguistic realism (Crystal, Fletcher, & Garman, 1976; Milroy & Milroy, 1985). In attempting to establish testing instruments with strong psychometric characteristics, the current test design follows psychological, not linguistic, characteristics. As a result, the behavioral performances required on these tests are discrete and easily observable behaviors that are dissimilar to the behaviors observed in true communication. The tests typically focus on splinter skills that are only tangentially related to language. While this reliance on the modular construct of language and its resultant discrete point methodology makes formal test design possible, this practice removes the essential synergistic quality from language. This results in a focus on artificial behaviors that have relatively little to do with real communication (Crystal, 1987; Duchan, 1983; Leonard, Prutting, Perozzi, & Berkley, 1978; Muma, 1978; Oller, 1983).

Another indication of the lack of linguistic realism is the emphasis on superficial aspects of language structure to the virtual exclusion of other dimensions of language during testing. While recent research in language assessment stresses the importance of global analysis of language difficulty (Crystal, 1982; Douglas & Selinker, 1985; Miller, 1981) and numerous studies suggest that language-impaired individuals have functional difficulties (Fey & Leonard, 1983), intentional difficulties (Chapman, 1981), and discourse difficulties in various manifestations of language (Hedberg, Stoel-Gammon, Westby, & Yoshinaga, 1984), the current language tests are still syntactically oriented. In addition, other potential problems are not addressed.

The lack of linguistic realism has resulted in two other problems with the current assessment approach. First, this approach and its testing instruments do not properly consider variation in language. Instead, a set of "correct" structural forms are employed as potential indices for language impairment. This prescriptionistic view is problematic since the structural coding of meaning in spoken language is quite variable. Speakers use different registers or speaking styles based on contextual, social, and affective factors. Additionally, a speaker's range of structural coding (i.e., the observable vocabulary, phonology, morphology, and syntax) is based on that speaker's previous exposure to various dialects and speaking styles. An individual's pattern of structural coding, therefore, typically reflects that speaker's exposure to language structure rather than the speaker's language-learning capacity. This variation regarding both a speaker's exposure to language and that speaker's usage patterns are typically not considered in the scoring and interpretation of norm-referenced tests. This approach assumes that there is one proper or correct form that reflects on a speaker's underlying language proficiency and, therefore, production of that form is expected during assessment. Failure to produce the specified form may result in a negative evaluation of the speaker's proficiency.

Finally, the current tests are designed to reduce language description to a single number that describes a normative position or rank rather than information about the behavior or the process itself. Language is too complex to be described in this manner.

LACK OF AUTHENTICITY

The second major concern about the current assessment approach is based on the way that the language tests are designed. To ensure replicability of results for norm-referencing, language tasks are highly standardized. Stimuli, test administration, expected responses, and testing context are all rigidly controlled. Essentially, there is an attempt to reduce intervening variables by controlling the testing situation as much as possible. In adhering to this practice, however, the tests no longer work with authentic language (Seliger, 1982; Shohamy & Reves, 1985). The "language" under investigation is removed from naturally occurring situations where it functions optimally and where it can be influenced by contextual variables. As a result, many of the current tests are poor predictors of the language and communication abilities of the individuals being tested (Allen, Bliss, & Timmons, 1981; Bowerman, 1976; Connell & Myles-Zitzer, 1982; Fujiki & Willbrand, 1982; Mims & Camden, 1986; Prutting, Gallagher, and Mulac, 1975).

This criticism of the current testing approach has been discussed for nearly three decades (see e.g., Carroll, 1961). Despite that, there is an isolation of the language test to a contrived situation where the participants, the motivation, the topics, and the necessity to perform all conspire to make the task unlike real communicative interaction (Adler, 1981; Oller, 1983; Taylor, 1977).

POOR PSYCHOMETRIC STRENGTH

The third concern about the discrete point approach revolves around psychometric evaluations of the tests themselves. Numerous studies indicate that even though these tests strive for psychometric strength, they are not completely successful. Darley (1979) stated that of the 28 most widely used tests of language development, not one met acceptable criteria in all three of the essential areas of psychometric strength (i.e., validity, reliability, and normative application). More recently, McCauley and Swisher (1984) analyzed 30 English tests of language or articulation ability based on a set of 10 predetermined criteria of psychometric strength. None of the tests met all 10 essential criteria and not one demonstrated acceptable predictive validity or interexaminer reliability (with a correlation coefficient of .90 or better). In fact, on 8 of the 10 criteria, less than one-third of the tests met the predetermined standards. Other studies have addressed specific psychometric issues and also found significant problems (Lieberman & Michael, 1986; Olswang & Carpenter, 1978; Shorr, 1983; Shorr & Dale, 1984). These findings suggest that the current tests exhibit inability to adhere to their own conceptual approach.

INHERENT AND UNAVOIDABLE BIAS

While the three concerns just discussed apply to the current assessment approach in general, the last concern addresses issues involving LEP students directly: the inherent and unavoidable bias contained in these assessment air tools.

Language tests are biased toward the culture within which they were developed. Through their construction, all language tests have unique cultural elements built in. This must be the case since language behavior is acquired and used within a culture, and the actual tests are constructed within a specific cultural context. As a result, the experiences, expectations, beliefs, and artifacts of that culture are incorporated into the tests. This is unavoidable and is the main reason that culture-free tests are not possible. If true culture-free tests were developed, those tests could not function as language tests because language is unique to a culture (Berry, 1966; Bloom, 1981). Stripping cultural context, therefore, would strip the test of its validity.

There are ways, however, that evaluators can reduce the effects of test bias when working with groups outside of the mainstream culture. One way is to create tasks that are as natural as possible. By requiring performance on tasks that typically cross cultural boundaries, the examinee will have some experiential basis from which to operate (Oller, 1979; Scribner, 1979). Another way evaluators can reduce the potential bias is by building a flexibility of interpretation into the assessment process. That is, rather than use the results of the biased testing procedures to diagnose and place a LEP student, evaluators can use this information only as one source of data.

Due to the modular perspective of the current assessment approach, this approach to assessment does not attempt to reduce the inherent bias. First, because of the discrete point methodology and the strict standardization practices, the tasks required during testing are not at all natural. Students are expected to perform artificial tasks and to make out-of-context judgments during language assessment. In language testing, Kamhi and Koenig (1985) have argued that tools requiring language performance out of its normal communicative context are tapping meta-linguistic performance components rather than real communicative proficiency. This is especially problematic for LEP students because meta-linguistic skills are very much influenced by experience and cultural context (Feuerstein, 1979; Nelson, 1981; Olshtain & Blum-Kulka, 1985). Additionally, these less meaning-based activities require a different type of information processing that is also more difficult in a second language (Duran, 1985; McLaughlin, Rossman, & McLeod, 1983).

A second reason that the current approach is more prone to bias is that the belief in the autonomy of language, the use of norm-referencing, and the prescriptionistic view of language and communication do not allow for the flexibility of interpretation needed to overcome the bias inherent in the tests themselves. Normative data is used and comparisons are made between individuals and groups with the goal of differentiating on the basis of a numerical score. Although the problems with norm-referencing (especially when assessing nonmainstream students) is generally recognized, these problems are typically defended as a necessity for school placement and planning, or it is stated that the claims of bias are overexaggerated (Cole, 1981; Green, 1981; Reschly, 1981).

Lack of attention to the "natural" requirement in language testing (Oller, 1979) is another reason that the previously described test adaptations are not effective. Despite attempts at test adaptation, the research still demonstrates that the current assessment tools are ineffective when assessing LEP students. This point warrants discussion.

Ineffectiveness of Discrete Point Adaptations

The primary reason for the ineffectiveness of these adaptations is that a modified tool in another language or culture is only as good as its original version in English. Given the previous discussion, therefore, it is not surprising that these adaptations have not been successful. For example, in keeping with the modular perspective, one adaptation resulted in the construction of language-dominance tests that focused on specific components of language. Research has demonstrated, however, that performance on these discrete point dominance tests does not accurately reflect language dominance or proficiency in other manifestations of language usage (Gerken, 1978; Wald, 1981). Consequently, there are discrepancies between the findings of different discrete point tests of language dominance, and these tools exhibit poor predictive validity (Dieterich, Freeman, & Crandall, 1979; Payan, 1984; Ulibarri, Spencer, & Rivas, 1981). Just as with other discrete point tests, these dominance tests do not reflect language in reality.

Another demonstration of difficulties inherent in the modular perspective is the belief that direct structural translations of discrete point tests are easily accomplished. This fallacy is based on the lack of linguistic realism. As discussed by the Bay Area Bilingual Education League (BABEL) (1969), such translation efforts are problematic. Due to the modular approach to assessment and the way in which the discrete point tests are constructed, translation of these tests is complicated (Oller, 1979). These tools focus on specific aspects of English structure and use test formats requiring the use of specific types of linguistic relationships. For example, a test may require the student to listen to a sentence and then point to one of three optional pictures that best applies to the sentence stimulus. Typically, at least one of the pictures is designed as a distractor. That is, it is not the best match for the stimulus but it is close, differing only by the critical linguistic element isolated on this test item. Additionally, most of the discrete point tests are designed to become progressively more difficult as more items are completed. This allows for the use of a ceiling score for efficiency of administration.

When this type of test is translated, both the factive information and the distractor items must be successfully translated. Further, the relationships between the factive item and its linguistic and extralinguistic contexts have to be maintained at the same level in the second language as in the first language, the relationship between the distractor items and the factive item must be the same, and the distractor's relationship with its linguistic and extralinguistic contexts must have the same relationship across the two languages. If these relationships are not maintained, then the examiner may get a very different test than the one with which the translators began. Additionally, the level of complexity between each test item and all other test items must be maintained in the second language. This is necessary to maintain the overall progression toward more complexity that the test requires. In sum, successful discrete point test translation requires approximately the same linguistic register, the same frequency of vocabulary use, comparable phrasing and reference complexity, and the same relationships among the optional choices in the second language as was present in the first. It is little wonder that Oller stated:

While it may sometimes be difficult to maintain the factive content of one linguistic form when translating it into another language, this may be possible. However, to maintain the paradigm of interrelationships between linguistic and extralinguistic contexts in a set of distractors is probably not just difficult—it may well be impossible. (1979:89)

The work of several researchers tends to support this contention regarding the translation of discrete point tests (Briere, 1973; Condon, 1975; Rueda & Perozzi, 1977; Scoon, 1974). The attempts to view translation as a simple language exercise, therefore, are not realistic.

INVALIDITY OF THE UNDERLYING CONSTRUCT

Based on the previous concerns, the current assessment approach is not effective when testing LEP students for one primary reason: This approach lacks construct validity. Construct validation is the process of marshalling evidence in the form of theoretically relevant relations to support the inference that an observable response has a rational basis. This is accomplished by postulating an attribute of people assumed to be reflected in test performance and real life. This attribute is referred to as a construct and its importance in the assessment process has been discussed previously (see Chapter Three). For our purposes, it is important to note that this construct is essential to test interpretation and is the evidential basis for inferring a measure's meaning and using it to predict performance in the real world.

The current communicative assessment approach is based on a modular and autonomous construct of language proficiency that is not consistent with more recent theoretical models (see Chapter Three). The practical result is that many LEP students are inadequately assessed and inappropriately placed after language assessment. Clearly, there is need for another construct of language proficiency and an alternative approach to communicative assessment based on this construct. The remainder of this chapter will provide a descriptive approach to communicative assessment that fulfills this need.

A DESCRIPTIVE APPROACH TO COMMUNICATIVE ASSESSMENT

A new model of communicative assessment should address the problems inherent in the current approach and allow for different and more effective approaches to assessment. Additionally, this model needs to be clearly described. Larson (1978) emphasized that the majority of problems in assessment of functional communication result from conceptual ambiguity. To avoid such ambiguity and to remain consistent with the more contemporary theoretical constructs of language proficiency, a descriptive approach to communicative assessment should be used. Language and communication must not be treated as static, divisible, and autonomous. Rather, these complex human behaviors should be treated as dynamic, synergistic, and integrative with both intrinsic cognitive factors and extrinsic contextual features. Such an approach will more effectively limit the bias inherent in the communicative assessment of LEP students and will enable the evaluator to differentiate between language-learning impaired students versus normal second-language learners or individuals from culturally diverse backgrounds. The underlying perspective of this descriptive approach, its defining characteristics, and its clinical applications are discussed in the following sections.

SYNERGISTIC PERSPECTIVE

Consistent with the theoretical model proposed in Chapter Three, the descriptive approach to communicative assessment uses a synergistic perspective of language and communication. Language proficiency is considered a componentially complex, generative semiotic system that functions in an integrated fashion in many communicative contexts. That is, the components of language exist only as an integrated whole, and this whole system is unpredicted by the behavior of its parts taken separately (Fuller, 1982). Language and communication are revealed because some aspect of meaning, coded by grammatical structures for some purpose, is needed in a particular situation. While dimensions like form, content, and use may be focused on during the function of communication as a whole, these dimensions should not be separated in practice (see Chapter Three).

This perspective gives rise to two implications distinct from those of the modular perspective. First, language is not viewed as an autonomous system. It is an integrated system that is closely tied to other semiotic and cognitive abilities and is influenced by extraneous intervening variables. Consequently, task performance is highly influenced by factors such as motivation, fatigue, experience, anxiety, and learning. The language and communication behaviors assessed must be authentic.

Second, the internal structure of language proficiency is also integrated. The components of language (e.g., syntax, phonology, semantics, pragmatics, reception, and expression) are essentially terminological distinctions created in the mind for ease of discussion and analysis. They are not divisible and discrete in their functioning; they function holistically. Communication can only be assessed directly as it functions in naturalistic contexts, thus insuring linguistic reality.

As with the modular perspective, the synergistic perspective and its implications regarding the construct of language proficiency gives rise to a particular approach to assessment: the descriptive approach. As a means of comparing the synergistic perspective and its implications with the modular perspective, the descriptive approach to assessment will be typified by six overlapping characteristics that oppose those of the current assessment approach.

CHARACTERISTICS OF THE DESCRIPTIVE APPROACH

Pragmatic Methodology

Because language proficiency is considered from a synergistic perspective, the goal of the descriptive assessment approach (and the tests designed within this approach) is to collect data that are meaning-based and integrative. Rather than focusing on performance data that attempt to fragment language and communication into discrete points or components, communication is viewed as it functions holistically. That is, the dimensions of meaning, structure, and use are only viewed as they interact to produce real communication. The procedures used, therefore, are pragmatic in nature (Oller, 1979). This means that the performance tasks of interest are those that require attention to motivated meaning transmission in real activities. In real activities, the normal temporal constraints of communication and the numerous intrinsic and extrinsic variables that affect communication are in operation. The pragmatic methodology, therefore, stresses a focus on real communication.

Focus on Functional Aspects

The second characteristic of the descriptive approach is a focus on the functional aspects of communication. Rather than eliciting various aspects of superficial language structure to indicate potential language or communicative difficulty, the evaluator asks, "How proficient is this student as a communicator?" This question of proficiency is based on how well the student functions on three criteria: the effectiveness of meaning transmission, the fluency of meaning transmission, and the appropriateness of meaning transmission.

Effectiveness of Meaning Transmission. This criterion relates to the primary goal of communication: the formulation, comprehension, and transmission of meaning. As discussed by Oller and Damico (see Chapter Three), language as a semiotic system exists to achieve an understanding of what occurs in the world. When some aspect of this understanding is formulated into communication to relate that understanding to others, the individual's skill in handling this message (either as a speaker or hearer) is directly relevant to that person's proficiency. The key element, of course, is the message. Using a functional focus (regardless of how the message is formulated): If the meaning is transmitted, then communication is accomplished and the individual is effective.

Fluency of Meaning Transmission. Proficiency, however, depends on more than just getting the meaning across. A good communicator must also be a fluent transmitter of meaning in two ways. First, the individual must conform to the temporal constraints of language and communication so that the message is formulated and transmitted or comprehended within the expected time parameters. If this does not occur, then the flow of communication is affected, which will result in a devaluation of the individual's rating as a communicator. Second, fluency involves how well a communicator can repair an interaction if meaning transmission is not accomplished on the first attempt. As a speaker, can the student reformulate the message so that it is better comprehended by others? As a listener, can the student successfully ask for clarification or use contextual cues effectively if the initial message is incomprehensible? This ability to make repairs is an essential skill for a proficient communicator.

Appropriateness of Meaning Transmission. The third criterion of proficiency involves the appropriateness of meaning transmission. Realistically, language and communication are significantly influenced by the expectations that members of a linguistic community share regarding the communication norms of that community. Consequently, success and fluency in meaning transmission are not always enough. A student must also transmit meaning in a manner socially and culturally appropriate to the context within which the interaction is embedded (Fey, 1986). A student unable to use the appropriate structural code and stylistic register expected will not be as proficient a communicator as someone who can.

These three criteria allow the evaluator to comment on how proficient the LEP student is as a communicator. The way that this functional focus is incorporated into the actual descriptive assessment approach will be clarified as the remaining characteristics are detailed.

Variational Flexibility

The third characteristic of the descriptive approach is a reaction against the prescriptionism of the current assessment approach. Rather than ignore the dynamism of communication both in terms of individual variation and group differences, this assessment approach emphasizes the variability present in language and communication. Through the overlapping characteristics of functional focus, description, and the requirement for naturalistic data, the concept of variation in communication is incorporated into the assessment process. Variation is expected in the performance of every individual assessed, and it is described as an important component of that person's ability.

Description

To remain consistent with the synergistic perspective and its focus on the functionality and variation of real communication, detailed description of the student's communicative performance is required. The simple quantification of the current assessment approach cannot account for the complexity and dynamism observed in communication.

The descriptive characteristic requires a bilevel analysis paradigm. Through this bilevel analysis, the evaluator can function as the agent of the mainstream school to determine if the LEP student is a poor communicator in that environment and, at the same time, can function as an advocate for the LEP student. This is accomplished by conducting a descriptive analysis and, if needed, an explanatory analysis as a routine component of the descriptive assessment approach.

Descriptive Analysis. When a student is referred for language testing, the evaluator must function as an assessment agent of the school system and determine if the student is indeed experiencing language or communicative difficulty in the context of interest (e.g., the school). Regardless of the causal factors (e.g., a dialectal difference, a cultural difference, learning English as a second language, a language-learning impairment), if the student is not functioning effectively that fact must be documented. Based on the three criteria of proficiency discussed earlier, the evaluator asks, "In this context with its constraints, is this student a proficient communicator?" That is, at this level the evaluator comments on the success of actual communication in the domain of focus and from the mainstream perspective. Additionally, the actual determination of communicative difficulty (*not* a communicative disorder) must be justified through the description of those behaviors, giving credence to the determination of poor proficiency.

Explanatory Analysis. If the descriptive analysis does not reveal any communicative difficulties, then the evaluation is ended. The student's strengths and strategies can be described, and no communicative assistance will be required. If the descriptive analysis reveals any communicative problems, however, then the second level of analysis is required. This analysis, the explanatory analysis, seeks to determine the causal factors for the communicative difficulties noted in the descriptive analysis. It is at this level of analysis that the question of the differentiation between a language or cultural difference versus an intrinsic language-learning impairment is addressed. Also, here the evaluator takes the role of an advocate for the LEP student.

When conducting explanatory analysis, the evaluator starts with the belief that the communicative problems documented during descriptive analysis are actually due to factors other than an intrinsic language-learning disorder. Based on this orientation, the evaluator attempts to determine causality based on other factors such as cultural differences, first-language interference, the unreasonable expectations of others and the like. If extraneous causal variables are not indicated, then the evaluator must look more closely at the actual linguistic structure of the data to determine difficulty. For example, when assessing an LEP student, the problems noted in English will also be noted in the first language if there is a true language-learning difficulty. Additionally, there will typically be some underlying systematicity to the presenting problems, which will indicate a true intrinsic language-learning impairment. At the explanatory level, the underlying causes for the observed and described difficulties are explained and the most appropriate assistive or remedial measures are recommended.

Strong description using this bilevel analysis based on real and objective indices of communicative difficulty will enable the evaluator to function simultaneously as both the assessment agent for the schools and as the advocate for the LEP student, thereby ensuring (if needed) the most appropriate placement available.

Communicative-Referencing

When conducting descriptive analysis, it is necessary to have a basis for comparison to help determine the student's proficiency. That is, some guideline is needed to answer the question, "Is the student a good or poor communicator?" As previously discussed, norm-referencing is not very effective when dealing with communication. The alternative is communicative-referencing (Bloom & Lahey, 1978). This is a version of criterion-referencing that focuses on general communicative behaviors without making reference to norms or specific standards of performance. The researcher determines through a combination of observation, empirical documentation, and intuitive judgment as a native speaker which behaviors exhibited by communicators make for successful or unsuccessful communication. Once the behaviors are determined and can be used reliably and accurately to predict success in communication, these behaviors can serve as indices for language proficiency. The advantage of communicative-referencing as a basis for comparison is that the behaviors analyzed are actual behaviors that are important to success in the real world. This method results in a frame of reference that may serve as a comparison at least equal to that of normative-referenced description. It has other advantages, however, in that it is more adaptable to language variation, real communicative activities, and clinical planning and management while still being accountable. As discussed by Meehl (1954), as long as any descriptive methodology can be proven effective actuarially, accountability need not be based on norm-referencing.

Natural Observation

Finally, communicative assessment should be accomplished in natural-istic settings where true communicative performance is occurring and is influenced by contextual factors rather than in an artificial situation set up to meet the requirements of standardization. Natural observation is consistent with the theoretical model proposed by Oller and Damico (see Chapter Three) and with the emphasis on relativism in behavior analysis (Muma, 1978). To view language and communication as they function in real situations, it is also necessary to view language in its three major manifestations: use of communication in (1) oral monologic, (2) oral dialogic, and (3) contextually constrained situations. These three manifestations of communicative performance are actually general cate-gories reflecting the different uses of communication for different pur-poses and in different situations (Canale 1983; Luria, 1981).

Oral Monologic Communication. This manifestation refers to com-munication that is preplanned to some extent. During these communica-tive situations, the speaker has had time to prepare some type of planned discourse (Ochs, 1977) or the discourse is preplanned through some type of external framework (e.g., visual cues during picture de-scription or a previously narrated story). Due to this preplanning, the speaker can present information in a consistent and logically structured form and highlight the most significant information without the listener forcing a change in the speaker's plan of meaning transmission. This type of communication is important for the relating of information and is a necessary skill in academics (Cummins, 1983; 1984; Westby, 1985). Examples of this type of communication are picture description (where the pictures serve as an external framework for planning, story telling, or narration) where the student has some opportunity to preplan and has certain schemas to guide the story (Applebee, 1978; Peterson & McCabe, 1983), and other forms of transactional speech (Brown, Ander-son, Shillcock, & Yule, 1984).

Oral Dialogic Communication. This manifestation may occur in the form of answers to questions or in the form of conversational discourse. Oral dialogic communication is different from the oral monologic mani-festation in several ways. First, this communication is unplanned. That is, utterances do not continually originate with an individual's ready-made internal motive, intention, or thought. Rather, the individual is responding to the motivations, intentions, or reactions of the other participant in the conversational dyad. Consequently, continual preplanning of content, structure, or purposes cannot occur. The individual must be ready to modify communication according to the flow of the situation and the contextual factors. Second, since there is greater context-embedding in face-to-face interaction, there is typically more shared knowledge, less need for explicit linguistic elaboration, and more opportunity for feedback and repair during communication (Cummins, 1983). The major example of oral dialogic communication is conversational discourse.

Contextually constrained Communication. The third major manifestation encompasses communication that is rigidly constrained either by the context or by the interactional format. In this manifestation, communication may be set in a context that requires strict adherence to a certain set of rules and expectations that are not applied in the other two manifestations. For example, in the classroom there are certain distinct interactional patterns between the teacher and the students that are very different from conversational discourse. To be a proficient communicator in the classroom, the student must adhere to these rules of academic or school discourse (Mehan, 1979; Ripich & Spinelli, 1985; Wilkinson, 1982). Similar contextual constraints may be seen in game playing (Terrell, 1985), discussion group interactions, reading group participation, and job interviews.

Although there is some overlap between these three manifestations, this tripartite division does allow for more in-depth description and does reflect clinical experience. By using this division, assessment becomes a more organized and descriptive process for use in naturalistic settings. The evaluator is able to consider different language styles, registers, and usages. To this extent, this tripartite division fits well with initial dichotomy between basic interpersonal communicative skills and cognitive/academic language proficiency skills described by Cummins (1980) and his subsequent refinement into a set of continua (Cummins, 1983), Westby's division along an oral-literate continuum (Westby, 1985), and numerous other divisions of language structure and usage (Bruner, 1975; Donaldson, 1978; Luria, 1981) that are reflected in clinical experience. This division allows for careful analysis of an individual's communicative strengths and weaknesses in these manifestations. Individuals may exhibit difficulties in all three manifestations, in any one separately, or in any combination of the three. Further, if there are specific strengths and weaknesses according to contextual or usage parameters, this division will aid in their description. Consequently, the assessment process becomes more flexible and allows for performance variation.

CLINICAL APPLICATION OF THE DESCRIPTIVE APPROACH

Just as with the current modular approach, the descriptive approach and its synergistic perspective structure the assessment process and the assessment procedures used in communicative evaluation.

Assessment Process

The synergistic perspective directs the assessment process differently from the modular perspective. Rather than attempting to break communicative behavior into subcomponents or discrete points through the use of artificial testing procedures, communication is assessed as it functions holistically in its various manifestations and within naturalistic contexts. Once the evaluator receives the referral and carefully operationalizes the concerns of the referral source, the evaluation is initiated. As illustrated in Figure 5-2, this first requires conducting a *descriptive analysis:* That is, the evaluator asks, "In the present domain of interest, how proficient a communicator is this individual?" To determine this, the evaluator chooses communicative assessment procedures that will allow the description of communication as its functions in the three previously detailed manifestations: oral monological language use, oral dialogic language use, and the use of contextually constrained communication. These assessment procedures typically focus on all aspects of communicative effectiveness (language and speech) together and allow for a determination of communicative proficiency based on the three criteria of effectiveness, fluency, and appropriateness. Once this level of descriptive analysis is completed, the evaluator decides whether there is a com-

Fig. 5-2. Descriptive Assessment Process

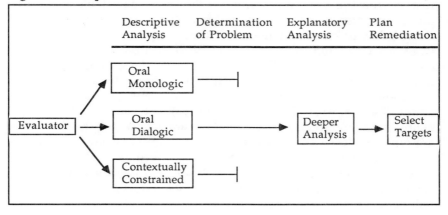

munication *difficulty* in one or more of the manifestations. This is determined by the presence of "problematic behaviors," which are identified by the descriptive assessment procedures. If no difficulties are noted, then the assessment process is completed and the evaluator can describe the individual's strengths and pattern of communication as evidence of communicative proficiency. If difficulties are noted in one or more of the manifestations, however, then the second type of analysis, explanatory analysis, is conducted.

At the explanatory level of analysis, the evaluator examines the difficulties noted during the descriptive analysis stage and attempts to determine *why* the individual had these particular difficulties in the manifestation(s) under scrutiny. Initially, extraneous variables are examined as potential explanations for these problematic behaviors (e.g., second-language acquisition phenomena or significant cultural differences). If no extraneous explanatory factors are noted, then a more systematic analysis of the actual linguistic data is initiated (see section titled "Explanatory Analysis Procedures"). Based on this analysis, the evaluator determines the underlying causes of the problematic behaviors identified during the descriptive analysis phase and can determine if a true intrinsic language-learning disorder exists. With this information, appropriate remediational strategies can be recommended.

In summary, the assessment process uses naturalistic and communicative-referenced descriptive procedures to analyze communication in a pragmatic fashion and then applies a bilevel analysis in the three communicative manifestations to differentiate between a language or cultural difference versus a language-learning disorder. This assessment process, therefore, is consistent with the synergistic perspective.

Descriptive Analysis Procedures

Just as with the assessment process, the assessment tools and procedures must also be more descriptive and able to analyze true communicative behavior in real situations to fit the synergistic perspective. Particularly since the mid-1970s, numerous tools and procedures have been developed to accomplish these objectives. At the descriptive analysis level, these procedures address the question of an individual's language proficiency in the domain of focus. In most situations in the United States, Canada, Australia, and Great Britain, the domain of focus is the mainstream English-language school system. Consequently, these tools are typically designed to look at proficiency in this context. It follows, therefore, that the tools and procedures described for descriptive analysis *will be culturally and linguistically biased toward the mainstream English-speaking culture.* It is during the explanatory analysis phase that this bias will be taken into account.

Oral Monologic Assessment. The assessment activities considered under this manifestation may be divided into three different types. Brown, Anderson, Shillcock, and Yule (1984) classified such transactional tasks according to an ascending scale of difficulty:

1. Static tasks: those requiring the speaker to describe static relationships among objects (e.g., a speaker instructing a hearer to follow routine directions)
2. Dynamic tasks: those involving dynamic relationships among people or objects, where the described entities change over time or location (e.g., narratives)
3. Abstract tasks: those requiring the communication of abstract notions (e.g., preplanned arguing or justification)

In keeping with this classification, the oral monologic assessment procedures will be discussed according to this division.

In a detailed study conducted for the Scottish Education Department, Brown and her colleagues (Brown, Anderson, Shillcock, & Yule, 1984) designed several *static* activities for descriptive assessment purposes. These tasks (the diagram-drawing task, the pegboard task, the playing cards task, and the object assembly task) are designed to allow for the manipulation of various dimensions (e.g., the number of entities included in a diagram) that act to increase or decrease the difficulty of the tasks. Consistent with the functional characteristic, these procedures are scored according to the ability of the student to transfer information (e.g., the entities in a diagram, their color and size, and their location) to a hearer and less emphasis is placed on the actual form of the information transfer. Although they were used for 14- to 16-year-olds, the tasks and their scoring protocols may be adapted for different age levels.

The majority of oral monologic assessment procedures developed and described focus on the *dynamic* tasks (i.e., narration and story telling). Effective procedures range from screening approaches involving story-reformulation tasks (Chappell 1980; Culatta, Page, & Ellis, 1983; Hamayan, Kwiat, & Perlman, 1985) to much more elaborate analyses. Westby & colleagues (1982; 1985; Westby, Van Dongen, & Maggart, 1989), Garnett (1986), Hedberg and Stoel-Gammon (1986), and Roth (1986) have demonstrated the clinical effectiveness of various types of analyses. Based on the work of Applebee (1978), for example, a narrative organizational analysis can be conducted that provides developmental stages according to the student's ability to produce a coherent text by linking concepts (chaining) to the central theme or topic of the story (centering). This approach enables the description of narratives according to six basic types of organization: heaps, sequences, primitive narrative, unfocused chain, focused chain, and narrative. Hedberg and Stoel-Gammon (1986) have suggested that this narrative level analysis procedure is particularly effective with students exhibiting limited verbal abilities.

A more elaborate type of descriptive narrative assessment involves the use of "story grammar" analyses (Peterson & McCabe, 1983; Stein & Glenn, 1979). This analysis approach describes the student's narrative performance according to a set of syntactic and semantic relation rules that operate to structure one's ability to transmit information in this dynamic activity. Although these analyses are typically more complex and time-consuming than a narrative level analysis, they are effective in describing the global organization of narratives, particularly at the upper elementary school and adolescent levels (Hedberg & Stoel-Gammon, 1986; Roth, 1986). In a forthcoming manual on narrative assessment, Westby (unpublished manuscript) provides a detailed and practical set of procedures for story grammar analysis including definitions, developmental data, analysis forms, optional analyses, and clinical procedures for implementing data collection.

In addition to narrative level analysis and story grammar analysis, several other methods are available to describe dynamic monologic tasks. Brown and her colleagues (1984) focused on four criteria that allowed them to develop a reliable and effective analysis procedure. As a result of their research, their scoring protocol focuses on referential explicitness, clarity in marking temporal shifts, clarity in marking locational shifts, and informational content. With a different focus, Merritt and Liles (1987) stressed both story generation and comprehension abilities by recommending several episode analysis approaches, responses to factual information from the stories, and responses to story grammar questions. Norris provides another perspective (1985; Norris & Bruning, 1988): She uses a number of problematic behaviors (e.g., hesitation phenomena, referential explicitness) and measures of cohesive unity and coherence as indices for potential difficulty. Finally, Johnston (1982) has also provided a practical application of narrative analysis for use in descriptive assessment and focuses on four different perspectives by using five clinically oriented questions:

1. Does the speaker's performance follow the typical story grammar model, including both a setting and a coherent episode structure?
2. How maturely is the narrative organized?
3. What does the narrative reveal about the narrator's knowledge of events and expectations about event sequences?
4. What linguistic means are used to create a cohesive discourse unit?
5. How sensitive is the narrator to the needs of the listeners?

By working through these questions and applying specific analysis techniques, the evaluator can produce a detailed description of a student's oral monologic communication.

Descriptive assessment of *abstract* tasks can also be accomplished. Brown and her colleagues (1984) have designed an opinion-expressing activity to obtain student-initiated talk that expresses and justifies an opinion and that can be scored against a common set of criteria. Scoring is more functional and less reliant on "proper" grammatical form. Based on their work, there seem to be five different types of responses that might be expected and may be scored accordingly. The least adequate performance is failure to produce a reply in response to the first opinion-seeking question. The next least adequate response involves description of the stimulus material rather than expressing an opinion. The scoring criteria then proceeds to providing an opinion but giving no reason and giving no alternative argument; expressing an opinion and giving a rationale but no alterative; and, finally, expressing an opinion with both a rationale and providing an alternative argument. Although this procedure has not been extensively studied, it appears to have potential for the assessment of abstract monologic communication.

Oral Dialogic Assessment. There are a number of procedures available to assess this communicative manifestation. Given the emphasis on conversation in language assessment, this is not surprising. For over a decade, speech-language pathologists have been recommending oral dialogic assessment procedures that are not highly standardized or norm-referenced (Holland & Forbes, 1986; Leonard, Prutting, Perozzi, & Berkley, 1978; Leonard & Weiss, 1983; Lund & Duchan, 1983; Muma, 1978; Rees, 1979). These procedures involve the description of behaviors that are necessary for effective, fluent, and appropriate meaning transmission in conversation. They may be classified according to the data collection procedures that they use (e.g., language sampling, rating scales and protocols, and direct observation). For organizational purposes, the procedures will be described according to this division.

The first major division involves the use of *language sampling* procedures: That is, the targeted student's conversation is audio-recorded, transcribed, and then analyzed. A number of analysis procedures are available that fit the focus of functional aspects of communication. Loban (1976), for example, emphasizes dimensions of clarity of expression, fluency, command of lexical expression, and comprehension. Blank and Franklin (1980) have developed an appropriateness scale to analyze spontaneous language samples; Larson and McKinley (1987) have structured an *Adolescent Conversational Analysis* that focuses on the role of the listener in conversation and the role of the speaker. This particular analysis includes language features, paralanguage features, communicative functions, and verbal and nonverbal rules.

Another language sample procedure that is effective in determining oral dialogic proficiency is *Clinical Discourse Analysis* (Damico, 1985a). This descriptive analysis tool employs a set of 17 communicative-referenced behaviors and the theoretical framework of H.P. Grice's Cooperative Principle (1975) to determine a speaker's conversational proficiency. For illustrative purposes, the 17 behaviors are listed, defined, and classified within the Gricean framework:

QUANTITY CATEGORY

1. **Failure to provide significant information to the listener:** The speaker does not provide the amount or type of information needed by the listener to achieve comprehension.
2. **The use of nonspecific vocabulary:** Indexical or deictic terms such as pronouns are used in a way that leaves the referent unspecified from the listener's point of view. The speaker tends to use terms such as *this, it, stuff, thing,* and *there,* when the listener has no clue about the point of reference.
3. **Informational redundancy:** This involves the continued and inappropriate fixation on a proposition. The speaker will continue to stress a point or relate a fact even when the listener has acknowledged its reception.
4. **Need for repetition:** Repetition is required prior to any indication of comprehension despite the fact that the material is not apparently difficult.

QUALITY CATEGORY

5. **Message inaccuracy:** An attempted communication involves the relating of inaccurate information.

RELATION CATEGORY

6. **Poor topic maintenance:** The speaker makes a sudden, inappropriate change in the topic without providing transitional cues to the listener, which usually results in confusion.
7. **Inappropriate response:** The individual's response indicates radically unpredictable interpretation of meaning. It is as

though the individual were operating on an independent discourse agenda. The result is that the contribution does not further the conversation.

8. **Failure to ask relevant questions:** The individual does not seek clarification of information that is unclear.

9. **Situational inappropriateness:** This behavior tends to account for a generalized lack of relevance. The speaker's utterance is not only irrelevant to the discourse or the question asked, but it also may occur in an inappropriate social or interactional situation.

10. **Inappropriate speech style:** The speaker does not change the structural, lexical, or prosodic form of the utterance according to the needs of the listeners or the constraints of the situation. This may involve dialectal variation.

MANNER CATEGORY

11. **Linguistic nonfluency:** Speech is disrupted by frequent repetitions, pauses, or other hesitation devices. It is the frequency of the occurrence that is the distinguishing factor.

12. **Revision:** The speaker seems to come to dead ends in a maze, as if starting off in a certain direction, then coming back to a starting point and beginning anew after each attempt. There are false starts and self-interruptions.

13. **Delays before responding:** Communicative exchanges initiated by others are followed by pauses of inordinate length (more than 2 seconds) at turn-switching points.

14. **Failure to structure discourse:** Due to poor content organization, the discourse is confusing even though all the necessary propositional content is present.

15. **Turn-taking difficulty:** The participant in the conversational interaction does not attend to the cues necessary for the appropriate exchange of conversational turns. This results in one of two possible outcomes. First, the individual does not allow others to add information so there are interruptions or consistent and inappropriate bids for the turn. Second, the individual does not read the switching cues appropriately and does not continue the interaction by picking up the turn as expected.

16. **Gaze inefficiency:** The individual's use of eye contact is inappropriate to the context (it is inconsistent or absent).

17. **Inappropriate intonational contour:** The speaker's ability to

embellish or "color" meaning through the use of linguistic suprasegmentals (i.e., pitch levels, vocal intensity, and other inflectional contours) is poor.

Research has indicated that these behaviors are effective in identifying students with communicative difficulty (Damico & Oller, 1980; Damico, Oller, & Storey, 1983). When asking the question, "Is this individual a proficient communicator in the mainstream context?" the frequent occurrence of one or more of these behaviors necessitates a negative response.

The second division of descriptive oral dialogic assessment procedures are those using *rating scales or protocols*. These procedures allow the evaluator to observe the student during conversational interactions and then to rate or describe individual aspects of the student's behavior according to a set of reliable and valid indices of communicative difficulty. For example, Norris (1989) has developed a very extensive profile system for young children. This tool, *Systematic Assessment of Early Communicative Development*, is designed to describe communicative development by examining the interrelated functioning of the cognitive, social, and semiotic domains. Rather than using only communicative-referenced behaviors with this younger age range, Norris has merged these behaviors with developmental data to create a profile system with nine different components that is consistent with the synergistic perspective. Bretherton, Synder, and colleagues (Bretherton & Beeghly, 1982; Bretherton, McNew, Synder, & Bates, 1983; Synder, Bates, & Bretherton, 1981) have also developed a descriptive procedure for preschool children. This tool is an interview protocol to be used with the parents or caretakers of the preschooler, and it has a demonstrated concurrent validity with oral language sampling data.

There are a number of rating scales and protocols available for school-age speakers. Simon (1979) has suggested a "functional-pragmatic approach" that focuses on communicative proficiency by identifying features of competence and incompetence in the three communicative domains of form, function, and style. This procedure is very effective in determining proficiency from the mainstream perspective. Damico and Oller (1985) have modified some of their earlier work to create a rating scale screening instrument that is also effective with school-age speakers. This tool, *Spotting Language Problems* (SLP), uses seven of the behaviors previously described under *Clinical Discourse Analysis* to screen students for communicative difficulties. SLP has demonstrated strong reliability and validity with both monolingual English and bilingual populations (Bishop, 1988; Damico & Oller, 1985).

Several other rating scales or protocol procedures have been used successfully with LEP students. The *Spanish Language Assessment Procedures: A Communication Skills Inventory* (Mattes, 1985) is designed to focus on descriptive assessment using natural observation and some criterion-referenced behaviors. This tool provides information on both structural and functional aspects of communication. Mattes and Omark (1984) have also provided a shorter observational protocol that uses 20 communicative behaviors. This tool, *Bilingual Oral Language Development* (BOLD), is effective for commenting on the functional dimension of oral dialogic communication. Similarly, Cheng (1987) has designed several protocols involving both verbal and nonverbal behaviors that are helpful in the descriptive assessment of Asian LEP students.

The descriptive communicative protocol most widely known and used at present, however, is the *Pragmatic Protocol* (Prutting & Kirchner, 1983, 1987). This tool has been found to be very reliable and valid (Duncan & Perozzi, 1987; Prutting & Kirchner, 1987) and has been applied successfully in differentiating between language disorders versus language differences (Ferrer & Damico, 1988).

The final division of oral dialogic tools involves *direct and on-line observation*. Although this data collection approach is still relatively new in the assessment of communicative ability, it holds promise. These procedures involve the direct observation of a student's communicative interaction and the real-time and immediate coding of the communicative behaviors observed. Consequently, these procedures can provide detailed and objective data on the speaker's performance rather than just a final judgment of sufficient/insufficient or appropriate/inappropriate communicative performance.

Three direct observational approaches are currently available. The first is the *Environmental Communication Profile* (Calvert & Murray, 1985). This technique is designed to analyze oral dialogic interactions in school settings. It focuses on three aspects of these interactions: the function of the speaker's communicative act, the type of communicative act, and the antecedent environmental event that "cues" the interaction. Using 10-minute samples taken over a period of days, descriptions are made and can be evaluated to determine effectiveness of the interactions. This allows for identification of problem areas in communicative interaction; the procedure has strong reliability indices.

The second direct observational tool is the *Social Interactive Coding System* (SICS). This tool was designed by Rice, Sell, and Hadley (in press) to describe the speaker's verbal interactive status (i.e., initiation, repetition, verbal and nonverbal responses, ignoring, and the language used) in conjunction with the setting, the conversational partner, and the activities in which the speaker is engaged. This tool requires a 20-minute observational period during which the evaluator observes and codes freeplay for 5 minutes and then takes a 5-minute break to fill in any codes that might have been missed. This "5 minutes on, 5 minutes off" format is followed for four consecutive cycles until the 20 minutes of direct observation is accomplished.

Although this procedure was developed for use with preschool children, it has direct application for the description of oral dialogic behavior in the school-age population and the observation sheet designed for this tool has the advantage of highlighting code-switching behavior. When dealing with LEP populations, this tool appears especially promising. Current data suggest that *SICS* has strong validity and reliability indices.

The third direct observational procedure is *Systematic Observation of Communicative Interaction* (SOCI) (Damico, 1985b). This tool was designed to employ a balanced set of low-inference and high-inference items to achieve a reliable coding of illocutionary acts, verbal and nonverbal problematic behaviors, and a determination of the appropriateness of the student's communicative interaction. This tool uses the problematic verbal behaviors described in *Clinical Discourse Analysis* and a set of problematic nonverbal behaviors and illocutionary acts. Once trained to identify and code the behaviors, the evaluator observes the student for 12 minutes and codes the interactions observed each 10 seconds. This yields 72 coded cells of data per observation. The evaluator observes the student from four to seven times, which allows for sufficient data to make representative descriptions of behavior.

Research has indicated that this tool can be applied with high reliability (Damico, 1985b). Two reliability studies have been conducted and have demonstrated both strong interobserver reliability and temporal reliability of this tool. SOCI has also been shown to possess strong discriminant validity and concurrent validity indices. It should be noted that this tool was designed for the school-age student and older; consequently, it is not appropriate for preschool children.

Contextually Constrained Assessment. This manifestation of communication is diverse due to the large number of potential contexts that are constrained for communicative purposes. While the other two manifestations are generic (e.g., basic conversational skills hold in many contexts), this manifestation presents many contextually unique skills and rules that could be assessed. Since the focus here is on school-related activities, however, this discussion focuses on contexts within the academic setting and on oral communicative interactions. Discussions of other types of academically oriented assessment are located in Chapters Six and Seven.

The most important communicative aspects under this manifestation involve the student's ability to interact according to the rules of school discourse, or "teacher talk." Numerous sets of behaviors have been detailed to comment on this contextually constrained interaction. These communicative-referenced behaviors range from a few behaviors for screening purposes (Archer & Edward, 1982) to much more comprehensive lists (Bassett, Whittington, & Staton-Spicer, 1978). Many of the behaviors described in research situations have been modified into lists for easy clinical use. Nelson (1985), for example, provides a set of behaviors that can be used to document poor communicative proficiency in the classroom environment. Similarly, the clinical question formats of Vetter (1982) and Creaghead and Tattershall (1985) are helpful in orienting the evaluation toward communicative behaviors necessary for classroom interaction.

In addition to evaluating general classroom discourse, there are descriptive assessment procedures that focus on other communicative aspects in this constrained contextual setting. Calfee and Sutter-Baldwin (1982), for example, assess discussion group settings and the skills needed in this unique context whereas Larson and McKinley (1987) have designed a *Curriculum Analysis Form*, which allows for analysis of the student's comprehension, attitudes in the classroom, utilization of textbooks, and understanding of test-taking behaviors.

Perhaps the most comprehensive discussion of classroom communicative abilities and suggestions for descriptive analysis is the *Classroom Communication Screening Procedure for Early Adolescents* (CCSPEA) (Simon, 1989). This manual is designed to identify students with potential classroom-communication difficulties based on a combination of criterion-referenced and communicative-referenced behaviors. Aimed particularly at students making the transition from elementary school to secondary school, the CCSPEA focuses on the wide range of communicative behaviors needed to understand and complete assignments, to comprehend the language of the classroom, and to formulate and reason during classroom discussions and assignments. This tool may be used as a group-screening procedure and has specific recommendations for further descriptive evaluation if needed.

Although they are less naturalistic, there are two other assessment approaches that fit effectively under this communicative manifestation. The first involves use of "cloze techniques." In cloze techniques, a reading passage or an oral text is supplied to the student with every nth word deleted (e.g., every seventh word). The student is expected to "fill in" these blanks by using the surrounding linguistic context to supply meaning. To perform this task, it is reasoned that the student must use an internalized system of grammatical and lexical knowledge to restore meaningful text (Oller, 1979). As discussed by Oller (1979), Hamayan, Kwait, and Perlman (1985) and others (Mattes & Omark, 1984; Streiff, 1978), cloze procedures are pragmatic testing approaches that accurately reflect on the student's underlying language proficiency. As demonstrated by Laesch and van Kleeck (1987), cloze techniques are effective measures within this communicative manifestation. In a study comparing a cloze procedure with more discrete point language tests, these researchers demonstrated significant correlations between their cloze procedure and the *California Test of Basic Skills*. The cloze procedure was more effective in measuring the language needed in academic tasks, and it discriminated between subjects with varying degrees of proficiency.

The second approach involves a relatively new assessment procedure in speech-language pathology that is similar to the the concept of dynamic assessment (Feuerstein, 1979). That is, the targeted students are provided with a reasonable opportunity to learn an invented language rule or language behavior and are evaluated according to their ability to efficiently and effectively learn the rule. Perozzi (1985) has reported a variation on this idea in a pilot study to determine the learning potential for a group of bilingual language-handicapped students and determined that approach held promise. Connell (1986) more directly applied the idea to an assessment format and demonstrated the potential of this approach with monolingual language-disordered students. More recently, Roseberry and Connell (1988) have applied this technique to the differentiation between language different versus language disordered Spanish-speaking students. By teaching an invented English morphological rule and analyzing subject responses to the generalization phase of the task, they found significant differences between LEP students with and without specific language impairment. Although this approach is still being developed, it appears to hold great potential, especially within this communicative manifestation.

The tools listed and discussed under the heading of "Descriptive Analysis Procedures" are based on the communicative proficiency of the LEP student *within the mainstream context*. These tools are effective in identifying communicative difficulties in the three manifestations but are not sufficient by themselves to determine whether or not an individual has a communication or language disorder. To make that determination, the second stage of the bilevel analysis must be taken: explanatory analysis.

Explanatory Analysis Procedures

Once a student is found to have communication difficulties at the descriptive level, the evaluator initiates this level of analysis. The question of interest at this point is, *"Why* do we see the problematic behaviors which identified the student as a poor communicator during descriptive analysis?" To answer this question, the evaluator must determine whether the problematic behaviors are due to factors extrinsic to the student or due to an intrinsic learning deficit. The true language-learning disabled student will have intrinsic explanatory factors.

To conduct an explanatory analysis of a LEP student, the evaluator must have more information on the student than just the data from the descriptive analysis procedures. Data collection is one essential component of explanatory analysis. Additionally, once the data is available, the evaluator must know what questions to ask in order to conduct the explanatory analysis. This is the second essential component. These two components will be discussed separately. In practice, of course, they are usually simultaneous activities.

Data Collection Component. To answer the questions necessary for explanatory analysis of the previously identified problematic behaviors, the evaluator must know something of the LEP student's history, environment, and current social, familial, and academic circumstances. This requires collecting more data on the student in one of several ways. First, the evaluator might conduct a case history interview or a set of prepared questions can be answered by reliable sources familiar with the student (e.g., a parent or guardian, an older sibling, a community social worker, a priest or minister). Chapters Four, Six, and Seven of this book have excellent lists of questions that might be used for this purpose. Additionally, Cheng (1987), Mattes and Omark (1985), Gallagher (1983), and Adler and Birdsong (1983) have all designed lists or questionnaires that are effective for collecting the essential background information.

A second type of data collection procedure involves the evaluation of the student's interactional environments. Two tools are available for this purpose. Peck (1989) has created a procedure for describing the student's interactional environments at the dyadic level, the situational level, and the contextual level. Ortiz (1988) has developed a questionnaire for evaluating the student's educational context. This questionnaire consists of 25 questions that revolve around the issues of cultural pluralism, parent participation, shared governance, academically rich programs, skilled use and training of teachers, personal attention to students, and student responsibility for student affairs. This tool is especially beneficial in commenting on the presence or absence of an empowering environment. Although it is designed in a yes/no format, the tool can be used to guide more detailed description.

A third data collection type emphasizes the importance of the student's family. Although there are numerous observational scales and protocols designed to describe this special environment, the work of Deal, Trivette, and Dunst (1988) is particularly relevant. These researchers have developed a number of scales that comment on specific aspects of family functioning. Some of their work is designed to take cultural and socioconomic differences into account.

Finally, there are a number of evaluators who have advocated the use of qualitative description to collect the data necessary for explanatory analysis (Omark, 1981a). Using modified ethnographic techniques that help ensure a triangulation of the data base and a detailed description of the student in numerous interactional contexts, these researchers have provided some practical assessment ideas. Of particular interest is the work of Bauman (1971) and Ripich and Spinelli (1985); they have proposed assessment frameworks that embrace some ethnographic principles. Currently, the most complete ethnography of language assessment is the work of Kayser (1987) who described three Mexican-American students labelled as language disordered. She has proposed some communicative assessment procedures that do make use of ethnographic techniques.

Once the data necessary for the explanatory analysis is collected, the evaluator begins analyzing the previously described problematic behaviors from the descriptive analysis procedures and looks for explanations. As previously discussed, the evaluator should begin with the assumption that the documented problematic behaviors are due to extrinsic factors until these possibilities are reasonably eliminated. When dealing with the assessment of LEP students, this helps prevent bias against these students. The explanatory analysis proceeds with the evaluator asking a series of questions.

Questions Applied to Explanatory Analysis. In analyzing the problematic behaviors revealed during descriptive analysis, the evaluator should apply two general sets of questions. First, regarding extrinsic explanation:

1. Are there any overt variables that immediately explain the communicative difficulties in English? Among the potential considerations:
   a. Is the student a monolingual speaker of another language with limited exposure to English?
   b. Are the documented problematic behaviors occurring at a frequency level that would be considered within normal limits or in random variation?
   c. Were there any procedural mistakes in the descriptive analysis phase that accounts for the problematic behaviors?

d. Is there an indication of extreme test anxiety during the observational assessment in one context but not in subsequent ones?

e. Is there significant performance inconsistency between different contexts within the targeted manifestation?

2. Does the student exhibit the same types of problematic behaviors in the first language as in English?

This is a critical question. The advantage of the descriptive assessment procedures based on functional aspects of communication is that they can be more easily translated into the student's first language and applied according to the structural characterisitics of that language. For example, the frequent use of nonspecific vocabulary might be coded differently in Hmong, but the underlying functional problem is one that can still occur. The native speaker can be trained to identify the functional concept according to the structural characteristics unique to the targeted language. If the same types of problems are not noted in the student's first language as in English, then there is no intrinsic language or communicative impairment (see Chapter Three). It is important, therefore, that tools be designed in other languages to fit within the descriptive assessment model, preferrably to match those developed in English. As previously discussed, this type of functional, rather than structural, translation will be more effective and will result in more valid assessment tools. The work of Ortiz and her colleagues (Ortiz & Maldonado-Colon, 1986; Ortiz & Wilkinson, 1987), Bishop (1988), and Damico and Oller (1985) hold promise in this regard.

3. Is there evidence that the problematic behaviors noted in English can be explained according to normal second-language acquisition or dialectal phenomena?

If the English difficulties can be explained by interference factors between the first language or dialect and English, or because of interlanguage or rule fossilization, or code-switching behavior, then the student is likely a normal language learner in the process of acquiring English as a second language (see Chapter Two). There are several excellent demonstrations of how the evaluator can analyze the English data for these phenomena. Wolfram (1985) has described this procedure in the case of the phonologic system and Leonard and Weiss (1983), Cheng (1987) and others (Corder, 1981; Wiener & Lewnau, 1982) provide some demonstration of grammatical comparisons. One particularly interesting approach has been described by Terrell, Arensberg, and Rosa (1986). These evaluators compared the surface structural productions of a child referred for language problems with the surface forms produced by the student's parent. This "Parent-Child Comparative Analysis" is consistent with the focus on extrinsic explanations for descriptive data and holds great promise.

Over the last several years, numerous researchers have provided first-language acquisition and language usage data in various languages that can be helpful in making cross-linguistic comparisons. In Spanish, Anderson and Connell (1987) have provided data on personal pronoun development. Savich, Matsuda, and Garcia (1986) have discussed pragmatic development. Maez (1985), Canfield (1981), Eblen (1982), and others (Bailey & Allen, 1983; Cancel, 1976; Dato, 1983; Hall-Olsen & Ocampo, 1983; Iglesias, Cohen, & Gutierrez-Clellen, 1985) have conducted studies in phonology. Data have also been provided in Mandarin (Cheng, 1987; Wang, Phillips, Kuo, & Chen, 1984; Wang, Phillips, Kuo, & Hwang; 1984); French (McNutt, Doehring, Lanoix, Van Engelen, Tourigny, Bergeron, & Dudley, 1987); and dialectal English (Cole & Taylor, 1987; Haynes & Moran, 1987).

4. Is there any evidence that the problematic behaviors noted in English can be explained according to cross-cultural interference or related cultural phenomena?

As detailed in Chapter Four, there are numerous ways that cross-cultural interference can result in problematic behaviors in all three manifestations of communication. The evaluator should focus on differences due to culture-specific expectations, culture-specific experiences, and culture-specific learning and interactional patterns. Britton and Britton (1981), Tannen (1984), and Varonis and Gass (1985) provide some examples in oral dialogic communication. Cheng (1987), Iglesias (1985), and Philips (1983) discuss classroom and learning-style interferences. Heath (1983; 1986) and Westby (in press) discuss cultural differences in narratives.

5. Is there any evidence that the problematic behaviors noted in English can be explained according to any bias effect that was in operation before, during, or after the descriptive analysis phase?

Evaluators must consider intentional or unintentional bias when analyzing the data obtained from the descriptive analysis phase. Bias can be noted in several areas: In the classroom, bias on the part of the teacher, aide, or other students can have an effect. Additionally the teaching materials or teaching procedures may reflect bias as may the assessment process itself. The ancillary personnel in the school or the evaluator may be biased, which could affect the referral process, the assessment procedure, the interpretation of results, and the placement decision. Each of these possibilites should be considered. Niklas Miller (1984b) has provided an excellent discussion on this topic and Taylor and Payne (1983) and Adler and Birdsong (1983) give clinically related procedures to address this issue at the explanatory level.

If there are no extrinsic explanations for the data obtained during the descriptive analysis phase of the assessment process, then there must be a greater suspicion that the targeted student does have an intrinsic language-learning impairment. If this is so, the student should exhibit some underlying linguistic systematicity that can account for the majority of the problematic behaviors noted in the descriptive assessment phase. *If the initial five questions cannot explain the problematic behaviors*, then the final question and the analysis needed to answer this question should be conducted.

6. Is there any underlying linguistic systematicity to the problematic behaviors that were noted during the descriptive analysis phase?

This question reflects directly on the issue of intrinsic explanatory factors. To answer this question, the evaluator conducts a modified co-occurring structure analysis (Muma, 1978). This analysis typically requires the collection of communicative data in a form that lends itself to analysis (e.g., language sample or narrative transcriptions, detailed written observations). The evaluator takes only those interactional turns that contain problematic behaviors and tries to determine if these problematic behaviors are the result of some type of difficulty with the syntagmatic and paradigmatic dimensions of language. That is, since the problematic behaviors are only manifestations of a potential language-learning impairment, the evaluator must attempt to determine the underlying linguistic causes. Routine syntactic analysis or other forms of analysis will not demonstrate any systematicity to the data unless the evaluator focuses only on those points where problems occur (the problematic behaviors). By conducting systematic co-occurring analysis of the problematic behaviors, the evaluator can typically account for 70 to 80% of these behaviors on the basis of one or several linguistic operations. The following steps should be conducted:

a. Ensure that no overt factors account for the problematic behaviors.
b. Isolate the turns or utterances that contain the problematic behaviors.
c. Perform a systematic linguistic analysis on these data points looking for consistency in the appearance of problematic behaviors based on syntagmatic and/or paradigmatic factors. Several systematic analyses have been found to be effective when conducting a co-occurring analysis of the problematic behaviors.

In the syntagmatic dimension of language (i.e., the dimension that characterizes the ordered arrangments of phonemes, morphemes, and propositions), there a number of strong tools available (Bloom & Lahey, 1978; Muma, 1978; Miller, 1981). For example, Miller and Chapman (1983) have developed a computerized system for analyzing a number of structural parameters. This tool, *Systematic Analysis of Language Samples*, analyzes structural, lexical, and functional aspects of communication (e.g., turn taking, ratio of speaking to listening, and frequency usage of designated structures), and it has sufficient flexibility to allow for some modification in its analysis program. This enables the evaluator to request additional types of analyses. Another particularly effective procedure is Crystal's grammatical analysis profile system known as the LARSP (1979; 1982; Crystal, Fletcher, & Garman, 1976). Based on the notion of linguistic profiles that are descriptions of "just those features of a person's (or group's) use of language which will enable him to be identified for a specific purpose" (1982:1), this analysis system enables the evaluator to determine if the problematic behaviors are due to an increase in grammatical complexity at the phrasal, clausal, or discourse levels. This analysis system is extensive and enables detailed explanatory analysis. Similarly, the work of Halliday and Hasan (1976) in coherence and cohension, Brown and Yule (1983) on information structure, and Stubbs (1983) on exchange structures may also be used to comment on the syntagmatic dimension.

In the paradigmatic dimension of language (i.e., the dimension that characterizes the ordered categorization, classification and use of the sets of semantically related terms that can occur in the same context), the semantic profiling system known as PRISM (Crystal, 1982) is helpful. This system enables the evaluator to determine if an increase in semantic complexity at the lexical or grammatical levels can account for the problematic behaviors. Other descriptions of the paradigmatic dimension may also be revealing: for example, analysis according to linguistic displacement. As one example, Blank, Rose, and Berlin (1978) have specified four levels of perceptual-language distancing that allow for the systematic analysis of communication into levels of abstraction. Frequently, this classification can reveal systematic expressions of problematic behavior. Another area of analysis is seeking explanation based on the student's level of metalinguistic awareness. As detailed by van Kleeck and colleagues (Schuele & van Kleeck, 1987; van Kleeck, 1984; van Kleeck & Schuele, 1987), a student's ability to understand and comment at a metalinguistic level has significant implications in discourse and in the classroom.

If the evaluator follows the sequence of the questions for explanatory analysis, many of the students will not need a detailed co-occurring linguistic analysis. Their problematic behaviors will be explained by extrinsic variables. Consequently, these students will stand less chance of being misidentified as language impaired when they only exhibit language or cultural differences. Table 5-1 summarizes the procedures and measures used for this bilevel descriptive assessment paradigm.

Table 5-1. Summary of Procedures Used in Descriptive Communicative Assessment of LEP Students

Descriptive analysis
  Oral monologic communication
    Static tasks
      Object description
      Giving directions
    Dynamic tasks
      Story reformulation
      Narrative analysis
    Abstract tasks
      Opinion-expressing
  Oral dialogic communication
    Language sample analysis
    Rating scales and protocols
    Direct and systematic observation
  Contextually constrained communication
    School discourse analysis
    Curriculum analysis
    Cloze techniques
    Modified dynamic assessment
Explanatory analysis
  Data collection
    Case history
    Environmental interactional analysis
    Family interactional analysis
    Ethnographic observation

Table 5-1. *(continued)*
  Application of explanatory questions
    Extrinsic variables
      Problems due to overt explanatory variables?
        Monolingual speaker of language other than English
        Frequency level of occurrence within normal limits
        Procedural mistakes during assessment
        Extreme test anxiety
        Assessment contextual factors
      Does student exhibit problems in both languages?
      Problems due to normal L2 or dialectal phenomena?
      Problems due to cross-cultural interference?
      Problems or interpretation of problems due to bias?
    If these five questions do not explain the problematic behaviors:
    Intrinsic variables
      Is there an underlying linguistic systematicity?
      Syntagmatic analysis
        Bloom and Lahey analysis
        Muma analysis
        SALT
        LARSP
        Coherence and cohesion
        Information structure analysis
        Exchange structure analysis
      Paradigmatic analysis
        PRISM
        Perceptual language distancing
        Metalinguistic analysis

CONCLUSIONS

Progressively over the last several decades, professionals involved in communicative assessment have recognized the problems inherent in the modular approach to language proficiency and its assessment. With the use of the synergistic perspective, however, many of the problems noted earlier vanish. Pragmatic and naturalistic description enable more valid and reliable assessment that is both effective in describing communication problems in the domain of focus and in differentiating between language and cultural differences versus language impairment.

This chapter has reviewed the two approaches and has recommended the synergistic perspective and the descriptive approach. Numerous tools and procedures have been discussed and placed within a descriptive framework. Through the descriptive approach, the evaluator can perform effective assessment activities that account for diversity rather than penalize for it. Consequently evaluators can function as agents of the school system and as advocates of the students that they serve.

Culturally and linguistically diverse students need not be victims of the system of communicative assessment; rather, they can benefit from the testing process and the appropriate remediation that it generates.

REFERENCES

Acevedo, M. A. (1986). Assessment instruments for minorities. In F. H. Bess, B. S. Clark, & H. R. Mitchell (Eds.), *Concerns for minority groups in communication disorders.* (American Speech-Language-Hearing Association Reports 16), (pp. 46–51). Rockville, MD: American Speech-Language-Hearing Association.

Adler, S. (1981). Testing: Considerations in cultural differences. *Seminars in Speech, Language, and Hearing, 2,* 77–90.

Adler, S., & Birdsong, S. (1983). Reliability and validity of standardized testing tools used with poor children. *Topics in Language Disorders, 3,* 76–87.

Allen, D. V., Bliss, L. S., & Timmons, J. (1981). Language evaluation: Science or art? *Journal of Speech and Hearing Disorders, 46,* 66–68.

Anastasi, A. (1976). *Psychological testing* (4th Ed.). New York: MacMillan.

Anderson, R. T., & Connell, P. J. (1987). Personal pronoun development in Spanish-speaking preschoolers. A paper presented at the American Speech-Language-Hearing Association convention. New Orleans, November.

Applebee, A. N. (1978). *The child's concept of story.* Chicago: University of Chicago.

Archer, P., & Edward, J. R. (1982). Predicting school achievement from data on pupils obtained from teachers: Towards a screening device for disadvantaged. *Journal of Educational Psychology, 74,* 761–770.

Arnold, K. S., & Reed, L. (1976). The grammatic closure subtest of the ITPA: A comparative study of black and white children. *Journal of Speech and Hearing Disorders, 41,* 477–486.

Bailey, S. I., & Allen, E. J. (1983). Spanish articulatory development in six-year-old Mexican children. A paper presented at the American Speech-Language-Hearing Association convention. Cincinnati, November.

Bassett, R. E., Whittington, N., & Staton-Spicer, A. (1978). The basics in speaking and listening for high school graduates: What should be assessed? *Communication Education, 27,* 300–307.

Bauman, R. (1971). An ethnographic framework of the investigation of communicative behaviors. *Asha, 13,* 334–340.

Bay Area Bilingual Education League. *Bilingual testing and assessment. Proceedings of Bay Area Bilingual Education League (BABEL) Workshop and Preliminary Findings. Multilingual assessment program.* ERIC Document Reproduction Service No. 065 225 (1969).

Berry, J. (1966). Temne and Eskimo conceptual skills. *International Journal of Psychology, 1,* 207–229.

Bishop, S. (1988). *Identification of language disorders in Vietnamese children.* San Diego: San Diego State University. Unpublished master's thesis.

Blank, M., & Franklin, E. (1980). Dialogue with preschoolers: A cognitively based system of assessment. *Applied Psycholinguistics, 1,* 127–150.

Blank, M., Rose, S., & Berlin, L. (1978). *The language of learning.* New York: Grune & Stratton.

Bloom, A. H. (1981). *The linguistic shaping of thought: A study on the impact of language on thinking in China and the West.* Hillsdale, NJ: Laurence Erlbaum Associates.

Bloom. L., & Lahey, M. (1978). *Language development and language disorders.* New York: J. Wiley & Sons.

Boehm, A. (1971). *Boehm test of basic concepts.* New York: The Psychological Corporation.

Bowerman, M. (1976). Semantic factors in the acquisition of rules for word use and sentence construction. In D. Morehead & R. Morehead (Eds.), *Normal and deficient child language* (pp. 99–180). Baltimore: University Park Press.

Bretherton, I., & Beeghly, M. (1982). Talking about internal states: The acquisition of an explicit theory of mind. *Developmental Psychology, 18,* 906–921.

Bretherton, I., McNew, S., Synder, L., & Bates, E. (1983). Individual differences at 20 months: Analytic and holistic strategies of language acquisition. *Journal of Child Language 10,* 293–320.

Briere, E. (1973). Cross-cultural biases in language testing. In J. W. Oller & J. C. Richards (Eds.), *Focus on the learner: Pragmatic perspectives for the language teacher.* (pp. 214–230). Rowley, MA: Newbury House.

Britton, L. P., & Britton, E. C. (1981). *Cultural traits of Asian students with implications for testing.* Sacramento: California State Department of Education.

Brown, G., Anderson, A., Shillcock, R., & Yule, G. (1984). *Teaching talk: Strategies for production and assessment.* Cambridge: Cambridge University Press.

Brown, G., & Yule, G. (1983). *Discourse analysis.* Cambridge: Cambridge University Press.

Brown, L., & Bryant, B. B. (1984). The why and how of special norms. *Remedial and Special Education, 5,* 52–61.

Bruner, J. S. (1975). Language as an instrument of thought. In A. Davies (Ed.), *Problems of language and learning* (pp. 61–82). London: Heinemann.

Burt, M., Dulay, H., & Hernandez-Chavez, E. (1976). *Bilingual Syntax Measure.* New York: Harcourt, Brace, Jovanovich.

Calfee, R., & Sutter-Baldwin, L. (1982). Oral language assessment through formal discussion. *Topics in Language Disorders, 2,* 45–55.

Calvert, M. B., & Murray, S. L. (1985). Environmental Communication Profile: An assessment procedure. In C. S. Simon (Ed.), *Communication skills and classroom success: Assessment of language-learning disabled students* (pp. 135–165). Austin, TX: PRO-ED.

Canale, M. (1983). From communicative language pedagogy. In J. C. Richards & R. W. Schmidt (Eds.), *Language and communication* (pp. 2–28) London: Longman.

Cancel, C. A. (1976). Lisping in Spanish: A defect or a dialectal trend? *International Journal of Oral Myology, 2,* 94–97.

Canfield, D. L. (1981). *Spanish pronunciation in the Americas.* Chicago: University of Chicago Press.

Carroll, J. B. (1961). Fundamental considerations in testing for English proficiency of foreign students. In *Testing the English proficiency of foreign students* (pp. 31–40). Washington, DC: Center for Applied Linguistics.

Carrow, E. (1974a). Assessment of speech and language in children. In J. McLean, D. Yoder, & R. Schiefelbrusch (Eds.), *Language intervention with the retarded* (pp. 52–88). Baltimore: University Park Press.

Carrow, E. (1974b). *Carrow elicited language inventory.* Boston: Teaching Resources.

Carrow E. (1974c). *Test of auditory comprehension of language–Spanish version*. Hingham, MA: Teaching Resources.

Carrow, E. (1974d). *Austin Spanish articulation test*. Hingham, MA: Teaching Resources.

Carrow-Woolfolk, E. (1985). *Test of auditory comprehension of language-revised*. Allen, TX: DLM Teaching Resources.

Chapman, R. (1981). Exploring children's communicative intents. In J. Miller (Ed.), *Assessing production in children* (pp. 112–136). Baltimore: University Park Press.

Chappell, G. E. (1980). Oral language performance of upper elementary school students obtained via story reformulation. *Language, Speech, and Hearing Services in Schools, 11*, 236–251.

Cheng, L.L. (1987). *Assessing Asian language performance*. Rockville, MD: Aspen.

Chinn, K. (1980). Assessment of culturally diverse children. *Viewpoints in Teaching and Learning, 56*, 50–63.

Cole, L. (1980). Black child language: The development of Black English grammar. A miniseminar presented at the American Speech-Language-Hearing Association convention. Detroit, November.

Cole, N. S. (1981) Bias in Testing. *American Psychologist, 31*, 1067–1077.

Cole, P. A., & Taylor. O. L. (1987). Morphological characteristics of language in learning disabled Black children. A paper presented at the American Speech-Language-Hearing Association Convention. New Orleans, November.

Compton, A., & Kline, M. (1983). *Compton speech and language screening evaluation: Spanish adaptation*. San Francisco: Carousel House.

Condon, E. C. (1975). The cultural context of language testing. In L. Palmer & B. Spolsky (Eds.), *Papers on language testing: 1967–1974* (pp. 204–217). Washington, DC: TESOL.

Connell, P. (1986). Teaching subjecthood to language-disordered children. *Journal of Speech and Hearing Disorders, 29*, 481–492.

Connell, P., & Miles-Zitzer, C. (1982). An analysis of elicited imitation as a language evaluation procedure. *Journal of Speech and Hearing Disorders, 47*, 390–396.

Corder, S. P. (1981). *Error analysis and interlanguage*. Oxford: Oxford University Press.

Crane, B. J. (1976). *Crane oral dominance test, Spanish/English*. Trenton, NJ: Motivational Learning Programs.

Creaghead, N. A., & Tattershall, S. S. (1985). Observation and assessment of classroom pragmatic skills. In C. S. Simon (Ed.), *Communication skills and classroom success: Assessment of language-learning disabled students* (pp. 105–134). Austin, TX: PRO-ED.

Critchlow, D. E. (1974). *Dos Amigos verbal language scales*. San Rafael, CA: Academic Therapy Publications.

Crosland-Real, M. (1978). *Los Niños, a screening test of communicative disorders, English/Spanish*. Downey, CA: Office of Los Angeles County Superintendent of Schools.

Crystal, D. (1979). *Working with LARSP*. New York: Elsevier.

Crystal, D. (1982). *Profiling linguistic disability*. London: Edward Arnold.

Crystal, D. (1987). Towards a "bucket" theory of language disability: taking account of interaction between linguistic levels. *Clinical Linguistics and Phonetics, 1*, 7–22.

Crystal, D., Fletcher, P., & Garman, M. (1976). *The grammatical analysis of language disability*. London: Edward Arnold.

Culatta, B., Page, J., & Ellis, J. (1983). Story telling as a communicative performance screening tool. *Language, Speech, and Hearing Services in Schools, 14,* 66–74.

Cummins, J. P. (1980). The cross-lingual dimensions of language proficiency: Implications for bilingual education and the optimal age question. *TESOL Quarterly, 14,* 175–187.

Cummins, J. P. (1983). Language proficiency and academic achievement. In J. W. Oller, Jr. (Ed.), *Issues in language testing research* (pp. 108–130). Rowley, MA: Newbury House.

Cummins, J. P. (1984). *Bilingualism and special education: Issues in assessment and pedagogy.* Austin, TX: PRO-ED.

Damico, J. S. (1985a). Clinical Discourse Analysis: A functional language assessment technique. In C. S. Simon (Ed.), *Communication skills and classroom success: Assessment of language-learning disabled students* (pp. 165–204). Austin, TX: PRO-ED.

Damico, J. S. (1985b). *The effectiveness of direct observation as a language assessment technique.* Albuquerque, NM: University of New Mexico. Unpublished doctoral dissertation.

Damico, J. S., & Oller, J. W., Jr. (1980). Pragmatic versus morphological/syntactic criteria for language referrals. *Language, Speech, and Hearing Services in Schools, 9,* 85–94.

Damico, J. S., & Oller, J. W., Jr. (1985). *Spotting language problems.* San Diego: Los Amigos Research Associates.

Damico, J. S., Oller, J. W., Jr., & Storey, M. E. (1983). The diagnosis of language disorders in bilingual children: Pragmatic and surface-oriented criteria. *Journal of Speech and Hearing Disorders, 48,* 385–394.

Danhauer, J. L., Crawford, S., & Edgerton, B. J. (1984). English, Spanish and bilingual speakers' performance on a Nonsense Syllable Test (NST) of speech sound discrimination. *Journal of Speech and Hearing Disorders, 49,* 164–168.

Darley, F. L. (1979). *Evaluation of appraisal techniques in speech and language pathology.* Reading, MA: Addison-Wesley.

Dato, D. P. (1983). On universal processes in normal and deviant Spanish phonological development. A paper presented at the American Speech-Language-Hearing Association convention. Cincinnati, November.

Day, E. C., McCollum, P. A., Cieslak, V. A., & Erickson, J. G. (1981). Discrete point language tests of bilinguals: A review of selected tests. In D. R. Omark and J. G. Erickson (Eds.), *The bilingual exceptional child.* (pp. 129–161). Austin, TX: PRO-ED.

Deal, A., Trivette, C., & Dunst, C. (1988). Family Functioning Style Scale. In C. Dunst, C. Trivette, & A. Deal, *Enabling and empowering families: Principles and guidelines for practice* (pp.179–184). Cambridge, MA: Brookline Books.

Deal, V. R., & Rodriguez, V. L. (1987). *Resource Guide to Multicultural Tests and Materials in Communicative Disorders.* Rockville, MD: American Speech-Language-Hearing Association.

DeAvila, E., & Duncan, S. E. (1981). *Language Assessment Scales.* San Rafael, CA: Linguametrics Group.

Dieterich, T. G., Freeman, C., & Crandall, J. S. (1979). A linguistic analysis of some English proficiency tests. *TESOL Quarterly, 13,* 535–550.

Donaldson, M. (1978). *Children's minds.* Glasgow: Collins.

Douglas, D., & Selinker, L. (1985). Principles for language tests within the "discourse domains" theory of interlanguage. *Language Testing, 2,* 205–226.

Duchan, J. (1983). Language processing and geodesic domes. In T. Gallagher &

C. Prutting (Eds.), *Pragmatic assessment and intervention issues in language* (pp. 83–100). Austin, TX: PRO-ED.

Duncan, J. C., & Perozzi, J. A. (1987). Concurrent validity of a pragmatic protocol. *Language, Speech, and Hearing Services in Schools, 18,* 80–85.

Dunn, L. M., & Dunn, L. M. (1982). *Peabody picture vocabulary test.* Circle Pines, MN: American Guidance Service.

Duran, R. P. (1985). Influences of language skills on bilinguals' problem solving. In J. W. Segal, S. F. Chipman, & R. Glaser (Eds.), *Thinking and learning skills: research and open questions,* Vol 2. (pp.187–208). Norwood, NJ: Lawrence Erlbaum.

Eblen, R. E. (1982). Some observations on the phonological assessment of Hispanic-American children. *Journal of the National Student Speech Language Hearing Association, 10,* 44– 54.

Evans, J. (1976). *Spanish/English language performance screening.* Monterey, CA: CTB McGraw Hill.

Evard, D., & Sabers, D. (1979). Speech and language testing with distinct ethnic-racial groups: A survey of procedures for improving validity. *Journal of Speech and Hearing Disorders, 44,* 255–270.

Ferrer, J., & Damico, J. S. (1988). Language difference vs. language disorder: A pragmatic approach. A paper presented at the Symposia on Culturally Diverse Exceptional Children. Council for Exceptional Children. Denver, October.

Feuerstein, R. (1979). *The dynamic assessment of retarded performers: The Learning Potential Assessment Device, theory, instruments, and techniques.* Baltimore: University Park Press.

Fey, M. E. (1986). *Language intervention with young children.* Austin, TX: PRO-ED.

Fey, M. E., & Leonard, L. B. (1983). Pragmatic skills of children with specific learning impairment. In T. M. Gallagher and C. A. Prutting (Eds.), *Pragmatic assessment and intervention issues in language* (pp. 65–82). Austin, TX: PRO-ED.

Foster, R., Gidden, R., & Stark, J. (1969). *Assessment of children's language comprehension.* Palo Alto, CA: Consulting Psychologists Press.

Foster, R., Gidden, R., & Stark, J. (1978). *Assessment of children's language comprehension—Spanish version.* Palo Alto, CA: Consulting Psychologists Press.

Fredrickson, C. K., & Wick, J. W. (1976). *Short test of linguistic skills.* Department of Research and Evaluation, Board of Education, Chicago.

Fujiki, M., & Willbrand, M. L. (1982). A comparison of four informal methods of language evaluation. *LSHSS, 13,* 42–52.

Fuller, B. (1982). *Synergetics.* New York: MacMillan.

Gallagher, T. M. (1983). Pre-assessment: A procedure for accommodating language use variability. In T. M. Gallagher and C. A. Prutting (Eds.), *Pragmatic assessment and intervention issues in language* (pp. 1–29). Austin, TX: PRO-ED.

Gardner, M. F. (1980a). *Receptive one word picture vocabulary test,* Spanish edition. Novato, CA: Academic Therapy Publications.

Gardner, M. F. (1980b). *Expressive one word picture vocabulary test,* Spanish edition. Novato, CA: Academic Therapy Publications.

Garnett, K. (1986). Telling tales: Narratives and learning-disabled children. *Topics in Language Disorders, 6,* 44–56.

Gerken, K. C. (1978). Language dominance: A comparison of measures. *Language, Speech, and Hearing Services in Schools, 9,* 187–196.

Goldman, R. W., Fristoe, M., & Woodcock, R. W. (1970). *Goldman-Fristoe-Woodcock Test of Auditory Discrimination.* Circle Pines, MN: American Guidance Service.

Green, B. F. (1981) A primer of testing. *American Psychologist, 36,* 1001–1011.

Grice, H. P. (1975). Logic and conversation. In P. Cole & J. Morgan (Eds.), *Syntax and semantics: Speech acts,* Vol. 3 (pp. 41–59). New York: Academic Press.

Grill, J., & Bartel, N. (1977). Language bias tests: ITPA Grammatic Closure. *Journal of Learning Disabilities, 10,* 229–235.

Hall-Olsen, K., & Ocampo, G. (1983). Phonological processes evident in the speech of Spanish speaking children. A paper presented at the American Speech-Language-Hearing Association convention. Cincinnati, November.

Halliday, M. A. K., & Hasan, R. (1976). *Cohesion in English.* London: Longman.

Hamayan, E., Kwiat, J., & Perlman, R. (1985). *Assessment of language minority students: A handbook for educators.* Arlington Heights, IL: Illinois Resource Center.

Hammill, D. D., Brown, V. L., Larsen, S.C., & Wiederholt, J. L. (1980). *Test of adolescent language.* Allen, TX: DLM.

Harris, G. (1985). Considerations in assessing English language performance of Native American children. *Topics in Language Disorders, 5,* 42–52.

Haynes, W. O., & Moran, M. J. (1987). Phonological development in Black English. A paper presented at the American Speech-Language-Hearing Association convention. New Orleans, November.

Heath, S. B. (1983). *Ways with words.* Cambridge, MA: Cambridge University Press.

Heath, S. B. (1986). Taking a cross-cultural look at narratives. *Topics in Language Disorders, 7,* 84–94.

Hedberg, N. L., & Stoel-Gammon, C. (1986). Narrative analysis: Clinical procedures. *Topics in Language Disorders, 7,* 58–69.

Hedberg, N. L., Stoel-Gammon, C., Westby, C. E., & Yoshinga, D. (1984). Discourse analysis: Methods, research findings and implications. A miniseminar presented at the American Speech-Language-Hearing Association convention, San Francisco, November.

Hemingway, B. L., Montague, J. C., Jr., & Bradley, R. H. (1981). Preliminary data on a revision of a sentence repetition test for language screening with Black first grade children. *Language, Speech, and Hearing Services in Schools, 12,* 153–159.

Hoffman, M. N. H. (1934). *The measurement of bilingual background.* New York: Columbia University.

Holland, A., & Forbes, M. (1986). Nonstandardized approaches to speech and language assessment. In O.L. Taylor (Ed.), *Communication disorders in linguistically diverse populations* (pp. 49–66). Austin, TX: PRO-ED.

Hresko, W. P., Reid, D. K., & Hammill, D. D. (1981). *The test of early language development.* Austin: PRO-ED.

Hresko, W. P., Reid, D. K., & Hammill, D. D. (1982). *Prueba del Desarrollo Inicial del Lenguaje.* Austin: PRO-ED.

Ickes, W. K., & Brown, J. (1976). A translation of the Peabody Picture Vocabulary Test into Mex-Tex. *Tejas, 2,* 16–20.

Iglesias, A. (1985). Cultural conflict in the classroom: The communicatively different child. In D. N. Ripich & F. M. Spinelli (Eds.), *School discourse problems* (pp. 79–96). Austin, TX: PRO-ED.

Iglesias, A., Cohen, L., & Gutierrez-Clellen, V. (1985). Phonological complexity of spoken Spanish. A paper presented at the American Speech-Language-Hearing Association convention, Washington, D.C., November.

Jakobovits, L. (1968). Dimensionality of compound coordinate bilingualism. *Language Learning, 18*, 28–49.

James, P. (1975). *James language dominance test*. Austin, TX: Learning Concepts.

Johnston, J. R. (1982). Narratives: A new look at communication problems in older language-disordered children. *Language, Speech, and Hearing Services in Schools, 13*, 144–155.

Juarez, M., Hendrickson, S. A., & Anderson, M. P. (1983). Critique of discrete point tests. In J. P. Gelatt & M. P. Anderson (Eds.), *Bilingual Language Learning System Institutes Manual*. Rockville, MD: American Speech-Language-Hearing Association.

Kamhi, A. G., & Koenig, L. A. (1985). Metalinguistic awareness in normal and language-disordered children. *Language, Speech, and Hearing Services in Schools, 16*, 199–210.

Kayser, H. G. (1987). A study of three Mexican American children labeled language disordered. *NABE Journal, 12*, 1–22.

Kirk, S., McCarthy, J., & Kirk, W. D. (1971). *Illinois test of psycholinguistic abilities*. Los Angeles: Western Psychological Services.

Labov, W. (1983). Recognizing Black English in the classroom. In J. Chambers, Jr. (Ed.), *Black English: Educational equity and the law* (pp. 29–55). Ann Arbor, MI: Karoma Publishers.

Lado, R. (1961). *Language testing*. New York: McGraw-Hill.

Laesch, K. B., & van Kleeck, A. (1987). The cloze test as an alternative measure of language proficiency of children considered for exit from Bilingual Education. *Language Learning, 37*, 171–189.

Larson, C. E. (1978). Problems in assessing functional communication. *Communication Education, 27*, 304–309

Larson, V. L., & McKinley, N. L. (1987). *Communication assessment and intervention strategies for adolescents*. Eau Claire, WI: Thinking Publications.

Lee, L. (1970). *The Northwestern Syntax Screening Test*. Evanston, IL: Northwestern University Press.

Lee, L. (1974). *Developmental Sentence Analysis*. Evanston, IL: Northwestern University Press.

Leonard, L. B., Prutting, C., Perozzi, J., & Berkley, R. (1978). Nonstandardized approaches to the assessment of language behaviors. *Asha, 20*, 371–379.

Leonard, L. B., & Weiss, A. L. (1983). Application of nonstandardized assessment procedures to diverse linguistic populations. *Topics in Language Disorders, 3*, 35–45.

Lieberman, R. J., & Michael, A. (1986). Content relevance and content coverage in tests of grammatical ability. *JSHD, 51*, 71–81.

Loban, W. (1976). *Language development: K-12*. Urbana, IL: National Council of Teachers of English.

Lund, N. J., & Duchan, J. (1983). *Assessing children's language in naturalistic contexts*. Englewood Cliffs, NJ: Prentice-Hall.

Luria, A. R. (1981). *Language and cognition*. New York: J. Wiley and Sons.

Maez, L. (1985). The acquisition of the Spanish sound system by native Spanish-speaking children. In E. E. Garcia & R. V. Padilla (Eds.), *Advances in bilingual education research* (pp. 3–26). Tucson, AZ: University of Arizona Press.

Mares, S. (1980). *Pruebas de Expression Oral y Percepcion de la Lengua Espanola*. Downey, CA: Office of the Los Angeles County Superintendent of Schools.

Mason, M. A., Smith, B. F., & Henshaw, M. M. (1976). *La Meda: Medida Espanola de Articulacion*. San Ysidro, CA: San Ysidro School District.

Matluck, J. H., & Mace, B. J. (1973). Language characteristics of Mexican-American children. *Journal of School Psychology, 11*, 365–386.

Mattes, L. J. (1985). *Spanish language assessment procedures: A communication skills inventory*. San Diego: Los Amigos Research Associates.

Mattes, L. J., & Omark, D. R. (1984). *Speech and language assessment for the bilingual handicapped*. Austin, TX: PRO-ED.

McCauley, R. J., & Swisher, L. (1984). Psychometric review of language and articulation tests for preschool children. *Journal of Speech Hearing Disorders, 49*, 34–42.

McLaughlin, B., Rossman, T., & McLeod, B. (1983). Second language in learning: An information-processing perspective. *Language Learning, 33*, 135–159.

McNutt, J. C., Doehring, D. G., Lanoix, H., Van Engelen, J., Tourigny, S., Bergeron, M., & Dudley, J. G. (1987). Phoneme development in Francophone-Quebecoise children aged 1–6 to 9–11. A miniseminar presented at the American Speech-Language-Hearing Association convention. New Orleans, November.

Meehl, P. E. (1954). *Clinical versus statistical prediction*. Minneapolis, MI: University of Minnesota Press.

Mehan, H. (1979). *Learning lessons: Social organization in the classroom*. Cambridge, MA: Harvard University Press.

Mercer, J. R. (1979). *SOMPA: System of Multicultural Pluralistic Assessment*. New York: Psychological Corporation.

Mercer, J. R. (1983). Issues in the diagnosis of language disorders in students whose primary language is not English. *Topics in Language Disorders, 3*, 46–56.

Mercer, J. R. (1984). What is a racially and culturally nondiscriminatory test? A sociological and pluralistic perspective. In C. R. Reynolds & R. T. Brown (Eds.), *Perspectives on bias in mental testing* (pp. 293–356). New York: Plenum Press.

Mercer, N. (Ed.). (1981). *Language in school and community*. London: Arnold.

Merritt, D. D., & Liles, B. Z. (1987). Story grammar ability in children with and without language disorder: Story generation, story retelling, and story comprehension. *Journal of Speech and Hearing Research, 30*, 539–552.

Miller, J. (1981). *Assessing language production in children*. Baltimore: University Park Press.

Miller, J., & Chapman, R. (1983). *SALT: Systematic analysis of language transcripts, User's manual*. Madison: University of Wisconsin.

Miller, N. (1984a). *Bilingualism and language disability: Assessment and remediation*. Austin, TX: PRO-ED.

Miller, N. (1984b). Some observations concerning formal tests in cross-cultural settings. In N. Miller (Ed.) *Bilingualism and language disability: assessment and remediation* (pp. 107–114). Austin, TX: PRO-ED.

Milroy, J., & Milroy, L. (1985). *Authority in language: Investigating language prescription and standardization*. London: Routledge & Kegan Paul.

Mims, H. A., & Camden, C. T. (1986). Congruity and predictability between two measures of nonstandard dialect usage on four grammatical forms. *Journal of Speech and Hearing Disorders 51*, 42–52.

Moog, J. S., & Geers, A. F. (1979). *Grammatical analysis of elicited language*. St. Louis, MO: Central Institute of the Deaf.

Muma, J. R. (1978). *Muma assessment program*. Lubbock, TX: Natural Child Publications.

Musselwhite, C. R. (1983). Pluralistic assessment in Speech-Language Pathology: Use of dual norms in the placement process. *Language, Speech, and Hearing Services in the Schools, 14,* 29–37.

Nelson, N. W. (1981). Tests and materials in speech and language screening. *Seminars in Speech, Language and Hearing, 2,* 11–36.

Nelson, N. W. (1983). Black English sentence scoring: A tool for nonbiased assessment. A paper presented at the American Speech-Language-Hearing Association convention. Cincinnati, November.

Nelson, N. W. (1985). Teacher talk and child listening—fostering a better match. In C. S. Simon (Ed.), *Communication skills and classroom success: Assessment of language-learning disabled students* (pp. 65–104). Austin, TX: PRO-ED.

Nelson-Burgess, S., & Meyerson, J. (1975). MIRA: A concept in receptive language assessment of bilingual children. *Language, Speech, and Hearing Services in Schools, 6,* 24–28.

Newcomer, P., & Hammill, D. (1977). *Test of linguistic development.* Austin, TX: Empiric Press.

Norris, J. A. (1985). *Pragmatic criteria and the prediction of reading achievement: An examination of qualitative language differences.* Lincoln: University of Nebraska, Unpublished doctoral dissertation.

Norris, J. A. (1989). A process approach to early communicative assessment/ intervention. A paper presented at the American Speech-Language-Hearing Association convention. St. Louis, MO, November.

Norris, J. A., & Bruning, R. (1988). Cohesion in the narratives of good and poor readers. *Journal of Speech and Hearing Disorders, 53,* 416–424.

Norris, M. K., & Juarez, M. (1985). Further evidence for development of local norms for minority populations. A paper presented at the American Speech-Language-Hearing Association convention, Washington, D.C., November.

Nye, C. (1987). Assessing language development in Native American Navajo children. A paper presented at the American Speech-Language-Hearing Association convention. New Orleans, November.

Oakland, T. (Ed.). (1977). *Psychological and educational assessment of minority children.* New York: Brunner/Mozel.

Ochs, E. (1977). Planned and unplanned discourse. In T. Givon (Ed.), *Syntax and Semantics, Vol. 12 Discourse and Syntax* (pp. 51–80). New York: Academic Press.

Oller, J. W., Jr. (1979). *Language tests at school.* London: Longman.

Oller, J. W., Jr. (1983). Testing proficiencies and diagnosing language disorders in bilingual children. In D. R. Omark & J. G. Erickson (Eds.), *The bilingual exceptional child* (pp. 69–88). Austin, TX: PRO-ED.

Olshtain, E., & Blum-Kulka, S. (1985). Cross-cultural pragmatics and the testing of communicative competence. *Language Testing, 2,* 16–30.

Olswang, L. B., & Carpenter, R. L. (1978). Elicitor effects on the language obtained from young language-impaired children. *Journal of Speech and Hearing Disorders, 43,* 76–88.

Omark, D. R. (1981a). Pragmatics and ethnological techniques for the observational assessment of children's communicative abilities. In J. G. Erickson & D. R. Omark (Eds.), *Communicative assessment of the bilingual bicultural child* (pp. 249–284). Baltimore: University Park Press.

Omark, D. R. (1981b). Conceptualizations of bilingual children: Testing the norm. In J. G. Erickson & D. R. Omark (Eds.), *Communicative assessment of the bilingual bicultural child* (pp. 99–114). Baltimore: University Park Press.

Ortiz, A. A. (1988). Evaluating educational contexts in which language minority students are served. *Bilingual Special Education Newsletter, 7,* 1–4, 7.

Ortiz, A. A., & Maldonado-Colon, E. (1986). Reducing inappropriate referrals of language minority students to special education. In A. C. Willig & H. F. Greenberg (Eds.), *Bilingualism and learning disabilities: Policy and practice for teachers and administrators* (pp. 37–50). New York: American Library Publishing.

Ortiz, A. A., & Wilkinson, C. Y. (1987). *Limited English proficient and English proficient Hispanic students with communication disorders: Characteristics at initial assessment and at reevaluation.* Austin, the University of Texas, Handicapped Minority Research Institute on Language Proficiency.

Padilla, A. M. (1979). Critical factors in the testing of Hispanic Americans: A review and some suggestions for the future. In R. W. Tyler & S. H. White, (Eds.), *Testing, teaching and learning* (pp. 219–243). Washington, D.C.: The National Institute of Education.

Payan, R. (1984). Language assessment for bilingual exceptional children. In L. M. Baca & H. T. Cervantes (Eds.), *The bilingual special education interface* (pp. 125–137). St. Louis, MO: Times Mirror/Mosley.

Peck, C. A. (1989). Assessment of social communicative competence: Evaluating environments. *Seminars in Speech and Language, 10,* 1–15.

Perozzi, J. A. (1985). A pilot study of language facilitation for bilingual language-handicapped children: Theoretical and intervention strategies. *Journal of Speech and Hearing Disorders, 50,* 403–407.

Peterson, C., & McCabe, A. (1983). *Developmental psycholinguistics: Three ways of looking at a child's narrative.* New York: Plenum Press.

Philips, S. U. (1983). *The invisible culture.* New York: Longman.

Prutting, C., Gallagher, T., & Mulac, A. (1975). The expressive portion of the NSST compared to a language sample. *Journal of Speech and Hearing Disorders, 40,* 40–48.

Prutting, C. A., & Kirchner, D. M. (1983). Applied pragmatics. In T. M. Gallagher & C. A. Prutting (Eds.), *Pragmatic assessment and intervention issues in language* (pp. 29–64). Austin, TX: PRO-ED.

Prutting, C. A., & Kirchner, D. M. (1987). A clinical appraisal of the pragmatic aspects of language. *Journal of Speech and Hearing Disorders, 52,* 105–119.

Rees, N. (1979). Breaking out of the centrifuge. *Asha, 21,* 992–997.

Reschly, D. J. (1981). Psychological testing in educational classification and placement. *American Psychologist, 36,* 1094–1102.

Rice, M. L., Sell, M. A., & Hadley, P. A. (in press). The Social Interactive Coding System (SICS): An on-line, clinically relevant descriptive tool. *Language, Speech, and Hearing Services in Schools.*

Ripich, D. N., & Spinelli, F. M. (1985). An ethnographic approach to assessment and intervention. In D. N. Ripich & F. M. Spinelli (Eds.), *School Discourse Problems* (pp. 199–217). Austin, TX: PRO-ED.

Rosenberry, C., & Connell, P. J. (1988). *Assessment of language-impaired Spanish-speaking children.* A paper presented at the American Speech-Language-Hearing Association convention, Boston, November.

Roth, F. P. (1986). Oral narrative abilities of learning-disabled students. *Topics in Language Disorders, 7,* 21–30.

Rueda, R. (1987). Social and communicative aspects of language proficiency in low-achieving language minority students. In H. Trueba (Ed.), *Success or failure? Learning and the language minority student* (pp. 185–197). New York: Newbury House.

Rueda, R., & Perozzi, J. A. (1977). A comparison of two Spanish tests of receptive language. *Journal of Speech and Hearing Disorders, 42,* 210–215.

Samuda, R. (1975). *Psychological testing of American minorities: Issues and consequences.* New York: Harper & Row.

Savich, P. A., Matsuda, M. M., & Garcia, M. (1986). Pragmatic language skills in Hispanic preschool children. A paper presented at the American Speech-Language-Hearing Association convention. Detroit, November.

Schuele, M., & van Kleeck, A. (1987). Precursors to literacy: Assessment and intervention. *Topics in Language Disorders, 7,* 32–44.

Scoon, A. (1974). *The feasibility of test translation—English to Navajo.* Unpublished doctoral dissertation, University of New Mexico, Albuquerque.

Scribner, S. (1979). Modes of thinking and ways of speaking: Culture and logic reconsidered. In R. O. Freedle (Ed.), *New directions in discourse processing,* Vol. 2 (pp. 223–234), Norwood, NJ: Ablex.

Seliger, H. W. (1982). Testing authentic language: The problem of meaning. *Language Testing, 2,* 60–73.

Semel, E., & Wiig, E. (1987). *Clinical evaluation of language fundamentals–Revised.* San Antonio, TX: The Psychological Corporation.

Shohamy, E., & Reves, T. (1985). Authentic language tests: Where from and where to? *Language Testing, 2,* 48–59.

Shorr, D. N. (1983). Grammatical comprehension assessment: The picture avoidance strategy. *Journal of Speech and Hearing Disorders, 48,* 89–93.

Shorr, D. N., & Dale, P. S. (1984). Reflectivity bias in picture–pointing grammatical comprehension tasks. *Journal of Speech and Hearing Research, 27,* 549–555.

Shutt, D. L. (1974). *Shutt primary language indicator test (SPLIT), Spanish/English.* Phoenix: Citizens Press.

Silvaroni, N. J., & Maynes, J. O., Jr. (1975). *Oral Language Evaluation.* D. A. Lewis Associates, Clinton, MD.

Simon, C. S. (1979). *Communicative competence: A functional-pragmatic approach to language therapy.* Tucson, AZ: Communication Skill Builders.

Simon, C. S. (1989). *Classroom communication screening procedure for early adolescents: A handbook for assessment and intervention.* Tempe, AZ: Communi-Cog Publications.

Stein, N. L., & Glenn, C. G. (1979). An analysis of story comprehension in elementary school children. In R. O. Freedle (Ed.), *New directions in discourse processing* (pp. 53–120). Hillsdale, NJ: Erlbaum.

Strieff, V. (1978). Relationships among oral and written cloze scores and achievement test scores in a bilingual setting. In J. W. Oller, Jr. & K. Perkins (Eds.), *Language in education: Testing the tests* (pp. 65–102). Rowley, MA: Newbury House.

Stubbs, M. (1983). *Discourse analysis: The sociolinguistic analysis of natural language.* Chicago: University of Chicago Press.

Synder, L., Bates, E., & Bretherton, I. (1981). Content and context in early lexical development. *Journal of Child Language, 8,* 565–582.

Tannen, D. (1984). The pragmatics of cross-cultural communication. *Applied Linguistics, 5,* 189–195.

Taylor, O. (1977). Sociolinguistic dimension in standardized testing. In M. Saville-Troike (Ed.), *Linguistics and anthropology* (pp. 257–266). Washington, D.C.: Georgetown University Press.

Taylor, O., & Payne, K. T. (1983). Culturally valid testing: A proactive approach. *Topics in Language Disorders, 3,* 1–7.

Terrell, B. Y. (1985). Learning the rules of the game: Discourse skills in early childhood. In D. N. Ripich & F. M. Spinelli (Eds.), *School discourse problems* (pp. 13–27). Austin, TX: PRO-ED.

Terrell, S. L., Arensberg, K. E., & Rosa, M. R. (1986). Parent–child comparative analysis: A proposed method for nondiscriminatory assessment. A paper presented at the American Speech-Language-Hearing Association convention. Detroit, November.

Toronto, A. S. (1972). *Southwestern Spanish articulation test.* Austin: National Educational Laboratory.

Toronto, A. S. (1973). *Screening test of Spanish grammar.* Evanston, IL: Northwestern University Press.

Toronto, A. S. (1976). Developmental assessment of Spanish grammar. *Journal of Speech and Hearing Disorders, 41,* 150–169.

Toronto, A. S. (1977). *Toronto Tests of Receptive Vocabulary.* Austin: National Educational Laboratory.

Toronto, A. S., Leverman, D., Hanna, C., Rosenzweig, P., & Maldonado, A. (1975). *Del Rio language screening test.* Austin: National Educational Laboratory.

Toronto, A. S., & Merrill, S. (1983). Developing local normed assessment instruments. In D. R. Omark & J. G. Erickson (Eds.), *The bilingual exceptional child* (pp. 105–122). Austin, TX: PRO-ED.

Ulibarri, D. M., Spencer, M. L., & Rivas, G. A. (1981). Language proficiency and academic achievement: A study of language proficiency tests and their relationship to school ratings as predictors of academic achievement. *NABE Journal, 5,* 47–80.

van Kleeck, A. (1984). Assessment and intervention: Does "meta" matter? In G. Wallach & K. Butler, (Eds.), *Language learning disabilities in school-age children* (pp. 179–198). Baltimore: University Park Press.

van Kleeck, A., & Schuele, M. (1987). Precursors to literacy: Normal development. *Topics in Language Disorders, 7,* 13–31.

Varonis, E. M., & Gass, S. M. (1985). Miscommunication in native/non-native conversation. *Language in Society, 14,* 327–343.

Vaughn-Cooke, F. B. (1986). Theoretical frameworks and language assessment. In F. H. Bess, B. S. Clark, & H. R. Mitchell (Eds.), *Concerns for minority groups in communication disorders.* (American Speech-Language-Hearing Association Reports 16) (pp. 33–39). Rockville, MD: American Speech-Language-Hearing Association.

Vetter, D. K. (1982). Language disorders and schooling. *Topics in Language Disorders, 2,* 13–19.

Wald, B. (1981). On assessing the oral language ability of limited English proficient students: The linguistic bases of the non-comparability of different language proficiency assessment measures. In S. S. Seidner (Ed.), *Issues in language assessment. Foundations and research* (pp. 117–126). Evanston, IL: Illinois State Board of Education.

Wang, F. N., Phillips, P. V., Kuo, J., & Chen, J-W. (1984). Mandarin Chinese misarticulation: Error analysis. A paper presented at the American Speech-Language-Hearing Association convention. San Francisco, November.

Wang, F. N., Phillips, P. V., Kuo, J., & Hwang, H. (1983). Articulation development in Mandarin-speaking preschool children in Taiwan. A paper presented at the American Speech-Language-Hearing Association convention. Cincinnati, November.

Watson, D. L., Grouell, S. L., Heller, B., & Omark, D. R. (1987). *Nondiscriminatory assessment test matrix,* Vol. 2. San Diego: Los Amigos Research Associates.

Werner, E. O., & Kresheck, J. D. (1974). *Structured photographic language test.* Sandwich, IL: Janelle Publications.

Westby, C. E. (1982). Cognitive and linguistic aspects of children's narrative development. In L. Bradford (Ed.), *Communicative disorders: An audio journal*, 7, 1.

Westby, C. E. (1984). Development of narrative abilities. In G. P. Wallach & K. G. Butler (Eds.), *Language learning disabilities in school-age children* (pp. 103–127). Baltimore: Williams & Wilkins.

Westby, C. E. (1985). Learning to talk—talking to learn: Oral–literate language differences. In C. S. Simon (Ed.), *Communication skills and classroom success: Therapy methodologies for language-learning diabled students* (pp. 181–218). Austin, TX: PRO-ED.

Westby, C. E. (in press). Cultural variation in story telling. In L. Cole & V. Deal (Eds.), *Communication disorders in multicultural populations*. Washington, DC: American Speech-Language-Hearing Association.

Westby, C. E. Story grammar analysis. Unpublished manuscript.

Westby, C. E., Van Dongen, R., & Maggart, Z. (1989). Assessing narrative competence. *Seminars in Speech and Language*, 10, 63–76.

Wiener, F. D., & Lewnau, L. E. (1982). Differentiating language profiles of normal/language impaired Black English speakers. A miniseminar presented at the American Speech-Language-Hearing Association convention. Toronto, November.

Wiener, F. D., Lewnau, L. E., & Erway, E. (1983). Measuring language competency in speakers of Black American English. *Journal of Speech and Hearing Disorders*, 48, 76–84.

Wiener, F. D., Simon, A. J., & Weiss, F. L. (1978). *Spanish picture vocabulary test: An adaptation of the PPVT for New York City's Spanish-speaking Puerto Rican population*. ERIC Document Reproduction Services, ED 009964.

Wilkinson, L. C. (Ed.). (1982). *Communicating in the classroom*. New York: Academic Press.

Wing, C. S. (1974). Evaluating the English articulation of nonnative speakers. *Language, Speech, and Hearing Services in Schools*, 5, 143–151.

Wolfram, W. (1985). The phonologic system: Problems of second language acquisition. In J. M. Costello (Ed.), *Speech disorders in adults* (pp. 59–76), Austin, TX: PRO-ED.

Young, L. W. L. (1982). Inscrutability revisited. In J. J. Gumperz (Ed.), *Language and social identity* (pp. 72–84). Cambridge: Cambridge University Press.

Zachman, L., Huisingh, R., Jorgensen, C., & Barrett, M. (1976). *Oral language sentence imitation screening test*. Moline, IL: LinguiSystems.

Zimmerman, I., Steiner, V., & Pond, A. (1976). *Preschool Language Scale—Spanish*. Columbus, OH: Charles E. Merrill.

Zirkel, P. A. (1974). A method for determining and depicting language dominance. *TESOL Quarterly*, 8, 7–16.

CHAPTER 6

Educational Assessment

NANCY CLOUD

In assessing limited English proficient (LEP) students, evaluators attempt to understand the student's current level of performance across academic areas as well as the variables that have contributed to the student's current educational status. This means that while direct assessment of the student is of utmost importance to establishing an appropriate intervention plan, so too is an accurate assessment of all of the student's previous educational experiences.

Direct assessment of a LEP student implies that the examiner will select appropriate measures or techniques based on the student's proficiency in both the first and second languages (L1/L2), the student's age, the pattern of disability, the cultural and experiential background, and the specific purpose of each assessment planned. A student's performance is best understood in context; this implies that when interpreting results, the examiner will consider various contextual factors.

First, the evaluator should consider the nature and extent of the student's current and previous educational experiences. These experiences may play an important role in the student's current performance due to the previous knowledge base provided, the pedagogical methods employed, the attitudes and expectations expressed by teachers and other school-related personnel, and the successes and failures experienced by the student. Researchers have found that such experiences greatly affect a student's performance and potential in the classroom (Bruck, 1984; Cummins, 1986; Skutnabb-Kangas, 1981; Spindler, 1987). Second, evaluators must be aware of the impact of the student's language, culture, test-taking experiences, and the pattern of disability performance when selecting the particular educational assessment method or technique. As documented by Philips (1983) and Bloom (1981), LEP students may have particular difficulties during the assessment process due to cultural or linguistic differences rather than to learning difficulties. For example, the concept of assessment as a measure of educational accomplishment and a potential measure of self-worth may not be shared by some cultures; consequently, performance may be affected by this difference in perception (Deyhle, 1987). Third, the evaluator must consider the student's motivational and emotional status both before and during the assessment process. Many norm-referenced techniques are designed with the assumption that students will be motivated to perform to the best of their abilities and that they are unaffected by their emotional status. This is not always the case; it is even more unlikely if the target of assessment is a LEP student who may view the assessment process as a barrier to educational opportunity (Padilla, 1979; Rivera, 1983). Fourth, the evaluator should consider the student's academic preparation and orientation of other family members who provide support to the student. Issues regarding home valuation of education, encouragement during adversity, and insights provided about school by parents and siblings can have a powerful effect on motivation and coping abilities (Bronfenbrenner, 1986; Skutnabb-Kangas & Toukomaa, 1976). Finally, to understand performance in context, the amount of disruption that has occurred in the student's education due to illness, mobility, migration, or other factors should be addressed. Academic difficulty may reflect mobility or lack of opportunity rather than lack of potential.

This chapter assists service providers in planning, administering, and interpreting valid educational assessments of LEP students with special education needs. It treats both topics raised in this introduction: how to conduct academic assessment with LEP exceptional students and how to interpret the outcomes of such assessments appropriately. Two major factors when considering the academic assessment of LEP students will be discussed first: the impact of language proficiency on academic achievement and the problem of interrupted schooling. After these factors are considered, the assessment process itself will be discussed beginning with the contextual variables that need to be included in the assessment of educational background. This will establish a framework within which direct assessment methods can be described meaningfully.

IMPACT OF LANGUAGE PROFICIENCY AND TEST-TAKING SKILLS ON ACADEMIC ACHIEVEMENT

Various researchers have documented the influence of students' language competence on academic test performance (Cummins, 1982; Nadeau & Miramontes, 1987; Politzer, 1983; Ulibarri, Spencer & Rivas, 1981). These investigators have demonstrated a relationship between the degree of oral language proficiency developed and reading achievement scores; between native language development and achievement in both the primary and second languages; and the need for a special type of academic English language proficiency to ensure academic success in English (i.e., what Cummins (1982) calls Cognitive/Academic Language Proficiency). Politzer (1983) goes on to suggest that English linguistic competence is not only directly involved in English achievement measures, but the learning of a second language may in itself constitute (or at least involve) a "scholastic" achievement.

In order to properly interpret academic performance, then, evaluators must make an accounting of the students' language proficiency in both languages. Further, both communicative competence and cognitive/academic linguistic abilities must be considered.

The language proficiency debate has been particulary acute surrounding the reclassification and bilingual program exit process. LEP students may be at great risk of academic failure or of being erroneously referred to special education services if they are prematurely reclassified as English proficient when they have not in fact developed the necessary proficiency to succeed in an English-medium academic environment (Cummins, 1984). Once lack of English proficiency is ruled out as depressing student achievement, other factors such as learning disabilities may be sought. A number of studies that have looked at the reclassification process in transitional bilingual education programs have cautioned that a combination of indicators must be used (rather than English language proficiency or English reading achievement alone) to determine readiness to transition, among them: L1 reading proficiency, months of English reading instruction, English vocabulary, English listening comprehension, and teacher ratings based on native language performance (Fischer & Cabello, 1981; Nadeau & Miramontes, 1987; Nava-Hamaker, 1981).

The lack of test-taking experience among minority students has also been demonstrated to affect test performance by a number of researchers (summarized in Powers, 1982). For example, Dreisbach and Keogh (1982) demonstrated that Spanish-speaking kindergarten students who were trained in test-taking skills performed better than their untrained peers, whether tested in Spanish or English on a standardized readiness measure. These researchers concluded that the consideration of test-wiseness of youngsters is important in any assessment program. A variety of test-wiseness training procedures have been suggested to overcome possible poor performance that can result when students lack test-taking skills (Bernal, 1977; Frierson, 1977; Gifford & Fluitt, 1980; McPhail, 1981).

STUDENTS WITH INTERRUPTED SCHOOLING

LEP students of all ages are entering school in the United States with diverse educational backgrounds. To limit bias in educational assessment, evaluators need to consider each student's individual background. One aspect of educational background that has an impact on academic preparation and performance is continuity of educational experience. For students whose schooling has been significantly interrupted, this variable must be considered. These students are so different from the American norm that it is worthwhile to describe their cases separately.

PRIMARY, SECONDARY, AND TERTIARY MIGRATION

Often LEP students resettling in the United States do so having lived for various periods of time in other countries under various conditions. Many refugee families have experienced such multiple-phase resettlement processes. This may mean that students have been educated in a variety of languages and educational systems, or that they have received only a sporadic education; in some cases, students have had no formal education. Some children were born under adverse health and medical conditions, increasing their "at-risk" status for particular disabling conditions. All of these possibilities must be explored in order to adequately interpret the results of achievement testing.

REVERSE MIGRATION OF PUERTO RICAN, MEXICAN, AND OTHER LINGUISTICALLY DIVERSE STUDENTS

Many LEP students' families frequently move back and forth between the parents' place of birth and a resettlement community of relatives and friends on the United States mainland. These frequent interruptions to the student's schooling may result in the student's inability to function successfully in either environment. This problem is receiving more and more recognition of both sending and receiving school officials. For example, the frequent migration of Puerto Rican youngsters between urban northeastern United States school districts and Puerto Rico has prompted the development by the Educational Testing Service of an *Educational Passport* to facilitate the exchange of information about the student between the sending and receiving school systems.

There are similar patterns of frequent migration for Mexican students in the west and southwest United States and for Dominican and Haitian students in the northeast. These students are at further risk of lower achievement levels since they may remain marginal in both societies. They may never be fully accepted as a part of either society, which dramatically affects their self-esteem and motivation to achieve. In evaluating the school performance of such students, evaluators must consider the effects of reverse migration on achievement.

SPECIAL PROBLEMS OF REFUGEE AND MIGRANT STUDENTS IN THE UNITED STATES

Mobility, marginality, health and nutritional status, separation from family, and loss of family members are special circumstances that affect the achievement of migrant and refugee students. These conditions are often unacknowledged. Necessary health and counseling services or training for teachers is unavailable, and the schools are ineffective because students' other needs are going unmet. Alienation and withdrawal are common responses to the prolonged periods of stress and confusion and to the fragmentation of social and family structures experienced by refugee and migrant students (Jacobs, 1987; Trueba, 1987). An unfortunate yet inescapable outcome of alienation and withdrawal is school failure.

Evaluators must consider all aspects of the student's life in these cases in order to accurately interpret the results of educational testing. In particular, the medical, emotional, and health status of the student must be fully evaluated. Also, these students' experiences may be so different from those needed for good performance on United States achievement measures that the tests will be ineffective with such youngsters. Thus, background information is essential if adequate assessment is to occur.

EDUCATIONAL BACKGROUND ASSESSMENT

Education is both a formal and informal process that occurs at school and at home. When evaluators assess educational performance, they must analyze the complete range of educational environments that have contributed to current performance levels. This means that they must understand the academic preparation and orientation of family members who assist the student at home as well as the previous and current classroom environments in which the student has been educated.

FAMILY / HOME FACTORS

Many factors related to the home environment have been documented to affect the achievement of linguistically diverse students including: socioeconomic status (SES), number of years in the United States, value placed on academic achievement, years of schooling and literacy level of the parents, and language use for mediation or caretaking purposes.

SES has a well-established relationship to the level of academic achievement (Dreisbach & Keogh, 1982). Depressed levels of achievement are commonly associated with lower SES conditions and the many stresses and barriers this introduces into the educational process. While it is important not to assume that all lower SES students are low achievers or doomed by their SES level to a cycle of academic failure, the overrepresentation of low SES students in compensatory programs and in drop-out statistics demonstrate the "at-risk" status commonly held by lower SES students in United States schools.

The number of years the family has been in the United States is also associated with student achievement (Politzer, 1983). Higher scores on achievement measures designed for pupils in United States schools and administered in English also are commonly thought to be due to the acculturation process (Ramirez, 1983). This relationship may be an indirect one in that length of residence in the United States is likely to be related to higher levels of acculturation and English language proficiency, both important predictors of academic achievement (Deyhle, 1987; Ulibarri, Spencer & Rivas, 1981).

Another variable related to achievement is the value placed on education by the family and in the larger ethnic community. The level of emphasis placed on education might be governed by factors such as economic conditions, education level of the parents, sex of the child, the degree to which the family believes that education will guarantee their child's advancement in society, and the degree to which the family believes their child is being offered a quality education.

Of special importance in understanding academic achievement of linguistically diverse students with disabilities is the quality and amount of mediation their parents provide. According to the theory of structural cognitive modifiability (Feuerstein, 1980), when parents provide adequate mediation to their children, higher achievement levels result. In cases where parents provide mediation in a language in which they are proficient and transmit the full extent of the culturally determined knowledge they possess, adequate intergenerational transmission occurs to ensure the success of children. However, when parents experience cultural and linguistic ambivalence or rejection and reduce the quantity and quality of the mediation they offer by providing it in a second language in which they are not proficient or by withholding the transmission of traditionally determined beliefs, values, and knowledge, children's cognitive and linguistic development suffers. Because of the minority status of many linguistically diverse families, negative attitudes held about native language use, and assimilationist values promoted in many areas in the United States, parents of linguistically diverse students may feel pressured to switch to the language and cultural content of the host country. Cummins (1981) has warned that in cases where the quality and quantity of mediation provided the child is affected by this switch, negative consequences will occur in the child's academic performance.

It is also common for parents of handicapped children who experience failure (when attempting to mediate to their child with disabilities) to reduce mediation attempts out of frustration or out of a belief that mediation is impossible. In some cases, professionals may encourage parents to offer less mediation to children out of a belief that they are helping parents set more "realistic" goals. When home-based mediation is reduced, negative consequences are likely to result for the child, especially when needed mediation is not available from other sources (Feuerstein, 1980).

Because of the many home variables related to achievement, evaluators must gather information about this important educational context in which the student participates. The questionnaire that follows is an example of the type of data-gathering efforts that would help evaluators to better understand the complex variables in the home environment that contribute to the student's current level of performance.

HOME BACKGROUND QUESTIONNAIRE

1. How many years has the family been in the United States _____?

2. What is the birthplace of the parents (guardians)?

    Mother: _____

    Father: _____

3. In what language did each parent/guardian receive most of his/her education?

    Mother: _____

    Father: _____

4. How many years of schooling did each parent (guardian) complete?

    Mother: _____

    Father: _____

5. What language do the parents (guardians) speak at home most of the time?

    Mother: _____

    Father: _____

6. What language does the student speak with his/her parents?

    Mother: _____

    Father: _____

7. What language does the student most often speak with brothers and sisters? (List each sibling and language)

Sibling	**Language**
_____	_____
_____	_____
_____	_____

8. What language does the student most often speak with his/her friends or play-mates? _____

9. In which language are television and radio programs most often received in the home? _____

10. In which language is most print media (books, magazines, newspapers) in the home? _____

11. Does the family receive a daily newspaper? If so, in what language?

_____

12. To what magazines does the family subscribe? _____

13. Does the child receive any periodicals under his/her own name? If so, in what language? _____

14. How many hours per week is the child read to? _____

In what language(s)? _____

15. How many hours per week does the child observe the parents reading? __

In what language(s)? _____

16. How many hours does the child read per week? _____

For what purposes? _____

In what languages(s)? _____

17. If the child reads regularly for pleasure, what are the child's current interests?

_____

18. How many years of schooling has the student received in a language other

than English? _____

CLASSROOM ENVIRONMENT

In addition to collecting data on the home to understand the student's current performance levels, evaluators should also consider the current classroom environment in which the student participates to determine if there are factors that might help in interpreting achievement status. Variables such as teacher expectations and expertise, teaching and learning style match, opportunity to participate, acceptance by peers and adults, and appropriateness of instructional activities and materials all affect student performance (see e.g., Goodlad, 1983). In order to understand the child's reading achievement, the following questionnaire may be administered to assess the factors present in the current classroom environment that would help explain performance.

CLASSROOM ENVIRONMENT QUESTIONNAIRE

1. Describe the print available in the classroom (newspapers, magazines, news-

letters, readers, textbooks, stories, novels, poetry) _____ .

2. How many minutes per day is the student read to? _____

In what language(s)? _____

3. How many minutes per day does the student read? (Note if silent or aloud.)

_____

In what language(s)? _____

4. Is reading being formally taught? _____

By what methods? _____

In what language(s)? _____

5. For what purposes does the student read in the classroom (personal, informal,

education, or pleasure)? _____

6. Does the class use the library? _____

   For what purposes? _____

   How often? _____

7. Describe the writing activities in which the student engages (e.g., copying, completing sentences, answering questions, journals, essays, reports). ____

   _____

8. How many minutes per day does the student write? _____

   In what language(s)? _____

9. Is writing being formally taught? _____

   By what method? _____

   In what language(s)? _____

10. What is the student's attitude toward reading (e.g., positive, confident, eager, negative, self-conscious, tentative)? _____

11. What is the student's attitude toward writing (e.g., positive, confident, eager, negative, self-conscious, tentative)? _____

12. How does the instructor view this student as a reader (e.g., strong, weak, motivated, eager, tentative)? _____

13. How does the instructor view the student as a writer (e.g., strong, weak, motivated, eager, tentative)? _____

PREVIOUS EDUCATIONAL EXPERIENCES

As previously mentioned, the students' educational history is the key to understanding the current profile of performance. Some LEP students were born in the United States, whereas others resettled in the United States as immigrants, refugees, or as the children of migrant workers. Some have been involved in a continuous educational process, whereas others have interrupted and fragmented schooling backgrounds. Some attained proficiency in their native language and experienced academic success in their home countries prior to coming to the United States, whereas others did not attain a strong foundation in the native language prior to beginning schooling experiences in English.

All of these possibilities have consequences for student achievement. Considerable evidence exists to demonstrate that students with high achievement levels in language-related and academic content areas in their native language will also experience academic success in English (Toukomaa & Skutnabb-Kangas, 1977). Correspondingly, students with low literacy and achievement levels in the native language also exhibit low achievement levels in English. The significance of this finding to assessment efforts is that when children have proficiency in non-English languages, accurate assessment of native language literacy and achievement levels is essential if evaluators are to interpret achievement levels attained in English. In all cases, then, evaluators need information about the previous education to properly interpret the results of direct assessment of the student.

Evaluators should seek information about the student's educational history from knowledgeable informants. The following questions might be asked of parents (guardians) and previous teachers.

PREVIOUS EDUCATIONAL EXPERIENCES QUESTIONNAIRE FOR PARENTS/GUARDIANS

1. Are there any known medical problems that interfere with learning? _____

2. At what age did the student begin school? _____

3. Was attendance consistent? _____

   If it was interrupted, why? _____

4. Has the student ever been retained? _____

5. Where has the student attended school (countries, districts, schools)? _____

6. In what language(s) has the student been educated? _____

7. Does the student attend afterschool, community-based, or church school programs? _____

8. Have family members lived most of their lives in rural or urban areas? _____

9. What was the last grade completed by parents/guardians?

   Mother: _____

   Father: _____

10. In what language are parents best able to assist the student at home with schoolwork?

    Mother: _____

    Father: _____

PREVIOUS EDUCATIONAL EXPERIENCES QUESTIONNAIRE
FOR TEACHERS

1. What were the number of absences each month in school?

   _____   _____

   _____   _____

   _____   _____

   _____   _____

   _____   _____

2. Was the student ever considered for retention? _____

3. What was the nature of the student's academic performance in each basic subject (e.g., strong or weak)?

   _____   _____

   _____   _____

   _____   _____

4. Has the student ever participated in special programs or received special services (e.g., counseling, speech/language, reading laboratory, bilingual/ESL education services)?

   _____

5. What methods and materials were used in the program? How did the student perform using these methods and materials?

   _____

This section has shown that there are a variety of factors to consider other than disabilities when interpreting the performance of LEP students on measures of achievement. In the next section, formal and informal procedures for the assessment of academic achievement of language minority students will be reviewed. Regardless of the technique employed, evaluators should remember that many variables will contribute to and explain performance. Therefore, careful consideration of each factor is required in order to plan an appropriate programmatic response.

FORMAL ASSESSMENT

When students are limited in English proficiency, thereby precluding meaningful use of achievement measures in English, norm-referenced achievement measures may be administered in non-English languages to establish general levels of academic functioning and possible points of difficulty in broad areas such as reading comprehension or arithmetic computation (Plata, 1982). While considerable cautions and criticisms have been alleged against dual-language standardized tests (the most important of which will be summarized at the end of this section), their sensitive use may be warranted as a first step in analyzing student achievement. In addition, such comparative data may be required by state or local regulations. Several measures in non-English languages will be described next as representative of a particular type of formal test available for use with LEP students. Other measures of each type are listed in Appendix B.

NORM-REFERENCED READING TESTS IN NON-ENGLISH LANGUAGES

Bateria Woodcock Psico-Educativa en Espanol (Woodcock-Johnson Psycho-Educational Battery)

This measure, as with other nationally normed achievement tests, is broad in scope. While the reading assessment components are the focus of interest in this section, the reader should note that it includes 17 subtests. Ten of these can be used to assess broad cognitive ability; a combination of 10 other subtests can be given to measure scholastic aptitude, and 7 of the 17 subtests can be administered to measure actual achievement. In the case of reading achievement, the following subtest clusters would be useful: *Reading Achievement Cluster*, including the Letter-word Identification, Word Attack, and Passage Comprehension subtests; and the *Reading Aptitude Cluster*, including the Visual-Auditory learning, Antonyms-Synonyms, and Analogies subtests. This battery can be used with Hispanics aged 3 through adult. Criticisms of this measure include these: The word-analysis subtest is a meaningless indicator of word-analysis skills since it is based on nonsense syllables and words; there are too few items per skill area tested; it gives little diagnostic information on low-functioning students; and it is complicated to score. It also suffers from all of the criticisms alleged against dual-language tests where the original was constructed in English and the Spanish is based on that version. Strengths include these: It is individually administered; it includes a cross-representation of Spanish-speaking groups in its development; and it includes an instructional implications profile.

Other measures of this type include the *Spanish Assessment of Basic Education* (SABE), the *Interamerican Tests of Reading* and the *Moreno Spanish Reading Comprehension Test*. All are dual-language, nationally normed, reading achievement tests for Spanish/English bilinguals (see Appendix B).

NORM-REFERENCED MATHEMATICS TESTS IN NON-ENGLISH LANGUAGES

The Spanish Assessment of Basic Education (SABE)

As mentioned in the last section, several dual-language achievement measures exist that cover more than one content area. The *Spanish Assessment of Basic Education* (SABE), published in 1987 as a successor to the CTBS Español, is a Spanish language achievement-test battery. It is designed to parallel the content of, and is linked statistically to the Comprehensive Tests of Basic Skills (CTBS) Forms U and V and the California Achievement Tests (CAT) Forms E and F. SABE was designed to measure achievement levels of pupils in United States bilingual programs and of "immigrant" students entering American schools in reading and mathematics. In the case of mathematics evaluation, it measures mathematics computation, concepts and applications, grades 1 to 8. The mathematics computation subtests in SABE are identical to those of the CTBS U. The concepts and applications test items were also adapted directly into Spanish from CTBS U (*User's Guide*, Preliminary Edition, pp. 9–10).

Coyne (1979) and Bradley (1984) discuss problems encountered by LEP students on translated or adapted math tests: the processes and paradigms, vocabulary, and symbol use may vary from that used in the students' home country, creating confusion and depressing performance. Examples of such difficulties present in SABE include the use of the United States paradigm for division $3\sqrt{33}$; the inclusion of formats unusual outside of the United States, such as number sentences (7 + 4 $\square$ 10 or $\square$ × 4 = 24); and item content in the problem-solving and measurement sections that solely relate to the United States context (e.g., monetary system, measurement system). In all cases, a student could have the skills required but be unable to respond due to format or content issues. As well, the layout and format of the tests, use of separate answer sheets, and timed testing conditions are also known to depress performance. The publishers of SABE have responded to this second issue by providing Practice Tests for all levels of SABE; use of these tests is highly recommended. Another positive feature of SABE is the objective performance indexes, which report the level of mastery for each objective the test measures, allowing a more criterion-referenced interpretation of performance for each student. Individual administration and a task analysis interpretation could improve the insights gained from the test with special needs students.

The *Bateria Woodcock* and the *Interamerican Test of Reading and Number* are other examples of this type of dual-achievement measure that include an assessment of mathematical abilities (see Appendix B).

NORM-REFERENCED TESTS IN OTHER AREAS IN NON-ENGLISH LANGUAGES

Early Assessment and Remediation Laboratory (EARLY)

The EARLY contains 23 tasks and covers gross motor, fine motor, language, visual discrimination, and memory. It was developed by the Chicago Board of Education to improve the screening and identification of young learning-disabled students. The Spanish directions are well written, and the follow-up remediation activities assist in linking assessment to intervention. Criticisms include that it is built on an information processing model that targets deficits in the student instead of in the total instructional environment; the so-called developmental milestones may be culturally and experientially biased; and it favors field independent learners.

CAUTIONS AND CRITICISMS OF A STANDARIZED OR NORM-REFERENCED TESTING APPROACH

Standarized tests are believed to underestimate linguistically diverse students' abilities. These students' low performance on such measures can be attributed to the following factors:

1. Test content (Mercer, 1979) and test construction problems, such as underrepresentation of minority groups in the item development, selection, and norming process (Bernal, 1977; Green, 1972; Nuttall, Landurand, & Goldman, 1984), as well as translation and curricular relevance problems (Cabello, 1983).
2. Test use problems: the effect of examiner and situational factors such as timed test and group administration on test performance (Garcia & Zimmerman, 1972).

3. Student-related characteristics such as cultural, experiential (especially test-taking experience), and language biases (Cabello, 1983; Dreisbach & Keogh, 1982; Matluck & Mace, 1973; Nava-Hamaker, 1981; Nuttall, Landurand, & Goldman, 1984; Zirkel, 1972).

Even if these problems did not exist, the information gained from standardized tests would be criticized as not being precise enough for planning specific teaching programs (Plata, 1982). Additionally, diagnostic applications are rarely made since evaluators do not know why a student missed a particular item when students are tested according to standardized procedures.

Finally, most standardized tests in non-English languages are adapted from (if not directly translated from) English language forms of the same instrument. Such tests are criticized as containing the same cultural/experiential item bias as the English versions on which they are based and of lacking equivalence in intent, difficulty level, style, and tone to the English versions upon which they are based (Cabello, 1983; Carsrud, 1980; Cervantes, 1975).

With all of these serious criticisms against standardized tests in non-English languages, it is easy to understand why a variety of alternatives have been proposed to circumvent their use. These alternatives will be described next.

INFORMAL ASSESSMENT

Ambert and Dew (1982) include under the rubric of "informal testing" all measures that are not standardized or norm-referenced. They cite these common examples: informal reading inventories, cloze procedures, miscue analyses, criterion-referenced tests (CRT), mastery tests based on grade level or course objectives, and task analyses. These authors claim that informal testing has several advantages:

(1) it does not compare the child's performance to the performance of others but rather tries to locate it on an objective skill continuum and to chart individual progress, (2) the techniques are very diagnostic-prescriptive in nature, which helps define an instructional plan of action, (3) the procedures can be implemented using any language or combination of languages, (4) the methods are less intimidating than formal tests because they are used routinely by the child's teacher in a familiar setting, and (5) they can be structured to measure more subtle changes in performance than do standardized tests. Its drawbacks are that (1) instructors are often inadequately prepared to construct valid informal measures, (2) it is more time-consuming to plan instruction based on individual assessments than to teach predetermined grade-level subject matter, (3) decision-makers are sometimes reluctant to place value in locally developed assessment procedures, and (4) informal testing generally requires a commitment to ongoing assessment, whereas norm-referenced testing typically occurs only once or twice a year. (p. 59)

This section covers five types of informal assessment as examples of what might be done to supplement or substitute for standardized tests: commercial CRTs in non-English languages, district developed instruments in non-English languages, cloze testing with content area text material (L1 and L2), performance analysis, and learning style analysis.

COMMERCIAL CRITERION-REFERENCED TESTS IN NON-ENGLISH LANGUAGES

Baca and Cervantes (1984) state that the purpose of educational assessment is to gather information about the student's functional educational skills so that the results can be directly translated into prescriptive intervention strategies. They claim that unless the test results are directly related to instruction, the effort has been wasted. The goal of criterion-referenced assessment is precisely that of establishing a direct relationship between test results and instruction. According to Plata (1982), results of criterion-referenced tests are best used by practitioners when the aim is to individualize educational programs for students. These tests can aid teachers in: (1) pinpointing the strengths and weaknesses of specific students for whom they are responsible; (2) determining the starting place for the student's instruction; (3) selecting teaching materials to accomplish stated objectives in the student's individualized education program; (4) monitoring the student's progress academically, vocationally, or socially; and (5) reporting on the student's progress to parents, administrators, and the students themselves.

While the use of CRTs is encouraged, there are limitations. Kirk, Kliebhan, and Lerner (1978) and Davis (1974) outline them:

1. A disproportionate amount of time must be spent monitoring students, keeping records, and doing paperwork.
2. Hard-to-measure qualities, such as appreciation or attitude toward reading, may be overlooked.
3. Students who test at an acceptable criterion level for a specific skill may be unable to transfer that skill to another situation.
4. Students may test at an acceptable criterion level on a specific skill one day but be unable to perform that skill a few days later.
5. The hierarchy, or ordered sequence of skills, selected by the test maker may be inappropriate for a particular student. Moreover, test makers do not agree about a specific sequence.
6. Determining the appropriate criterion for proficiency may be difficult. That is, 60% proficiency may be sufficient for some skills, whereas in other skills a 95% proficiency may be required.

7. The sequence of skills to be learned does not take into account the unique strengths and weaknesses of a specific student. This is particularly important for slow and disabled learners as well as for bilingual handicapped students.
8. Criterion-referenced tests must be well constructed in order to determine valid and reliable content-referenced interpretation.

In addition to these weaknesses, there are other concerns regarding criterion-referenced tests. Careful attention must be given to the following questions concerning who determines the objectives of the assessment; who sets the behavioral criterion levels; if the test items accurately reflect the behavioral criterion levels assumed; what constitutes a sufficient sample of items at each criterion level; and whether the test scores obtained effectively describe an individual's response pattern. These are all issues essential to the underlying construct validity of the CRT measures (see Plata, 1982, for a discussion of these concerns). With these points in mind, an example of this type of measure will be given: *The Brigance Diagnostic Assessment Of Basic Skills–Spanish Edition.*

The major purposes of the *Brigance Diagnostic Assessment of Basic Skills– Spanish Edition* are to screen for dominant language; to determine grade-level placement (seven grade-level screens); to identify specific strengths and weaknesses in readiness, speech, listening, reading, language arts and math; and to track a student's progress in his/her instructional program.

The assessment system covers 10 areas: readiness, speech, functional word recognition, oral reading, reading comprehension, word analysis, listening, writing and alphabetizing, numbers and computation, and measurement. It contains 102 diagnostic basic skill assessments. The tests are designed for all Hispanic groups and regional variations of vocabulary are provided to facilitate administration with students from different Spanish-speaking backgrounds.

The system is based on the *Comprehensive Inventory of Basic Skills in English.* While considerable caution was exercised in the adaptation process, undoubtedly some content and format bias remains. The publisher states that a national group of advisors (which included authorities in the Spanish language), linguists, and educators participated in the adaptation process by critiquing and revising items for potential inclusion. A questionnaire was mailed to 10,000 educators involved in bilingual, ESL, migrant, and bilingual special education programs to ascertain which of the 183 assessments from the *Comprehensive Inventory of Basic Skills* (K through 8) were appropriate for inclusion. In addition, 150 field testers reviewed each assessment (once adapted) for content validity, clarity of directions, Spanish grammatical structure, and Spanish word choice.

Skill sequences were developed by researching different publishers' Spanish and English texts to determine the sequence and grade levels at which skills are most frequently taught and when competency should be expected. Grade notations are given to indicate these levels on the examiner pages and in the student record book for specific assessments. [(Spanish basal series were analyzed to determine the grade sequence noted.)] The publisher claims the instrument is culturally fair, since regional terms and expressions are provided to make the instrument more appropriate for use with all Hispanic youngsters. The test was field tested throughout the United States and in Latin America in hospitals/clinics and a variety of school settings.

The strength of the system is that it monitors student progress in functional skills development from grades K through 6, is individually administered, and provides considerable diagnostic guidance to teachers. Weaknesses include the fact that it was constructed from an English test and that it may not correlate perfectly to a particular district's curriculum content sequence in Spanish and English.

DISTRICT-DEVELOPED INSTRUMENTS IN NON-ENGLISH LANGUAGES

Many districts have noted a need for developing local instruments that measure content area achievement in their high-incidence LEP students' native languages. A variety of instruments have been developed by districts including Chicago's Short Test of Linguistic Skills, which assesses reading achievement, grades 3 through 8, in 11 languages; Seattle's kindergarten through twelfth-grade reading, math, and social studies achievement tests in five languages; Hayward's kindergarten through sixth-grade Bilingual Management System in Portuguese, Spanish and English; and Boston's Cloze Test to measure reading achievement, grades 2 through 8, in 10 languages (see Appendix B). These tests vary in terms of their technical properties (reliability and validity) and diagnostic capability. Practitioners who use locally developed instruments in the educational assessment of LEP students need to understand the strengths and limitations of each measure employed to ensure that use of such instruments is accomplished in a nonbiased manner. The previously described content, construction, administration, and student-related factors that create biases in standardized measures may also exist in locally developed measures; therefore, an appropriate level of caution is encouraged.

Commerical publishers have also developed placement or mastery testing materials in Spanish to accompany their Spanish basal reading series. Examples include Santillana's Reading Management System; Crane's Placement/Diagnostic Tests; Addison Wesley's CRTs and end of book tests; and Houghton-Mifflin's placement and assessment tests.

CLOZE TESTING WITH CONTENT AREA MATERIAL

Since commercial criterion-referenced tests and instruments are designed independently of specific school districts, there is no guarantee that the content will match local curricula. Thus, it may be preferable to base assessment on locally determined classroom materials. One procedure designed for this application is the cloze procedure, which can help determine which level and series in reading, science, or social studies will prove useful in a particular student's individualized education program.

In order to establish the readability of a particular reading or content area textbook in English or the native language for a specific student, the cloze testing procedure is recommended. In this procedure, a self-contained passage is chosen out of a book that is at the student's expected grade level. The text could be a story or a chapter from a content area book. Words are blanked out of the text systematically (every *n*th word), and the student's task is to fill in those blanks. Specific conditions need to be met in the construction, administration, and interpretation of a cloze test (see Cohen, 1980, for a description of the procedures).

The cloze procedure is an easy and quick way for teachers to assess the reading difficulty of texts they intend to use with particular students. One positive feature of the cloze procedure is that it is not based on direct translation of specific English or L1 words and structures. Rather, it focuses on the underlying meaning relationships and concepts taught in the educational setting (Oller, 1979). Since this is the case, cloze procedures can be applied across many languages. Cloze techniques have been used in Czech, French, Spanish, Italian, German, Japanese, Polish, Swedish, Thai, Vietnamese, Navajo, and Apache with equal success to that obtained in English. Assessment procedures related to the actual classroom materials that will be used are favored over measures with only general curricular relevance (Cabello, 1983).

PERFORMANCE ANALYSIS

An intuitively appealing approach to academic assessment involves the concept of performance analysis: that is, using informed, on-going observation during actual academic tasks to determine a student's strengths and weaknesses (Mercer & Yssledyke, 1977). This is accomplished by noting the occurrence of behaviors that can act as "windows" into the academic task of interest (Goodman & Goodman, 1977). These behaviors focus on the processes used by the student in the academic task rather than on the end product. As an illustration, in reading miscue analysis, the types of errors noted (e.g., various word substitutions) can give important information regarding the student's interpretation of the meaning of a passage. This assessment approach is different than those previously discussed in that the evaluator observes and/or works with the student during the academic task of interest and attempts to determine how, when, and why the student experiences difficulty. This can only be accomplished, however, by close observation and awareness of certain behaviors that reflect on the process of learning. In the areas of reading and story telling, Norris (1985) has identified a number of behaviors that appear to provide insight into the deep level of semantic processing during reading and story telling activities. By noting these behaviors during the task of interest (e.g., reading), the evaluator can determine what aspects of the reading process are causing the child difficulty and can formulate strategies to overcome these problems (Norris, 1988).

Performance analysis can be used with any academic task *if* the evaluator has valid processing indices for the academic task. By noting these behaviors in their performance context, the evaluator can make inferences regarding the underlying problems and confirm these assumptions by attempting to overcome the difficulties. In this regard, performance analysis is a test-teach-test approach (Piazza, 1979).

The following outline is provided to aid performance analysis in mathematics and to demonstrate a variety of areas in which intervention could lead to improvement in student performance.

A. Potential indices of difficulty
  1. Output: Quantity and/or quality of the student's work
  2. Distractability during task
  3. Avoidance of activity
  4. Requests for assistance
  5. A spatial or sequential pattern of response
  6. Frustration
  7. Response delays
  8. Self-corrections
B. Potential contextual factors
  1. Computational abilities
  2. Conceptual knowledge
  3. Self-confidence
  4. Motivation
  5. Problem solving approach
    a) Perseverance
    b) Appreciation of patterns
    c) Task-presentation preference
    d) Language-use preference
    e) Strategies employed
    f) Investigative behavior used
    g) Communication abilities
    h) Record-keeping skills

By focusing on possible indices of difficulty within the actual performance context, performance analysis can give evaluators a better understanding of the academic abilities of the student. This approach is inherent in miscue analysis in reading (Goodman & Goodman, 1977) and in numerous other assessment techniques involving discussion group activities (Calfee & Sutter-Baldwin, 1982), writing activities (Isaacson, 1985), and prereferral activities (Graden, Casey, & Bonstrom, 1985).

LEARNING STYLE ANALYSIS

One instructional dimension receiving increasing attention in promoting and ensuring student achievement is matching instruction to the students learning style. A student's learning style may be defined as the consistent pattern of behavior and performance used by that student in the educational domain: that is, the manner in which the individual approaches, manipulates, and attempts to overcome any learning task. According to some researchers (Ross, 1985; Sokolov, 1972), a student's learning style is actually a composite of that person's internal neurological and personality traits linked with culturally mediated traits learned through social interactions with others. To ensure that an individual benefits optimally from academic instruction, it is helpful for evaluators to link the teaching strategies that are used with the student's learning style.

The objective of learning style analysis should be to determine which style most closely resembles the student's and then to determine if the educational strategies used in the academic situation are consistent with this style. There are a number of techniques that can be used in learning style analysis (see Burke-Guild & Garger, 1985). The work of Dunn (1983a; b; c), Hodges (1983), Hopkins (1978), and Carbo (1982a; b) offer learning style analyses for general educational activities, mathematics, and reading activities, respectively. Additionally, there are inventories such as the *Learning Styles Inventory* (Dunn, Dunn, & Price, 1979), which has been translated into Spanish; the *Myers-Briggs Type Indicator* (Myers & Briggs, 1976); and the *Gregorc Style Delineator* (Gregorc, 1982). Each of these tools may determine the learning style of the LEP student and appropriate teaching strategies can be implemented.

CONCLUSIONS

The majority of existing procedures for educational assessment are designed for students from a high-incidence language background with high-incidence disabilities. Less abundant are procedures for high-incidence language-background students with lower-incidence handicapping conditions or low-incidence language background students with high-incidence disabilities. Least available are assessment procedures for low-incidence language groups with low-incidence disabilities. This means that standardized, criterion-referenced, and locally developed procedures are most abundant for mildly handicapped Hispanic students. Fewer resources exist for educators assessing moderate and severely impaired youngsters of all language backgrounds. Few resources exist for educators serving students with low-incidence handicapping conditions from low-incidence language backgrounds.

Above and beyond the question of availability of measures or applicable techniques are the interpretation issues discussed in the first half of this chapter. These factors make appropriate educational assessment of LEP students with special needs a challenge to educators serving such students. Success can only be attained through the combined and concerted efforts of all parties involved: parents, teachers, and assessors.

REFERENCES

Ambert, A., & Dew, N. (1982). *Special education for exceptional bilingual students: A handbook for educators.* Milwaukee: Midwest National Origin Desegregation Assistance Center, The University of Wisconsin–Milwaukee.

Baca, L. M., & Cervantes, H. T. (1984). *The bilingual special education interface.* St. Louis: Times Mirror/Mosby.

Bernal, E. M., Jr. (1977). *Adapting asssessment procedures to specific population characteristics: The Chicano child.* (ERIC Document Reproduction Service No. ED 145 943).

Bloom, A. H. (1981). *The linguistic shaping of thought: The impact of language on thinking in China and the West.* Hillsdale, NJ: Lawrence Erlbaum Associates.

Bradley, C. (1984). Issues in mathematics education for Native Americans and directions for research. *Journal for Research in Mathematics Education, 15*(2), 96–106.

Bronfenbrenner, U. (1986). Alienation and the four worlds of childhood. *Phi Delta Kappan, 66,* 430–436.

Bruck, M. (1984). The suitability of immersion education for children with special needs. In C. Rivera (Ed.), *Communicative competence approaches to language proficiency assessment: Research and application* (pp. 123–133). Clevedon, England: Multilingual Matters.

Burke-Guild, P., & Garger, S. (1985). *Marching to different drummers.* Alexandria, VA: Association for Supervision and Curriculum Development.

Cabello, B. (1983). A description of analysis for the identification of potential sources of bias in dual language achievement tests. *NABE Journal, 7,* 33–51.

Calfee, R., & Sutter-Baldwin, L. (1982). Oral language assessment through formal discussion. *Topics in Language Disorders, 2,* 45–55.

Carbo, M. (1982a). Be a master reading teacher. *Early Years. 12,* 39–42, 47.

Carbo, M. (1982b). Teaching reading the way children learn to read. *Early Years, 12,* 43–47.

Carsrud, K. E. (1980). *Evaluation of achievement outcomes: Austin's experience* (Publication No. 80. 33). Austin, TX, Austin Independent School District. (ERIC Document Reproduction Service No. ED 193 006).

Cervantes, R. A. (1975). *Problems and alternatives in testing Mexican-American students.* Washington, D.C., National Institute of Education. (ERIC Document Reproduction Service No. ED 093 951).

Cohen, A. (1980). *Testing language ability in the classroom.* Rowley, MA: Newbury House.

Coyne, M. (1979). Math the universal language? *Bilingual Education Service Center Newsletter, 7*(1), 11–12.

Cummins, J. (1981). Minority students and learning difficulties: Issues in assessment and placement. In *Summary Proceedings of a Working Institute on Bilingual Special Education* (pp. 3–34). Boulder, CO: Bueno Center for Multicultural Education, University of Colorado, Boulder.

Cummins, J. (1982). Tests, achievement, and bilingual students. *FOCUS, 9.* Rosslyn, VA: National Clearinghouse for Bilingual Education.

Cummins, J. (1984). *Bilingualism and special education: Issues in assessment and pedagogy.* Austin, TX: PRO-ED.

Cummins, J. (1986). Empowering minority students: A framework for intervention. *Harvard Educational Review, 56,* 18–35.

Davis, F. B. (1974). Criterion-referenced testing: A critique. In W. Blanton, R. Farr, and J. Tuinman (Eds.), *Measuring Reading Performance.* Newark; DE: International Reading Association.

Deyhle, D. (1987). Learning failure: Tests as gatekeepers and the culturally different child. In H. T. Trueba (Ed.), *Success or failure? Learning and the language minority student* (pp. 85–108). New York: Newbury House.

Dreisbach, M., & Keogh, B. K. (1982). Test-wiseness as a factor in readiness test performance of young Mexican-American children. *Journal of Educational Psychology, 74,* 224–229.

Dunn, R. (1983a). Now that you know your learning style: How can you make the most of it? *Early Years, 13*(6), 49–54.

Dunn, R. (1983b). Now that you understand your learning style . . . What are you willing to do to teach your students through THEIR individual styles?, *Early Years, 13*(7), 41–43, 62.

Dunn, R. (1983c). You've got style: 21 elements that determine your learning style. *Early Years, 13*(6), 26–31.

Dunn, R., Dunn, K., & Price, G. E. (1979). *Learning styles inventory.* Lawrence, KS: Price Systems, Inc.

Feuerstein, R. (1980). *Instrumental enrichment: An intervention program for cognitive modifiability.* Baltimore, MD: University Park Press.

Fischer, K. B., & Cabello, B. (1981). *Predicting student success following transition from bilingual programs.* Report #CSE-R-161. National Institute of Education, Washington, D.C. (ERIC Document Reproduction Service No. ED 222 091).

Frierson, H. T. (1977). *Test-taking intervention: Its effects on minority student's MCAT scores.* (ERIC Document Reproduction Service No. ED 206 687).

Garcia, A. B., & Zimmerman, B. J. (1972). The effect of examiner ethnicity and language on the performance of bilingual Mexican-American first graders. *Journal of Social Psychology, 87,* 3–11.

Gifford, C. S., & Fluitt, J. L. (1980). How to make your students test-wise. *The American School Board Journal, 167*(10), 29.

Goodlad, J. I. (1983). *A place called school: Prospects for the future.* New York: McGraw-Hill.

Goodman, K. S., & Goodman, Y. M. (1977). Learning about psycholinguistic processes by analyzing oral reading. *Harvard Educational Review, 47*, 317–333.

Graden, J. L., Casey, A., & Bonstrom, O. (1985). Implementing a prereferral intervention system: Part II. The data. *Exceptional Children, 51*, 487–496.

Green, D. R. (1972). *Racial and ethnic bias in test construction, Final Report* (ERIC Document Reproduction Service No. ED 056 090).

Gregorc, A. (1982). *Gregorc Style Delineator.* Maynard, MA: Gabriel Systems, Inc.

Hodges, H. L. B. (1983). Learning styles: Rx for mathphobia. *Arithmetic Teacher, 30*(7), 17–20.

Hopkins, M. H. (1978). The diagnosis of learning styles in Arithmetic. *Arithmetic Teacher, 25* (7), 47–50.

Issacson, J. (1985). Assessing written language skills. In C. S. Simon (Ed.), *Communication skills and classroom success: Assessment of language-learning disabled students* (pp. 403–424). San Diego: College Hill Press.

Jacobs, L. (1987). *Disability or cultural differences: A study of four Hmong third grade students in a California resettlement community.* Santa Barbara: Social Process Research Institute, University of California.

Kirk, S. A., Kliebhan, J. M., & Lerner, J. W. (1978). *Teaching reading to slow and disabled learners.* Boston: Houghton Mifflin.

Matluck, J. H., & Mace, B. J. (1973). Language characteristics of Mexican-American children: Implications for assessment. *Journal of School Psychology, 11*, 365–386.

McPhail, I. P. (1981). Why teach test-wiseness? *Journal of Reading, 25*, 32–38.

Mercer, J. R. (1979). *System of Multicultural Pluralistic Assessment Technical Manual.* New York: The Psychological Corporation.

Mercer, J. R., & Ysseldyke, J. (1977). Designing diagnostic-intervention programs. In T. Oakland (Eds.), *Psychological and educational assessment of minority children* (pp. 70–90). New York: Brunner/Mazel.

Myers, I. B., & Briggs, K. C. (1976). *Myers-Briggs Type Indicator.* Palo Alto, CA: Consulting Psychologist Press.

Nadeau, A., & Miramontes, O., (1987). *The reclassification of limited-English proficient students: Assessing the interrelationship of selected variables.* Presentation at the 16th Annual International Bilingual Bilcultural Education Conference (NABE), Denver, CO.

Nava-Hamaker, M. L., (1981). *Academic achievement of LEP students after reclassification: A southern California Study.* (ERIC Document Reproduction Service No. ED 221 313).

Norris, J. A. (1985). *Pragmatic criteria and the prediction of reading achievement: An examination of qualitative language differences.* Unpublished doctoral dissertation, University of Nebraska, Lincoln.

Norris, J. A. (1988). Using communicative strategies to enhance reading acquisition. *The Reading Teacher, 47*, 668–673.

Nuttall, E. V., Landurand, P. M., & Goldman, P. (1984). A critical look at testing and evaluation from a cross-cultural perspective. In P. C. Chinn (Ed.), *Education of Culturally and Linguistically Different Exceptional Children* (pp. 42–62). Reston, VA: ERIC Clearinghouse on Handicapped and Gifted Children.

Oller, J. W., Jr. (1979). *Language tests at school.* Rowley, MA: Newbury House.

Padilla, A. M. (1979). Critical factors in the testing of Hispanic Americans: A review and some suggestions for the future. In R. Tyler & S. H. White (Eds.), *Testing, teaching, and learning* (pp. 219–243). Report of a conference on research on testing, National Institute of Education, Washington, D.C.

Philips, S. (1983). *The invisible culture: Communication in the classroom and on the Warm Springs Indian Reservation.* New York: Longman.

Piazza, R. (1979). *Three models of learning disabilities.* Guildford, CN: Special Learning Corporation.

Plata, M. (1982). *Assessment, placement, and programming of bilingual exceptional pupils: A practical approach.* Reston, VA: ERIC Clearinghouse on Handicappped and Gifted Children.

Politzer, R. L. (1983). Linguistic and communicative competence of Mexican-American pupils and their relation to motivation, length of residence, and scholastic achievement. *Bilingual Education Paper Series, 6*(9). (Also ERIC Document Reproduction Service No. ED 255 047).

Powers, S. (1982). *The effect of test-wiseness on the reading achievement scores of minority populations.* Final report. (ERIC Document Reproduction Service No. ED 222 549).

Ramirez, M., III. (1983). *Psychology of the Americas: Mestizo perspectives on personality and mental health.* New York: Academic Press.

Rivera, C. (Ed.). (1983). *An ethnographic/sociolinguistic approach to language proficiency assessment.* Clevedon, England: Multilingual Matters.

Ross, D. (1985). *Learning styles.* (ERIC Document Reproduction Service, ED 269 201).

Skutnabb-Kangas, T., & Toukomaa, P. (1976). *Teaching migrant children's mother tongue and learning the language of the host country in the context of the socio-cultural situation of the migrant family.* Helsinki: The Finnish National Commission for UNESCO.

Skutnabb-Kangas, T. (1981). Guest worker or immigrant: Different ways of reproducing an under-class. *Journal of Multilingual Multicultural Development, 2,* 89–115.

Sokolov, A. N. (1972). *Inner speech and thought.* New York: Plenum Press.

Spindler, G. (Ed.). (1987). *Education and the cultural process: Anthropological approaches* (2nd ed.). Prospect Heights, IL: Waveland Press.

Toukomaa, P., & Skutnabb-Kangas, T. (1977). *The intensive teaching of the mother tongue to migrant children of preschool age and children in the lower level of comprehensive school.* Research Reports 26. Tampere: Department of Sociology and Social Psychology, University of Tampere, Finland.

Trueba, H. T. (1987). *From cultural differences to learning handicaps: An ethnographic study of four minority children.* Santa Barbara: Office for Research on Educational Equity, Linguistic Minority Research Project, Graduate School of Education, University of California.

Ulibarri, D. M., Spencer, M. L., & Rivas, G. A. (1981). Language proficiency and academic achievement: A study of language proficiency tests and their relationship to school ratings as predictors of academic achievement. *NABE Journal, 5*(3), 47–80.

Zirkel, P. A. (1972). Spanish-speaking students and standardized tests. *Urban Review, 5/6,* 32–40.

CHAPTER 7

Assessment
of Cognitive Ability

WAYNE H. HOLTZMAN, JR.
AND
CHERYL YELICH WILKINSON

Cognitive assessment rests on the assumption that a sample of an individual's behavior can be used to predict that person's future learning. For this prediction to be accurate, the behavioral sample should represent the individual's best performance and incorporate a number of chances for the individual to show knowledge in a variety of areas.

When the individual to be assessed is limited English proficient (LEP) but is being examined in an environment where English is the predominant language, the chance for optimal performance is threatened. This chapter will review research and theory related to cognitive assessment with culturally different populations, particularly those who are limited in English proficiency and provide guidelines regarding such assessments. The focus will be on assessment as it is carried out for school-age individuals, the group for whom handicapping conditions are most frequently identified (Mercer, 1973).

Further, the chapter mainly focuses on cognitive assessment of students with mild handicaps such as learning disabilities and mild mental retardation. While the identification of more severely handicapped LEP students is a priority, these handicaps are usually easier to diagnose due to their more pronounced physiological and developmental components. When a mild handicap is suspected, the differentiation between an intrinsic handicapping condition versus a cultural/language difference as the causal factor for school problems becomes more difficult to determine. Finally, this chapter is written from the perspective that assessment must serve several purposes, including identification of the handicapping condition, provision of a basis for educational planning, and fulfillment of the legal and procedural requirements for special education. Therefore, although some critics have suggested that traditional IQ tests are inappropriate for culturally diverse and LEP students, strengths and weaknesses as well as possible modifications of IQ tests are reviewed here because those same traditional tests best fulfill some current legal guidelines. Similarly, innovative approaches to cognitive assessment that do not fulfill all legal requirements but that may generate expanded information for identification and planning also are included. The chapter concludes with a case demonstration of how cognitive assessments that both provide information and fulfill legal requirements can be conducted.

TASK OF ASSESSMENT

The objective of assessment should be the fairest, most accurate evaluation of the student possible. Assessment should have high-quality, appropriate educational interventions as its cornerstone. It should not be an isolated activity but should be regarded as an effective means of providing information to school personnel so that they can provide the best possible instructional settings and educational programs. In referring to his nondiscriminatory testing model, Tucker (undated, cited in DeBlassie & Franco, 1983) believes that nonbiased testing "simply means reducing the chance that a child is incorrectly placed in special classes and increasing the use of intervention programs which facilitate his or her physical, social, emotional, and academic development" (p. 51). To accomplish this objective is the task of assessment. In the cognitive area, one important component involves IQ testing.

IQ TESTING

General Purposes

Perhaps the most common reason for IQ testing is to determine eligibility for special education classes. Criteria for classification into different special education categories vary, and admission often is at least partially determined by the student's IQ scores. Indeed, without the IQ scores it would not be possible to legally classify a student as mentally retarded or learning disabled. A second common use of IQ tests is to obtain information concerning a student's "intellectual potential" and a profile of the individual's abilities in different areas. There is a high correlation between IQ scores and academic achievement, so information from an IQ assessment can aid in predicting future school achievement. When all the assumptions of cognitive assessment are met, parents and teachers can learn about the relative strengths and weaknesses of student's intellectual abilities.

LEGAL REQUIREMENTS

Almost all handicapping conditions require IQ assessment. To be classified as mentally retarded, a student must demonstrate an IQ score that falls more than two standard deviations below the mean. More severe retardation is indicated if the IQ is more than three standard deviations below the mean. To be classified as learning disabled, a student's IQ must fall within the normal range. In addition, it must fall at least one standard deviation above a standardized achievement test score, so that a discrepancy exists between the individual's intellectual functioning and academic achievement. A handicapping condition of emotional disturbance likewise requires an IQ score within the normal range. IQ scores are less important to the classification of the physically handicapped and multihandicapped, but IQ tests nonetheless frequently are administered to these students. A comprehensive IQ assessment is not required for individuals who are speech and language handicapped, but it is important that they show evidence of normal intellectual functioning. Short screening instruments such as the Test of Nonverbal Intelligence (TONI) or the Peabody Picture Vocabulary Test–Revised (PPVT-R) typically are used with these students (see Chapter Five).

Until the passage of PL 94-142 in 1975, there were no legal guidelines regarding language requirements for IQ assessment. In the early 1970s, however, there were several judicial decisons involving IQ testing for the assessment of minority groups, including culturally and linguistically different students, and their impact continues to affect assessment practices. *Baca and Cervantes (1984)* name *Arreola v. Board of Education (1968), Diana v. State Board of Education (1973),* and *Covarrubias v. San Diego Unified School District (1970)* as three of the most important cases. Casso (1973) notes that in each case, retests indicated that the plaintiff students were not mentally retarded and had been misplaced. Furthermore, it was determined that these students suffered damage from the misplacement. In the landmark Diana case, the school districts involved agreed to begin testing students in the primary language, administering nonverbal tests and ensuring that additional data would be collected and used in the assessment process.

With the passage of PL 94-142, however, a mandate was established that unless it is "clearly not feasible to do so," assessments must be carried out in the student's native language. The native language is defined as the language that the individual understands best and is not necessarily the language spoken by the parents. Noncompliance with this guideline is a violation of the law, and school districts should not give themselves much liberty in this regard. The burden of proof falls on the school district to justify why it is not feasible to conduct testing in the student's native language.

Controversy and change in the area of assessment have continued in the 1980s. Allegations of test bias and discrimination against minority groups have been heard with increasing frequency, and the courts have continued their involvement in testing issues. For example, the recent decision in the Larry P. v. Riles case has resulted in a chaotic situation for California's public school system. The original suit was filed in 1971 on behalf of black students in California, but legal directives were not handed down until 1987. It is now against California law for black students to be placed in special education on the basis of IQ tests. This case and others like it have resulted in changes in local school district practices: Many districts are hesitant to use IQ tests with LEP students, which has resulted in a dilemma for assessment personnel who have relied on IQ tests in the past. Informal tests, classroom observations, criterion-referenced tests and nonstandardized instruments, with which assessment personnel are not as familiar, are being used instead. Some districts have been experimenting with tools such as the Learning Potential Assessment Device (LPAD) (Feuerstein, 1979) as innovative, nonbiased assessment instruments that show promise for use with LEP and culturally different students, but these tools do not yet have sufficient data to warrant their exclusive use.

Given the best current data and the legal requirements for LEP assessment, no instrument is a panacea for the complex problem of conducting cognitive assessment of LEP students fairly and equitably. The instruments of cognitive assessment, therefore, must be supplemented with careful preparation and regard for the complexities of the evaluative process and the LEP population. It is appropriate, therefore, to suggest some general guidelines that should be considered when conducting cognitive assessment with this population.

GUIDELINES FOR ASSESSING THE LEP STUDENT

Assessment personnel are continuously faced with the task of gathering information about LEP students in a way that both fulfills legal requirements and provides adequate data for decision making. Inherent in these two conditions is the idea of avoiding potential bias. Specifically, the assessment personnel should monitor the potential effects of bias (either conscious or unconscious) in the referral process, in the actual assessment activities, and during the interpretation of the assessment data since these stages seem particularly susceptible. While this task is complicated, the following guidelines may be used to ensure more effective, nonbiased procedures at each of these stages: insistence on prereferral intervention, use of situational analysis, direct observation as a portion of the assessment process, establishment of language dominance prior to assessment, use of a dual-language testing strategy, informed selection of a test battery, and careful data interpretation.

PREREFERRAL INTERVENTION

A truly nonbiased assessment begins in the regular classroom. Before students are referred for testing, they should be exposed to appropriate instruction and educational interventions of different types in their regular learning environments (Heller, Holtzman, & Messick, 1982). This is necessary because the process of assessment frequently implies that the problem is inherent in the student rather than in the educational techniques applied. Since this is not always the case, the implication should not be made unless there is a basis for such a claim: that is, unless it has

Table 7-1. Assessment guidelines for limiting bias during cognitive
evaluations of LEP students

1. There must be an insistence on prereferral intervention before
   initiation of formal assessment request.
2. Assessment personnel should use situational analysis prior to
   formal assessment.
3. Direct observation of the student in the classroom environment
   should constitute a portion of the assessment process.
4. The student's language dominance should be determined prior
   administration of formal intelligence tests.
5. Assessment personnel should use a dual-language testing
   strategy.
6. Informed selection of the appropriate test battery should occur for
   each individual student.
7. Care should be taken in the interpretation of the assessment data.

been demonstrated that alternative instructional strategies as well as
behavioral techniques, social support, and counseling intervention have
been used and the student still experienced difficulty. Of particular relevance for LEP students is the inclusion of evidence showing that instruction in the native language has been attempted over a sufficient period
of time (Barona & Santos de Barona, 1987). The use and documentation
of these procedures may be referred to as *prereferral intervention*. Along
with the other prereferral procedures described in Chapter Four, this is a
first step in ensuring valid cognitive assessment as a safeguard against
unnecessary full-fledged assessment of LEP and other students. Many
LEP students are referred for assessment at the first sign of trouble,
before the potential benefits and risks of a special placement can be
weighed against alternative solutions.

    Prereferral intervention is important to consider for any individual,
but it is even more important for LEP students because the normal process of second-language acquisition may easily be confused with a communication disorder or learning disability. Similarly, the decision making process may be influenced by the expectations or biases that the
teacher or others in the classroom environment may hold toward the
LEP student.

    Prereferral intervention primarily involves the classroom teacher who
refers the individual for testing. Along with support personnel, the
teacher has a major responsibility in determining whether prereferral
interventions are successful. If a LEP student is experiencing difficulty in
academic areas, the teacher should review curriculum materials to determine their appropriateness for the student's cultural and linguistic background. If materials are not at an apppropriate instructional level, differ-

ent materials can be introduced. It is also important to review the type of teaching method that is being used. If a phonics approach to reading is inadequate, for example, global sight word approach or communicative reading strategies (Norris, 1988) could be tried. The teacher may choose to evaluate the student's performance through task analysis by breaking down the task into its component parts. The teach-test-reteach-retest process also can help to monitor the child's progress. Specialized personnel such as a Title I reading teacher, counselor, or math teacher can collaborate with the teacher at the prereferral stage. In some cases, it may be desirable for the student to be transferred to a different regular classroom if there is incompatibility between the language usage, personalities, or cognitive styles of the teacher and student in question. Only after various educational and behavioral interventions have been attempted should the individual be referred for a formal assessment.

The role of the assessment specialist is to monitor the prereferral intervention to determine if appropriate and sufficient approaches have been attempted and documented. If this is not the case, the responsible teacher can receive recommendations and guidance. Only after alternative approaches have been attempted and failed is a formal cognitive assessment necessary.

SITUATIONAL ANALYSIS

Even after referral, the school psychologist or educational diagnostician should evaluate background information carefully to confirm that the referral is appropriate (see Chapter Four). This step involves analysis of the actual referral situation and ensures that the referral does not reflect lack of knowledge or prejudice. Some teachers refer a disproportionate number of minority group students (including LEP students) because of their own inappropriately low expectations, frustration with unsuccessful teaching methods, lack of experience with this population, or unconscious racism. For example, a simulated study of vignettes found that teachers were willing to recommend special education placement for significantly more students who possessed certain "unattractive" physical attributes, even though all students were described as equal in intelligence and achievement (Ysseldyke & Algozzine, 1983). The assessment specialist is responsible for acting as a safeguard against such potential bias at the referral stage.

DIRECT OBSERVATION

School psychologists and educational diagnosticians must protect themselves against potential bias during the assessment process. Too often there is a tendency for assessment personnel to unconsciously lower their own expectations regarding the abilities of a student simply because the student is referred. One way for assessment personnel to overcome such referral acquiescence (Damico, 1988) is to observe the LEP student in several different educational contexts before initiating formal testing procedures. This will provide information about how the individual works independently and how the student relates to teacher and peers. Assessment personnel also may gain insight into how discrepant the student's behavior is from that of other students in the classroom environment. Alessi and Kaye (1983) call this approach "norm-referenced observation." The school psychologist or educational diagnostician can then "calibrate" the expectations of the student against those for that student's peers. Additionally, assessment personnel should consider whether problems might be alleviated by a behavior modification intervention within the regular classroom. All recommendations, both academic and behavioral, should be communicated to the student's parents so that they have the opportunity to provide input (further reducing the chance of bias) and, if necessary, can help implement any needed changes.

ESTABLISHING LANGUAGE DOMINANCE

Assessment personnel should never assume that an individual is bilingual or speaks proficient English on the basis of hearsay, physical appearance, or assumptions derived from tangential information such as the student's surname. Decisions made from such information are frequently based on prejudice. Formal language assessments in both the native language and in English should be carried out for all LEP students upon referral, and previous assessments should not be used unless they are less than 6 months old (Ortiz et al., 1985). Since Cummins (1984) and others have shown that there are differences between an individual's language use for communication versus the language needed to perform in the classroom, information regarding an individual's use of school-related language (cognitive academic linguistic proficiency) is as important or more important than knowing the student's level of conversational language skill (basic interpersonal communication skills). Because the language tests ordinarily used for placement in bilingual education programs focus more on conversational language, teachers and assessment personnel should not place undue emphasis on placement test scores derived solely from conversational formats. Rather, they should try to estimate the student's academic language proficiency through analysis of the language skills needed in the classroom and other learning situations. This may involve informal assessment approaches (see

Chapters Four and Five). If the LEP student is bilingual, an estimate of the individual's academic language proficiency should be obtained for each language.

DUAL-LANGUAGE TESTING

One way to avoid potential bias based on inappropriate assumptions about a student's language abilities is for assessment personnel to use a dual-language testing strategy. When using this strategy, the question to ask with most LEP students is not whether to test in both languages, but which language to test in first. The dominant language of the individual should be used for initial testing, but testing in the weaker language should also be performed. To test a student's IQ only in the dominant language gives the assessor an incomplete picture of the individual's abilities and ignores information that has been learned and stored in the other language. In order to limit bias in assessment, students must have every opportunity to demonstrate their competencies. In using this strategy, it is of utmost importance to use certified bilingual examiners who have been trained in performing bilingual assessments for dual-language testing. Because of the need to test in two languages, the time required for the assessment is increased. Therefore a school psychologist cannot complete an assessment in a single two-hour testing session. The amount of time devoted to the assessment of LEP students, however, should not be the issue. The primary objective is that the assessment be valid and of high quality. Misplacement of a LEP student in a special education class because of an inadequate assessment is unfair, affects the individual's educational future, and may cause the school district to bear the added expense of special services for a student who does not need them. The added cost of the dual-language assessment strategy to school districts may result in lower long-term costs.

INFORMED SELECTION OF A TEST BATTERY

Given the many potential problems demonstrated when using standardized tests in assessing LEP students, the importance of assessment personnel's using a combination of standardized instruments and informal tests and procedures cannot be overemphasized. The qualitative data obtained from informal instruments and procedures should be integrated with the quantitative information obtained from standardized tests to produce a richer profile of the LEP student's abilities. Standardized instruments should, as much as possible, be selected to closely match the demographic and cultural aspects of the individual being assessed. Care should be taken to select standardized instruments that do not make use of inappropriate normative samples or culturally biased test content (see Chapter Five). When nonbiased standardized instruments are not available, modifications of the traditional approaches or informal procedures should supplement the more formal standardized instruments.

It is best not to rely on the results of only one IQ test to determine the intellectual functioning of any individual, particularly those who are LEP or culturally different. If mental retardation is suspected in an LEP individual, school psychologists should use the results of at least two IQ tests and measure the student's level of adaptive behavior. This lessens the potential biases of the individual tests.

CAREFUL TEST INTERPRETATION

Interpretation of test results that occur both at placement committee meetings and in psychological reports must be carefully accomplished for LEP students if proper placement is to be assured. When making initial placement decisions, it is particularly important to guard against bias. Numerous studies have indicated that placement decisions are frequently made on the basis of factors other than actual test data (Bergin, 1980; Cummins, 1984; Nuttall, Landurand, & Goldman, 1984). For example, there are instances when test results can be clearly explained by linguistic or cultural differences but these facts are ignored or suppressed due to lower expectations or prejudice. At times, however, test data are suppressed or ignored because the student is bilingual or LEP and the placement committee is uncertain about how the language issues should be addressed. Consequently, many students are inappropriately placed in special education programs or prevented from such placement when it is appropriate.

One way to avoid bias at this stage is to ensure that appropriate personnel are present during test interpretation. Although PL 94-142 requires that an assessment representative be present at placement meetings, it does not set any further requirements. For LEP students, the assessment representative should be fluent in the student's native language, familiar with the child's culture, and trained in bilingual assessment. This individual should aid the other personnel in the proper interpretation of the test data, given the knowledge of the student's performance and the student's cultural, linguistic, familial, and educational background.

To be able to communicate assessment results effectively in writing is another important consideration when attempting to avoid bias. The way in which information is presented in the psychoeducational report is critical if the reader is to understand and use it. If the report is unclear, contains technical inaccuracies or jargon, adds irrelevant or omits relevant information, it likely will be misinterpreted.

Possible report recipients include parents, teachers, principals and other school personnel, physicians, social welfare agencies, and law enforcement personnel. Students also may read the report at some point, especially if they are enrolled in junior high or high school. These individuals come from a wide variety of backgrounds and educational levels, and each may be using the report for a different purpose. Since the school psychologist does not know who may need to use the report in the future, the report should be written to communicate information as clearly and as straightforward as possible. Often, parents of LEP students either cannot read English or lack formal education altogether. In these cases, the school psychologist should ensure that the opportunity is provided for a parent conference in the native language to discuss the results and implications of the report. This conference should be separate from the placement meeting.

Psychoeducational reports should describe assessment procedures in sufficient detail so that no doubt remains concerning how the assessment was conducted. The report should document, for example, whether a test was administered bilingually through an interpreter, or whether a certified bilingual examiner was used. The language of testing for each instrument and the order of the test administrations should be recorded. If "testing the limits" was performed or if informal tests or procedures were implemented, this also should be documented. Caution should be used in interpreting a LEP student's IQ scores if the test norms are based on English speakers. If standardized procedures have been adapted during testing, norm-referenced scores should not be reported. Statements about the student's linguistic or cultural background should be carefully phrased so as not to be pejorative. All educational recommendations evolving from the assessment should be specific and should include suggestions about the language of instruction as well as suggestions for teaching approaches. It is better to offer no recommendations than to use broad, difficult to follow recommendations. Recommending that the student be instructed using "a multisensory approach" or that the student be provided "individualized instruction to meet his or her needs" will not provide teachers with sufficient insight to improve the individual's educational treatment plan. In formulating recommendations for LEP students, psychologists should consider the multiple settings in which these individuals may be served. A LEP student found to be mildly handicapped probably will receive instruction in both a regular bilingual and a special education classroom. Further, the same student may be mainstreamed into a regular monolingual classroom for some activities. Recommendations to facilitate the coordination of content and instructional approaches across settings should be included for all LEP students.

APPROACHES TO COGNITIVE ASSESSMENT

While prereferral procedures combined with nontraditional testing procedures may meet the needs of some LEP students, there will always be individuals for whom traditional psychoeducational assessment information is needed. This section reviews available options for cognitive assessment in light of their advantages and disadvantages for the evaluation of LEP students.

TRADITIONAL APPROACHES

Two tests of cognitive skills have been used most frequently by schools during the past 50 years. These are the Stanford-Binet and Wechsler Scales. Both scales have been renormed on several occasions; however, their basic structure has endured. This section will discuss briefly these two tests and their use and examine the principles that have guided their construction. Problems inherent in these instruments for LEP students will be highlighted.

The Stanford Binet

The Stanford-Binet Intelligence Scale–Revised has its roots in the Binet-Simon Scale developed in 1905 (Hagen, Sattler, & Thorndike, 1985). It is used to test persons from age 2 to adult. Stanford-Binet subtests are arranged by age and show a progressive increase in difficulty level. The examiner usually begins testing at the examinee's chronological age level and continues until basal and ceiling criteria are reached. It is assumed that an examinee would pass all tests below the basal level and fail all tests above the ceiling. The Stanford-Binet is regarded as a heavily verbally laden scale; however, since reliability is adequate at the upper and lower ranges of IQ, the Stanford-Binet is still used when a student may be gifted or mentally retarded. This is true even if the student is LEP (Holtzman, Jr., Ortiz, & Wilkinson, 1986).

The Wechsler Scales

As with the Stanford-Binet, the Wechsler Intelligence Scales have been renormed several times since their initial development. The scale used with school-aged individuals is the Wechsler Intelligence Scale for Children–Revised (WISC-R) (Wechsler, 1974). In contrast to the Stanford-Binet, in which the age of the examinee determines which subtests are administered, all examinees are administered the same subtests, which are grouped into Verbal and Performance scales.

The WISC-R is the most frequently used test for the cognitive evaluation of school-aged children and is often administered to LEP students. Two studies that examined assessment practices for Hispanic LEP students with either learning disabilities or mental retardation (Ortiz et al., 1985; Holtzman, Jr., Ortiz, & Wilkinson, 1986) found that 92% of the learning disabled students and 66% of the mentally retarded students received the WISC-R as part of their initial evaluation. Upon reevaluation, all of the LEP learning disabled students were administered the WISC-R (Wilkinson & Ortiz, 1986).

TRADITIONAL IQ SCALES AND THE LEP STUDENT

Since the Stanford-Binet and Wechsler Scales often are administered to LEP students, and since important decisions are based on the IQs obtained from them, much has been written about their suitability for culturally different individuals. More recently, their appropriateness for LEP students also has been considered. Besides matching the test's language to the individual, concerns have centered on two major areas: (1) the model of testing on which the tests are based, and (2) other potential sources of test bias, including cultural and socioeconomic bias and lack of representation of LEP students in norming samples.

Test Development and Indicators of Quality

Both the Stanford-Binet and WISC-R have been developed and renormed following accepted procedures for norm-referenced tests. Items that best correlate with success on a subtest or the full instrument, and that represent varying levels of difficulty, are selected. Cummins (1984) believes that this norming process biases IQ tests against minority groups. Because the standardization sample represents minority groups in limited numbers, the items that appear to meet the criteria for good items will reflect the learning and experience of the majority. In addition to the representativeness of the norming sample, the quality of a norm-referenced test is judged by its reliability and validity as well as its long-term stability. Research on the WISC-R suggests that reliability and validity are adequate for minority populations. Dean (1977) reports reliability coefficients for the WISC-R that are similar to those reported in the test manual for a sample of 53 Hispanic students tested over a 1-year period. A similar study (Dean, 1979) found WISC-R scores to be acceptable predictors of Iowa Test of Basic Skills (ITBS) achievement scores for a sample of 49 Mexican-American students, with verbal scores showing a stronger relationship to achievement than did performance scores. Oakland (1983) also reports high correlations between WISC-R scores and later reading and math scores on the California Achievement Test for a sample that included approximately 130 Mexican-American students. However, the influence of limited English proficiency on test reliability and validity (especially for tests administered in English) has not been determined.

The long-term stability of IQ tests for culturally or linguistically different populations has received little research attention. Wilkinson and Ortiz (1986) report significant decreases in Hispanic LEP LD students' Verbal IQ scores between school triannual evaluations. However, it cannot be concluded from this that the IQs of all LEP students are similarly unstable.

Cultural and Socioeconomic Bias

It often is suggested that traditional psychoeducational tests contain items that are biased against certain groups while favoring middle-class mainstream students. Cultural bias also occurs when tests are translated. For example, when English WISC-R Verbal Scale items are translated to Spanish on the Escala de Inteligencia Wechsler para Ninos–Revisada (EIWN-R; Wechsler, 1982), the difficulty level of some items changes across languages. The connotation of a word in one language may be slightly different from that of its counterpart in another. The Vocabulary subtest of the WISC-R especially is affected by this problem.

Differences in cultural value systems can create problems as well. For example, the Comprehension subtest of the WISC-R attempts to measure social reasoning and ability to function appropriately in society. The middle-class child from the United States would likely agree that it is usually better to give money to an organized charity than to a street beggar. In some third world nations, however, giving money to a street beggar would be considered better because charities are filled with corruption and the lack of a welfare system ensures that most of these beggars truly are in need of financial assistance.

The issue of cultural bias has been given serious consideration in the formulation of testing guidelines. School districts need to be aware of possible allegations of cultural bias in the instruments that they use, since PL 94-142 has mandated that culturally biased instruments should not be used to make special education placement decisions.

Representation of LEP Students in Norming Samples

A frequent criticism of IQ tests is that their norms are based largely on mainstream students in the United States, and consequently, may be inappropriate for use with culturally or linguistically different students (Barona & Santos de Barona, 1987). The Hispanics included in the WISC-R standardization procedure (Wechsler, 1974) were not a representative sample since a disproportionate number of them appeared to be more elevated in socioeconomic status than the general Hispanic population. Unfortunately, no IQ test exists to date that has been normed for wide-spread use with LEP students. Consequently, school personnel should use extreme caution whenever interpreting the results of IQ tests to parents and to other professionals.

The best alternative for a standardization sample for culturally and linguistically different students is one based on local norms for sub-groups of interest. However, students' language proficiency as well as their native language must be considered in norming. One should not confuse LEP with English-proficient members of any bilingual group. Only to the extent that the subjects from the standardization sample are similar in relevant characteristics to the students of interest is it appropriate to use even local norms with these individuals.

Bias versus Fairness

The controversy over whether IQ tests are biased against culturally different individuals, and therefore appropriate to use in assessing their cognitive abilities, is an ongoing one. Because several interpretations of what constitutes test bias have been proposed, the answer to the question of whether tests are biased is both "no" and "yes."

Proponents of a psychometric view of bias (e.g., Clarizio, 1982) believe that IQ tests are not biased if they have similar statistical properties for all groups. Jensen (1974) downplays the influence of culture in explaining the differential performances of ethnic and racial groups and stresses the predictive validity of a test as particularly important. Since IQ tests have been shown to have similar reliabilities, validities, and factor structures for Anglos and minority groups (Gutkin & Reynolds, 1980), advocates of this position conclude that they are suitable for the assessment of culturally different students. Others (e.g., Mercer, 1979) use a "fairness" definition of bias. This definition argues that since both tests and schools stress the use of English and incorporate the assumptions of mainstream American society, a test can appear to be psychometrically valid while still overlooking the student's learning potential.

At present, it is not possible to conclude whether IQ tests are psychometrically biased against LEP students, since research that considers the interaction of language proficiency and test properties has not been carried out. Traditional IQ tests can be considered biased from a fairness definition because they have been found to contain items that are culturally specific.

MODIFICATIONS OF TRADITIONAL APPROACHES FOR THE LEP STUDENT

The problems with traditional IQ tests that have been discussed have led researchers and assessment personnel to seek means of making the scores of LEP and culturally different students more accurate and interpretable. Suggested methods include translations of tests, recategorizations of scores, testing of limits, nonverbal IQ tests, and statistical corrections of scores.

Translations of Traditional Tests

The problem of how best to assess an individual's IQ in the native language is difficult to solve. Even if a bilingual examiner is available, appropriate instruments are scarce. The majority of IQ tests have been developed in the United States, and translations into other languages have been conducted with varying degrees of success. Different translated versions of the WISC-R have been developed for use with Puerto Ricans, Cuban-Americans, and Mexicans. Standardized instructions and subtest items in Spanish for the EIWN-R were carefully prepared by consulting Hispanic experts in various regions of the United States. The final published version of the EIWN-R contains several options for phrasing test items and instructions to meet the linguistic needs of subcultural groups without violating standardized procedures. Unfortunately, only isolated local norms exist. No national Spanish norms are available, and norms for LEP Hispanics do not exist. Therefore, although a Spanish IQ test administration can be carried out, its results cannot be interpreted. The situation is even worse for other groups such as Cambodians or Vietnamese who do not as yet have access to standardized IQ tests in their native languages.

At least two ways of translating a test are available to a bilingual examiner, including the use of a script or impromptu translation. With a script, the examiner is not distracted by having to think about how to translate each item. The quality of the script notwithstanding, it provides a means of ensuring that all students tested by the examiner are exposed to the same linguistic stimuli, and the script can be used by other examiners as well. Impromptu translations should be discouraged since they lack the advantages just mentioned and may bias the difficulty level of test items to an unknown degree.

Since there are few certified examiners for languages other than English, school districts commonly hire paraprofessional interpreters to help in the administration of IQ tests. This can be an acceptable practice if the district carefully hires, trains, and supervises such individuals, and if English-based norms are not used when test results are interpreted. The use of an interpreter also allows the examiner to observe the student functioning in the native language under controlled conditions. Too often, however, these individuals are allowed to function with little supervision and with minimal or no training in test administration procedures. They may be fluent native speakers but still not understand the importance of adhering to instructions in the test manual. By not giving the student sufficient time to respond to an item, by teaching the student, or by providing inappropriate verbal and nonverbal cues, the interpreter can alter the test situation. If this occurs, the information obtained is less useful. Furthermore, if the interpreter is permitted to use impromptu translation of test items, there is no guarantee that the translation will be correct or appropriate (see Chapter Four for further discussion on the use of interpreters).

A study by Swanson and DeBlassie (1979) shows the importance of the language used or different test administration conditions in determining test scores. Students classified as Spanish dominant were tested using the WISC-R under one of three experimental conditions: with an English-speaking monolingual examiner, with an English-speaking monolingual examiner plus an interpreter, or with a fluent Spanish-speaking examiner. The highest scores on the Verbal scale were obtained from the English administration while the highest scores on the Performance scale were obtained from the Spanish administration. The English administration using an interpreter showed mixed effects and only sometimes resulted in higher scores than the Spanish administration. We speculate that the presence of the interpreter may have inhibited the student's performance on the Performance scale. The results of this study must be interpreted cautiously, however, since no formal assessment of the subjects' language proficiency was obtained.

Recategorization of WISC-R Scores

The interpretation of the WISC-R Verbal Scale score poses great difficulty when the student is LEP. A large difference between the Verbal and Performance scale scores is considered to be diagnostically significant. Obtaining a higher score on the Performance scale than the Verbal scale has been associated with mental retardation, reading difficulties, and learning disabilities (Sattler, 1974). In the case of LEP students, however, this discrepancy may simply show that less knowledge of English is needed to carry out performance tasks. A small number of studies have tried to identify patterns on the WISC-R that are typical for linguistically/culturally different versus handicapped children. Leton (1972) found culturally different Hawaiian students, who had been referred to special education, to have average IQs and average scores on the Bender Gestalt Visual Motor Test but a distinct pattern on the WISC-R when compared to learning disabled students. Leton interpreted these scores as evidence of lack of a learning disability.

Bannatyne (1974) proposed a recategorization of WISC-R subtests based on factor analytic studies. Among the factors he describes is Acquired Knowledge, which is intended to measure readiness for school but that also encompasses effects of acculturation outside the mainstream culture. This factor includes the Information, Arithmetic, and Vocabulary subtests. A Conceptualizing Ability factor, which includes the Comprehension, Similarities, and Vocabulary subtests, may also be sensitive to cultural influence. While Bannatyne's system is interesting, the two factors that may be culturally influenced include all of the Verbal subtests, essentially leaving the examiner with a Performance IQ only.

Cummins (1984) examined the WISC-R profiles of 428 referred Canadian students from minority-language backgrounds. He reported that typically, these students achieved higher scores on the Performance than on the Verbal scale. Within the Verbal scale, scores on the Arithmetic and Digit Span subtests were higher than scores on other subtests. Cummins suggests that deviations from this pattern by a language-minority student are significant. A low Performance, Arithmetic, or Digit Span score may indicate visual processing or auditory memory difficulties. Examination of score patterns to try to infer whether scores are depressed by culturally bound items is probably important when a LEP student is tested in English. However, recategorization of scores should not take the place of native language assessment or other ways of assessing cognitive functioning. Examination of a small number of subtests does not produce as reliable a score as does examination of an entire scale, and the idea of analyzing patterns of WISC-R subtests has been questioned (Kramer, Henning-Stout, Ullman, & Schellenberg, 1987).

Testing the Limits

One purpose of standardized tests is to ensure that all students are tested under similar conditions so that their performances can be compared with those of students in the standardization sample. But what if the examiner wishes to determine what the individual can learn under different, more flexible sets of conditions? To study an individual's performance in this manner is called "testing the limits." Teachers behave similarly whenever they try different curricula and teaching strategies with students who are not succeeding in their classes. They want to provide the best conditions for learning so that the individual can make optimal use of intellectual abilities. Likewise, the examiner may wish to provide the best conditions for showing what a child is able to do.

Testing the limits is an informal procedure in which the examiner purposefully violates standardized administration conditions in some way. This could involve substituting more comprehensible, less formal vocabulary in test instructions or items to see if the student's performance improves. Or, it might include administering items above the student's obtained ceiling to see if any of them can be mastered. Still another example would be to teach items to the student or to provide positive reinforcement to motivate the student to a higher level of performance. Unfortunately, most examiners never attempt to test the limits, even though it could be a useful clinical strategy with all students, particularly those who are LEP, since they may have difficulty performing well under the linguistic constraints of standardized conditions.

Nonverbal IQ Tests

Culturally and linguistically different students tend to perform poorly on verbal IQ tests. For example, Gerken (1978) found that Mexican-Americans obtained higher scores on nonverbal than verbal tests. Some researchers have therefore suggested that nonverbal IQ scores should be stressed in the assessment of LEP students (Wilen & Sweeting, 1986). It makes sense to emphasize nonverbal tests in cases where LEP students must be tested by English-speaking examiners. On the other hand, the usefulness of nonverbal tests is limited since only a partial measure of the student's intellectual ability is obtained and no measure of global IQ or of verbal abilities can be calculated. Verbal tasks have been found to predict school achievement better than nonverbal tasks do, so that using nonverbal IQ scores to predict LEP students' academic achievement must be done with caution. A better use of nonverbal IQ tests would be as screening instruments for students who are suspected of having below average cognitive development. Even in this case, the examiner should investigate the robustness of the instruments selected in order to choose appropriate ones. Some advantages and disadvantages of the more common nonverbal IQ tests used with LEP children are mentioned in the following section.

The WISC-R Performance Scale consists of five subtests that measure different nonverbal abilities. Thus, a pattern of strengths and weaknesses is obtained in nonverbal areas. Although Performance scale items do not require verbal expression, the examinee must follow standardized verbal instructions. Limited English proficient students who are not test-wise or who come from cultures where speed and accuracy is not highly valued may obtain low scores on the WISC-R Performance Scale because all subtest items are timed. In some cases, bonus points are provided for fast performance. Despite the above, the Performance Scale of the WISC-R is one of the better instruments for use with LEP students.

The Leiter International Performance Scale (Leiter, 1979) was originally thought to be culture-fair and has been used with many cultural groups. The original version was standardized on Hawaiian natives in about 1929, but Americans were included in a later revision. Although the notion of culture-free or culture-fair tests no longer is accepted, the Leiter Scale continues to be used with students who have limited verbal abilities. A variety of nonverbal abilities are included (e.g., visual discrimination, classification, sequencing). One advantage of this test is that only short instructions are required. While the test materials are colorful and interesting to students, they are heavy to carry. One of the biggest problems with the Leiter in the past has been that the norms for students in the United States clearly were inadequate (Oakland & Matuszek, 1977). Rather than supplanting other tests, the Leiter Scale can supplement information obtained from other sources if the score is interpreted cautiously.

The Progressive Matrices (Ravens, 1960) was developed in Great Britain largely as a measure of nonverbal abstract reasoning, classification, concept formation, and spatial abilities. Unlike most tests, norms have been established for several countries. It can be administered either to individuals or to groups. Although this test was once thought to be culture-fair, it has been shown to be biased against certain groups from non-European backgrounds and is susceptible to practice effects and educational level of examinees. In addition, very little psychometric information is reported in the manual (Anastasi, 1968). Thus, the Progressive Matrices test is better for assessing nonverbal abstract reasoning abilities than for obtaining a comprehensive measure of nonverbal IQ.

Some of the nonverbal subtests of the Stanford-Binet Intelligence Scales are helpful, especially for very young or retarded students. At the early age levels, all subtests are either nonverbal or require receptive as opposed to expressive language. If the examiner is not fluent in the student's native language, only the nonverbal subtests can be administered at each successive mental age level until it is clear that a ceiling has been reached. Although an IQ score is not obtained (since verbal subtests were not administered), much information could be obtained by examining age levels at which nonverbal subtests were passed.

There are two other nonverbal instruments that differ from others in that they were normed on handicapped populations. The Columbia Mental Maturity Scale, Third Edition (Burgemeister, Blum, & Lorge, 1972) was developed for use with individuals afflicted with cerebral palsy. It measures the individual's ability to classify objects. The examinee is asked to study several drawings of common objects and point to the one that does not fit logically. The test is good for screening purposes, particularly for Hispanic students (Wilen & Sweeting, 1986). The Hiskey-Nebraska (Hiskey, 1966) is a more comprehensive test of nonverbal abilities and was developed for use with deaf individuals. Separate norms exist for deaf and hearing populations, and the test can be used with children between the ages of 3 and 17. Pantomime and practice items are used, and subtests are not timed. Thus, this is an appropriate test to use with LEP students and is especially appropriate for deaf individuals from non-English speaking homes.

A more recent addition is the Test of Nonverbal Intelligence (Brown, Sherbenou, & Johnsen, 1982). The examiner mimicks the instructions and refrains from speaking during the test administration. It is similar to the Columbia Mental Maturity Scales and usually takes between 15 and 20 minutes to complete. Because of the short administration time and lack of language, some school districts have begun to include this instrument in their standard assessment battery. It also has been used as a screening device for LEP students who have been referred to speech-language pathologists. One should note, however, that it only measures a limited number of nonverbal abilities.

Regardless of which nonverbal tests are chosen, it is critical that assessment personnel not overemphasize any one test for diagnostic or placement decisions. None of these tests measure global IQ, and since they were normed on different groups of students, the extent of their usefulness for LEP populations has yet to be demonstrated. They should only be interpreted within a broad context.

Mercer's Estimated Learning Potential (ELP)

The development of the ELP was the outcome of a series of research studies that began with an examination of the prevalence of mental retardation in Riverside, California (Mercer, Butler, & Dingman, 1964). Results of this study led Mercer (1971) to study the labeling process and to design a system of assessment that she believed incorporated a variety of critical perspectives for the assessment of minority group students. The System of Multicultural Pluralistic Assessment (SOMPA; Mercer & Lewis, 1977) was normed on a sample of California children aged 5 to 12 years and includes both a student assessment and a parent interview. The student assessment is composed of physical dexterity tasks, the Bender Visual Motor Gestalt Test, a weight by height index, visual and auditory screenings, and the WISC-R. The parent interview includes the Health History Inventories, the Sociocultural Scales, and the Adaptive Behavior Inventory for Children.

When given to members of minority cultures, the WISC-R is scored in the traditional fashion to provide a comparison of the student's functioning to the expectations of the "school culture." WISC-R results are also used along with the Sociocultural Scales to calculate the ELP, which is a second estimate of intellectual functioning based on the student's sociocultural characteristics, including family size, family composition, SES, and urban acculturation. Rather than comparing the student's performance to the WISC-R's norming sample, the ELP compares performance to that of students with the same sociocultural characteristics. However, it should be noted that this comparison is statistically generated rather than coming from a norming sample.

One of the arguments against the use of the ELP is that the SOMPA's norms include only Anglo, Black, and non-LEP Hispanic students. The norms for Hispanic children may not be appropriate when a child is LEP, in that the SOMPA System requires that the WISC-R be administered in English (Wilen & Sweeting, 1986). Another concern about the use of the ELP is that the standardization of the SOMPA took place in California, and thus, its norms may not be applicable to other places. Buckley and Oakland (1977) found that regression weights used to predict the ELP differed between California and Texas. Oakland (1983) reports that the ELP does not predict school achievement as accurately as the uncorrected WISC-R. In general, while the approach to cognitive assessment taken by the SOMPA is an interesting one, the ELP has not been widely used by school systems.

INNOVATIVE APPROACHES TO COGNITIVE ASSESSMENT

Besides the traditional approaches and their modifications, attempts have been made to measure cognitive abilities through innovative procedures. These procedures incorporate conceptualizations of intelligence and theories of learning other than those on which more traditional tests are based, allowing them to minimize the use of verbal abilities in most cases. Additionally, since they have been developed recently, they generally are more relevant for culturally different students. Minority groups have been included as part of the target population, and items in some tests have been reviewed for cultural bias. While innovative procedures show promise for use with LEP students, their utility with these groups has yet to be proven.

The Cartoon Conservation Scales (CCS)

The Cartoon Conservation Scales (De Avila, 1977) is based on the cognitive-developmental theories of Jean Piaget. Piaget postulates that children proceed through a series of cognitive stages, each of which is characterized by the ability to use certain types of logic in thinking about problems and relationships between objects. One important concept that the child develops is conservation, which is the recognition that quantities remain constant despite their form.

The CCS measures eight Piagetian concepts: conservation of number, length, substance, distance, and volume; horizontality of water, egocentricity/perspective, and probability. The scales are intended for use with students in kindergarten through eighth grade. Problems are presented through a story illustrated by a cartoon. English and Spanish story scripts are provided, and the test manual contains suggestions about how to translate the test stories into any language. Approximately 60% of the norming sample for the CCS had Spanish surnames, making the test particularly suitable for use with Mexican-Americans (Bernal, 1980). While Mexican-Americans generally score lower than Anglos on tests such as the WISC-R, De Avila and Havassy (1974) found that Mexican-Americans scored at levels that were appropriate for their chronological age and that were equal to a control sample of Anglos on the CCS. Other research has suggested that the CCS may be useful in identifying gifted LEP children (Cohen, De Avila, & Intili, 1981) and may be used to suggest prescriptive classroom activities (Bernal & De Avila, 1976).

While the CCS represents a promising approach for LEP students, it is not without drawbacks. Dew (1979) cites reviews that find that although the test appears linguistically and culturally appropriate for Cuban, Puerto Rican, and Mexican-American students, some words from the Spanish translation might need to be changed for each group. Other reviews cited by Dew note that young children may have trouble following test directions since items are not given in a sequential order. The test has no verbal component, so the problems with nonverbal tests that were discussed previously also are present with the CCS. Most importantly, the relationship between scores on the CCS and school achievement has not been fully examined. Until more is known about how CCS scores relate to school functioning, it is probably not an appropriate test to use for identifying handicapping conditions.

Feuerstein's Learning Potential Assessment Device (LPAD)

The major purposes of the LPAD are to assess the degree to which a student's cognitive structures can be modified and to ascertain the conditions needed to make cognitive modifications. The instrument is intended for use with children and adolescents. The LPAD differs greatly from traditional approaches to cognitive assessment since norm-referenced comparisons are absent, and the testing situation is flexible rather than uniform. The examiner should serve as a teacher for the student and should prevent, rather than document, failure. The LPAD is based on work in Israel with refugee children (Feuerstein et al., 1986). Because these children differ in learning opportunities from children on whom traditional tests are normed, their IQs are uniformly low. Feuerstein developed the LPAD in order to accurately separate the handicapped from those who could be taught to function independently in Israeli society.

According to Feuerstein, adequate cognitive development is the result of an individual receiving enough mediated learning experiences to be able to interpret incoming information and to learn from direct experience. Mediated learning is defined as an interaction that incorporates the elements of: (1) meaning (i.e., the learner is made to understand the significance of this learning event); (2) intentionality (i.e., the teacher is emotionally invested in transferring meaning to the learner and will do what is needed to accomplish this); and (3) transcendence (i.e., what is learned goes beyond specific content to a principle that can be applied outside the learning situation). While factors such as genetic conditions, language differences, socioeconomic status, or home culture are important, they are only important because they promote or deny access to mediated learning.

In an LPAD administration, the examiner seeks to identify one or more cognitive deficits, to teach by mediation a strategy that will correct the deficit, and then to ascertain how well the child can apply the strategy learned to new material. The test includes dot organization (in which hidden figures are found) and the Raven's Progressive Matrices. Cognitive functions are observed at three phases of problem solving: input, elaboration, and output. A total of 29 possible cognitive deficiencies across the three areas are considered. Feuerstein has also developed a remediation program called Instrumental Enrichment, which is intended to teach the types of cognitive functions examined in the LPAD.

The LPAD offers several advantages over traditional cognitive assessment procedures. It avoids some problems encountered in the assessment of LEP students in the freedom it accords in the test situation. If the examiner believes the student's native language (or the native language and English together) should be used, this can be done without violating standardized procedures. The tasks used in the LPAD were selected to minimize cultural bias. Since the most important outcome of the assessment is the determination of what the student can do with concepts learned in the test session, students are not penalized for their linguistic or cultural background. Finally, the LPAD provides information that can be used to plan further instruction.

However, those wishing to use the LPAD may encounter several difficulties. The test takes more time to administer than do traditional IQ tests; it must be given by an examiner who has been trained by an LPAD trainer. At present, the number of trainers in the United States is small, and training opportunities are limited. Additionally, the LPAD is hard to adapt to current legal requirements, its administration relies upon the clinical judgment of the examiner, and the same child might be given different tasks or a different sequence of tasks if tested by different people. This in turn gives rise to the possibility that one examiner will perceive a child to be handicapped while a second does not. It is difficult to determine what degree of cognitive deficit indicates a need for special education placement. As a result, the LPAD's procedures are not amenable to the traditionally used psychometric criteria of standardization, reliability, or validity. While this is not a problem to the instrument's authors, it precludes the determination of whether the instrument predicts future school achievement. Finally, the LPAD rests on theories that are only now beginning to be studied empirically. The relationship between correcting deficient cognitive functions as Feuerstein defines them and enhanced academic learning has not been established.

Overall, the newness of the LPAD to the United States prevents complete evaluation of its utility. While it is worthy of further use and study, its strengths and weaknesses have not been fully established at this time.

Informal Assessment Procedures

Although adaptations of traditional standardized tests for LEP students have been proposed, and new tests continue to be developed, at this time no one method of cognitive assessment for a LEP student is adequate. Similarly, when a standardized test has been used, the teacher or psychologist may wish to validate its results against some other observation. In these instances, it is desirable to gain further insight into the student's cognitive functioning through the individual's naturally occurring behavior. Informal cognitive assessment strategies (as described by Guerin & Maier, 1983) provide a basis for collecting and organizing information about students' cognitive functioning by determining whether they can perform a skill being observed at various levels of difficulty.

Informal information can be gathered from several sources. The most important of these is direct observation, which can be structured or unstructured. In a structured observation, a target for the observations is identified and recorded (e.g., how many times a certain behavior occurs) while an unstructured observation encompasses all that happens. Indirect information can be gathered using interviews with the student and others or from school records. Finally, student work samples can be analyzed to locate patterns of errors and correct answers. It is important to observe LEP students using both the native language and English, so that comparisons across languages can be made.

Guerin and Maier (1983) detail six skills that they believe are indicative of cognitive functioning: (1) categorization, (2) association, (3) sequencing, (4) time concepts, (5) size concepts, and (6) problem solving. They further suggest that play behavior and the ability to identify body parts should be observed for younger children, while older children's ability to listen or otherwise monitor incoming information should be observed.

Several possible comparisons can help to interpret observation results. The student can be compared to others of a similar age and background, or informal results can be compared to the results of standardized testing. Deficient skills can be used as a basis for lesson planning. When students are LEP, the informal assessment may help to identify gaps in English vocabulary. If tasks can be performed more readily using pictorial stimuli or the native language rather than English, the examiner will feel more confident that lack of English expression rather than lack of cognitive ability is hampering performance.

Informal assessment offers several advantages over standardized testing. It can be conducted by anyone, so the assessor can be someone with whom the student is familiar. Formal testing, which may be threatening to the student can be avoided, and the student can simply be observed while working on classroom tasks. Informal observations may be particularly helpful in finding areas where further instruction is needed.

The major disadvantage of informal observation is its reliance on the objectivity and perceptiveness of the observer since the quality of the assessment depends upon the observer's skills. Unless tasks are comprehensible and there is an understanding of the student's language and culture, results may be no more reflective of cognitive abilities than a biased IQ test. Additionally, results of informal assessments do not meet legal requirements for special education placement and, therefore, should not be interpreted in isolation from other information.

Kaufman Assessment Battery for Children (K-ABC)

The K-ABC (Kaufman & Kaufman, 1983) is a promising new assessment instrument. Its authors believe that intellectual abilities should be dichotomized into sequential and simultaneous processing skills. The K-ABC yields norm-referenced scores for each skill area and a combined Mental Processing Composite. An optional achievement scale also is available. Selected sequential and simultaneous processing subtests can be used to obtain a nonverbal standard score. This procedure is particularly useful whenever a LEP student is tested by a monolingual examiner.

The K-ABC manual contains a Spanish translation of test instructions as well as acceptable responses and states that any non-English language, signing, or other communication system shared by the examiner and the student may be used for test instructions and examinee responses. This feature makes the K-ABC potentially useful for testing various language groups. However, its usefulness is weakened by the requirement that test items be presented *only* in English if norms are to be used (Kaufman & Kaufman, 1983, p. 44).

The appropriateness of the K-ABC has been investigated for Hispanic LEP learning disabled students. Fourqurean (1987) found generally higher scores on the K-ABC than on the WISC-R; this may reduce the number of Hispanic LEP children labeled mentally retarded. However, the higher scores may also make an achievement-IQ discrepancy more likely, so that more students are labeled learning disabled.

Cummins (1984) has proposed that the K-ABC is less culturally biased than the WISC-R, but others believe that the K-ABC does not tap the right aspects of intelligence (Sternberg, 1983). If important aspects of intelligence are being passed over, placement of students in special education based on K-ABC scores could be invalid. Notwithstanding some disadvantages, the K-ABC mental processing scales show promise for use with LEP students. If young children are to be tested, the K-ABC might be a better instrument to use than the WISC-R for several reasons. First, the subtest items are shown on large colored cards and are presented in a concrete, tangible fashion. Children seem to like the visual materials and may attend better to the tasks. In addition, verbal instructions are less formal and are shorter than the WISC-Rs. The practice items included with each subtest may be important for LEP children who have had little or no experience working on structured test-like tasks. These items provide immediate feedback so that children can better understand what is expected of them and increase their level of test-wiseness.

CASE STUDY

The following case study is presented in two versions. The first description is similar to what occurs typically in many school districts. The second description includes prereferral procedures and informal instruments as well as standardized tests. It also demonstrates how information from cognitive assessments might provide information about school problems.

DESCRIPTION #1

Juan is an 8-year-old LEP student referred for testing due to low academic achievement. He is the youngest child in a family of eight siblings. He was enrolled for his first school year in a bilingual kindergarten class and is now repeating first grade. He has been steadily increasing his level of proficiency in English but still is Spanish-dominant. Although he has been receiving academic instruction in Spanish, he still is functioning at beginning first-grade level. His bilingual classroom teacher says that he seems distractible and has difficulty working independently and completing assignments.

The results from the Bender Visual Motor Gestalt Test indicate normal perceptual-motor functioning. Juan made only two minor errors in reproducing the various geometric designs that were shown to him on cards. The EIWN-R (Spanish WISC-R) yielded IQ scores in the average range on the Performance and Full Scales and in the low average range on the Verbal scale. The highest scores were obtained on subtests measuring nonverbal abstract reasoning for designs and perceptual abilities and spatial organization needed to assemble puzzles. The lowest scores were obtained on subtests that measure immediate auditory memory for digits, immediate visual memory for symbols, and oral numerical reasoning. Performance on the Bateria Woodcock (in Spanish) was at beginning first-grade level in all areas. Juan identified all letters of the alphabet presented to him but was able to call correctly only four words from the reading list. He was able to compute simple written addition and subtraction problems but became confused when he was given word problems.

A significant discrepancy exists between Juan's measured level of IQ and his academic achievement in reading and mathematics. It is recommended that he be placed in a bilingual special education resource room setting to receive individualized instruction as a learning disabled student. A multisensory approach to teaching is recommended so that he will be able to improve his level of retention of basic skills.

DESCRIPTION #2

Juan is an 8-year-old LEP student referred for testing due to low academic achievement. He is the youngest child in a family of eight siblings. He was enrolled for his first school year in a bilingual kindergarten class and is now repeating first grade. He has been steadily increasing his level of proficiency in English but still is Spanish-dominant. A recent administration of the Language Assessment Scales earlier this year confirmed that Spanish is his stronger language. Although he has been receiving academic instruction in Spanish, he still is functioning at beginning first-grade level. His bilingual teacher has tried two alternative reading series with few signs of improvement but noted that his attention span has improved somewhat while using the latest series. She has used a phonics approach with Juan, but she has not attempted to use a more global approach. He still is somewhat distractible and has some difficulty working independently and completing assignments. A classroom observation conducted by the examiner confirmed that Juan was not attending adequately to his work.

The results from the Bender Visual Motor Gestalt Test indicate normal perceptual-motor functioning. Juan made only two minor errors in reproducing the various geometric designs that were shown to him on cards.

Since Spanish is Juan's stronger language, intellectual functioning first was measured by the administration of the Spanish version of the WISC-R (EIWN-R). Later, the Verbal scale of the WISC-R was readministered in English in order to obtain a more complete estimate of Juan's IQ. A composite score on the Verbal scale was obtained by including all items that had been answered correctly in one or both languages. The Performance Scale IQ score fell within the average range and the Verbal and Full scale IQ scores fell within the low average range of intellectual functioning. These IQ scores should be interpreted with caution, since the norms are based upon the English version of the WISC-R. Norms for the Spanish version were not available. Juan's highest scores were obtained on subtests measuring nonverbal abstract reasoning for designs and perceptual abilities and spatial organization needed to assemble puzzles. The lowest scores were obtained on subtests that measure immediate auditory memory for digits, immediate visual memory for symbols, and oral numerical reasoning. In order to obtain additional information, the Test of Nonverbal Intelligence (TONI) also was administered. The IQ score was slightly higher, but similar to the Performance Scale IQ score of the EIWN-R. The score fell within the upper limits of the average range.

Since the lowest scores on the WISC-R are related to poor attention span, distractibility and immediate memory problems, the assessor decided to re-administer these subtests under less stringent conditions to determine the severity of the deficit. On the Digit Span subtest, Juan was instructed to try the mnemonic device of visualizing the numbers in his head. Three repetitions of each item were presented, with praise given for effort. The time limit was disregarded on the Oral Arithmetic subtest, and items were repeated several times, if appropriate. These informal procedures had no effect in improving Juan's performance. Better results occurred, however, on the Coding subtest, which measures immediate visual memory for symbols. The time limit was disregarded, and Juan was told to concentrate only on one number-symbol relation at a time. He was to locate all boxes with the same number and write their respective symbols above them in the empty boxes. After performing this practice exercise, he was re-administered the subtest under timed conditions. His performance improved, and he was able to remember the symbols much better after having been exposed to the visual stimuli multiple times.

The Bateria Woodcock was administered to Juan in Spanish. An English language achievement test ordinarily would be administered as well, but this procedure was not followed because Juan had never been exposed to any English instruction in academic areas. Performance was at beginning first-grade level in all areas. On Bateria subtests, Juan correctly identified all letters of the alphabet that were presented to him but was able to call correctly only four words from the reading list. He was able to compute simple written addition and subtraction problems but became confused when he was given word problems. Next, the examiner showed Juan a short list of words that were from his basal reader. He was able to call correctly several of them with apparent uncertainty and missed several others. He tried to sound out all words but had much difficulty in combining syllables. His sound-letter recognition was poor.

In conclusion, a significant discrepancy exists between Juan's measured level of IQ and his academic achievement in reading and mathematics. School personnel should consider the option of placing him in a bilingual special education resource room setting to receive individualized instruction as a learning disabled student. Juan's regular classroom teacher may wish to collaborate with the special education teacher in planning Juan's instructional program, particularly in reading. Given his auditory memory deficits (which may also involve deficits in auditory processing), it might be wise to plan to teach Juan to read by using a visual, global approach. Much repetition of visual stimuli should be accompanied by positive reinforcement for effort, and he should be praised for attending to his work.

CONCLUSIONS

As greater attention is placed on the process of assessing LEP students for special education placement and remediation, the issue of cognitive assessment will become more critical. Due to the emphasis placed on cognition and intelligence in our society (Gould, 1981) and on the importance afforded cognitive assessment in educational placement, the measurement of cognitive ability and potential appears more important than other areas of assessment for both political and educational reasons. Consequently, this area of assessment should be carefully undertaken.

As demonstrated in this chapter, there are instruments and approaches that can limit the effects of bias on cognitive assessment. However, changes in testing practices alone rarely will be adequate to correct the problem of special education misplacement due to poor cognitive assessment. In addition to tools and methods, assessment personnel should develop an attitude of objectivity and exploration when approaching the task of cognitive assessment, particularly when LEP students are involved. Only by careful analysis of the student's background, the performance expectations, the assessment tasks required, and the student's actual performance during all relevant activities can assessment personnel make reasonable, appropriate, and accurate decisions.

REFERENCES

Alessi, G. J., & Kaye, J. H. (1983). *Behavioral assessment for school psychologists.* Kent, OH: National Association of School Psychologists.

Anastasi, A. (1968). *Psychological testing* (3rd ed.). New York: Macmillan.

Baca, L. M., & Cervantes, H. T. (1984). *The bilingual special education interface.* St. Louis: Times Mirror/Mosby College Publishing.

Bannatyne, A. (1974). Diagnosis: A note on recategorization of the WISC scaled scores. *Journal of Learning Disabilities, 7,* 272–274.

Barona, A., & Santos de Barona, M. (1987). A model for the assessment of limited English proficient students referred for special education services. In S. H. Fradd & W. J. Tikunoff (Eds.), *Bilingual education and bilingual special education: A guide for administrators* (pp. 183–209). Austin, TX: PRO-ED.

Bergin, V. (1980). *Special education needs in bilingual programs.* Arlington, VA: National Clearinghouse for Bilingual Education.

Bernal, E. M. (1980). *Methods of identifying gifted minority students.* Report 72, ERIC Clearinghouse on Tests, Measurements and Evaluation. Princeton, NJ: Educational Testing Service.

Bernal, E. M., Jr., & De Avila, E. A. (1976, May). *Assessing gifted and average children with the Cartoon Conservation Scales.* Paper presented at the Fifth Annual International Bicultural Bilingual Conference, San Antonio, TX.

Brown, L., Sherbenou, R. J., & Johnsen, S. K. (1982). *Test of Nonverbal Intelligence: A Language-Free Measure of Cognitive Ability.* Austin, TX: PRO-ED.

Buckley, K., & Oakland, T. (1977, August). *Contrasting localized norms for Mexican American children on the ABIC.* Paper presented at the annual meeting of the American Psychological Association. San Francisco, CA.

Burgemeister, B. B., Blum, L. H., & Lorge, I. (1972). *Columbia Mental Maturity Scale.* New York: Harcourt Brace Jovanovich.

Casso, H. (1973). *A descriptive study of three legal challenges for placing Mexican American and other linguistically and culturally different children into educably mentally retarded classes.* Unpublished doctoral dissertation, Amherst: University of Massachusetts.

Clarizio, H. F. (1982). Intellectual assessment of Hispanic children. *Psychology in the Schools, 19*(1), 61–71.

Cohen, E. G., De Avila, E., & Intili, J. A. (1981). *Executive summary: Multicultural improvement of cognitive ability.* Report to State of California Department of Education.

Cummins, J. (1984). *Bilingualism and special education: Issues in assessment and pedagogy.* Clevedon, Avon, England: Multilingual Matters.

Damico, J. S. (1988). The lack of efficacy in language therapy. *Language, Speech and Hearing Services in Schools, 19,* 51–66.

Dean, R. S. (1977). Reliability of the WISC-R with Mexican-American children. *Journal of School Psychology, 15,* 267–268.

Dean, R. S. (1979). Predictive validity of the WISC-R with Mexican-American children. *Journal of School Psychology, 17,* 55–58.

De Avila, E. A. (1977). *The Cartoon Conservation Scales (CCS).* San Rafael, CA: Linguametrics.

De Avila, E. A., & Havassy, B. E. (1974). *Intelligence of Mexican-American children: A field study comparing neo-Piagetian and traditional capacity and achievement measures.* Austin, TX: Dissemination Center for Bilingual Bicultural Education.

DeBlassie, R. R., & Franco, J. N. (1983). Psychological and educational assessment of bilingual children. In D. R. Omark & J. G. Erickson (Eds.), *The bilingual exceptional child* (pp. 55–68). Austin, TX: PRO-ED.

Dew, N. (1979). *Available intelligence tests for limited English speakers.* Arlington Heights, IL: Bilingual Education Service Center.

Feuerstein, R. (1979). *The dynamic assessment of retarded performers: The learning potential assessment device, theory, instruments, and techniques.* Baltimore: University Park Press.

Feuerstein, R., Rand, Y., Jensen, M., Kaniel, S., Tzuriel, D., Shachar, N. B., & Mintzker, Y. (1986). Learning potential assessment. In R. E. Bennett & C. A. Maher (Eds.), *Emerging perspectives on assessment of exceptional children* (pp. 85–106). New York: The Haworth Press.

Fourqurean, J. M. (1987). A K-ABC and WISC-R comparison for Latino learning-disabled children of limited English proficiency. *Journal of School Psychology, 25,* 15–20.

Gerken, K. C. (1978). Performance of Mexican-American children on intelligence tests. *Exceptional Children, 44,* 438–443.

Gould, S. J. (1981). *The mismeasure of man.* New York: W. W. Norton.

Guerin, G. R., & Maier, A. S. (1983). *Informal assessment in education.* Palo Alto, CA: Mayfield Publishing Company.

Gutkin, T. B., & Reynolds, C. R. (1980). Factorial similarity of the WISC-R for Anglos and Chicanos referred for psychological services. *Journal of School Psychology, 18,* 34–39.

Hagen, E., Sattler, J. M., & Thorndike, R. L. (1985). *Stanford Binet Intelligence Scale* (4th ed.). Chicago: Riverside.

Heller, K. A., Holtzman, W. H., & Messick, S. (1982). *Placing children in special education: A strategy for equity.* Washington, DC: National Academy Press.

Hiskey, M. S. (1966). *Hiskey-Nebraska Test of Learning Aptitude: Manual.* Lincoln, NE: Union College Press.

Holtzman, W. H., Jr., Ortiz, A. A., & Wilkinson, C. Y. (1986). *Characteristics of limited English proficient Hispanic students in programs for the mentally retarded: Implications for policy, practice and research.* Austin, TX: The University of Texas, Handicapped Minority Research Institute on Language Proficiency.

Jensen, A. (1974). How biased are culture-loaded tests? *Genetic Psychology Monographs, 90,* 185–244.

Kaufman, A. S., & Kaufman, N. L. (1983). *Interpretive manual. Kaufman Assessment Battery for Children.* Circle Pines, MN: American Guidance Service.

Kramer, J. J., Henning-Stout, M., Ullman, D. P., & Schellenberg, R. P. (1987). The viability of scatter analysis on the WISC-R and the SBIS: Examining a vestige. *Journal of Psychoeducational Assessment, 5*(1), 37–47.

Leiter, R. G. (1979). *Leiter International Performance Scale: Instruction manual.* Chicago: Stoelting Company.

Leton, D. A. (1972). Discriminant analysis of WISC profiles of learning-disabled and culturally disadvantaged pupils. *Psychology in the Schools, 9,* 303–308.

Mercer, J. R. (1971). Sociocultural factors in labeling mental retardates. *Peabody Journal of Education, 48*(3), 188–203.

Mercer, J. R. (1973). *Labeling the mentally retarded: Clinical and social system perspectives on mental retardation.* Berkeley, CA: University of California Press.

Mercer, J. R. (1979). *System of Multicultural Pluralistic Assessment Technical Manual.* New York: The Psychological Corporation.

Mercer, J. R., Butler, E. W., & Dingman, H. F. (1964). The relationship between social-developmental performance and mental ability. *American Journal of Mental Deficiency, 69,* 195–205.

Mercer, J. R., & Lewis, J. F. (1977). *System of Multicultural Pluralistic Assessment.* New York: The Psychological Corporation.

Norris, J. A. (1988). Using communicative strategies to enhance reading acquisition. *The Reading Teacher, 47,* 668–673.

Nuttall, E. V., Landurand, P. M., & Goldman, P. (1984). A critical look at testing and evaluation from a cross-cultural perspective. In P. C. Chinn (Ed.), *Education of culturally and linguistically different exceptional children* (pp. 42–62). Reston, VA: ERIC Clearinghouse on Handicapped and Gifted Children.

Oakland, T. (1983). Concurrent and predictive validity estimates for the WISC-R IQs and ELPs by racial-ethnic and SES groups. *School Psychology Review, 12,* 57–61.

Oakland, T., & Matuszek, P. (1977). Using tests in nondiscriminatory assessment. In T. Oakland (Ed.), *Psychological and Educational Assessment of Minority Children* (pp. 52–69). New York: Bruner/Mazel.

Ortiz, A. A., Garcia, S. B., Holtzman, W. H., Jr., Polyzoi, E., Snell, W., E., Jr., Wilkinson, C. Y., & Willig, A. C. (1985). *Characteristics of limited English proficient Hispanic students in programs for the learning disabled: Implications for policy, practice and research.* Austin, TX: The University of Texas, Handicapped Minority Research Institute on Language Proficiency.

Ravens, J. C. (1960). *Guide to using the Standard Progressive Matrices.* London: Lewis.

Sattler, J. M. (1974). *Assessment of children's intelligence—revised reprint.* Philadelphia, PA: W. B. Saunders Company.

Sternberg, R. J. (1983). Should K come before A, B, and C? A review of the

Kaufman Assessment Battery for Children (K-ABC). *Contemporary Education Review, 2* (3), 199–207.

Swanson, E. N., & DeBlassie, R. R. (1979). Interpreter and Spanish administration effects on the WISC performance of Mexican-American children. *Journal of School Psychology, 17,* 231–236.

Wechsler, D. (1974). *Manual for the Wechsler Intelligence Scale for Children–Revised.* New York: The Psychological Corporation.

Wechsler, D. (1982). *Manual para la Escala de Inteligencia Wechsler–Revisada.* New York: The Psychological Corporation.

Wilen, D. K., & Sweeting, C. V. (1986). Assessment of limited English proficient Hispanic students. *School Psychology Review, 15,* 59–75.

Wilkinson, C. Y., & Ortiz, A. A. (1986). *Characteristics of limited English proficient and English proficient learning disabled Hispanic students at initial assessment and reevaluation.* Austin, TX: The University of Texas, Handicapped Minority Research Institute on Language Proficiency.

Ysseldyke, J.E., & Algozzine, B. (1983). Diagnostic classification decisions as a function of referral information. *Journal of Special Education, 13,* 429–435.

CHAPTER 8

The Nonbiased Individualized Educational Program: Linking Assessment to Instruction

ANN C. WILLIG AND
ALBA A. ORTIZ

The ultimate goal of assessment is to determine the most effective instructional setting for a student and to obtain information that will serve as a basis for developing an Individualized Educational Program (IEP) that will meet the unique needs of the student who receives special education services. The Education for All Handicapped Children Act of 1975 (PL 94-142) contains detailed requirements of what should be included in an IEP (*Federal Register*, August 4, 1982, p. 33840):

- A statement of the present levels of educational performance

- Annual goals, including short-term instructional objectives

- Specific educational services to be provided

- The extent to which the student will be able to participate in regular education programs

- The projected date for initiation and anticipated duration of services

- Appropriate objective criteria and evaluation procedures and schedules for determining, on at least an annual basis, whether instructional objectives are being achieved.

There are no requirements in PL 94-142 specific to the development of IEPs for language-minority students. Consequently, for these students, educators frequently fail to consider cultural/linguistic learner characteristics and their effects on the teaching-learning process. Just as essential as nonbiased assessment for cultural and linguistic minorities is the development and implementation of nonbiased IEPs.

ADAPTING IEPS FOR EXCEPTIONAL LANGUAGE-MINORITY STUDENTS

Ambert and Dew (1982) suggest that, in addition to the requirements of PL 94-142, IEPs for exceptional language-minority students should specify: (1) instructional strategies that take into account linguistic facility, academic skill levels, modality, and cognitive style preferences; (2) the language(s) of instruction; (3) curricula and materials designed specifically for linguistically and culturally diverse populations; and (4) motivators and reinforcers that are compatible with the learner's cultural and experiential background. Consequent to a comprehensive assessment process that includes assessment of all of a student's linguistic skills, one of the first questions to be addressed in the IEP is the language of instruction.

SELECTING THE LANGUAGE OF INSTRUCTION

Legislation such as the Bilingual Education Act (1968) and litigation such as Lau v. Nichols (1974) mandate that schools offer programs for limited English proficient (LEP) students so they are not excluded from participation in school activities and can learn English in a logical, sequential manner (see Chapter One). In bilingual education programs, students learn basic skills and academic content in the native language so they do not fall behind their English-speaking peers in academic areas. Instruction in English as a second language is included as a component of bilingual education and provides sequential instruction so that students learn English as quickly and effectively as possible. In transitional programs, students move into a full English language curriculum when it is determined that they are proficient in English.

When LEP students are found to be eligible for special education services, they do not lose their right to bilingual education. Exceptional LEP students have the right to pedagogically sound programs that not only meet needs associated with their handicapping condition(s) but that also accommodate their language status.

For minority students who are academically at risk, strong promotion of native language conceptual skills will be more effective in providing a basis for the acquisition of English literacy than will be initial content instruction in English (Cummins, 1984). Instruction in English academic skills should not be initiated if students are experiencing difficulty mastering such skills in their native language. Difficulty in the native language indicates that the student is not ready to make the transition from native language instruction to content instruction in the second language. A premature transition will create additional learning difficulties for these students. Thus a critical aspect of developing an IEP for a linguistically diverse student is determination of the language in which instruction will produce optimal results. The basis for this determination should be data from the comprehensive language assessment.

The comprehensive assessment should have provided data that allow comparison of the level of skill the student possesses in the native language and in English, that is, the student's relative language proficiency or language dominance. For each of the student's languages, the language assessment should describe both conversational skills and mastery of the more complex, abstract dimensions of language related to literacy development. Both types of data are essential for planning the language of instruction and language intervention strategies.

Generally, exceptional LEP students who are dominant in a language other than English should receive content instruction in that language in addition to a sequential program of English language instruction. Students dominant in English should be instructed in English. If no clear dominance can be established, other variables should be taken into consideration, including: (1) the student's age, (2) the student's language preference, (3) motivation, (4) previous language experiences, and (5) parents' attitudes or wishes. In addition, special considerations are necessary for those students placed in special education because of a true language disability and for linguistically diverse students who do not appear to be LEP but who cannot handle instruction in mainstream classrooms.

For students whose language skills are not consistent with their chronological age, developmental norms, or the usage patterns in the language to which they have been exposed, designating the language of instruction is particularly important. Too often, educators assume that if a student has not acquired language, it will not matter whether English or the native language is used for instruction. They opt for instruction in English to ensure that students can communicate in English. However, if students have not acquired the language of their parents or caretakers through the normal process of language acquisition, there is little likelihood that they will be able to acquire English skills any more readily (Bruck, 1978). Such individuals especially need a language foundation in the familiar language that can provide a conceptual basis for skill development in English. Thus, linguistically diverse students who have not realized normal language development in the language of their own home or speech community should receive special education in that language. Language-handicapped students reared in homes where English is predominant should receive instruction in English.

Linguistically diverse students who are not eligible for bilingual education or English as a second language programs because of apparent proficiency in English are usually placed in English-based programs. Because these speakers have managed to acquire conversational skills in English, they appear to have the linguistic abilities necessary to handle the complex, context-reduced language used by teachers and found in textbooks and other instructional materials. When they begin to experience difficulty, lack of English proficiency is ruled out as a possible cause of the problem. However, informal communication ability bears little relationship to academic achievement (Cummins, 1984; Saville-Troike, 1984). While these bilingual students demonstrate good interpersonal communication skills in English, they may need more time to obtain the cognitive academic language proficiency required for mastery of literacy skills (Cummins, 1984). Because these students are not eligible for bilingual education or English as a second language classes, both regular classroom and special education teachers must realize that linguistically diverse students who appear to be proficient in English may still require a language development program in English to assure that all aspects of their English skills are commensurate with those of Anglo peers.

LANGUAGE-USE PLAN

Because handicapped students are likely to receive services from several instructional or related services personnel, it is important to develop a language-use plan as part of the IEP. The language-use plan essentially describes who will be using which language, for what purpose, and in which skill or subject. Usually, for each objective specified in the IEP, a person is designated as responsible for instruction leading to attainment of that objective. The IEP of a bilingual student should additionally specify for each objective the language in which instruction or other services will be provided. The program should include not only the language to be used by special education and regular classroom teachers but also by speech pathologists, counselors, occupational and physical therapists, migrant education teachers, and remedial program personnel. Specifying the language of instruction for each aspect of the IEP will ensure that instruction is consistent with the student's language status and that instructional personnel will not be working at cross purposes.

TYPE OF LANGUAGE INTERVENTION REQUIRED

Beyond choosing the language of intervention and developing a language-use plan, the IEP should also specify the *type* of language intervention required. Some students will have intact language skills and will require simply that teachers help them refine and expand their linguistic abilities. This type of language intervention can be characterized as *language enrichment*, in that a decision has been made that the student's language proficiency is adequate for academic instruction. Language enrichment can be provided in the native language, in English, or in both languages depending upon the student's language dominance and proficiencies. Other students will require *language development* programs. It is not unusual for students from lower socioeconomic status environments to experience difficulty because their language skills, although adequate for communication in their homes and communities, do not match the type of language spoken by teachers and found in textbooks (Fradd, 1987; Wong-Fillmore, 1986). The teachers' task, in such cases, is to provide a language development program that allows students to handle the academic language demands of the classroom. If the student is LEP and has access to a bilingual program, language development is provided in the student's native language. If the student is in the regular classroom receiving instruction in English, then language development is provided in English. Students with communication disorders will need *language remediation*. As indicated previously, it is critical that these students receive special education services in their native language.

Where this is not possible and the only option available is to teach handicapped students in English, special education instruction must be modified.

Choice of the language of instruction applies to instruction in academic skills and content areas. In addition to content instruction, regardless of the language of that instruction, all LEP students will require instruction in English language skills, commonly referred to as English as a second language (ESL) instruction. ESL instruction must be specified in the student's IEP, and special educators must become familiar with current practice and research in second language teaching.

According to Krashen (1982), language acquisition is optimal when sufficient input is provided that is comprehensible, interesting, relevant, and not necessarily in grammatical sequence. Methods such as the Total Physical Response (Asher, 1979) or the Natural Approach (Krashen & Terrell, 1983), seem to be more effective because they allow students to develop comprehension skills, attempt to reduce student anxiety, and provide comprehensible input. An advantage for many handicapped students is that these methods offer simplified language codes and involve students actively in the learning process.

Recent approaches to teaching academic English stress the development of vocabulary and skills related to academic content or content-based ESL. One such approach (Chamot & O'Malley, 1987) promotes the development of academic English through a careful sequence beginning with academic vocabulary and content that is highly contextualized and comprehensible and that requires a low level of cognitive demand. Throughout the sequence, contextualization is gradually reduced while the cognitive demand of the content is gradually increased. The ultimate goal is that a student acquire the cognitive-academic English skills necessary to deal with the regular school curriculum.

APPROPRIATE PLACEMENT ALTERNATIVES

An IEP adapted to the needs of language-minority students must include not only specifications concerning language uses and language interventions, it must also specify the appropriate program placement for the student. This decision, too, is based upon data provided by the comprehensive assessment.

In reaching this decision, the placement committee must determine the "least restrictive environment" ensuring that, to the maximum extent possible, the handicapped student is educated with nonhandicapped peers. Separate classes or schooling should occur only when the nature or severity of the handicap is such that education in regular classes with supplementary aids and services cannot be achieved satisfactorily (Federal Register, 1977).

The concept of "least restrictive environment" often is ignored when placement decisions are made for LEP students. However, all language-minority students should have access to a continuum of placement alternatives that will provide the highest likelihood of success. For LEP students, this continuum must include opportunities for mainstreaming into bilingual education and ESL classes. When students are mainstreamed into bilingual education programs, bilingual teachers must be assisted by special educators and they must receive training to adapt instruction to meet needs associated with the handicapping condition. By the same token, special education and related services personnel must be trained to assure that specialized instruction is linguistically and culturally relevant.

PLANNING INSTRUCTIONAL APPROACHES FOR THE LEP STUDENT

The development of a comprehensive IEP that includes all of the language and placement considerations just discussed still may not guarantee that the student's individual needs will be met. There is evidence that the most prevalent approaches to instruction in special education can exacerbate rather than remediate the LEP student's problems (Wilkinson & Ortiz, 1986). Thus the selection of an instructional approach is one of the key aspects of the whole planning process.

Zigmond and Miller (1986) suggest that special educators should rely on teaching effectiveness research to guide their selection of instructional interventions to be incorporated into IEPs for handicapped students. Bickel and Bickel (1986) and Heller, Holtzman, and Messick (1982) have indicated that the concepts and procedures identified through teaching effectiveness research are not necessarily contingent but are germane to any setting. Referring to strategies of direct instruction, Heller et al. note that children who are categorized as learning disabled, mildly mentally retarded, and low achievers in compensatory education all "seem to prosper best under the same kind of instruction" (p. 86).

The above suggestions imply the need for a reexamination of the literature on effective teaching with special consideration given to the needs of LEP students. The remainder of this chapter will review research relevant to the selection of optimal instructional approaches, and several specific approaches to instruction for LEP students will be described. The focus will be on language arts, since this is the content area most frequently addressed in IEPs for language-minority students. Wilkinson, Willig, and Ortiz (1986) found that for learning disabled Hispanic students, the most frequently selected goals and objectives on the IEP were all reading related and included both word recognition and comprehension skills. For mentally retarded students, highest priority rankings for annual goals were also in language arts with oral expression and reading receiving greatest emphasis. That report concluded that it is essential for teachers to develop skills in using those strategies and approaches most effective for teaching language arts to language-minority students.

RESEARCH-BASED PRESCRIPTIONS FOR EFFECTIVE INSTRUCTION

Two major philosophical approaches to instructional research have produced two types of prescriptions for effective teaching. The first are empirically based prescriptions that evolve from process-product studies in which discrete components of instructional processes, as observed in typical classrooms, are quantified and correlated with achievement (the product). Through this approach, a number of discrete components of traditional teaching practices in the public schools have been found to be related to gains in student achievement, and prescriptions for effective teaching have been based on these findings.

The second group of prescriptions are more holistic in nature and derive from theory and research on developmental processes in language and cognition. Teaching recommendations evolving from this school of research are based on an attempt to align instructional processes with current theory on cognitive and linguistic development. Each of these approaches will be reviewed briefly.

Process-Product Research

Findings from research on effective teaching in regular classrooms (reviewed by Brophy & Good, 1986) can be grouped into several categories including: the quantity and pacing of instruction; the organization of activities; the way in which teachers present information to classes; ways in which teachers respond to correct or incorrect information from students; characteristics of seatwork and homework; and characteristics of effective instruction in specific contexts, such as different grade levels or where students are of lower socioeconomic status (SES). Of particular relevance to the needs of LEP students are Brophy and Good's conclusions that low-SES and low-achieving students need more control and structuring from teachers, more review, drill, and practice, and more lower-level questions. While Brophy and Good acknowledge that such a prescription may lead to lesser amounts of material coverage, they believe the advantage lies in better mastery of the material covered.

This type of prescription reveals the approach to learning that many process-product researchers hold: that learning is linear in nature and successful learning of any skill requires a sequential mastery of subskills or components of the task. The better the subskills, the greater the possibility for learning a complete task. Instruction based on this approach is typical in the special education classroom, where task analysis and the teaching of component skills in segmented units predominates.

The major process-product study that has focused specifically on bilingual learners was conducted by Tikunoff and his associates (Tikunoff, 1985). Using observations and interviews, Tikunoff studied 58 bilingual teachers who had been described by school personnel as effective teachers and 232 of their LEP students. Instructional features that appeared to be effective with LEP students were typical of process-product findings with emphasis on direct instruction by the teachers and a linear approach to learning. The identified effective instructional features included such things as the use of clear communication to students, with explanations, outlines, and demonstrations of materials; maintenance of task focus, appropriate instructional pacing; promotion of student involvement; communication of expectations for students' success; monitoring of students' progress; provision of immediate feedback to promote student success; the use of both of the languages of the student; the integration of academic skills development with English language development; and responsiveness to the student's home culture.

Cazden (1984) has taken issue with Tikunoff's findings. She points out these findings do not define optimal teaching since alternative types of instruction were not observed. Additionally, she notes that the teaching characteristics observed by Tikunoff left little room for student initiative in that the form and content of the products the students were expected to produce were prescribed by teachers over 90% of the time.

Cazden's reservations also apply to the process-product literature in general, since much of the focus of such studies has been on instruction where the teacher controls and prescribes most of the instructional activities. Alternative types of instruction are observed less frequently in studies conducted in schools simply because they are found less frequently. However, the theoretical literature and research on innovative programs offers some compelling alternatives.

Theoretical Approaches to Teaching and Learning

In contrast to the empirically based prescriptions for effective teaching, holistic models are based on attempts to develop a theoretical framework for teaching and learning and to assess or prescribe teaching effectiveness on the basis of theory. Instructional models that are aligned with current theory and research on the acquisition of language include the "reciprocal interaction" model (Cummins, 1984) and the "instructional scaffolding" model (Langer & Applebee, 1986). These models stand in contrast to those based on the linear notion of learning, where one proceeds through an orderly and sequential mastery of subskills that will ultimately comprise a whole. The major focus of theory-based models is the purposeful nature of learning, where the learner actively seeks to learn skills or information in pursuit of a relevant goal. Components of any learning task are always seen in the context of their relation to the whole task or goal, and learning includes a constant shifting of focus between the whole task and its component subskills. The teaching of subskills (e.g., spelling, phonics, and parts of speech) in isolation, where they are not related to a contextualized whole, is considered to undermine student interest (Simmons, 1986).

In addition to a focus on purposeful and contextualized learning, the theoretically based approaches generally stress the importance of substantive (i.e., "real") interaction between the teacher and learner in both oral and written forms, with a mutual exploration of ideas rather than one-way transmission from teacher to student. In this type of relationship, the teacher helps the student to relate new knowledge to what the individual already knows. Cummins (1984) calls this "reciprocal interaction"; Langer and Applebee (1986) call it a "communicative relationship"; and Feuerstein (1979) calls it "mediation." These models also stress the necessity of building new abilities on skills already possessed by the student, without rejecting what the student brings to the classroom.

Cummins (1984) explicitly describes additional components of his model that are also implicit in the Langer and Applebee (1986) model. For example, Cummins discusses the need for the teacher to relinquish control of student learning and replace it with guidance and facilitation. In both writing and speech, the focus of instruction should be on meaning and ideas rather than the correction of surface errors, as these ultimately will self-correct for the student who has sufficient meaningful interaction with adult models. Langer and Applebee talk about the student's "ownership of learning," where students' own ideas and thoughts are allowed expression in their writing and communication. Cummins additionally encourages collaborative activities and student–student communication, believing that such interaction is crucial for the LEP student who needs practice in meaningful communication.

Contrasting the Two Prescriptions

When we compare these two prescriptions to instruction, those based on theory of language learning appear most appropriate. The models suggested by Cummins and by Langer and Applebee are consistent with the current paradigm of both first and second language acquisition, which stresses that language learners are active learners who, when exposed to sufficient language input from others, devise hypotheses about rules, test them out, modify them, and gradually construct their own language (Krashen, 1982). Additionally, these models incorporate those important aspects of learning in general and language learning specifically that Oller refers to as the Pragmatic Naturalness Constraints (1983; also see Chapter Three). According to Oller, in addition to the need for comprehensible input, learners also must have access to material that is meaningful and grounded in real context. For this to occur, it is necessary that the material used and the instructional strategies themselves be well-structured, student-initiated, highly motivating, progress in a sequential fashion, and make use of the learner's expectancies regarding the consequences of interaction. The process-product prescriptions derived from empirical observation are less grounded in theory and do not incorporate these constraints as effectively.

The antithetical nature of the empirical and theoretical models is most apparent when one compares the statements of Brophy and Good (1986) concerning low-SES and low-achieving students with those of Cummins (1984) concerning low achievers. Recall that the recommendations of Brophy and Good, based on findings from process-product research, call for more control and structure, more review, drill and practice, and more lower-level questions from the teacher. In contrast, Cummins (1984), Smith (1982), and Holdaway (1979) suggest that the way to make tasks easier is to adjust the context by increasing the number of contextual cues to meaning rather than fractionating the task to simpler and less meaningful segments.

In sum, the writings of Cummins and other major researchers who address the nature of instruction for LEP students stress the need for instructional models that have as a basis theory and research on the developmental processes of language and cognition. A number of specific approaches to teaching that are in line with current theory on language and literacy development have been described in the literature. Brief descriptions of several of these, in the following section, will illustrate the essence of holistic approaches.

Holistic Teaching Approaches

Whole Language Approach To Literacy. One approach to teaching writing, language arts, and reading consists of encouraging children to read and write daily from their first days of school, even prior to formal reading instruction. This approach, promoted by the work of Goodman

(1986), Graves (1983), Holdway (1979), and Smith (1982), emphasizes a number of the key components: Activities must have a purpose for the student; they must be rich in context; they must build on the experience of the student; they must be under the control of the student (thereby always being linguistically and culturally relevant); and they must be grounded in meaningful reciprocal interaction with the teacher and peers.

Graves' (1983) approach to teaching writing is a good example of applying the following key components. Students are allowed to control their own writing by choosing their own topics. They are also encouraged to invent their own spellings. Teachers hold intermittent individual conferences with each student as a piece of writing develops, maintaining writing folders for each student's work, establishing a writing community environment in the classroom, and integrating language arts and mechanical skills instruction with the natural writing process. The individual student–teacher writing conferences, which form the core of the teaching, focus on mechanics such as handwriting, spelling, punctuation, and grammar. Conferences usually revolve around the teacher's asking students to teach the teacher about the subject or topic of the student's writing, thereby creating a situation of true reciprocal interaction. Over time, the students' spellings approximate and finally adhere to standard forms, just as students' oral language gradually approximates and adheres to adult oral language. Student control over their own writing visibly affects intrinsic motivation.

Graves emphasizes that writing and language arts need not be taught in isolation, and that time taken up with meaningless activity sheets can be replaced with writing sessions out of which all other language activities emerge. It is also important for students to have an audience beyond the teacher during the writing process. For example, it helps if the students share their writing with others through daily whole-class discussion or the incorporation of their work into a class library for the use of their classmates. It has been noted that when children write and draw daily, their reading test results improve; talking and listening skills are enhanced; and spelling, handwriting, and other writing conventions develop appropriately (Walshe, 1982).

The Dialogue Journal. The dialogue journal (Staton, 1980, 1983) is similar to Graves' approach in that students are required to write on a regular basis on topics of their own choosing and are encouraged to focus on the meaning or intent of the communication rather than the surface forms of language. Written entries are entered into a journal by the students on a daily or regular basis, and these entries are answered by the teacher, who responds in the journal. The student's entry takes the form of a personal letter to which the teacher responds on a daily basis. Journal entries by students take the form of comments on questions and may be about class assignments, personal problems, or personal experiences. The teacher's response includes addressing the topic chosen by the student, answering questions, asking questions, and expressing views. Staton (1980) points out that the immediacy of the teacher's response creates strong motivation for the students to write and ask questions. In responding to the journal entries, the teacher's focus is on the communicative intent of the writing, and errors in the student's language are not corrected. Instead, the correct written form may be modeled in the teacher's written response, just as correct forms of oral language are modeled in caretaker speech. Thus, the dialogue journal provides one means of implementing true reciprocal interaction between student and teacher in writing. It is this written modeling and the meaningful interaction that motivate and demonstrate to the student how to self-correct and approximate adult writing standards.

Consistent use of the dialogue journal can increase the amount of writing that children do; improve grammar, spelling, and other mechanics of writing; improve student's ability to ask questions to receive clarification on subject matter (Staton, 1980); increase students' reading levels by a minimum of three grade levels in one year; and improve morale and self-esteem (Hayes & Bahruth, 1985). Furthermore, it opens up the lines of communication between student and teacher to a degree seldom found in traditional-style classrooms, and it provides a mechanism for LEP students to explore their concerns and problems with adjustments to a new culture.

Fernald's Contextual Approach. A method that integrates reading, spelling, and writing and that is similar to (and predates many of the current "innovative" methods) is that developed by Fernald (1945). The Fernald methods for teaching reading, spelling, writing, math, and other school subjects were developed specifically for students with reading or learning disabilities or those who were not achieving in school. The material to be read or written about is initially determined by the student, ensuring both experiential and cultural relativity. Students are encouraged to write about topics of their choice, and typed copies of the student's writing are used for reading material in the initial stages of reading. The use of words as whole units, rather than segmented parts, and the use of words in context are also integral parts of the Fernald method.

Fernald differs from Graves in that correct spelling of words to be written is demanded, even in the first draft of a writing. Students are taught to ask the teacher for any words they want to write, and the teacher writes out the word in a large, bold, pen, on a blank word card. The student is then encouraged to trace the word on the card using a finger. When the word has been traced in its entirety as many times as necessary for students to feel they can write the word, the word is incorporated into the work in progress. Once a student has learned to write a word using the word card provided by the teacher, the student stores the card in a personal word file that is organized by alphabetical tabs in a box. In this way, each student has his or her own store of personally relevant words, which can be reviewed whenever necessary. The alphabetical filing also provides a means by which the student learns the alphabet and reference skills. Whenever a student completes a piece of writing, it is typed within 24 hours and used as reading material for that student. This approach contains all of the qualities that have been stipulated in the theoretically based models of effective instruction: The teacher is a facilitator for a student's learning to read and write material that is of interest, and all reading, writing, and language mechanics are learned in a purposeful, meaningful context. Furthermore, the student's own ideas and perceptions are always culturally and experientially relevant.

Language Experience. The language experience approach exemplifies still another holistic approach. Although the most apparent focus of this approach is reading instruction, Stauffer (1980) points out that it actually encompasses all of the communication arts of reading, writing, listening, and speaking. Again, the emphasis is on learning in context. Students' own language and experience provide a context for the students' first reading material, which is developed through oral discussion of situations and experiences that have been structured and provided by the teacher.

The basic format of the language experience approach, as presented by Stauffer (1980), is that material to be used for reading is dictated to the teacher by the students after they have experienced a teacher-structured situation. A printed copy is made of the dictations, and this copy becomes reading material. Just as with the types of writing projects described earlier, the dictations can be reproduced on large charts, placed in notebooks, or "published" as illustrated books.

Stauffer also discusses possible modifications of Fernald's (1945) technique in conjunction with the language experience approach so that Fernald's approach would be appropriate for the nonhandicapped learner. The modifications appear to be equally appropriate for LEP students who are learning to read or write in either language. Stauffer suggests that each student keep a copy of the dictations in a notebook, thereby building up a personal reader. In order to liberate the nonhandicapped learner from Fernald's word tracing, students can underline words in their dictations that they can read, recognize, or write.

As with the other approaches just discussed, the language experience approach encompasses the major characteristics of instruction that has been described by Cummins (1984) as most appropriate for LEP students, both handicapped and nonhandicapped. The emphasis on context—and the use of student's own experience as a basis for language development, reading, and writing—ensures both experiential and cultural relativity. Furthermore, in classrooms with a great deal of ethnic heterogeneity, language experiences can be structured to promote cross-cultural understanding and to assist a student in learning about the dominant culture.

Reading as a Communicative Process. A final strategy for language and literacy instruction for LEP students in special education is the approach to reading as a communicative process. As described by numerous researchers, students may experience real difficulty with literacy when faced with formal reading instruction (Goodman, 1986; Smith, 1982). Due to poor initial instruction, lack of exposure to reading in the home, or language diversity, students are confounded by the attempts to teach reading through the use of phonic rules, word analysis skills, and other strategies. These students, however, can benefit from an approach that teaches them that reading is a communicative or interactional language process (Norris, 1988). Through the use of techniques termed *communicative reading strategies*, students are taught to actively participate in communication through written language. These strategies allow the students to learn not only about written language but also to understand oral communication to a much greater extent.

In communicative reading strategies, the teacher becomes a facilitator in the reading process, taking the role of the author and a mediator between the text and the student. In effect, the teacher uses the context of the written word and the text-appropriate pictures in the reading material to scaffold meaning and interaction for the student. This technique uses the teacher as a interactant to make what is incomprehensible, comprehensible (Krashen, 1982).

Once students learn to use and appreciate reading as a communicative task, the inclusion of story reading in the classroom can further enhance their experience of oral and written language. Hayes and Bahruth (1985) have described their use of a story hour in a fifth-grade class of migrant students where reading levels improved an average of three grade levels in 1 year. Along with daily reading of stories to students, the authors extended the activity to include discussions and reciprocal telling of stories by students. Stories were selected for their interest value for this particular class (primarily fifth-grade boys from Mexican-American migrant families). Selection also included consideration of the complexity and length of the stories, with a gradual increase in both. The authors describe an enthusiastic response by the students, who began to request loan of the books that had been read.

In addition to the theoretically based holistic approaches to language and literacy development described above, other aspects of instruction have been developed that comply with the need for interaction and collaboration between LEP students. These are specific types of cooperative learning groups that will be described in the following section.

COOPERATIVE LEARNING GROUPS

Cooperative learning refers to a variety of classroom techniques in which students work on learning activities in small groups in a structure that encourages mutual cooperation. Typically, groups consist of four to five members and are heterogeneous in regard to sex, ethnicity, and/or ability. Slavin's (1986) techniques focus primarily on the acquisition of basic skills and include the formation of classroom teams, each consisting of four or five students. Each team is responsible for the learning of all of its members and rewards are earned by teams rather than individuals.

Slavin (1986) and his colleagues have developed a number of cooperative learning structures to be used for various academic goals. One that may well be applied in the special education classroom is what Slavin calls Student-Teams Achievement Divisions (STADs). STADs consist of five major components: class presentations, team study sessions, quizzes, individual improvement scores, and team recognition. The class presentation, which is usually direct instruction by the teacher, is followed by the team study sessions. During these sessions, students discuss problems, compare answers, and correct teammates' misconceptions. After three to four periods of teacher presentation and team practice, students take individual quizzes and earn points for their teams based on how much their quiz scores exceed their average on past performance. Thus students can contribute maximum points to their team if they show improvement over past performance. Teams earn recognition in the form of certificates, printing of results in weekly class newsletters by the teacher, or other rewards.

The feature of Slavin's cooperative learning groups that is in accord with the recommended practices for teaching LEP students is the promotion of collaborative interaction among the students. Although the approach definitely promotes skill-building through practice and student-student drills, the collaboration inherent in the approach provides opportunity for increased student interaction. When used in groups of mixed language proficiency and in classrooms that also use the holistic approaches described in this paper, the Slavin approach appears to hold promise for LEP students in special education.

The cooperative learning methods designed by De Avila, Cohen, and Intili (1981) differ from those of Slavin in that their focus is on discovery learning as opposed to direct instruction in basic skills. Finding Out/ Descubrimiento is a discovery-oriented elementary school math/science program developed particularly for bilingual classes. Students become involved in hands-on science activities and experiments in small groups. Individual roles are assigned within the groups, such as secretary, time-keeper, or making sure everyone understands and gets their questions answered. Cooperation and verbal interaction are important aspects of this program as students work to solve problems together. Materials are available in English and Spanish so that monolingual and bilingual students can work together cooperatively.

This approach contains many elements that illustrate principles of contextualized, relevant instruction, and the materials could easily be used for the promotion of language development. The group problem-solving activities could be used for language-experience sessions or for writing topics. When used in this way, the approach includes all of the characteristics of holistic instruction for LEP students, including the integration of language development with broader subject matter.

In sum, the approaches described above are all grounded on current theory and research in the area of language and literacy acquisition and illustrate promising approaches to instruction for exceptional LEP students. In addition to including the instructional characteristics deemed essential for LEP students, such as personal and cultural relevance, salience of context, promotion of student control over learning and reciprocal interaction in the classroom, these approaches operationalize the key ingredient of special education and the IEP: individualization. As will be argued below, individualized instruction to date has probably been more of an ideal than a reality. Consideration of the current state of affairs concerning individualized instruction in special education only serves to highlight the need for approaches such as those described above.

INDIVIDUALIZING INDIVIDUALIZED INSTRUCTION: A FINAL CONSIDERATION FOR THE IEP

The majority of referrals to special education are made by regular teachers and staff who believe the student will benefit from instruction that is highly individualized both in terms of content and teachers' time. In many instances, this assumption may not hold. Not only is evidence sparse concerning the benefits of matching teaching approaches to particular student characteristics that have been identified through assessment (Zigmond & Miller, 1986), but there are also a number of practical demands placed on special education teachers that make it extremely difficult to individualize instruction in an effective manner. These include both the heterogeneous nature of special education groups and problems in scheduling student attendance in the resource room.

HETEROGENEITY

In contrast to the typical mainstream classroom teacher, the special education teacher usually works at any given time with a group of students who span two to six grade levels and who represent an even larger range of functional levels. Typically, these students also represent several special education categories. For example, it is not atypical to have in one partially self-contained classroom students who had been diagnosed as behaviorally disturbed, mildly mentally retarded and learning disabled, or deaf. Resource rooms observed by Willig, Wilkinson, and Polyzoi (1985) typically contained a similar mix of students, although learning disabled students tended to predominate in this setting.

The difficulty of providing individualized instruction in a classroom with this degree of heterogeneity is augmented further when an additional range of individual differences is included that are cultural and linguistic. The teacher must be able to plan instruction that accounts not only for individual learning differences and functional levels but also for a range of language diversity where each student demonstrates a different pattern of proficiencies across at least two languages. In many instances, the teacher must accomplish all of this without an aide.

SCHEDULING

For the teacher in the resource room, dealing with the heterogeneity of the students is even more complex due to variations in the scheduling of students' attendance in the room. Students may be assigned to the special education resource room for 1 hour per week to several hours every day. This creates a constant turnover of students in the room with a small core of more consistent attenders. Exacerbating this problem is the fact that scheduling is frequently based on the agenda of instruction in the regular classroom and is not tied to the capabilities of the special education teacher to handle the additional diversity caused by the scheduling. For example, Haynes and Jenkins (1986) reported that students assigned to special education resource rooms for individualized help with reading actually received less reading instruction than nonspecial education students. Local policy dictated that students were to attend the resource room at the time the content or skill with which they had difficulty was taught in the regular classroom. Since the special education teachers had to assume responsibility for a number of students representing a large range of individual needs at the same time, the students were deprived of the very instruction for which they needed additional help. Haynes and Jenkins' findings are by no means singular. Similar situations, with the same type of scheduling policies, have also been reported by special education teachers (Willig, Wilkinson, & Polyzoi, 1985), suggesting that the pattern may be prevalent.

HOW TEACHERS ATTEMPT TO INDIVIDUALIZE INSTRUCTION

Most special education teachers use a combination of strategies in attempting to provide individualized instruction. At times, they may form small group activities, assign individual seatwork, or teach the same lesson to the whole class while varying their expectations for each student's completion of work related to the lesson. A number of problems with these strategies leads to questions concerning their effectiveness. For example, Willig and Swedo (1987) noted that small group activities usually place a strain on the teacher who must manage both the group and the remaining students in the room. The group activities observed by Willig and Swedo tended to be interrupted frequently for the teacher's provision of feedback or communications to students not included in the group. In one instance, a student receiving individual reading instruction spent 10 of 12 minutes of allocated individual reading time waiting by the teacher's side while the teacher attended to other students' needs.

The strategy of providing homogeneous instruction for the whole class while holding different expectations for students also presents problems. The differing expectations frequently concern work quantity, such as telling students they need do only half of the problems or answer fewer questions. Expectations that vary primarily for work quantity indicate to students that the teacher's expectations are lower for them than for the other students and may reinforce or further lower student self-perceptions of ability.

If the goal of individualized instruction is too idealistic when it is conceived of as a matching of different strategies, content, and teacher time to students' differences, then alternative approaches to instruction in the special education classroom must be devised. Approaches to instruction for LEP students in special education that allow for individual differences in ways that enhance rather than assault the student's self-confidence, that ease the problems of classroom management, and that make classroom activities relevant to each student in terms of that individual's level of functioning, language, culture, and background experiences are needed. These approaches are more apt to be found in theory-based rather than empirically based literature, as has been described throughout this chapter. Until special education teachers can make these approaches part of their teaching repertoire, LEP students will continue to be frustrated by instruction that does not meet their needs. Students at risk will continue to become students lost.

REFERENCES

Ambert, A., & Dew, N. (1982). *Special education for exceptional bilingual students: A handbook for educators.* Milwaukee: Midwest National Origin Desegregation Assistance Center.

Asher, J. (1979). *Learning another language through actions: The complete teacher's guidebook.* Los Gatos, CA: Skyoak Productions.

Bickel, W. E., & Bickel, D. D. (1986). Effective schools, classrooms, and instruction: Implications for special education. *Exceptional Children, 52*(6), 489–500.

Bilingual Education Act. (1968). Sections 702 et seq., 20 U.S.C.A., Sections 880b et seq., P.L. 90–247.81 Stat. 783.

Brophy, J., & Good, T. (1986). Teacher behavior and student achievement. In M. C. Wittrock (Ed.), *Handbook of research on teaching* (pp. 328–375). New York: Macmillan.

Bruck, M. (1978). The suitability of early French immersion programs for the language disabled child. *Canadian Modern Language Review, 34,* 884–887.

Cazden, C. B. (1984). *Effective instructional practices in bilingual education.* Unpublished manuscript.

Chamot, A. U., & O'Malley, J. M. (1987). The cognitive academic language learning approach: A bridge to the mainstream. *TESOL Quarterly, 21*(2), 227–249.

Cummins J. (1984). *Bilingualism and special education: Issues in assessment and pedagogy.* Clevedon, Avon, England: Multilingual Matters.

De Avila, E., Cohen, E. G., & Intili, J. A. (1981). *Multicultural improvement of cognitive abilities.* Final report to the California State Department of Education.

Federal Register. (August 23, 1977). Washington, DC: U.S. Government Printing Office.

Federal Register. (August 4, 1982). Washington, DC: U.S. Government Printing Office.

Fernald, G. M. (1945). *Remedial techniques in basic school subjects.* New York: McGraw-Hill.

Feuerstein, R. (1979). *The dynamic assessment of retarded performers: The Learning Potential Assessment Device, Theory, Instruments and Techniques.* Baltimore: University Park Press.

Fradd, S. H. (1987). Accommodating the needs of limited English proficient students in regular classrooms. In S. H. Fradd & W. J. Tikunoff (Eds.), *Bilingual education and bilingual special education* (pp. 133–182). Austin, TX: PRO-ED.

Goodman, K. (1986). *What's whole about whole language?* Portsmouth, NH: Heinemann.

Graves, D. H. (1983). *Writing: Teachers and children at work.* Exeter, NH: Heinemann.

Hayes, C. W., & Bahruth, R. (1985). Querer es poder. In J. Hansen, T. Newkirk, & D. Graves (Eds.), *Breaking ground: Teachers relate reading and writing in the elementary school.* Portsmouth, NH: Heinemann.

Haynes M. C., & Jenkins J. R. (1986). Reading instruction in special education resource rooms. *American Educational Research Journal, 23*(2), 161–190.

Heller, K. A., Holtzman, W. H., & Messick, S. (Eds.). (1982). *Placing children in special education: A strategy for equity.* Washington, DC: National Academy Press.

Holdaway, D. (1979). *The foundations of literacy.* Sydney, Australia: Ashton Scholastic.

Krashen, S. (1982). Bilingual education and second language acquisition theory. In *Schooling and language minority students: A theoretical framework.* Los Angeles: Bilingual Education Evaluation, Dissemination, and Assessment Center.

Krashen, S., & Terrell, T. (1983). *The natural approach: Language acquisition in the classroom.* Oxford, England: Pergamon Press.

Langer, J. A., & Applebee, N. (1986). Reading and writing instruction: Toward a theory of teaching and learning. In *Review of Research in Education.* Washington, DC: American Educational Research Association.

Lau v. Nichols. 414 U.S. 563, 1974.

Norris, J. (1988). Using communcation strategies to enhance reading acquisition. *The Reading Teacher, 41*(7), 668–673.

Oller, J. W. Jr. (1983). Some working ideas for language teaching. In J. W. Oller, Jr. & P. Richard-Amato (Eds.), *Methods that work: A Smorgasbord of ideas for language teachers* (pp.3–19). Rowley, MA: Newbury House.

Saville-Troike, M. (1984). What really matters in second language learning for academic achievement? *TESOL Quarterly, 18*(2), 199–219.

Simmons, W. (1986). Beyond basic skills: Literacy and technology for minority schools. In R. D. Pea & K. Sheingold (Eds.), *Mirrors of minds: Patterns of experience in educational computing.* Norwood, NJ: Ablex.

Slavin, R. E. (1986). *Using student team learning.* Baltimore: Johns Hopkins University.

Smith, F. (1982). *Understanding Reading.* NY: Holt, Rinehart and Winston.

Staton, J. (1980). Writing and counseling: Using a dialogue Journal. *Language Arts, 97* (5), pp. 514–518.

Staton, J. (1983). Dialogue journals: A new tool for teaching communication. *ERIC/CLL News Bulletin,* No. 6(2) pp. 1–2.

Stauffer, R. G. (1980). *The language experience approach to the teaching of reading,* 2nd ed. NY: Harper & Row.

Tikunoff, W. J. (1985). *Applying significant bilingual instructional features in the classroom.* Rosslyn, VA: National Clearinghouse for Bilingual Education.

Walshe, R. D. (1982). *Donald Graves in Australia: "Children want to write . . .".* Exeter, NH: Heinemann.

Wilkinson, C. Y., & Ortiz, A. A. (1986). Reevaluation of learning disabled Hispanic students: Changes over three years. *Bilingual Special Education Newsletter, 5*(1), 3–6.

Wilkinson, C. Y., Willig, A. C., & Ortiz, A. A. (1986). *Goals and objectives targeted in Individualized Educational Programs developed for exceptional limited English proficient and English proficient Hispanic students.* Austin, TX: Handicapped Minority Research Institute.

Willig, A. C., & Swedo, J. J. (1986). *Improving teaching strategies for exceptional Hispanic limited English proficient students: An exploratory study of task engagement and teaching strategies.* Paper presented at the annual meeting of the American Educational Research Association. April, Washington, DC.

Willig, A. C., Wilkinson, C. Y., & Polyzoi, E. (1985). *Interim report for the development of teaching strategies for use with LEP children who are receiving services for LD and MR.* Austin, TX: Handicapped Minority Research Institute.

Wong-Fillmore, L. (1986). Teaching bilingual learners. In M. C. Wittrock (Ed.), *Handbook of research on teaching*, 3rd ed. (pp. 648–685). New York: Macmillan.

Zigmond, N., & Miller, S. (1986). Assessment for instructional planning. *Exceptional Children, 52*(6), 501–509.

CHAPTER 9

Implementing Assessment in the Real World

JACK S. DAMICO
AND
ELSE V. HAMAYAN

When assessing the communicative, academic, and cognitive abilities of limited English proficient (LEP) students for possible special education services, evaluators are frequently placed in a perplexing situation. On the one hand, they recognize the importance of assessment in the school system. On the other hand, these professionals understand the problems inherent in the current approach to assessment and the potential for inappropriate identification of some LEP students as having special needs that go beyond the normal second language development process. While evaluators recognize the need for assessment, they are cognizant of the difficulties noted in many of the current communicative, academic, and cognitive assessment techniques and guidelines used with LEP students.

Direct experience with these students during assessment frequently leaves the evaluator with questions regarding the validity of the testing process (Cole, 1985; Damico, 1988; Howard, 1982). Research indicates that a large number of LEP students have been misidentified as having a special need and placed into special education programs inappropriately (Ortiz & Maldonado-Colon, 1987) or have been omitted from special education programs when such placement was appropriate (Bergin, 1980). Further, many professionals believe that the assessment process itself is inherently biased against LEP students because the process tends to primarily locate problems within the student rather than within the poor educational practices of our school systems or the larger home and societal contexts that the student is in (DeBlassie & Franco, 1983; Figueroa, 1983; Rueda & Mercer, 1985; Seymour & Miller-Jones, 1981). The overall result is that current approaches to assessment frequently hold negative consequences for LEP students rather than providing the benefits evaluators should expect (Cheng, 1987; Cummins, 1986; Miller, 1984; Sinclair & Ghory, 1987; Trueba, 1983).

Given the importance of communicative, academic, and cognitive skills to school success (Cazden, 1986; Heath, 1983; Norris & Bruning, 1988), the provision of these skills to LEP students in the most effective manner is crucial; education is a primary mechanism for enculturation and mobility in our society (Apple, 1982; Ogbu, 1978). Evaluators play a very important role vis-à-vis LEP students: within a school setting they function as "gatekeepers" to determine what type of assistance LEP students should receive (Cummins, 1981; Deyhle, 1987). Consequently, these professionals have an obligation to function as advocates for any student evaluated, ensuring that misidentification does not occur (Erickson & Walker, 1983). The problems inherent in assessment confound this obligation. As a result, evaluators acting as student advocates are reluctant to initiate the assessment process. They view the current state of practice in communicative, academic, and cognitive assessment as biased against LEP students and may desire to avoid the entire testing procedure. In doing so, however, evaluators are caught in a dilemma: They realize that they must act as agents for the schools and function to make a placement decision. At the same time, evaluators feel that they should act as advocates for LEP students. Due to the current approach to assessment, however, they are prevented from fulfilling both roles simultaneously.

The chapters of this volume demonstrate how this assessment dilemma could be overcome. By recognizing the actual problems that exist while assessing LEP students and by gaining more information on the complexity of assessment when dealing with these students, alternative assessment approaches appear more appropriate. In Chapter One the actual context of assessment with LEP students was provided. By establishing the historical and legal context and then linking it with behavioral considerations, a greater appreciation for alternative solutions was established. In the next three chapters, specific information needed to recognize the complexity of assessment in the LEP population was presented. Systematic and unique characteristics of the second language acquisition process and the practical implications of moving between two languages and different cultures were discussed and then tied to a consistent theoretical paradigm that views language proficiency as a holistic and synergistic process. Together, these three chapters demonstrate that language proficiency is determined by an interaction between the student's intrinsic abilities, experiences and motivations and that all aspects of the assessment process are dependent on the student's underlying language proficiency. The next four chapters then discuss actual techniques that may be used to overcome the assessment dilemma. Each of these chapters integrates the theoretical foundations and practical considerations of the previous chapters to provide alternative solutions. Overall, the three chapters on assessment approaches (Chapters Five, Six, and Seven) and the chapter on instructional implications (Chapter Eight) stress a more holistic, naturalistic, and descriptive approach to assessment and intervention. Taken together, these eight chapters provide a theoretical framework, necessary information, and practical suggestions for limiting the bias inherent in the assessment of LEP students.

In the real world, however, theory, information, and technique are only as good as their implementation. This chapter discusses three issues that relate to the successful implementation of the information provided in the first eight chapters: the necessity for advocacy, the process of implementation, and taking individual responsibility.

ADVOCACY IN THE ASSESSMENT PROCESS

To successfully implement the assessment approaches suggested in this volume, the evaluator must become advocacy oriented. The purpose of assessment should be to continually operate in the student's best interest, and this purpose must be reflected in the attitudes and the behaviors of the evaluator. Based on what is known about the complexity of the assessment process and the difficulties inherent in crossing linguistic and cultural boundaries, evaluators should ensure that there is as little bias in the actual assessment process as is possible. Additionally, if bias is present, the evaluator should recognize its existence and modify the interpretation of test results and placement decisions to overcome this bias. The evaluator must be a primary advocate for the student.

This is not a simple matter. As numerous educators, researchers, and commentators have suggested, the educational process appears to be a primary method by which the dominating society "disables" students from dominated social groups (Cummins, 1986; 1989; Gould, 1981; Mehan, Hertweck, & Meihls, 1986; Mercer, 1973; Ogbu, 1978). Nowhere is this phenomenon clearer than it is with students whose primary language is other than English and who have a lower than optimal proficiency in English, the language of instruction. The disabling attitude is exhibited quite clearly in the label most commonly used for these students: limited English proficient—a label that focuses on the negative aspect of not being proficient in a language rather than focusing on the positive aspect of adding one language on to an existing one. Limited English proficient students are seen as entering school at a disadvantage, with little esteem for either the valuable resource of potential bilingualism or for the students' ability to communicate in a language, other than English, which they bring with them to school.

Through interactions with educational personnel, these students experience a loss of control over their own lives and the ability, confidence, and motivation to succeed academically. Based on the implicit or explicit role definitions relayed to these students by their interactions with the educational personnel, they typically lose confidence in their cultural and linguistic identity. This lack of confidence results in the loss of the ability to deal with any problems that might confront them in the normal course of academic activities. Because of the values and beliefs mediated to them, therefore, these students become impaired—not due to some intrinsic cognitive or perceptual impairment but because of the attitudes, biases, and practices of the dominating society.

According to Cummins (1986; 1989), when this insidious process occurs, it is initiated by a number of institutional characteristics including the assessment process. Due to the attitudes held about the students' culture and language, the way in which the school interacts with the students' communities, and the pedagogical practices and materials that are used, the students become disabled, and academic performance and interactional ability are impaired (Sinclair & Ghory, 1987). At this point, however, these behaviors are not typically seen as a product of the prejudice or biases against these students. Rather, these behaviors are viewed as an indication of some type of personal failure on the part of the student. Frequently, a referral is made to special education because the problem is considered to be due to some intrinsic cognitive, perceptual, or emotional problem rather than to normal second language learning difficulties. The blame for the academic or interactional difficulties, therefore, is shifted to the students and for the wrong reasons. If the assessment process maintains these beliefs and biases (when no actual intrinsic impairment does exist), then the cycle of extrinsic disabling of these culturally and linguistically diverse students from dominated societal groups is complete.

One of the areas about which evaluators need to educate others in the district relates to the entire process of normal second language learning. Teachers in particular, need to be aware of the difficulties that second language learners normally encounter as part of the language development process. As teachers are often the persons who initiate a referral or prereferral process, they need to know when it is appropriate to sound the alarm and when it is appropriate to wait for the normal second language learning process to even out. It is easy to forget how complex and difficult it is to attain proficiency in a second language, and expectations tend to be rather high that students start functioning in an academic setting using a language in which they are not optimally proficient.

Developing an advocacy-oriented attitude in assessment, however, allows the evaluator to check the disabling process. The attitude requires an initial assumption that the evaluator will closely analyze the potential *extrinsic* causal factors as carefully as the potential *intrinsic* factors that might have resulted in the academic or behavioral difficulties noted at the time of referral. A realistic and objective view should be taken with an orientation that in this group of students it is possible that the academic or interactive difficulties are not due to an intrinsic impairment in the student but, rather, due to that student's reaction to the disabling characteristics of the school system. Therefore, to an extent the perception of difficulty is initially switched from the student to the system. This transfer is essential when working with culturally and linguistically diverse students (particularly those from dominated societal groups). The assessment process should not be a means of ". . . legitimizing the location of the 'problem' in the students" (Cummins, 1986:21).

In playing the role of the advocate, the evaluator also has a certain responsibility toward the student's parents. This responsibility involves both giving and taking information, either directly or through a trained interpreter. In giving information, the evaluator needs to orient the parent as to the reasons for the assessment and the actual assessment procedure. When the assessment is completed, the evaluator needs to explain to parents in culturally sensitive ways both the results of the assessment and the placement decision that was made. Being an advocate of parents in the assessment procedure also means allowing them to voice their concerns. Language minority parents, who themselves are not very comfortable with English, are often reluctant to discuss their children's education with school professionals, especially if their children have been identified as having some kind of academic difficulty. They may have to be persuaded that their viewpoint is of utmost importance to school staff, and that they are able to provide a perspective that the experts at school do not have. Parents also need to be consulted in order to obtain information about their child's background, about their culture, and about their home environment. Involving parents in the assessment process is of utmost importance: first, the parents can be a source of valuable information about their children; and second, they can help provide support to the child during the assessment process by alleviating some of the anxiety that is bound to accompany testing. Thus, the evaluator has to be an advocate of the parents so that they in turn can become advocates of their own children.

It is important, of course, to realize that as an advocate for the student and the parent, the evaluator must be objective and must work within the educational system. Advocacy is not solely a political stance nor is it an excuse for conducting only a cursory examination before routinely placing the blame on the school system. Many culturally and linguistically diverse students do have real intrinsic cognitive and perceptual impairments; to ignore this fact is just as damaging to these students as would be the misidentification of other students as impaired. Students are best served when the evaluator works within the system with a circumspective attitude toward bias that is reflected in the assessment practices and the interactions with the students and other professionals. A true advocate has the influence and ability to work within the system for positive results. By adopting this advocacy-oriented approach and using the knowledge and strategies described throughout this volume, the use of the assessment process as a major component in the disabling process can be reduced.

THE IMPLEMENTATION PROCESS

Another essential issue when attempting to reduce bias in the assessment process is the way in which the alternative approaches to assessment are implemented (Damico, 1987). It is not enough to know what you as an evaluator want to do; you must also know how to actually get others to accept your ideas for assessment; then you must demonstrate the effectiveness of your ideas. Since the process of implementation involves these two stages, each will be discussed.

GAINING ACCEPTANCE

In setting up the alternative assessment approaches, the evaluator must gain the acceptance for these approaches from at least three sources: school administrators, other evaluation personnel, and teachers. Administrators typically include the special education or assessment supervisor, the bilingual, ESL, or Title VII supervisor, and the principal. Although there are other administrators ranging from the superintendent of the district to special education coordinators and assistant principals, these individuals typically play a smaller role in determining the day-to-day implementation of activities and procedures. Of the administrators, the principal can most easily make things happen or hinder changes in the school. Consequently, the evaluator must secure the support of this administrator. The bilingual, ESL, or Title VII coordinator or supervisor is also important because this person will probably be more sensitive to the needs of the culturally and linguistically diverse population than will the other administrators.

Support from the other evaluation personnel is also key since the testing procedures and interpretation of results will affect their work with the students. Usually, these individuals are aware of the problems with the current assessment methods, however, and they are willing to consider alternative approaches, especially if they are approached in the right way. Finally, since the teachers are the referring agents and the "consumers" of the assessment results, they must believe in the alternative assessment procedures and the recommendations that arise from the assessment process. Without their support, it will be difficult to implement change.

When gaining acceptance of the alternative assessment procedures with each of these individuals, the evaluator must approach the implementation task with three major objectives: careful preparation, effective presentation, and initial flexibility and patience.

When suggesting new or alternative methods of assessing, it is important to *prepare for acceptance of the approaches*. Any change in operating procedure is more likely to be accepted if there is a perceived need for the change. If the need is not present, then the likelihood of acceptance is typically poor. Consequently, it might be better for an evaluator to put off implementation of new approaches for a while rather than present the new ideas when others are not predisposed toward them.

The evaluator can gain acceptance by keeping two points in mind. First, the need for the change in assessment approach must be described to all concerned. This is accomplished by demonstrating that the current methods of assessment are less effective and the alternative approaches can overcome the bias and resulting problems generated by the traditional assessment procedures. Demonstrations of the impact of assessment can focus on the individual student in assessment or the group of culturally and linguistically diverse students as a whole. For example, the evaluator can show how the actual responses that the individual student produces in the testing situation are reasonable ones given the student's cultural background but not acceptable from the perspective of the formal test. On an individual basis, the evaluator can also prepare for implementation by gradually linking the two testing approaches together. There are two advantages to this strategy. Compared to one another, the alternative assessment procedures will typically be more effective and more appealing to other professionals and parents because more realistic information and more naturalistic data are collected. Further, the way that the data are analyzed is more consistent with the commonsense approach that cultural and linguistic difference should be accounted for. The second advantage is that, by linking the two approaches, there is an exposure effect. That is, the other professionals will grow accustomed to hearing reports of the alternative procedure when the testing results are presented. Consequently, they will gain more experience with these procedures and learn to expect them. It is important that when using alternative assessment tools the evaluator should constantly exploit the strengths and advantages of these approaches—and with culturally and linguistically diverse students the strengths will be substantial.

Another way to prepare for acceptance of the alternative approach is to identify the failure of the traditional approach with CLD students. A simple demonstration of the percentages of culturally and linguistically diverse students identified as impaired versus the mainstream students when using traditional tools is a very effective strategy. For example, in a recent needs assessment in a school district, one of the authors found that 72% of all LEP students and 37% of poor black students were referred for special education testing as compared to 9% of the mainstream white students. Of the students referred, the percentages of placement into special education were 82% (LEP), 76% (black), and 34% (white). Clearly, unless ethnicity is linked to impairment (which, of course, it is not), there is distinct bias in the assessment process in this district. Fortunately, this district was eager to modify their approach to assessment.

The second point to keep in mind when gaining acceptance of the approach is that evaluators must build the perception that they are best suited to suggest alternative approaches to assessment if the traditional approaches are modified. If someone unaware of the needs of this population is simply informed of the problems, the solution may be different but not much better. Different traditional tests might be substituted, for example, or the normative standards for different populations might be changed for interpretative purposes. There might even be the imposition of a testing moratorium when dealing with this population of students, which is rarely a good idea. The key to establishing the evaluator as an individual with realistic and effective solutions is that individual's credibility: that is, demonstrating that the evaluator has the background, knowledge, and interest to offer solutions. This credibility can be established as a consequence of making the need for the alternative approaches known.

Once the need for the alternative approaches is established and the evaluator has sufficient credibility, then the alternative approach to assessment should be proposed and the second objective in gaining acceptance should be remembered: The alternative solution should be *well prepared, clear, and nonthreatening*. This is necessary because even when there is a predisposition toward looking for alternative solutions, the evaluator must demonstrate that the solutions offered are serious ones. Being able to present a well-considered solution in clear language with supportive figures that show cost effectiveness and a benefit to all involved will typically succeed. The solutions should be presented in a written format that details the need for the change, the overall objectives, an outline and description of the approach and methods, a time line for implementation, and an accountability scheme. Experience suggests that the proposal should be no more than four or five pages in length, primarily in outline form with a brief narrative summary as a cover page. Once the written document is prepared, the evaluator should be prepared to verbally present the proposal in a clear, concise, defensible, and nonthreatening style.

The final objective for the evaluator when implementing the alternative assessment approach is to be *flexible and patient*. Even if the appropriate individuals agree with the needed changes, there may be a transitional period before the changes are accepted and implemented. The evaluator must recognize that implementation of the proposed modifications may be a slow, uneven process. If the evaluator is persistent, understanding, and patient, however, the changes will generally occur.

EFFECTIVE IMPLEMENTATION

Once the alternative approach to assessment is accepted, this approach must be placed into effective operation. This will involve dissemination of the new approach to others through inservice and the establishment and effective use of this newly accepted assessment approach.

When *disseminating the information through inservice* on the new approach, the actual determination of who should attend and how the inservice will be conducted depends on local circumstances. Several points, however, should be remembered. First, the changes should be presented as a clear and concise description. Second, the inservice should focus on why the change is needed. This is usually self-evident, particularly if appropriate preparation has occurred. Third, there should be a focus on the mutual concerns of the evaluators, educators, and parents when the inservice is presented. The changes will be most effective if you can demonstrate "what it will mean to me" from the perspective on all involved. Finally, explain the actual assessment process and procedures that will be used. Specific information will make everyone more comfortable with the proposed changes.

Once the information is disseminated, then the alternative process should be *established and effectively used*. In the final analysis, the assessment approach is only as effective as the evaluator allows it to be. A set process should be established and followed. This process, of course, will vary according to the characteristics and needs of the individual schools or school districts. Here, too, several points should be remembered. First, despite the changes needed for local implementation, the core of the changes should remain within the concept of synergy, collection of naturalistic, appropriate, and complete data, and a reliance on valid and descriptive measures. Second, be sure that when a referral is received either by the prereferral committee or the evaluator that the referral receives an immediate response. Third, when discussing the student under consideration, target the concerns expressed by the referring agent and the needs of the student. Fourth, use effective and proven assessment tools and procedures that are consistent with the defined approach. The three assessment chapters in this volume provide a number of acceptable procedures. Fifth, make certain that the data collected and the interpretations made are shared with the concerned professionals and the parents. Sixth, as discussed in chapter eight, evaluators should engage in a process of mutual problem solving over how the identified problems may be overcome when discussing educational planning. Finally, engage in periodic evaluation of the ongoing assessment approach to determine its effectiveness and your implementation of the approach.

The linking of the information in the first eight chapters with an advocacy orientation and effective implementation procedures will ensure the reduction of the biasing effects of assessment. For each of these components to be used, however, there is one final component, perhaps the most important one. The individual professional must take responsibility for the changes if they are to occur.

TAKING INDIVIDUAL RESPONSIBILITY

The issues involved with the assessment of LEP students and other students from culturally and linguistically diverse backgrounds are interesting. Numerous studies have been conducted, workshops and conferences have been convened, and reports, articles, and books have been written on the topic. Doubtless, this issue is an important one that will receive even more attention in the future. In reality, however, all the books and conferences are of little significance. The real importance lies at the level of the individual student and that student's evaluator. Regardless of all the studies, nothing matters unless changes are made to benefit actual students in real situations. For this to occur, all professionals involved in the assessment of culturally and linguistically diverse students must take on the individual responsibility of making changes in their own situations. This process of becoming responsible requires several decisions on the part of individual evaluators.

First, evaluators must decide for themselves the importance of the issues discussed in this book and in others. They must weigh the theoretical models with the empirical data and their own experiences to determine what they really believe regarding this issue. Once decided, they must endeavor to make their practice fit their beliefs. Each individual must, therefore, engage in a process of *personal redefinition*.

Second, if they determine that changes are needed, evaluators must decide to modify their perceptions of where the problems exist. The problems discussed in these chapters do not typically reside in the student but in the system. Implementation barriers, if present, will not be due to the alternative assessment procedures themselves but to the educational environment's acceptance of them. Once evaluators realize these facts, they can more easily modify their individual situations to make the necessary changes. This necessitates a *flip in perception*.

Third, evaluators must decide to take the obligation for changing their environments into their own hands. They must modify their activities and interactions to shape their professional environments in order to meet their needs and those of their students. Individually, evaluators must move beyond the attitude of learned helplessness and implement change: They must become *change agents.*

Finally, change must be accomplished through well-established and well-conceived procedures to ensure effective and cooperative changes. Evaluators must decide to become more knowledgeable about the issues and techniques that are available so that their attempts to implement change are based on systematic and organized procedures. Further, they must be able to share this information with others to defend their position and convince others of the utility and power of their beliefs. They must *use information as a tool.*

CONCLUSIONS

Taken together, the three issues in this chapter (i.e., becoming a student advocate, carefully planning implementation, and taking individual responsibility) and the information in the previous eight allow evaluators to overcome the professional dilemma of having to pit the best interests of the student with the responsibilities of the job. These professionals can act as both agents of the educational system and advocates for the culturally and linguistically diverse students they serve. In effect, this empowers the evaluators as well as the students. As Jim Cummins has stated, ". . . educators can empower students only if they themselves are empowered; in other words, only if they are secure in their own personal and professional identities and confident that they have the ability and administrative support to help students succeed academically" (1989).

REFERENCES

Apple, M. (1982). *Cultural and economic reproduction in education.* London: Routledge Kegan Paul.

Bergin, V. (1980). *Special education needs in bilingual programs.* Washington, DC: Office of Bilingual Education.

Cazden, C. B. (1986). Classroom Discourse. In M. C. Wittrock (Ed.), *Handbook of research on teaching* (pp. 432–463). New York: Macmillan.

Cheng, L. L. (1987a). English communication competence of language minority children: Assessment and treatment of language "impaired" preschoolers. In H. Trueba (Ed.), *Success or failure? Learning and the language minority student* (pp. 49–68). New York: Newbury House.

Cheng, L. L. (1987b). *Assessing Asian language performance.* Rockville, MD: Aspen.

Cole, L. (1985). Minority concerns: Progress and challenge. A miniseminar presented at the American Speech-Language-Hearing Association Convention. Washington, DC, November.

Cummins, J. P. (1981). The entry and exit fallacy in bilingual education. *NABE Journal, 4,* 26–60.

Cummins, J. P. (1986). Empowering minority students: A framework for intervention. *Harvard Educational Review, 56,* 18–36.

Cummins, J. P. (1989). *Empowering minority students.* Sacramento, CA: California Association for Bilingual Education.

Damico, J. S. (1987). Addressing language concerns in the schools: The SLP as consultant. *Journal of Childhood Communication Disorders, 11,* 17–40.

Damico, J. S. (1988). The lack of efficacy in language therapy: A case study. *Language, Speech, and Hearing Services in Schools, 19,* 51–67.

DeBlassie, R. R., & Franco, N. J. (1983). Psychological and educational assessment of bilingual children. In D. R. Omark & J. G. Erickson (Eds.), *The bilingual exceptional child* (pp. 56–68). Austin, TX: PRO-ED.

Deyhle, D. (1987). Learning failure: Tests as gatekeepers and the culturally different child. In H. E. Trueda (Ed.), *Success or Failure? Learning and the language minority student* (pp. 85–108). Cambridge, MA: Newbury House.

Erickson, J. G., & Walker, C. L. (1983). Bilingual exceptional children: What are the issues? In D. R. Omark & J. G. Erickson (Eds.), *The Bilingual Exceptional Child* (pp. 3–22). Austin, TX: PRO-ED.

Figueroa, R. (1983). Test bias and Hispanic children. *Journal of Special Education, 17,* 431–440.

Gould, S. J. (1981). *The mismeasure of man.* New York: W. W. Norton.

Heath, S. B. (1983). *Ways with words.* Cambridge, MA: Harvard University Press.

Howard, D. (1982). Pitfalls in the multicultural diagnostic remedial process: A Central American experience. *Journal of Multilingual Multicultural Development, 3,* 41–46.

Mehan, H., Hertweck, A., & Meihls, J. L. (1986). *Handicapping the handicapped: Decision making in students' educational careers.* Palo Alto: Stanford University Press.

Mercer, J. (1973). *Labelling the mentally retarded.* Los Angeles: University of California Press.

Miller, N. (1984a). *Bilingualism and language disability: Assessment and remediation.* Austin, TX: PRO-ED.

Miller, N. (1984b). Some observations concerning formal tests in cross-cultural settings. In N. Miller (Ed.), *Bilingualism and language disability: Assessment and remediation* (pp. 107–114). San Diego: College Hill Press.

Norris, J. A., & Bruning, R. (1988). Cohesion in the narratives of good and poor readers. *Journal of Speech and Hearing Disorders, 53,* 416–424.

Ogbu, J. (1978). *Minority education and caste: The American system in cross-cultural perspective.* New York: Academic Press.

Ortiz, & Maldonado-Colon, E. (1986). Reducing inappropriate referrals of language minority students to special education. In. A. C. Willig & H. F. Greenberg (Eds.), *Bilingualism and learning disabilities: Policy and practice for teachers and administrators* (pp. 37–50). New York: American Library Publishing.

Rueda, R., & Mercer, J. (1985). A predictive analysis of decisionmaking with limited English proficient handicapped students. Third Annual Symposium: Exceptional Hispanic children and youth. *Monograph Series, 6,* 1–29.

Seymour, H. N., & Miller-Jones, D. (1981). Language and cognitive assessment of Black children. *Speech and Language: Advances in basic research and practice, 6,* 203–263.

Sinclair, R. L., & Ghory, W. J. (1987). Becoming marginal. In H. T. Trueba (Ed.), *Success or failure? Learning and the language minority student* (pp. 169–184). Cambridge, MA: Newbury House.

Trueba, H. T. (1983). Adjustment problems of Mexican-American children: An anthropological study. *Learning Disabilities Quarterly, 5,* 395–415.

Appendices

The following appendices list available language and educational tests and measures. Given the main thrust of the book chapters toward more descriptive, informal and multi references assessment within a pragmatic and synergistic framework, these appendices should not be taken as an indication that a test single is adequate for the assessment of bilingual students with exceptional needs. This is not the case. The volume editors and the individual chapter authors make their beliefs and practices known within each individual chapter. The reader is directed to those discussions and urged to combine a number of alternative assessment procedures with more standard ones in order to capture the most vivid and valid representation of a student.

It is important that a volume on assessment try to influence with persuasion and not omission. Consequently, a number of procedures inconsistent with the primary practices of the authors in this volume have been listed in the appendices in the spirit of comprehensiveness and fairness. The reader is encouraged to evaluate these procedures in light of the discussions presented. It should be noted that little psychometric data is provided. Assessing the psychometric strength of tests is a complicated process that involves close analysis of the individual tests' technical manuals and scrutiny of the empirical studies that provide the reliability and validity data. The reader is encouraged to determine psychometric strength based on their own investigations of these data.

Appendix A

Annotated Bibliography of
Communicative Ability Tests

Nancye Roussel
Louisiana State University

The tests listed below are available to speech-language pathologists for the assessment of communicative ability in limited English proficient (LEP) populations. In keeping with the different approaches to communicative assessment discussed in Chapters Three and Five, each test or instrument has been listed as either a discrete point, integrative, or pragmatic instrument. Additionally, each test is listed as either norm-referenced or descriptive. While the author of Chapter Five stresses a descriptive approach to communicative assessment, the tools listed in this appendix are included on the basis of availability and not on the basis of psychometric strength or theoretical consistency.

All-India Institute of Medical Sciences Test Battery
Developed by S. Bhatnagar
Available from Subhash Bhatnagar
       Department of Speech Pathology and Audiology
       Marquette University
       619 N. 16th—Room 210
       Milwaukee, WI 53233
 This battery of tests includes two discrete point tests for Hindi students. The first is a test of auditory comprehension of language and the second is a test of articulation. Both tests are norm-referenced, but the development of these tools is not completed; standardization of the test battery is still progressing. Consequently, little reliability or validity data are available.

Assessment of Phonological Processes—Spanish
Developed by B. Hodson
Available from Los Amigos Research Associates
       7035 Galewood
       San Diego, CA 92120
 This discrete point tool identifies articulation errors from the descriptive perspective of phonological processes. The student's productions are primarily elicited through a confrontational naming task using both pictures and real objects. Single-word productions are the primary focus of the test.

Austin Spanish Articulation Test
Developed by E. Carrow-Woolfolk
Available from DLM Teaching Resources
        One DLM Park
        Allen, TX 75002
Range: 3 years and up
    The purpose of this discrete point test is to assess the production of Spanish consonants, vowels, diphthongs, and clusters in isolated words. The test is administered using a standard sentence completion task with the target word pictured. Although designed within a norm-referenced paradigm, insufficient normative data are available. One favorable feature of the test is the symbolic scheme for recording Spanish phonemes.

Babel Chinese Proficiency Test
Developed by B. Jew
Available from Bay Area Bilingual Education League
        Berkeley Unified School District
        2134 Martin Luther King Jr. Way
        Berkeley, CA 94704

Basic Elementary Skills Test
Developed by Gamez-Huebner, Watson, and Omark
Available from Los Amigos Research Associates
        7035 Galewood
        San Diego, CA 92120
Range: K through Middle School
    This integrated tool focuses on language and educational achievement. It consists of tests for mathematics, spelling, reading, and written language. Designed as a criterion referenced test, BEST was normed on 500 Spanish-speaking LEP students and over 270 other LEP students. Reliability indices and concurrent validity of this test are strong. The test is available in Spanish, Arabic, Cambodian, Chinese, Farsi, Vietnamese, Hmong and Laotian.

Basic Inventory of Natural Language
Developed by C. H. Herbert
Available from Checkpoint Systems
        1520 N. Waterman
        San Bernadino, CA 92404
Range: Grades K through 12

This integrative test, administered in small group settings, is designed to assess natural oral monologic language production and provide measures of language dominance, fluency, and complexity of language structure. The student is encouraged to tell a story or talk about an experience to the other students using three types of stimulus materials. The student's performance is audiotaped and scored using a criterion-referenced scoring system focusing on fluency, syntax, and vocabulary. The weighting system used for scoring may penalize the child for differences in style that do not concern language proficiency. No validity or reliability information is reported. Norms are provided for Spanish and English only, but data are available on use of the test with many other languages.

Ber-Sil Spanish Test
Developed by M. Beringer
Available from The Ber-Sil Company
                3412 Seaglen Drive
                Rancho Palos Verdes, CA 90274
Range: 4 through 12 years
                13 through 17 years (experimental version)
This discrete point test is a screening measure of receptive language assessing comprehension of Spanish vocabulary and a limited number of verbal directions. The test also includes a section involving drawing and writing ability. The Spanish comprehension stimuli and instructions are presented by audiotape. The experimental secondary version assesses vocabulary, grammar, punctuation, spelling, and basic math. Although designed within a norm-referenced paradigm, there is only limited reliability, validity, and normative data for the original version of the test, and no psychometric data are available for the secondary version. The test is available in translated versions for speakers from China, Iran, Korea, and the Philippines.

Bilingual Language Proficiency Questionnaire
Developed by L. J. Mattes and G. Santiago
Available from Academic Communication Associates
                Publications Division, 2C
                P.O. Box 566249
                Oceanside, CA 92056
Range: Birth and up
This interview questionnaire is helpful when obtaining information about the developmental milestones and patterns of bilingual development including usage variables. Since the questionnaire obtains information for both English and Spanish, cross-linguistic comparisons are possible.

Bahia Oral Language Test
Developed by S. Cohen, R. Cruz, and R. Bravo
Available from Bahia Media Productions
P.O. Box 9337
North Berkeley, CA 94709
Range: Grades 5 through 12

This discrete point test is intended as a language-proficiency assessment tool. English and Spanish versions consist of 20 items per test based on three pictured settings and test the students' use of expressive syntax. Students' responses are scored with regard to morphological and syntactic correctness by comparing the responses to suggested scoring standards. The standard dialect for the Spanish version is Standard Mexican Spanish. The total correct is then translated to one of five proficiency levels in Spanish or English. Both versions appear to have adequate concurrent validity, test–retest reliability, and internal consistency.

Bilingual Syntax Measure
Developed by M. Burt, H. Dulay, and E. Hernandez-Chavez
Available from The Psychological Corporation
P.O. Box 839954
San Antonio, TX 78283-3954
Range: Level I   K through Grade 2
Level II Grades 3 through 12

These discrete point tests measure syntactic production in English and Spanish and can be used to determine some areas of language dominance, level of L_2 acquisition, and degree of maintenance/loss of the L_1. Each version consists of 20 questions about a series of seven pictures designed to elicit specific grammatical structures. The total raw score places the child at one of five levels of proficiency for each language. Validity information has not been reported, and reliability indices are low. Potential problems include the test's use of standard English syntax as the metric for measuring oral language proficiency and the validity of using a sequence of morpheme acquisition based on L_2 acquisition to assess L_1 proficiency.

Bilingual Syntax Measure—Chinese
Bilingual Syntax Measure—Tagalog
Developed by C. Tsang
Available from Asian-American Bilingual Center
Berkeley Unified School District
2134 Martin Luther King Jr. Way
Berkeley, CA 94709
Range: K through 12

Tests follow the format of the original Bilingual Syntax Measure.

Bilingual Two Language Battery of Tests
Developed by A. Caso
Available from Brandon Press
           17 Station Street
           Box 843
           Brookline Village, MA 02147

This discrete point, criterion-referenced battery is designed to measure a student's performance on articulatory production, comprehension, writing, and oral proficiency. The test is administered using a cassette tape presentation, first in the child's native language and then in English. The test is intended for use as a measure of progress. Consequently, it is recommended that it be administered twice a year for a period of 3 years. This tool is available in Spanish, Portuguese, French, and Vietnamese. Reliability and validity data are not available.

Boehm Test of Basic Concepts—Spanish Version
Developed by A. E. Boehm
Available from The Psychological Corporation
           P.O. Box 83954
           San Antonio, TX 78283-3954
Range: Grades K through 2

This discrete point test is designed as a screening measure of the student's comprehension of 50 basic concepts. The Spanish version is a direct translation of the English version that tests picture recognition vocabulary and can be administered individually or to an entire class. Norms are not available for the Spanish version. Questions have been posed concerning the theoretical basis of the English version of the test, the lack of predictive validity, the questionable content validity, and the low reliability scores. In addition, there is very little information concerning the validity, reliability, and utility of the Spanish version.

Brigance Assessment of Basic Skills—Spanish Edition
Developed by A. H. Brigance
Available from Curriculum Associates
           5 Esquire Road
           North Billerica, MA 01862-2589
Range: Pre-K through Grade 8

This instrument may be used to identify children needing referral for special testing, to determine instructional objectives, and to track student's progress. The test format includes 102 criterion-referenced tests in 70 subcategories and a Dominant Language Screening Form for assessing relative strength in English and Spanish. The administration procedures are relatively simple and may be given by a paraprofessional adept in Spanish. Reliability information is not included in the manual; some support for content validity is reported, but no other measures of validity are included. The language-dominance measure should be used with care as some of the tasks used for comparison of English and Spanish competence do not appear to be carefully matched for difficulty. The test is not normed, and no suggested levels of mastery are included.

Brigance Assessment of Basic Skills—Portuguese Edition
Developed by H. Grossman
Available from H. Grossman, Director
        Bilingual/Multicultural Special Education Programs
        Division of Special Education and Rehabilitation
        San Jose State University
        1 Washington Square
        San Jose, CA 95192
Range: Pre-K through Grade 8
This test battery is an adaptation of the English version of the Brigance.

Cantonese Test I
Available from Oakland Bilingual Education Program
        Oakland Unified School District
        1025 Second Avenue
        Oakland, CA 94606
This discrete point test is designed to assess the oral skills of Cantonese speakers. Little validity and reliability data are provided.

Chinese Oral Proficiency Test
Available from The National Hispanic University
        255 East 14th Street
        Oakland, CA 94606
Range: K through Grade 6
This integrative test is designed to measure language proficiency based on oral comprehension and word association tasks. The tool has little validity or reliability data available.

Chinese Test
Chinese Bilingual Test
Chinese Literature and Cultural Test
Developed by Antoinette Metcaff
Available from AB893 Chinese Bilingual Project
        San Francisco Unified School District
        135 Van Ness Avenue
        Room 1 Intake Center
        San Francisco, CA 94102

These three tools are designed as measures of language proficiency and language dominance, and as a measure of cultural knowledge in Chinese. The tools are primarily designed in a norm-referenced paradigm, but descriptive data are available. Little reliability or validity data are available.

Comprehensive English Language Test for Speakers of English as a Second Language
Available from CTB/McGraw-Hill International Book Co.
          300 West 42nd Avenue
          New York, NY 10036
Range: High school to adult
    This norm-referenced, discrete point tool is designed as an aid in placing students into English as a Second Language (ESL) programs and monitoring their progress in the acquisition of English as a second language. Reliability and validity figures are reported.

Comprehension of Oral Language Test—InterAmerican
Developed by H. T. Manuel
Available from Guidance Testing Associates
          William B. Travis Building
          1701 North Congress
          Austin, TX 78752
Range: Grades K through 1
    The discrete point test was designed to assess a student's ability to understand words and short phrases presented orally. Spanish and English versions that appear equivalent with respect to vocabulary and language demands are provided. The student marks the correct picture in a test booklet to correspond to the spoken stimulus. The test can be administered individually or as a group. No standardization data or data on reliability and validity are available in the manual. Only superficial advice is given on interpreting the test results.

Compton Phonological Assessment of Foreign Accent
Developed by A. J. Compton
Available from Institute of Language
          450 Mission at 1st Street
          Suite 504
          San Francisco, CA 94105
    This integrative test is a descriptive tool designed to lead the examiner through a detailed analysis of the oral productions of nonnative English speakers. This analysis is then used to design a treatment program for

overcoming phonological stabilization or fossilization. Data are obtained from single-word, phrasal, sentential, and conversational tasks.

Compton Speech and Language Screening Evaluation—Spanish
Developed by A. J. Compton and M. Kline
Available from Institute of Language
          450 Mission at 1st Street
          Suite 504
          San Francisco, CA 94105
Range: 3 through 6 years
    This discrete point, norm-referenced test is a direct translation of the English version. Using picture elicitation, a brief conversational sample, and repetition activities, the test screens students for problems with articulation, expressive and receptive vocabulary, memory, and receptive and expressive syntax and morphology.

Crane Oral Dominance Test—Spanish/English
Developed by B. Crane
Available from Crane Publishing Co.
          1301 Hamilton Avenue
          P.O. Box 3713
          Trenton, NJ 08629
Range: 4 through 8 years
    The purpose of this discrete point test is to determine a student's dominant language. It must be administered individually by a bilingual examiner. The examiner reads aloud a set of four pairs of words, and the student is required to repeat the words. The student may respond in any language. The examiner also asks a series of five questions regarding the language preferred when speaking to parents or siblings. The premise of the test is that the language in which the student thinks is the dominant language, and the ability to recall is directly related to the meaningfulness of the material to be recalled. Reliability and validity data provided are inconclusive.

Del Rio Language Screening Test
Developed by A. S. Toronto, D. Leverman, C. Hanna, P. Rosenzweig, and A. Maldonado
Available from National Educational Laboratory
          Publishers, Inc.
          P.O. Box 1003
          Austin, TX 78767
Range: 3 through 6 years
    This discrete point screening measure of Spanish and English receptive language is used for determining language dominance. Areas as-

sessed include receptive vocabulary, sentence repetition, memory for oral commands, and story comprehension. Test items were carefully selected to be culturally appropriate for the population of Del Rio, Texas. The standardization population of 384 normal children between the ages of 3 and 6 to 11 included English speaking Anglo-American, predominantly English-speaking Mexican-American and predominantly Spanish-speaking Mexican-American students. Norms are provided for each subpopulation group. While reliability indices appear adequate, the validity of the test is poor.

Developmental Assessment of Spanish Grammar
Developed by A. S. Toronto
Available from *Journal of Speech and Hearing Disorders 41*, 150–171
Range: 3 through 6 years
This discrete point procedure evaluates the grammatical skills of Spanish speakers and is intended to serve as a model for structuring language remediation. This tool uses a language-analysis method similar to the Developmental Sentence Scoring (Lee, 1971) to analyze the child's use of major syntactic structures in spontaneous speech. The procedure requires a corpus of 50 complete, consecutive, intelligible, different, and nonecholalic utterances. Each utterance is assigned a score. An average score is calculated and can be compared to norms. The procedure was standardized on 128 children of Mexican and Puerto Rican descent living in Chicago. Internal consistency and test–retest reliability were adequate. Validity scores were low. The DASG takes considerable time to administer and excludes many important Spanish grammatical features. In addition, the examiner must have a thorough knowledge of Spanish grammar.

Dos Amigos Verbal Language Scales
Developed by D. Critchlow
Available from Academic Therapy Publications
                20 Commercial Boulevard
                Novato, CA 94949
Range: Grades K through 6
This discrete point instrument was designed as a language-dominance measure. The examiner presents English and Spanish stimulus words arranged in order of increasing difficulty. The student's task is to give a word with an opposite meaning. The test should be administered individually by a bilingual examiner. Raw scores may be converted to percentiles, which are used to establish language dominance. The standardization of this norm-referenced tool is good. However, no reliability or validity information is presented in the manual. Some authorities sus-

pect that the test may underestimate Spanish dominance and that the task may be too difficult if the child does not understand the concept of opposite.

El Circo Assessment Series
Developed by Educational Testing Service
Available from CTB/McGraw-Hill Book Co.
                2500 Garden Road
                Monterey, CA 93940
Range: 4 through 6 years
   This discrete point test was developed to assess Spanish-speaking students' comprehension of simple math concepts and basic linguistic structures in English and Spanish. It is useful both as a screening measure and as a post-test to determine the success of intervention. The test appears to be carefully developed. Norms provided are based on a random, well-stratified sampling of Mexican-American, Puerto Rican, and Cuban children. The available validity and reliability data are adequate.

Expressive One Word Picture Vocabulary Test—Spanish
Developed by M. F. Gardner
Available from Children's Hospital of San Francisco
                Publications Department
                P.O. Box 3805
                San Francisco, CA 94119
Range: Lower level   2 through 11 years
            Upper level   12 through 16 years
   This discrete point, norm-referenced test focuses on numerical measures of single word expressive vocabulary and an estimate of fluency in English word production. Reliability appears adequate but validity indices are insufficient.

Flexibility Language Dominance Test—Spanish/English
Developed by G. D. Keller
Available from CTB/McGraw-Hill Book Co.
                2500 Garden Road
                Monterey, CA 93940
Range: 10 years and over
   This discrete point test was designed to measure linguistic dominance of Spanish/English bilinguals. The primary focus of the test is English/Spanish lexicon. The student is required to form legitimate English or Spanish words from five nonsense word presentations within a specified time period. Validity and reliability measures presented were inadequate. Other concerns about the test include inadequate administration, scoring and interpretation guidelines, as well as the fact that the test

ignores the broader linguistic, pragmatic, and sociolinguistic aspects of assessment of language proficiency.

FSI Oral Interview
Developed by Foreign Service Institute
Available from Educational Testing Services
                    Princeton, NJ
Range: Older students and adults
   This pragmatic procedure is designed to assess an individual's foreign language proficiency. In an interview setting, the test taker communicates with the interviewer in the target language, and overall proficiency is rated using a standardized rating scale. The procedure provides standardization of oral testing procedures and delineates aspects of performance that are to be observed. However, only one communicative speech style is assessed, and some findings indicate that there may be fluctuations in an individual's ratings due to differences in occasion, interviewer, speech style, and topic. Users should be cautious about making generalizations about a person's language competence based on a single interview.

Gloria and David Oral Language Assessment
Available from Institute of Cultural Pluralism
                    San Diego State University
                    School of Education
                    San Diego, CA 20735
Range: K through Grade 2
   This discrete point test is designed to assess a student's oral language ability in English and Spanish through a sentence repetition task. The student is required to repeat prerecorded sentences while viewing corresponding pictures through a filmstrip presentation. Problems include the direct translation of items from English into Spanish, use of unnatural intonation on English sentences, and the use of English intonation on Spanish sentences. In addition, all items are in present tense, so the test represents a limited portion of both English and Spanish syntax. While internal consistency and test–retest reliability scores are available, no validity data are reported.

Hannah-Gardner Test of Verbal and Non-Verbal Language Function
Developed by E. P. Hannah and J. O. Gardner
Available from Lingua Press
                    P.O. Box 3416
                    Iowa City, IA 52244
Range: 3.5 through 5.5 years

This discrete point instrument is a screening device for identifying Spanish and English speaking children with language deficits. Scores are obtained in the following categories: visual perception, conceptual development, auditory perception, linguistic development, a verbal summary score, a nonverbal summary score, and a total. The test must be administered individually. No information is available on norms, reliability, or validity.

Ilyin Oral Interview
Developed by Donna Ilyin
Available from Newbury House Publishers, Inc.
        68 Middle Road
        Rowley, MA 01969

This integrative instrument is designed to assess the ability of nonnative English speakers to communicate verbally with content and verbal accuracy. Two forms with 50 items each are provided. Students must answer questions with complete sentences about sequences of pictures. Utterances are scored on the basis of semantic appropriateness, grammatical structure, and intelligibility. No validity data are provided, and only tentative norms are included. The publisher recommends using local norms. The test has adequate internal consistency, but no data on test–retest reliability, equivalency of the two forms, or inter/intrajudge reliability are provided.

James Language Dominance Test
Developed by Peter James
Available from DLM Teaching Resources
        One DLM Park
        Allen, TX 75002
Range: Grades K through 1

This discrete point test assesses production and comprehension of Spanish and English vocabulary. The examiner presents 40 pictures in conjunction with the questions "What is this?" and "Where is the . . . ?" Questions are presented in English and Spanish. A total score, as well as the student's score on three special items to determine home language use, are used to place the child into one of five categories. Local norms were developed, but no information on subject selection criteria, reliability, or validity scores were reported.

Language Assessment Battery
Developed by Board of Education of the City of New York
Available from New York Board of Education
        OREA Scan Center
        49 Flatbush Avenue Extension
        Brooklyn, NY 11201

Range: Level I   K through 2
        Level II   Grade 3 through 6
        Level III   Grade 7 through 12

This test battery was designed to assess a student's relative "effectiveness" in English and Spanish. However, a large number of test items measures recognition of isolated sounds and words. Few items evaluate pragmatic functions of language or the child's discourse skills, which one would assume to be important in measuring overall effectiveness. The administration instructions are clearly given in the test manual, but scoring details are not as clearly stated. Culturally, most items on the test are aimed at students of Puerto Rican descent and may not be as appropriate for the Mexican-American population. The normative sample consisted of monolingual English-speaking and literate Spanish-speaking children from New York City. The test appears to have adequate internal consistency, but no other reliability or validity data are given.

Language Assessment Scales
Developed by E. A. DeAvila and S. E. Duncan
Available from CTB/McGraw-Hill Book Co.
                    2500 Garden Road
                    Monterey, CA 93940
Range: PreLAS   Pre-K through K
        Level I   Grade K through 5
        Level II   Grade 6 through 12

This discrete point instrument assesses auditory discrimination, vocabulary, phoneme production, sentence comprehension, and oral production in English and Spanish. It is designed to be used as a measure of language dominance. The examiner is provided with a set of sample data, and the child's output is compared to the examples and assigned a score. Criteria for assigning scores are not clearly explained in the manual. The total score obtained on each scale is used to place the child at one of five levels of proficiency in each language. The Spanish version was standardized on children from Mexican-American, Latin American, and Puerto Rican backgrounds. The English scales were standardized on English-speaking children living in the Southwest. Populations, however, were not drawn in a scientifically representative manner. Support for the validity of both the English and Spanish versions is inadequate.

Language Facility Test (Second Edition)
Developed by J. T. Daily
Available from Allington Corporation
                    P.O. Box 125
                    Remington, VA 22734
Range: 3 years and over

This discrete point instrument measures language proficiency in English or Spanish. Verbal responses are elicited using pictures provided in the test package. The student's responses are given a rating from 0 to 9, with 0 representing no response and 9 representing a well-organized story with imagination and creativity. Norms are available for ages 3 to 15. The test has high reliability, but there is no support for concurrent and construct validity. Indications are that the test may be more a measure of cognitive development than language proficiency.

Lindamood Auditory Conceptualization Test—Spanish
Developed by C. H. Lindamood and P. C. Lindamood
Available from DLM Teaching Resources
          One DLM Park
          Allen, TX 75002
Range: Pre-K and up
This discrete point test is designed to measure auditory perception and conceptualization of speech sounds. Though discussed in descriptive terms, this is primarily a norm-referenced tool with good reliability indices. The validity of this type of discrete point assessment tool is questionable.

Marysville Test of Language Dominance—Tagalog
Available from Marysville Reading Learning Center
          11th and Powerline
          Oliverhurst, CA 95961
Range: Grades K through 5
A discrete point test of language proficiency for Tagalog speakers. No reliability or validity data are provided.

MAT-SEA-CAL Oral Proficiency Tests
Available from Center for Applied Linguistics
          1118 22nd Street NW
          Washington, DC 20037
Range: Grades K through 5
An integrative test to determine the need for remedial instruction. Test is available for speakers of Chinese, Tagalog, Mandarin, and Cantonese.

Medida Espanola de Articulacion
Developed by M. Aldrich-Mason, B. Figueroa-Smith, and M. Martinez-Henshaw
Available from San Ysidro School District
          4350 Otay Mesa Road
          San Ysidro, CA 92073
Range: 4 through 9 years

This discrete point test assesses articulation of single words in Spanish. Picture stimuli and a sentence completion task is used to elicit the productions by the student. The standardization sample was locally obtained and is limited.

Multicultural Vocabulary Test
Developed by G. Trudeau
Available from Los Amigos Research Associates
　　　　　　7035 Galewood
　　　　　　San Diego, CA 92129
Range: 3 through 12 years
A discrete point test of expressive vocabulary using body parts as stimulus items. While the test appears suitable for many languages, it is poorly standardized in terms of actual implementation and scoring criteria. Additionally, this approach to assessment takes a superficial view of language and cultural proficiency.

Oral Language Proficiency Measure
Developed by El Paso Public Schools
Available from El Paso Schools
　　　　　　P.O. Box 2100
　　　　　　El Paso, TX 79998
Range: Grades 4 through 6
This integrative test is designed to assess proficiency in English and Spanish, determine dominant language, and place students in appropriate instructional programs. Students are asked a series of questions about three stimulus pictures. Scores are based on two criteria: number of words and number of grammatical responses. Scores are used to place the student in one of five levels of English and Spanish usage. Internal consistency is adequate, but no data on test–retest or intrajudge reliability were available. Some support for concurrent validity is presented, but no measures of predictive or construct validity are available.

Pictorial Test of Bilingualism and Language Dominance
Developed by D. Nelson, M. J. Fellner, and C. L. Norrell
Available from Stoelting Co.
　　　　　　620 Wheat Lane
　　　　　　Wood Dale, IL 60191
Range: Grades K through 2
This discrete point test provides measures of oral vocabulary for both Spanish and English as well as phonological, morphological, and syntactic development in both languages. The test is divided into two parts to test oral vocabulary and oral language production. The test must be administered individually by a bilingual evaluator. The student re-

sponds first in the language of preference and then is asked to respond to the same task in the other language. The test has adequate reliability and correlates positively with other measures of oral vocabulary.

Primary Acquisition of Languages (PAL) Oral Language Dominance Measure
Developed by Rosa Apodaca
Available from El Paso Schools
> P.O. Box 20100
> El Paso, TX 79998

Range: 4 through 9 years

This discrete point test is designed to determine structural proficiency in English and Spanish and to measure language dominance. The test must be administered individually by a bilingual evaluator. The instrument consists of 28 questions asked by the bilingual examiner. The student's responses are scored for acceptability and number of correct words in each response. Guidelines for scoring are given in the examiner manual. Normative data based on 202 students is provided. However, no demographic data on the normative population was included, and the reliability and validity indices appear inadequate.

Peabody Picture Vocabulary Test—Spanish
Developed by L. Dunn and L. Dunn
Available from American Guidance Service
> 753 Publisher's Building
> P.O. Box 99
> Circle Pines, MN 55014-1796

Range: 3 to 18 years

This discrete point test of single-word receptive vocabulary is a direct translation of the English version of the test. The format is similar in that the student is presented with plates containing four pictures. The examiner names one and the student must point to the proper picture. Although the reliability is fair, the validity of this test is poor. Additionally, more normative data are needed.

Preschool Language Assessment Instrument—Spanish Language Edition
Developed by M. Blank, S. Rose, and L. Berlin (Out of print)
Available from The Speech Bin
> 231 Clarksville Road
> P.O. Box 218
> Princeton Junction, NJ 08550-0218

Range: 3 through 6 years

This pragmatic test is designed to assess the student's ability to respond to tasks requiring comprehension and expression along a continuum of linguistic abstraction. Student performance is elicited through the use of pictures, brief questions, and instructions from the examiner. Rather than focusing on discrete points of language, however, the authors have conceptualized their tasks along a four-stage, developmentally relevant perceptual-language distancing principle. Additionally, the scoring criteria are both descriptive and norm referenced, although more normative data are needed. Reliability and validity indices are adequate.

Preschool Language Scale—Spanish
Developed by I. Zimmerman, V. Steiner, and R. E. Pond
Available from The Psychological Corporation
                        P.O. Box 839954
                        San Antonio, TX 78283-3954
Range: Birth to 6 years
   This discrete point, norm-referenced test measures both receptive and expressive language items divided into grammar, vocabulary, memory, attention span, temporal/spatial relations, and self-image. A direct translation of the English version, this tool has fair reliability and poor validity information.

Prueba del Desarrollo Inicial del Lenguaje
Developed by W. P. Hresko, D. K. Reid, and D. D. Hammill
Available from PRO-ED
                        8700 Shoal Creek Boulevard
                        Austin, TX 78758
Range: 3 through 7 years
   This discrete point test of expressive and receptive language follows the format of the Test of Early Language Development. Some items are direct translations of the English version. Scores may be converted to language quotients and percentiles. The test was standardized on 549 Spanish-speaking children from Mexico, Puerto Rico, and the United States. Subject selection criteria were not specified. Separate norms for the three standardization groups are provided. Reliability measures reveal adequate internal consistency, but information on validity is inadequate. The test appears useful in identifying children in need of more extensive testing, but because of the limited standardization sample, care should be taken using the norms provided.

Pruebas de Expresion Oral y Percepcion de la Lengua Española
Developed by S. Mares
Available from Division of Support Services
                        Office of L.A. County Superintendent of Schools
                        9300 E. Imperial Highway
                        Downey, CA 90242-2890
Range: 6 through 9 years

This discrete point test assesses the language abilities of Mexican and Mexican-American students living in Southern California. The test is administered entirely in Spanish. It includes five subtests that measure a student's auditory sequential memory, auditory association, encoding skills, story comprehension, and sentence repetition. Raw scores are converted to scaled scores. Percentiles should be available in the future. The standardization sample consisted of 674 Spanish-speaking students of Mexican heritage living in Southern California. Internal consistency, test–retest, interscorer, and item difficulty reliability were all within acceptable limits. No discriminative validity information was reported; content validity was based on review by recognized authorities. Although the test appears to be useful for the population for which it was designed, it is still in an experimental version and usefulness with other populations has not yet been determined.

Receptive One-Word Picture Vocabulary Test—Spanish
Developed by M. F. Gardner
Available from Children's Hospital of San Francisco
                      Publications Department
                      P.O. Box 3805
                      San Francisco, CA 94119
Range: 2 through 11 years
This discrete point, norm-referenced test focuses on numerical measures of single-word receptive vocabulary. It is a companion to the Expressive One-Word Picture Vocabulary Test and it is a direct translation of the English version of the test. Reliability indices are fair; validity is inadequate.

Screening Test of Spanish Grammar
Developed by A. S. Toronto
Available from Northwestern University Press
                      1735 Benson Avenue
                      Evanston, IL 60201
Range: 3 through 6 years
This discrete point, norm-referenced test is used as a screening measure for Spanish-speaking children with possible language deficiencies. It follows the same format and methods as the Northwestern Syntax Screening Test and consists of receptive and expressive subtests that assess the child's comprehension and production of increasingly complex syntactic structures. Items included take into account the acquisition sequence of Spanish syntax. The test was standardized on 192 children of Mexican-American and Puerto Rican descent from poor urban neighborhoods of Chicago. The test has weak correlation (0.55–0.64)

with the Developmental Assessment of Spanish Grammar and the data on reliability and validity are inadequate.

Short Tests of Linguistic Skills
Developed by C. K. Fredrickson and J. W. Wick
Available from Chicago Board of Education
            1819 W. Pershing Road
            Chicago, IL 60609
Range: 7 through 15 years

This discrete point test instrument evaluates listening, speaking, reading, and writing skills. It has parallel forms in English, Arabic, Chinese, Greek, Italian, Japanese, Korean, Pilipino, Polish, Spanish, and Vietnamese. Portions of the tests can be given simultaneously to an entire class, but the speaking portion must be administered individually by a native speaker. Detailed administration and scoring directions are presented in the manual, but no information on how to interpret the scores is given. The test may be a good screening instrument, but because of its brevity, it only provides approximate indications of the student's level.

Shutt Primary Language Indicator Test
Developed by D. L. Shutt
Available from School Division, McGraw-Hill Book Co.
            1200 NW 63rd Street
            P.O. Box 25308
            Oklahoma City, OK 73125
Range: Grades K through 6

This instrument is designed to determine language dominance between Spanish and English. Using a discrete point approach, the test consists of listening comprehension, verbal fluency, and reading comprehension subtests. The verbal fluency portion must be administered individually. The test is recorded on cassette tape, allowing administration by monolingual persons. No information on validity or reliability was available.

SOBER—Espanol
Developed by R. J. Carnejo
Available from SRA Inc.
            155 North Wacker Drive
            Chicago, IL 60606
Range: K through grade 3

This is a criterion-referenced test covering 10 to 30 objectives in four areas of reading: encoding, decoding, vocabulary, and comprehension. There are no data on reliability; no norms or suggested standards of mastery are presented in the manual. Although the test is presented as a test of reading, most of the test is presented orally and is more likely a test of readiness. The instrument appears to be effective for assessing children's entry skills and for measuring students' progress.

Southwestern Spanish Articulation Test
Developed by A. S. Toronto
Available from National Educational Laboratory Publishers, Inc.
P.O. Box 1003
Austin, TX 78757
Range: 3 years and up
This is a traditional articulation test for Spanish speakers that uses a picture-naming task to elicit single-word productions. As in most traditional tests, the productions are elicited to obtain the production of the consonants in the initial, medial, and final positions.

Spanish Articulation Measures
Developed by L. J. Mattes
Available from The Speech Bin
231 Clarksville Road
P.O. Box 218
Princeton Junction, NJ 08550-0218
Range: 3 years and up
A criterion-referenced articulation test designed to describe articulatory production through the use of phonological processes appropriate for Spanish speakers. The student's productions are obtained in several ways, including picture elicitation and spontaneous speech.

Spanish/English Language Performance Test
Developed by Southwest Educational Development Laboratory
Available from Southwest Educational Development Laboratory
211 E. 7th Street
Austin, TX 78701
Range: 4 through 5 years
This integrative measure of language dominance places each student in one of six language levels in English and Spanish. The test must be administered individually and by a bilingual examiner. The test consists of a 15-minute controlled interview in which the student is required to answer questions, name objects, follow directions, describe objects, and describe pictures. The child is placed in a language category based on the number of responses in each part of the test and the language in which the majority of responses are made. No validity or reliability measures are given.

Spanish/English Reading and Vocabulary Screening
Developed by Southwest Educational Development Laboratory
Available from Southwest Educational Development Laboratory
211 E. 7th Street
Austin, TX 78701
Range: Grades 1 through 8
This test is a language-proficiency screening measure to determine which version (Spanish or English) of the achievement test should be administered to the student. It is particularly appropriate when used in combination with the CTBS/S and/or CTBS Español achievement batteries. Problems with the test include substantial variability across forms, grade levels, and languages tested. In addition, there is no empirical evidence that the level of Spanish used is common across all regions of the United States. Potential users may want to develop local norms and classification rules based on the language-use patterns of the local bilingual population.

Spanish Language Assessment Procedures: A Communication Skills Inventory
Developed by L. J. Mattes
Available from Academic Communication Associates
P.O. Box 566249
Oceanside, CA 92056
Range: Grades K through 3
This pragmatic procedure assesses articulation, language, voice, and fluency of Spanish-speaking children. Criterion-referenced tasks and naturalistic observations are used to collect the information. Record forms for recording data are included. Norms for the articulation measure were obtained on a sample of Mexican-American children in southern California. Initial data suggest good reliability and validity indices.

Spotting Language Problems
Developed by J. S. Damico and J. W. Oller, Jr.
Available from Los Amigos Research Associates
7035 Galewood
San Diego, CA 92120
Range: 5 years and up
This pragmatic language screening measure is designed to identify students with potential communication problems. Although it is written in English, the tool has been used in a number of other languages (Spanish, Zuni, French, German, Vietnamese) with good success. Designed as a rating scale, the evaluator observes the students and comments on the student's effectiveness along seven dimensions of oral-dialogic language usage. Interpretation information is provided. This tool has strong validity and reliability indices.

SWCEL *Test of Oral Language Proficiency—Chinese*
Available from Southwestern Cooperative Educational Laboratory
> Attention: Dr. John A. Salazar
> 229 Truman, NE
> Suite A
> Albuquerque, NM 87108

A discrete point, norm-referenced test to assess the need for remedial instruction in Chinese students.

Test for Auditory Comprehension of Language—Spanish
Developed by E. Carrow
Available from DLM Teaching Resources
> One DLM Park
> Allen, TX 75002

Range: 3 through 6 years

This discrete point test assesses the comprehension of a wide range of language structures in both English and Spanish. It is a direct translation of the English version. When administering this test, the examiner provides an oral stimulus, and the student responds by pointing to one of three pictures on a picture plate. This is a norm-referenced test that can derive age equivalencies or percentiles. Norms are not provided for the Spanish version. Test–retest reliability is adequate; no other reliability or validity measures are provided.

Test of Grammatically Correct Spanish/English
Developed by Las Cruces Public Schools
Available from Las Cruces Public Schools
> 301 W. Amador Avenue
> Las Cruces, NM 88001

Range: Grades K through 4

This test was designed to compare the bilingual student's fluency in English with fluency in Spanish through the expressive modalities of writing and speaking. Each subtest consists of one task given in both languages. Students' responses are scored with regard to vocabulary, sentence patterns, grammar, and usage. Only the first two sentences of the response are scored. The test provides no information on the interpretation of raw scores, and no norms are provided. No data on reliability or validity of the procedure were available.

Test of Language Dominance
Developed by Max Luft
Available from Southwest Research Associates

P.O. Box 4092
Albuquerque, NM 87106
Range: Primary grades
This discrete point test attempts to accurately identify the child's dominant language and provide normative data regarding fluency in the child's two predominant languages. The test was simultaneously developed in English, Navajo, Spanish, Yupik, and Zuni. The first portion of the test measures receptive verbal ability and may be administered to a group. The second part tests expressive verbal ability and must be administered individually. The test administrator must be fluent in both of the languages being tested. The test has good reliability, but inadequate validity data are available.

Texas-Acevedo Screening of Speech and Language
Developed by M. A. Acevedo
Available from Bureau of Maternal and Child Health
            Texas Department of Health
            1100 W. 49th Street
            Austin, TX 78756
Range: 3 through 6 years
A discrete point screening test for articulation, receptive language, and syntax and morphology in English and Spanish.

Toronto Test of Receptive Vocabulary
Developed by A. S. Toronto
Available from National Educational Lab Publishers, Inc.
            P.O. Box 1003
            Austin, TX 78767
Range: 4 through 10 years
This discrete point test instrument assesses receptive vocabulary proficiency in both English and Spanish. Separate norms for Anglo-American, English-speaking Mexican-American, and Spanish-speaking Mexican-American students are included. The standardization sample was taken in San Antonio, San Marcos, and Temple, Texas. No other demographic information is available.

Woodcock Language Proficiency Battery—Spanish Form
Developed by R. W. Woodcock
Available from DLM Teaching Resources
            One DLM Park
            Allen, TX 75002
Range: 3 years through adult

This test assesses language dominance and, as a part of the larger Woodcock Spanish Psycho-Educational Battery, aids in assessing overall cognitive ability and scholastic achievement of Spanish-speaking individuals. An English form is also available for assessing the comparative proficiency of the child in the two languages. The test battery consists of eight subtests that measure oral and written language and reading skills. Scores may be converted to percentiles, grade equivalents, age equivalents, and standard scores. The test was standardized on 802 children from Costa Rica, Mexico, Peru, Puerto Rico, and Spain. Reliability and validity information are not available. The test can be used for identifying a student's strengths and weaknesses on a variety of language tasks. However, subtests in the Oral Language Battery require only one-word responses and, as such, sample only a small portion of the student's oral/verbal ability.

Appendix B

Annotated Bibliography of Academic Ability Tests

The tests listed below are available to assessment teachers and diagnosticians for the assessment of academic ability in limited English proficient (LEP) populations. These tools are listed on the basis of availability and not on the basis of preference and/or psychometric strength.

Analysis of Reading Skills—Spanish Version
Available from Houghton Mifflin Company
　　　　　　　　110 Tremont Street
　　　　　　　　Boston, MA 02107
Range: Grades K through 1
　This norm-referenced test focuses on skills in reading that are typically problematic for poor readers. This test was normed on Mexican, Puerto Rican, and Cuban Spanish speakers.

Basic Elementary Skills Test
Available from Los Amigos Research Associates
　　　　　　　　7035 Galewood, Suite D
　　　　　　　　San Diego, CA 92120
Range: Grades K through 9
　This test assesses arithmetic computation, spelling, reading, and writing in several languages (Arabic, Cambodian, Chinese, Farsi, Spanish, and Vietnamese).

Bateria Woodcock Psico-Educativa en Español
Available from DLM Teaching Resources
　　　　　　　　One DLM Park
　　　　　　　　Allen, TX 75002
Range: Ages 3 years to adult
　This nationally normed achievement test battery is designed to assess reading, mathematics, broad cognitive ability, scholastic aptitude, and actual achievement. Consisting of 17 subtests, numerous scores and clusters of scores may be used for interpretative purposes. This tool is a direct translation of the English language Woodcock-Johnson Psychoeducational Battery.

Bilingual Continuous Progress—Mathematics
Available from National Educational Laboratory Publishers, Inc.
　　　　　　　　P.O. Box 1003
　　　　　　　　Austin, TX 78767
Range: Pre-K through Grade 2

This norm-referenced test is designed to monitor progress in mathematics in Spanish-speaking students. Normed on Mexican students, this tool may be administered in a group setting or on an individual basis.

Bilingual Science Tests
Available from Curriculum Bureau
        Board of Education
        131 Livingston Street, Room 610
        Brooklyn, NY 11201
Range: Grades 5 through 8
These tests assess achievement in general science and chemistry. They are available in English and Spanish.

Brigance Diagnostic Assessment of Basic Skills—Spanish Edition
Available from Curriculum Associates, Inc.
        6 Esquire Road
        North Billerica, MA 01862
Range: Grades K through 6
This criterion-referenced battery is designed to screen for language dominance, determine grade-level placement, and identify specific strengths and weaknesses in reading readiness, reading skills, listening comprehension, writing, language arts, and mathematics. This battery was carefully constructed using the Comprehensive Inventory of Basic Skills as a model, but it is not a direct translation.

California Achievement Test
Available from CTB/McGraw-Hill Book Co.
        Del Monte Research Park
        Monterey, CA 93940
Range: Grades K through 12
This norm-referenced achievement test is designed to assess student achievement in the areas of reading, mathematics, and language arts. This tool is normed for speakers of English, Spanish (Mexican, Puerto Rican, and Cuban), and Chinese. It can be administered in a group setting or on an individual basis.

Cloze Tests 1980–1982
Available from Boston Public Schools
        Lau Unit
        26 Court Street, 8th Floor
        Boston, MA 02108
These cloze procedures are designed within particular content areas to assess instructional reading ability and mastery of the content area. Cloze tests have been developed in ten languages: Chinese, English,

French, Greek, Italian, Khmer, Laotian, Portuguese, Spanish, and Vietnamese.

Early Assessment and Remediation Laboratory
Available from Chicago Board of Education
                    Department of Research and Evaluation
                    2021 N. Burling Street
                    Chicago, IL 60614
Range: Pre-K through Grade 2
    This battery of 23 tasks is designed to screen and identify young students with potential learning disabilities. The tasks focus on gross and fine motor abilities, language skills, visual discrimination, and memory. It is available in Spanish and English.

Hayward Bilingual Management-Multicultural
Social Studies Criterion Referenced Test
Available from The Psychological Corporation
                    757 Third Avenue
                    New York, NY 10017
Range: Grades K through 6
    This criterion-referenced battery is designed to assess concepts related to geography, history, human characteristics, self-concept, and cultural differences in English, Spanish, and Portuguese. It is effective in monitoring a student's progress in social studies and can be given in a group setting and on an individual basis.

Hayward Bilingual Management Systems—
Spanish Math Criterion Referenced and Mastery Tests
Available from The Psychological Corporation
                    757 Third Avenue
                    New York, NY 10017
Range: Grades K through 6
    This criterion-referenced battery is designed to assess mathematical concepts and computations in English, Spanish, and Portuguese. It is effective in monitoring a student's progress in mathematics and can be given in a group setting and on an individual basis.

Inter-American Test of General Abilities (Test of Reading and Numbers)
Available from Guidance Testing Associates
                    P.O Box 28096
                    San Antonio, TX 78228
Range: Pre-K through Grade 12
    This battery assesses the ability to do academic work in general. It is available in both Spanish and English and may be administered either on an individual basis or in a group setting.

Inter-American Test of Reading
Available from Guidance Testing Associates
    P.O. Box 28096
    San Antonio, TX 78228
Range: Grades 1 through 12
 This nationally normed achievement test is designed to assess reading ability in both Spanish and English.

Math Achievement Tests
Available from Seattle Public Schools
    Bilingual Programs
    815 Fourth Avenue N.
    Seattle, WA 98109
Range: Grades K through 6
   Secondary (Pilot Test Edition)
 This test battery assesses the math skills commonly taught at each grade level. The pilot test edition assesses achievement in General Math, Algebra I, Geometry, and Algebra II. The test is available in Chinese, Ilokano, Korean, Pilipino, and Samoan.

Moreno Spanish Reading Comprehension Test
Available from Moreno Educational Company
    P.O. Box 19329
    San Diego, CA 92119
Range: Grades K through 6
 This nationally normed reading achievement test is available in Spanish and English.

New York State Mathematics Test
Available from New York State Education Department
    The University of the State of New York
    Albany, NY 12224
Range: Grades 3, 6, and 9
 This test assesses mathematical concepts, computation, and problem solving in Spanish and English.

Seattle Reading Test
Available from Seattle Public Schools
    Bilingual Programs
    815 Fourth Avenue N.
    Seattle, WA 98109
Range: Grades 1 through 12
 This test battery is designed to assess various aspects of the reading process (recognition of syllables and words, decoding, comprehension,

and word/phrase analysis). The tool is available in Chinese, Ilokano, Korean, Pilipino, and Samoan.

Short Test of Linguistic Skills
Available from Chicago Board of Education
                Department of Research and Evaluation
                2021 N. Burling Street
                Chicago, IL 60614
Range: Grades 3 through 8
   This battery evaluates reading, writing, speaking and comprehension skills although the emphasis is on the reading. Detailed administration and scoring directions are provided but little information is provided for interpretation purposes. Due to its brevity, this tool is best utilized as a screening tool. This tool has parallel versions in eleven languages (Arabic, Chinese, English, Greek, Italian, Japanese, Korean, Pilipino, Polish, Spanish, and Vietnamese).

Social Studies Achievement Tests
Available from Seattle Public Schools
                Bilingual Programs
                815 Fourth Avenue North
                Seattle, WA 98109
Range: Grades K through 6
                Secondary (Grades 7 through 12)
   This battery of achievement tests assesses social studies skills taught at each grade level. The Secondary version focuses on achievement in World History, U.S. History, and World Geography. This battery is available in Chinese, Pilipino, Samoan, and Korean.

Spanish Assessment of Basic Education
Available from CTB/McGraw-Hill Book Co.
                Del Monte Research Park
                Monterey, CA 93940
Range: Grades K through 12
   This achievement test battery is the successor to the Comprehensive Tests of Basic Skills—Espanol and is designed to measure achievement levels of pupils in U.S. bilingual programs and of immigrant students entering the United States. It assesses prereading and reading comprehension, language mechanics, spelling, math computation, concepts, and applications in both Spanish and English.

Stanford Early School Achievement Test
Available from The Psychological Corporation
757 Third Avenue
New York, NY 10017
Range: Grades K through 2
This norm-referenced test assesses general achievement in language arts and mathematics. Available in Mexican and Puerto Rican Spanish as well as in Navajo. Development of local norms are suggested.

Testing the Reading Ability of Cambodians
Available from the Center for Applied Linguistics
1611 N. Kent Street
Arlington, VA 22209
Range: Grade 1 through adult
This instrument is designed to assess the reading ability of Khmer-speaking individuals.

INDEX